THE
NOBEL PRIZE

A HISTORY OF GENIUS, CONTROVERSY, AND PRESTIGE

BURTON FELDMAN

Arcade Publishing • New York

1548929-736

FIRST EDITION

Library of Congress Cataloging-in-Publication Data

Feldman, Burton.
    The Nobel prize : a history of genius, controversy, and prestige / Burton Feldman.
        p. cm.
    Includes bibliographical references and index.
    ISBN 1-55970-537-X (hc)
    ISBN 1-55970-592-2 (pb)
    1. Nobel Prizes—History. I. Title.
AS911.N9 F38 2000
001.4'4—dc21   00—42002

Published in the United States by Arcade Publishing, Inc., New York
Distributed by Time Warner Trade Publishing

Visit our Web site at www.arcadepub.com

10 9 8 7 6 5 4 3 2 1

Designed by API

EB

PRINTED IN THE UNITED STATES OF AMERICA

Hu
APR -- 2002

THE
NOBEL PRIZE

For Peggy
My brave, life-loving, and witty wife,
and my life's treasure

Contents

molecular biology, literature in many genres and languages, peace awards from Teddy Roosevelt to Mother Teresa. To dare to survey and, at times, criticize prizes in six such intricate fields is to take one's life in one's hands. Specialists will notice imprecisions (or worse) despite every effort to be lucid and accurate. But when it comes to grasping the volatile, elusive, but potent matters of modern fame and authority bodied forth in the Nobel Prize, and how they modify and are modified by ourselves and our times, specialists are in the same leaky boat with the rest of us.

I owe debts of all kinds to many people. To Tug Yourgrau, first, whose gift for happiness is outdone only by his gift for generosity — I thank him for launching this book in the right direction. To Richard Seaver for believing in this book enough to want to publish it, showing that publishing is still an independent and courageous enterprise. To Webster Younce, my wizardly editor, for his wonderfully cheerful patience and benign surgeon's eye for improving my writing. To my other editor, Ann Marlowe, this book is blessedly in debt to her extraordinary skill, learning, and passionate dedication. To Baruch Hochman for his buoying humanity and a couple of helpful miracles. To Katherine Williams for a cherished friendship; no one helped as selflessly with this book. To Allen Mandelbaum, Robert Richardson, and Maria Katzenbach for early and lasting encouragement. To Elizabeth Richardson for her staunch support and her skill as a photographer. To David Markson and Werner Dannhauser for going out of their way to help. To Annie Dillard for a kindness and Garry Trudeau for a favor that saved me much work. To Roald Hoffmann, a Nobelist in chemistry, who has helped me understand the poetry of chemistry, and the chemistry of poetry. To Professor Ze'ev Rosenkrantz of the Einstein Archives at Hebrew University in Jerusalem for granting me permission to use Einstein's Nobel medal. To Tad Spencer and Tom Kite for help. To the Nobel Foundation for assistance, especially to Fredrick Skog. To Professor Milton Wainwright of Sheffield University for cordial assistance about his original research. I am indebted as well to too many others to name.

My debt to my wife would take a book longer than this one. I have had to settle for the dedication.

THE
NOBEL PRIZE

INTRODUCTION

The Nobel Prizes are the most coveted and most potent awards of our time. Only "Nobel Prize winner" bestows instant recognition, lifelong celebrity, and unrivaled authority around the globe. In the media the prizes, along with wars and politics and major disasters, command front-page and prime-time treatment. The public (though not always the experts) accepts the selections as supremely authoritative about the most important scientific discoveries, the "best" writers, the most significant peace work. To people bewildered by arcane science or strange literary experiments or "peace" perplexities, the Nobel annually declares with Olympian assurance what is of surpassing importance. In fields that few have the time or ability to follow, the prizes convey a sense that coherence somehow does exist out there.

To say "prizes" scarcely conveys the meaning of the Nobel awards. Some view these as only another scramble up the greasy pole of celebrity. But the Nobels are really knighthoods of a new and unusual kind, perhaps the only true aristocracy in our democratic, leveling age. Winning a war for Britain can make you a knight of that realm, but so can being a rich brewer or a winning jockey. To capture the Nobel's exalted sort of nobility, far greater achievements are needed. And why have an aristocracy unless it is very exclusive? The Nobel group is surely that. From 1901 through 1999 the Nobel Prize has bestowed only 687 awards upon its designees: for peace 87, medicine 169, literature 96, physics 159, chemistry 132, and economics 44. (These figures do not include nineteen awards to peace organizations such as the Red Cross; in many years, no awards were given: see chronology.) Millions may dream of being selected, but few are called and fewer are chosen — in literature and peace an average of one per year, in the sciences an average of fewer than two.

The Nobel confers its titles in a ceremony conducted by the king of Sweden. This ritual takes place always on 10 December, the anniversary of the death of Alfred Nobel, its benefactor. Two thousand dignitaries, tuxedoed and gowned, gather in the Stockholm Concert Hall. At 4 P.M. the ceremony begins. As the Stockholm

Philharmonic plays selections by Mozart and Mendelssohn (or Grieg and Sibelius), laureates from earlier years enter to applause. The king and queen take their places on the stage while the audience sings the Royal Hymn. Then appear the new laureates, also tuxedoed or gowned. They sit on the left of the stage in a fixed order of precedence, according to how Alfred Nobel listed their fields in his 1895 will — first physics, then chemistry, medicine, literature, and peace — with economics, an award established only in 1968, bringing up the rear. A great blue carpet covers the stage. At stage center, presiding over all, is an enlarged image of Alfred Nobel.

The investiture is brief, its script unchanging. One by one the laureates are named, rise, and come forward. A Swedish academician in the appropriate field delivers a brief laudatory description of the achievement honored, addressed to "Your Majesty, Your Royal Highnesses, ladies and gentlemen." To the laureate he then intones: "I now invite you to receive your prize from the hands of the king." The king shakes hands and presents the laureate with a leather box that contains a gold medal bearing a replica of Alfred Nobel's profile and engraved with the laureate's name (the economics medal somewhat disdainfully inscribes the laureate's name only on the rim), a diploma, and a certificate for the prize money, to be exchanged the next day for a check. The laureate steps back.

Later, in the Stockholm city hall, the king hosts a banquet where the plates are gold-leafed and decorated with replicas of the Nobel medals; the meat is traditionally venison, provided by the king's own hunters. Each laureate is toasted and returns the honor, speaking a few minutes in good spirits (Isaac Bashevis Singer, the Yiddish writer and 1978 Nobelist, said he liked writing Yiddish, that dying language, because he liked to write ghost stories). The next day, the laureates give a major address, in which the scientists explain their technical work and the writers and peace laureates speak as the spirit moves. The Israeli novelist S. Y. Agnon included all the animals in his thanks; the Italian dramatist Dario Fo handed out not the text of an address but a booklet of drawings. On following days there are celebrations in other Swedish towns. All the laureates stay up to a week at the Grand Hotel, as guests of Sweden.

The media meanwhile fill us in on what the Nobel institution decorously omits. We learn that the 1995 economics laureate, Robert Lucas of the University of Chicago, had agreed to pay half his

Nobel prize money to his ex-wife if he won within seven years of their divorce, specifically by 31 October 1995; he won in the seventh year on 10 October, when the announcements are made, and by that thin margin she got half the $600,000 award. All of Einstein's Nobel money of 1921 went to his ex-wife by prior agreement. The Indian government agreed not to tax Mother Teresa's 1979 Nobel Prize of $193,000, though she was based in Calcutta. But in 1923, when Fritz Pregl won in chemistry, the Austrian government took two-thirds of his $30,000 award in taxes. In 1986 the U.S. passed a law taxing Nobel awards as ordinary income, thus cutting heavily into American winners' receipts since then.

The molecular biologist Max Delbrück (Nobel in Medicine, 1969) donated his prize money to Amnesty International. Georg von Békésy (medicine, 1961) made the Nobel Foundation heir to his art estate worth almost half a million dollars, at least ten times what his actual prize had been worth. Delbrück also at first considered rejecting the prize as pointless and distracting, as did the physicists Paul A. M. Dirac and Richard Feynman. They all eventually accepted. Newspaper readers in 1946 learned that James B. Sumner, who shared that year's chemistry Nobel, had lost his left arm at seventeen while hunting; although left-handed, he trained himself to do laboratory work right-handed. King Gustav VI Adolf of Sweden, an ardent tennis player, was very curious about how Sumner managed to serve the ball during a game. In 1980 a repository of sperm from Nobel laureates was proposed for interested women. Three laureates were rumored to have enrolled and one even made his name public. But for lack of Nobelized sperm, the scheme dropped off.

Such tidbits, gossip, and a few scandals swirl about the prize. Child molesters do not usually make national news, but they do if one is a Nobel Prize winner: in 1996 a laureate in medicine was convicted of molesting a child he had brought to the U.S. from an overseas research trip that won him the prize. But even the most deserved fame sometimes reaches only so far. A famous football star happened to attend a speech by William Faulkner, was puzzled by the hushed attention, and asked the person next to him why. "He won the Nobel Prize." "Oh, the Mobil Prize," said the footballer, impressed.

The Nobel judges have also made mistakes. The wrong codiscoverer of insulin may have been honored in the Nobel Prize for Medicine of 1923. A mistaken cure for cancer was honored in 1926.

In 1952 the codiscoverer of streptomycin was omitted in the Nobel Prize for Medicine, although the evidence was on legal record and the Nobel jury could easily have obtained it. In 1912 Nils Dalén, a Swedish engineer, won the physics prize for improving lighthouse illumination, chosen over the great physicist Max Planck, among others.

But generally the science prizes are greatly admired, by those who understand them, and by the rest precisely because they don't. The literature awards, however, have sometimes raised gales of complaints, and several peace prizes have set off official repression or dissident protest.

And a far more unsettling question haunts all the prizes: Are blue ribbons, no matter how exalted, relevant to intellectual or artistic or even peace work? If the Nobels disappeared tomorrow, would it make the slightest difference? And if prizes are indeed useful, is the Nobel system the way to decide them? How excellent is the Nobel's own record? How much has it mattered? And whence these prizes that cause so much fuss?

The Nobel Prizes' celebrity is itself extraordinary. When the awards began, no one could have predicted it. Indeed, they have been forced to live up to their own unique success. This has not always been easy, but it has made the inner life of that institution far more interesting than one would have expected.

Alfred Nobel himself provoked most of the interest at first. Quite unexpectedly, even to his family, the inventor of dynamite left his entire immense fortune to fund the prizes. That an inventor should bequeath prizes for science might be expected, but a prize for literature was surprising, and a peace prize from a "merchant of death" was startling. Nobel died in 1896; five years later, the first Nobel Prizes were awarded. Only a few years after that, they began to spiral into ever-widening fame.

What helped here was an extremely lucky accident in 1903. In 1901 and 1902, what mainly interested the public and laureates was Nobel's glamorous name and the huge monies he bestowed. The literature and peace prizes drew most of the public attention, at least when one of the winners was a compatriot. But the first science prizes honored either already well-known discoveries, such as immunization against diphtheria and tetanus or Röntgen's discovery of X-rays back in 1895, or work like the synthesis of purines or electromagnetic theory, intelligible only to a few specialists. Much interest was prompted by national competition, as if the prizes were an exalted kind of modern Olympic Games, begun in 1896.

But interest of a different kind quickened dramatically in 1903 when the Nobel Physics Prize was shared by Henri Becquerel and Marie and Pierre Curie. Becquerel was a well-known professor in Paris, who had discovered radioactivity in uranium in 1896. But who were these Curies who had discovered two new radioactive elements?

The French press took it up partly because this was the first Nobel Prize awarded to French scientists: national pride was gratified. But the reporters, and then the world press, also found a most satisfying rags-to-riches story, which some then described as a minor national scandal.

The Curies turned out to be a devoted couple in early middle age (Pierre was forty-four, Marie thirty-six), shy, unworldly, utterly absorbed in their work. The reporters were captivated. This couple that had just won two-thirds of the munificent Nobel Prize, worth $40,000 in 1903 buying power, absentmindedly took meager meals when they remembered to eat. Marie, too busy with her science, had never bothered to learn to cook; Pierre never looked away from his experiments long enough to notice. She wore the plainest, most drab dresses. They lived in a little garret on the sixth floor, one hundred long steps up, so cold in winter that they had to sleep fully clothed.

Both also had drab jobs, though both had doctorates. Pierre taught at a small and obscure technical institute, and Marie in a girls' academy — a far cry from Becquerel at the grand Sorbonne. The reporters were especially taken with the shabbiness of the laboratory in which the great discoveries had taken place. It was a small decrepit workshop with greenhouse windows. There was no heat. The old walls and floor were damp, the roof dripped. The laboratory equipment was primitive and patched together — the ionization chamber was made from a jelly can, though Marie had luckily been able to borrow a good electrometer.[1] She had begun her work asking if the rays given off by Becquerel's uranium also came from other elements, and coined the word "radioactivity" to describe their common property. To test this, she begged and borrowed samples of every element she could from other scientists or obliging museums — and finally discovered that thorium was also radioactive. Working furiously, and meanwhile raising an infant daughter, Marie and Pierre also found the new radioactive elements polonium and radium.

To get more precise measurements and confirm Marie's findings, the Curies bought as much pitchblende and chalcite (uranium ores that contain minute traces of other radioactive elements) as they could afford. It was cheap, and so many gunnysacks of the stuff arrived that they had to expand their workshop across the back courtyard into a little shack. This shack was in even worse shape than the workshop: the walls were crumbling, drafts whistled through window cracks, the ceiling threatened to tumble down. But it had an old table, a blackboard, and a treasure — a cast-iron stove. The eminent German chemist and later Nobelist Wilhelm Ostwald, who visited this "laboratory" to pay his respects, could hardly believe he was at the right address; he described it as part stable and part potato cellar.[2]

Marie set out to purify radium. She did all the work herself. She filled iron cauldrons with the black ore, set them boiling, stirred the noxious mess with a long iron rod for hours, and did the tedious distillation procedure. The cauldrons were open and gave off nauseating fumes, so she moved them outside into the open courtyard. With every heavy rain, she had to push the cauldrons hastily back into the shed. The dirt, dust, and plaster from the shack tainted the purity of the distillations, forcing her to start over. Meanwhile she began to feel constantly fatigued and ill — the effects of radiation, which were of course then unknown. Her fingertips were soon painfully scorched from touching the radium.

But she and Pierre finally proved polonium and radium were new radioactive elements. Bits of scientific recognition came to them. In 1898 Marie won the Gegner Prize, worth almost what Pierre earned in a year. Pierre was made a member of the French Academy of Sciences after being rejected a few years earlier. Marie got the job in the girls' academy. In 1903, Pierre was appointed to a chair at the Sorbonne, where Marie received her Ph.D. in physics, summa cum laude — the first woman in Europe ever to earn a doctorate in science (first place in the science examinations, second place in mathematics).

In 1903, too, came the Nobel Prize. Theirs was a success story to delight any newspaper reader. The prize suddenly made them seventy thousand francs richer, almost twice their salaries for the next ten years. In 1891 Marie Skłodowska had been a penniless student just arrived from Poland to enroll in the Sorbonne. Now she and her husband were a pride of France's scientific community — and the French press insisted she was now entirely French.

While praising the Curies, the press could lament the stinginess with which France treated its scientific treasures. *Le Figaro* said: "We do not know our scientists, foreigners have to discover them for us."[3] The decrepit workshop, shack, and open courtyard were pictured and described over and over again, like icons. In fact, French science had not really stinted in funding the Curies' work, there was just not enough to buy them a good laboratory.

Marie Curie, more than Pierre, attracted attention. She was Polish and thus slightly exotic; she was a mother who was raising a daughter despite heroic hours stirring the boiling cauldrons; she was selfless, wholly absorbed in her quest for knowledge. It was not difficult to portray her as a kind of saint of science. At thirty-six, she was also fairly young. Indeed, compared to prizewinners in other fields often in their sixties or even eighties, she was refreshingly young, and a new face.

Radium with its mysterious rays and promise of curing any or all diseases helped swell the publicity. It was also recent enough news to compete with Marconi's new "wireless telegraphy" for popular attention.[4] Humorous and serious journals took it up. Loie Fuller, the American "art" dancer, performed a popular "radium dance" in Paris.

Marie welcomed the prestige from the prize. After Pierre's death, she was appointed to the Sorbonne to teach Pierre's courses — the first woman ever to teach at the Sorbonne. Other rich prizes came in, and she later made a successful tour of the United States to raise a large sum for her new laboratory. That Marie was a working scientist caused defenders of the home to berate her and feminists to defend her. One biographer, Susan Quinn, notes that this ambivalence about Marie likely was why four French scientists, including the great mathematician Poincaré and the 1908 physics laureate Gabriel Lippmann, tried to persuade the Nobel jury to exclude her from the prize by claiming the discoveries were Pierre's alone — which was untrue: Lippmann knew their joint work intimately.[5]

Like later laureates, the Curies found the celebrity at times infuriating, at times amusing. Marie's great fame from the physics prize was doubled when she won the Nobel chemistry prize in 1911, specifically for the discovery of radium and polonium. But her celebrity at that time almost brought her to disastrous public scandal — which in turn fed more publicity to the Nobel Prize.

By then a widow — Pierre had died in a street accident in 1906 — she had an affair with the renowned French physicist Paul Langevin, whose wife was madly jealous. Some Paris newspapers blared the affair and the wife's recriminations across their front pages. It was a media dream. Love letters were stolen, Langevin fought a duel with a journalist, the wife threatened Marie's life. The scandal might have cost Marie her second Nobel. But other newspapers rebuked the sensationmongers, Langevin reconciled with his wife, the threat of scandal faded. Marie kept a dignified silence and slipped away to Stockholm to collect her second prize.

Marie Curie thus became the first recipient of the Nobel Prize in both of its familiar aspects: honored for the importance of her work, but also instantly transformed into a worldwide celebrity. Because of her, newspapers around the globe changed their way of reporting the Nobel Prize, generating endless publicity, and thereby finally changing the meaning of the awards. We are by now used to idolizing accounts of Einstein. But soon after 1903, the press could be as extravagant about the Curies as later about Einstein. One paper hailed their study of radioactivity with these words: "Voilà, perpetual motion, the eternal sun, the supreme inexhaustible force have been at last found through the geniuses of Monsieur and Madame Curie, whose Nobel Prize fits them like a glove."[6]

The Curie story also demonstrated that the Nobel Prizes had been born at a very lucky time, when both science and literature were turning "modern" and thus increasingly incomprehensible to the public, and also when the media began its own great expansion and influence.

Journalists began to feature the personalities behind the prize. Interviewers poked into the laureates' private lives, charms and foibles, work habits, and opinions on all subjects, however unrelated to their special knowledge. This remains as true today. Reporters, expectedly enough, also saw what they chose to see. They habitually described Marie Curie as saintly and selfless, though her close friends saw her as refusing joy in life. "The soul of a herring," said Einstein, who admired her, sadly. She always wore a widow's black.

From the latest lottery winner to yesterday's pop star, ephemeral celebrity (Andy Warhol's "everyone is famous for fifteen minutes") now seems a fact of life. But the fame of a Nobel Prize is one of the scarcest and therefore most valuable, not only because great talent is rare, but in this race a miss is as good as a mile. Though up to three can share a single prize, the runners-up — however deserving, however possessed of true greatness — never appear on any Nobel list. The Nobel Prize does not teach the noble wisdom that the work is its own reward, but the harsher lesson that many may be truly worthy but very few will be chosen, and sometimes not even the most deserving.

In a single century, the unchosen "many" have multiplied many times over. In 1901 there were about a thousand active physicists in the world.[7] Today there may be as many as 200,000. So too with chemists and medical researchers. Judging by the vast increase in published matter, the number of poets and fiction writers in the world is immensely greater than in the nineteenth century, too large to count. As the pool of competitors increases, the Nobel Prize obviously becomes more difficult to win, but thus also more desirable as the only distinction by which one can rise above nearly all others.

The pre-Nobel nineteenth century perpetuated ancient methods for honoring scholars and artists. Princes gave out laurels, riches, titles, political rank. The pianist Franz Liszt, in his sensational virtuoso days of the 1840s, was regularly laden with ceremonial swords, medals, monetary tributes, trophies, keys to cities, not to mention a title of nobility. Scientists and artists also received once-in-a-lifetime celebrations. In 1890 the pioneering organic chemist August Kekulé von Stradonitz was grandly feted in Berlin on the twenty-fifth anniversary of his famous discovery of the benzene ring structure. In 1892 a more stupendous international jubilee was held for the great bacteriologist Pasteur on his seventieth birthday. Only a few years later, this was outdone by an even more spectacular commemoration for the chemist Marcellin Berthelot at which the president of the French Republic presented a flattering medal.[8] Kekulé and Pasteur died too soon for a Nobel Prize; Berthelot lived long enough, but never won.

Compared to these, the Nobel Prize ceremony is a modest and sober affair. Extravaganzas no longer suit science or literature. In the mid-1800s, scientists had often been gentlemen-amateurs, lone entrepreneurs (Alfred Nobel is a prime example), or government employees such as that prince of mathematicians Karl Gauss. Some were professors, but usually suffered low academic and social status.

At Yale the science students and faculty were not allowed to sit with regular students in chapel.[9] But toward the end of the nineteenth century, science became of crucial value to commerce, government, and the military. German and British industries set up research laboratories. Scientists entered universities as professors with high standing and began to set up that international network we now call "science." At the same time, literary scholars started becoming professors and launched societies and journals, turning themselves into professionals quite as respectable as lawyers, ministers, or doctors. The Nobel Prize is the child of all this. It is based in Swedish academic institutions, plus a Norwegian committee for the peace prize. Eminent professors and scholars dominate the Nobel committees.

But the Nobel ceremony is also and intrinsically a royal ceremony. The king's presence is symbolically indispensable. In 1901, when the first Nobel Prizes were conferred, many European nations still had monarchs. After World War I, the Swedish ruler kept his throne, if without real power, and his small country on the nothern periphery played a small part in a world dominated by the Great Powers. In the modern world, however, a king is a unique thing, and for Nobel purposes an item of incalculable iconic value.

The courtly ceremony over which today's King Carl XVI Gustav presides is, after all, a vestige of the vanished aristocratic past when princes rewarded artists or political favorites. The Nobel rite is performed for a modernity nostalgic for such older and vanishing glories. The king and queen, the gold medals stamped with Alfred Nobel's profile and his bas-relief dominating the dais, the royal blue carpet, the atmosphere of ancient nobility: all helps magically transform laboratory experiments and poems into world-commanding achievements, and for a moment makes its honored individuals imaginably heroic.

Nothing is more modern than how the Nobel Prizes marry such old-fashioned individual glory with the flatlands of democratic life — esoteric knowledge with popular opinion. As the works honored in science and, latterly, economics have grown increasingly remote and arcane to the general public, the Nobels have become the most important bridge between high intellectual achievement and the marketplace. Where comprehension fails, celebrity fills in.

The most dramatic novelty, of course, was the sizable fortunes the Nobel Prizes lavished on the laureates. By one estimate, the

French Academy of Sciences was disbursing a total of about 100,000 francs (approximately $20,000) per year from 1901 to 1910. But in 1901 *each* of the five Nobel Prizes was worth about 210,000 francs or $40,000.[10] The Nobels have remained the benchmark in prize money, though their value has gone up and down through the century along with inflations and recessions (see Appendix A). The sudden wealth raining on obscure scholars and impoverished artists also became one of the strongest arguments for the Nobels' integrity and authority. As early-Nobel historian Elisabeth Crawford notes, the public was likely to think that only truly worthy achievements could command prizes worth so much money.[11] The Nobel here stands as ancestor and prototype to the huge publicity generated by the MacArthur Foundation's so-called genius awards: why would anyone give five straight years of munificent support to anyone other than a "genius"?

The Nobel has its rivals, but none combines the wealth and prestige of the prize, the range of its subjects, and its century-long record. To be sure, the Templeton Prize for Progress in Religion, established by a wealthy Briton in 1972, is richer — precisely because its founder decreed that it should always be worth more than the Nobel Prize of the same year: in 1998, for example, the Templeton Prize was worth $1.24 million as against $978,000 per Nobel Prize. Unlike the Nobel, most awards specialize either in science or in the arts, with political honors excluded altogether. The (British) Royal Society is restricted to science. The Pulitzer Prize confines itself to journalism and a few of the arts; the Prix Goncourt, like the British Booker Prize (worth $31,500 in 1995), to literature. No award has the aura of the Nobel in literature or peace, though the Royal Society medals in science or the Fields Medals in mathematics are in some ways as prestigious or more among scientists than the Nobels — and harder to win, one might add. The Fields Medal, for example, is awarded only every four years, by the International Mathematical Union.

Other prizes have been created as alternatives to the Nobel.[12] The Wolf Prize, established in Israel in 1978, gives annual winners $100,000 each in physics, chemistry, medicine, mathematics, and the arts. Some awards, such as the Balzan Prize, are specifically set up for fields like sociology or political science for which no Nobel exists. Some specify no field, as with the Right Livelihood Award, founded in 1980. The Swedish Royal Academy of Sciences, which awards the Nobel Prizes in physics, chemistry, and economics, even administers an alternative to itself: the Schock Prize in Philosophy, which honors philosophy, mathematics, music, and fine arts. This award too is bestowed by the king of Sweden; in 1994 the American logician Willard van Orman Quine was the first recipient.

But new or old, the Nobel Prize still outranges them all. It was the first important regular prize to include not only the arts and sciences but politics in the form of "peace." It was an international prize. "No consideration whatsoever shall be given to the nationality of the candidates," commanded Alfred Nobel's will. Earlier literary awards had usually restricted eligibility to citizens of their nations, though the eminent scientific awards were open to foreigners. The Nobel's internationalism allowed it to include achievements anywhere in the world, to reap the harvest of all nations.

Inevitably, this appeal to international harmony — like the Olympics — has roused fierce national rivalries. Science may speak a transnational language, but each year, as the new Nobels are announced, national scorecards and rivalries are anxiously scrutinized. When the U.S. swept the prizes in all fields in 1976, the *New York Times* triumphantly headlined the event on its front page. When, in 1984, the European experimental physicists at the CERN laboratory outraced the U.S. to find the W and Z bosons, American editorialists lamented and warned of falling behind. The unsuccessful campaign to build the Superconducting Super Collider — at six billion dollars — involved hopes to regain the lead from the Europeans. Statistics are constantly paraded. Americans won 64% of all medicine Nobels in 1983–93, up from 1963–73, when the U.S. won only 50% of the medicine awards. In 1963–73 Americans took 55% of all prizes, but in 1983–93 only 48%, though the chemistry prizes rose from 33% to 60%. That must be progress, since science makes the technology which makes the "future." So far, it seems, the country is safe.

Luckily for Nobel celebrity, modern science became an international enterprise around 1900. Crawford describes a period of high international cooperation from the 1880s to 1914, followed by disruption from the First War through the Second War, and then cooperation again since 1945.[13] And since science speaks a language common to all nations, this helps explain why the Nobel record in the sciences has been so good — and the Nobel in literature not so good. Gauging the worth of writing requires knowing a particular language most fluently and intimately. But the world has scores of languages, though one would not guess this from the few major European languages that have taken almost all the prizes. The peace prizes, of course, cover every part of the globe: human conflict is the same everywhere, only worse.

Two other factors helped boost the Nobel to unmatched renown. Nobel's will contained a "most recent" clause, requiring awards to go only to the latest scientific discovery, invention, or improvement, or to literary works appearing during the "preceding year." This could clearly have become an unworkable requirement, and it was relaxed when the Nobel Statutes were drawn up in 1900. But this carried a danger. As mordantly stated by the Swedish chemist Svante Arrhenius (Nobel in Chemistry, 1903, and a force on the first science committees), the "worst thing would be for the prizes to develop into old-age pensions."[14] The literature prizes have come close.

Nonetheless, the "recent" requirement helped make the Nobel Prize an annual source of fresh and exciting news. The discovery of radium or the human genetic code or the transistor — or the Israeli/PLO accord — is newsworthy by any standard. Each fall, the public may hope to learn about astonishing breakthroughs, ingenious new techniques, a bold poet or peacemaker. Such novelty was soon expected in all the prize categories: "discoveries awarded the prize were expected to involve surprises, startling effects, leaps into the unknown."[15] But the literature judges, for the first half century or so, actually fought off such excitement by rejecting almost all "provocative" writers" (Ibsen, Joyce, D. H. Lawrence). Of course, startling novelties are rare. No matter. "Amazing" feats in sports also happen far between, yet all fans keep hoping and believing.

On the other side, annual awards can quickly wear out the supply of quality goods. The science prizes have an advantage here, since science progresses by refuting or refining its past successes. If particle physics stalls, there is still superconductivity, astrophysics, superstrings, and specialties yet aborning.

Peace laureates can always be found, since no one has any clear idea how to delimit that category. The Wright brothers were urged as peace laureates in 1909, Kaiser Wilhelm in 1910, Lindbergh after his solo trans-Atlantic flight, the American socialist Eugene Debs in 1924, Baron Pierre de Coubertin who founded the modern Olympic Games in 1896, several of the popes, Stalin's henchman Maxim

Litvinov in 1933. In 1977, U.S. congressman Les Aspin nominated Jerry Lewis for the Nobel Peace Prize for his muscular dystrophy fund-raising on TV; the winner that year was Amnesty International.

Even Hitler! At least, in 1934 the *New York Times* devoted an entire page, headlined HITLER NOMINATED FOR NOBEL PRIZE, to a long essay by Hamilton Fish Armstrong, then editor of the eminent journal *Foreign Affairs*. His point was that because Hitler had not invaded Austria in 1934 as he threatened, this "helped save the world, in 1934 at any rate, from war." Armstrong seems to have been writing with heavy-handed irony. But that the sober *Times* gave it so much space showed that the Nobel Prizes drew public attention.

The literature prizes are different. "Great" writers alone should win, but how to determine that? The Nobel abhors a vacuum: each year, a slot opens and another writer must be found to fill it. Nominees are of course never lacking. Margaret Mitchell was nominated for *Gone with the Wind* (and rejected). Charlie Chaplin was nominated in 1952 by the prominent Swedish literary critic Olof Lagercrantz, on the grounds that Chaplin was a major "screen author" because he wrote the scripts he acted in his films. Although Chaplin was rejected as primarily an actor rather than a playwright, the 1997 Nobel award went to the Italian Dario Fo, a famous comedian whose playwrighting, like Chaplin's, mainly consists of scripts for his own performances.

Many warn that the economics prize may soon, if not already, face a shortage of worthy candidates.

Certainly from Einstein's prize — in 1922 for the preceding year — the Nobel's prestige crucially rests on the prestige of its science prizes. Nuclear physics or transfer RNA may puzzle most people, but the wonder and dread inspired by the hydrogen bomb or cloning is inescapably real and obvious. Everyone grasps that these sciences embody vast and revolutionary might of uncertain kind. The violent power crouching in every stick of Mr. Nobel's dynamite made this point quite clear earlier.

Another reason is that the science juries have long chosen far more impressive laureates than have the literary judges. Planck, Rutherford, Einstein, Bohr, Heisenberg, Dirac, Pauling, Crick and Watson, Feynman — a steady procession of greatness or the nearest equivalent. Would the Nobel have much of an aura or any at all without those names? The literature prizes, after fifty years of ignoring the likes of Leo Tolstoy, Bertolt Brecht, James Joyce, and Virginia Woolf, can never catch up with the prestige of the science lists. The prizes in literature, peace, and economics are not unlike pale fires, shining more brightly in the reflected light of Einstein and company.

The Nobel Theater of Fame

When the Nobel Prize is awarded, no "short list" of top candidates is ever announced. The decision is final. Glaring mistakes or omissions have been made, but no award is ever reversed or altered, even when disputes inside the committees occasionally erupt into public sight.[16]

The effect is of magisterial authority and finality. The Bench is not to be approached. The decisions are rendered as if from eternity and for eternity. Those honored are forever of the Elect. Aesthetically, this is as it should be. Any sign of inner dissension spilling into public squabbling could bring the whole lofty drama abruptly down to earth. One should never look behind the scenes of any good theater. If one must have prizes for science and art, which is entirely debatable, they should come as from on high. The Nobel Foundation has always been shrewd about this.

The invisibility of the machinery heightens the majesty of the prizes. This machinery is so self-effacing that the decisions seem almost to issue not from mere Stockholm but from some timeless Realm of Objective Judgment. The Nobel Foundation has cultivated a very disciplined anonymity, though selecting the laureates is a process that involves hundreds of nominators and evaluators from around the world.

The small army of Swedish and Norwegian evaluators who filter this information are sworn to secrecy and have remained extraordinarily tight-lipped for almost a century, and so too the foreign colleagues in whom they doubtless confide. Leaks are extremely rare, and most apt to happen in that highly volatile category called, with unintentional irony, peace. A flagrant breach of Nobel secretiveness came when the 1994 peace committee awarded a share of the prize to the PLO leader Yasir Arafat. A committee member publicly denounced Arafat as a terrorist and resigned. Two members publicly resigned when the peace prize was awarded to Henry Kissinger and Le Duc Tho in 1973 for a cease-fire in the Vietnam War.

The most shocking breach of Nobel secrecy has come from outside. In 1995 the Swedish newspaper *Dagens Nyheter,* called the most influential in Sweden, printed seven articles charging the Nobel Prize in Medicine with corruption. *Dagens Nyheter* claimed that Fidia, an Italian pharmaceutical firm, had paid nine million dollars to the medicine judges to make Rita Levi-Montalcini a laureate: Fidia had funded her research since 1979 on nerve growth factors, and expected great profits if their researcher was a prizewinner. In fact she shared the prize in 1986. A Nobel committee member threatened to sue the newspaper. After two weeks of intense protests, *Dagens Nyheter* printed an editorial retraction, stating that bribery had not taken place. Informed sources speculate that the newspaper was trying to boost circulation.[17]

In Nobel committees as elsewhere, consensus is often hard to reach, much less unanimity. Friction often runs high, and certain committee members operate as power brokers, able to speed up a prize or delay one, sometimes for decades. So can powerful nominators: the great physicist Niels Bohr is reported to have personally stalled the physics prize to Feynman, Schwinger, and Tomonaga for almost fifteen years.

The identities of the all-important nominators are not publicly disclosed, nor of candidates. The science archives fifty years or older have been opened to outsiders,[18] but it may be a long time before anything very accurate is known about why Gandhi never won the peace prize, or why William Golding did win the literature prize. Still, it can come as a slight shock to peer behind the impassively majestic facade of the Nobel Foundation and catch sight of the prosaic Scandinavian professors who actually oil and run the grand machine.

The Nobel Foundation is a fair-sized industry. In 1994 the total expenditures on committees, staff, nominators, consultants, and others ran to six million dollars. The selection process is firmly institutional. The key work is done by committees usually of five or six members each, chosen, for literature, by the Royal Swedish Academy in Stockholm; for medicine, by the Karolinska Institute (Caroline Institute) in Stockholm; for physics, chemistry, and economics, by the Swedish Academy of Sciences in Stockholm; for peace, by the Norwegian Storting (parliament). These committees invite nominations from an international list of academics, eminent figures, and all former laureates. The Nobel science committees also seek nominations from directors of important laboratories or journals, and the literature committee from some writers. No candidate can be self-nominated, though many try it.

Nominations, due before 1 February, are sifted from a few hundred to about thirty. By summer, the committee elects its winner and sends the choice to the larger groups of the academies involved — in physics, for example, to all the physicists in the Academy of Sciences, then to the entire academy. The full group can overrule the committee recommendation and has done so. The final sessions can get rough: "We have finished murdering each other's candidates," one scientific member gleefully put it in the early years.[19]

The literature decisions are perhaps more contentious, but the setting is more elegant. After the committee has made its nomination, the eighteen members of the Swedish Academy meet to vote around an antique table.[20] Watched over by a bust of King Gustav III, founder of the Swedish Academy, they drop their ballots into a small silver pitcher. Gustav III ruled from 1771 to 1792, when he was assassinated at a masked ball — Sweden was a more romantic place back then. This stately voting is in keeping with the Swedish Academy's imitation of the brocaded airs of its model and ancestor, the Académie Française. Three members of the Swedish Academy resigned over the Rushdie affair, but have not had their resignations accepted, as appointment is for life. These three have not been attending meetings, but their votes still count if they exercise the right. In 1997 they apparently did not, and barely two-thirds of the members decided on the controversial Dario Fo that year.

The good news is telephoned to the laureate, to forestall leaks to the media. How well the hushed process works can be seen by how the world's experts usually guess wrong. For example, in 1995 the Norwegian media, which must be thought in the best position to hear leaks about the peace prize bestowed by the Norwegian peace committee, came up with these leading candidates: the Indonesian Catholic bishop Belo, the Kurdish leader Leyla Zana, former president Jimmy Carter, Mexican bishop Samuel Ruiz, Russian human rights activist Sergei Kovalyov, a Chinese dissident, negotiators for peace in Northern Ireland, and Doctors without Borders. In fact, the prize was shared by the British physicist–peace activist Joseph Rotblat and the Pugwash organization to control nuclear arms.

Nobel Monumentalism

The Nobel Foundation itself deserves a drama award for the way it glorifies its laureates. Its monumentalizing process begins with the citation that focuses the spotlight on the laureate's achievements alone — rarely are any colleagues, predecessors, or helpers mentioned. In this, the Nobel sanctions the kind of history that consists of great deeds and high majesty, with the rest of ordinary life ignored.

It is true that writers do their work alone. But the Nobels in physics, chemistry, and medicine can leave an unreal and romanticized impression of science.[21] No one can deny the moment of high individual triumph — Röntgen finding X-rays, or Max Planck discovering the quantum concept in 1900, so excited that he couldn't resist telling his young son that he had done something of which even Newton would be proud. But if science requires great talent, it also demands a vast collective effort. For a scientist, winning the prize requires working for years with stimulating colleagues and collaborators, and having an incessant exchange of ideas and suggestions in conferences, seminars, and hallways; scientists are doubtless the best-traveled of all scholars. The Nobel Prize dramatizes only the moment of success, not the perplexity and blunders, tips and hints, that are really the scientist's daily bread. Nor would one guess from the prizes how relentlessly competitive science is. The difference beween winning a Nobel and not can be a hairline. And the accidental makeup and views of prize committees can often be a decisive factor.

As Bertolt Brecht (never a Nobelist) once put it:

> Alexander the Great conquered the world.
> What? By himself? Hadn't he even a cook along?

The effect left by the Nobel awards is often like that, the lone heroic explorer on the stage magnified by the limelight, blocking out all else. The Nobel perpetuates the popular view of the lonely genius: Shakespeare, Mozart, Newton, Einstein do not abide our question.

Precisely because of this, the molecular biologist Max Delbrück was tempted to reject his 1969 prize. He relented, but later spoke blunt words about the Nobel Prize: "By some random selection procedure, you pick out a person and you make him an object of a personality cult. After all, what does it amount to?"[22] Maria Goeppert Mayer must also have asked herself what it amounted to when she shared the 1963 physics prize, and read in a San Diego newspaper — she was then teaching there — the headline: S.D. MOTHER WINS NOBEL PRIZE.

Responding to the Prize

During their first ten years, 1901–10, the Nobel Prizes were announced and awarded in Stockholm on the same day, 10 December. That meant the new laureates had to be secretly notified and then travel to Stockholm on a pretext or incognito. This proved hopelessly impractical and bothersome. And why such secrecy anyway? The more publicity, after all, the better.

Since then, the new Nobel Prizes have been announced each year in the fall. The usual practice now is that the medicine winners are named on 10 October. On successive days thereafter come the economics award, then physics and chemistry, then literature. The peace prize is usually announced last.

The responses follow a well-defined pattern. The new laureates typically declare themselves gratified, astounded, and humbled. The media translate the science awards into digestible terms for the lay audience. In science, colleagues almost always commend the selection for its new benefit to mankind or its deeper understanding of fundamental problems. Very few ever disagree with the choices, at least in public.

The literary and political (i.e., peace) communities do not always welcome their new laureates with a choir of approval. A member of the Swedish Academy once publicly resigned when William Golding won the literature Nobel. Literary laureates of small countries can become national heroes overnight by winning the prize; they can equally become targets of ideological or religious contempt. The Egyptian novelist Naguib Mahfouz (1988) has been continuously denounced for his "secularizing" work and status, and in 1994 was stabbed by a religious militant.

The peace prizes, since they involve political matters, naturally cause the most quarrels. Alfred Nobel set up the award to encourage "fraternity among nations . . . abolition or reduction of standing armies, or promotion of peace congresses." Political disputes regularly break out, as with the Soviet government's fury at Sakharov's peace award, or China's at the prize to the Dalai Lama for intimating that Tibet should regain its freedom from China. Mother Teresa was even accused of pandering to the rich and exploiting the sick for religious purposes.

In any case, a rude celebrity springs on every laureate. The media treat the new laureates like universal experts on almost anything under the sun: scientists are asked to comment on crime or poverty or religion, writers on foreign policy, peace laureates on the arts. In 1988 President Mitterand of France called a conference of laureates to "create an emergency committee with moral authority in crises around the world." Laureates reported a "pleasant exchange of ideas."[23]

Most bow out as quickly as possible, but a few move on to second careers as publicists for favorite causes. Linus Pauling (chemistry, 1954) even won a second Nobel, the peace prize in 1962, for his protests against H-bomb testing.

Of course, in the wake of the prize, other rewards stream in. Science laureates soon find their discoveries in up-to-date textbooks, funding gravitates to them, they are invited to endless congresses, conferences, advisory posts, committees, foundations, and institutes. The new literary laureates enjoy a certain rise in sales and renown — at least until the next year and the next laureate.

But such prestige brings its perils. The great bacteriologist Robert Koch, after winning the 1905 prize in medicine, was made an "Excellenz." But then, astounding the "entire German nation to whom he appeared almost a god," he suddenly divorced his wife and married a young actress. He was much reviled; it may even have contributed to his early death.[24]

Willy-nilly, all winners have the label "Nobelist" affixed to their names in life and in death. In his *Humboldt's Gift* Saul Bellow, himself a Nobelist in 1976, portrayed a Pulitzer Prize–winning writer who laments that his very obituary will become only another advertisement for that prize: "Pulitzer Prize-Winner Dies." Obituaries of Nobel laureates invariably make winning the prize the major event of that person's life.

Chewing Over the Bones

Nobel Prize winners are proudly and greedily claimed by their nations, universities, hometowns, political causes, professional organizations, and any other interested parties.

Nations are of course eager to claim winners, but this can often be confusing. Einstein was born in Germany but left there at sixteen and moved to Switzerland. He attended the Swiss scientific university, the ETH (Federal Institute of Technology, something like MIT or CalTech), and became a Swiss citizen. In 1914 he joined the Prussian Academy of Sciences in Berlin. When he won the physics prize for 1921, what nationality was he?

In fact, Swiss: that was his legal citizenship. Switzerland was where he grew up from age sixteen, was educated through his doctorate, worked for several years in the Swiss patent office and began teaching — and where he made his first great discoveries, including the one the Nobel honored. He kept lifelong Swiss citizenship even after taking U.S. citizenship. But with his Nobel Prize, Einstein's prestige was so great that the Germans were anxious to claim him as one of their own. They therefore declared that any member of the Prussian Academy of Sciences, by German law, had to be considered a German. The Swiss authorities thought otherwise. The Nobel Foundation finessed the problem by ignoring both the Swiss and the Germans; the Swedish ambassador to Germany presented the Nobel medal directly to Einstein in his home in Berlin. Nonetheless, Einstein is almost always described as German or German-American. Like all legends, the image of Einstein as German — thus a counter to the hateful face of Nazism — is destined to remain in the books.

National gamesmanship and honest confusion are involved here. Many laureates were refugees or émigrés at some point in their careers. The German physicist Max Born, who fled Hitler to Britain, is listed in the official Nobel history as British: he was indeed teaching in Edinburgh in 1954, the year he was awarded a long-delayed prize for work done almost thirty years before in Germany.

T. S. Eliot was born in Saint Louis, Missouri, but moved to England before World War I, and became a British citizen in 1927 at age thirty-five. His greatest poetry was written in Britain, and the Nobel Prize rightly lists him as British. Mother Teresa was born in Albania; she served as a young nun in Calcutta and became an Indian citizen; by any other criterion, she is "global." Reference works call her Indian.

The prize list makes little sense unless one knows not simply where but when the Nobel-winning work was done. Otherwise, topsy-turvy errors can result. One might conclude that the American novelist Pearl Buck (Nobel, 1938) was older and more famous than T. S. Eliot or Ernest Hemingway, since she became a laureate well before Eliot (1948) and Hemingway (1954). In fact, both were world-famous before she even began publishing. The Nobel that Max Born won in physics in 1954 seems to make him young enough to have been the student of Werner Heisenberg, who won the prize back in 1932. In fact Born was one of Heisenberg's teachers, a generation older, and an important collaborator on the theory that won Heisenberg his prize. The American biochemist Peyton Rous became a laureate in 1966 — for research done in 1911.

Schools claim any piece of a laureate they can. If the laureate studied there, taught there, did some research there, or was somehow affiliated, plaques or bronze scrolls or even oil portraits are apt to be in sight. Schools take Nobel glory very seriously, since a school's reputation can rise or fall thereby. The Business School of the University of Chicago advertises itself as having "more Nobel Prize winners than any other school." In the United States, the Nobelists in science come mainly from Harvard, Yale, Columbia, Chicago, MIT, CalTech, and Berkeley. The Bronx High School of Science in 1950 graduated two classmates who later shared the Nobel in physics — Steven Weinberg and Sheldon Glashow — while another graduate is the physics laureate Leon Cooper.

The laureate's hometown, whether Paris or Sauk Centre, Minnesota (Sinclair Lewis's birthplace), seizes the opportunity as well, commemorating its illustrious offspring by a bust or museum or street name. Tourist organizations remind all visitors that Nobelist X was born or lived or studied or taught or simply liked to vacation here. Books appear celebrating the Jews or Germans or British or Italians who have won Nobels. But Stockholm itself has no plaques or monuments to Alfred Nobel.

Through a Glass Darkly

Whether all these laureled "discoveries, inventions, and improvements" have proved themselves contributions "most materially of benefit to mankind" — to quote Alfred Nobel — remains an entirely open question. Science's contributions to war, pollution, social blight, and other problems have prompted a decline in the so-called religion of science. Literature's benefit to the world now often seems confined to a few rather than the multitude: film became by far the dominant popular art in the twentieth century. As for peace, little needs to be said about civilization's success in reining back war and armies. The Nobel's own influence — whether beneficial or corrupting to science, literature, and peace — is also entirely unsettled.

But no one could ever have accused Alfred Nobel of being unduly optimistic about any of this. It is to that unusual man we now turn.

1

The Founding Father

Alfred Nobel's life is a spectacular example of the new type that emerged in the nineteenth century, the capitalist whose energy, ambition, and ingenuity accepted no limits. Nobel invented a motto for himself: "My home is my work and my work is everywhere." He had no real homeland during his life. This famous Swede left Sweden at age nine and, for the rest of his life, returned only for very brief stays. Nor did he bother to maintain citizenship there. His brothers, too, were rootless, ever ready to migrate as they followed opportunities for profit. Alfred made his millions in the worldwide explosives industry. His father made his fortune, and lost it, manufacturing munitions for the Russian government. Alfred's two older brothers pioneered in the modern oil industry. Called the Russian Rockefellers, they opened up Russia's immense Baku oil fields, built a global enterprise, and became wealthier than Alfred.

What needs saying first about Alfred Nobel is that he was a singularly complicated man. He spoke Swedish, German, English, French, Russian, and Italian fluently, wrote plays and poems in English, and read far more widely in several languages than most informed people, to say nothing of millionaire inventors. In its time, his dynamite was the most destructive but also constructive weapon ever invented — indeed, one of the great inventions of the century. He gave a fortune to set up a peace prize. But the same man who created that award to alleviate human suffering had a mordant streak. He liked telling friends about his plan to set up a lavish mansion in Paris where prospective suicides could die amid luxury, rather than drown in the cold, filthy Seine. "A first-class orchestra" would play only "the most beautiful music."[1]

Inventor Becomes Millionaire

Alfred Nobel was born in 1833 in Stockholm, the third of four sons. The family traced itself back to peasants from a small town named Nobbelov, whence the name. But a seventeenth-century ancestor married into the family of an Uppsala University professor named Rudbeck, one of Sweden's famous early scientists, a researcher into the circulatory system. If the Nobels thereafter were poor, they remained educated. Alfred's grandfather was an army surgeon. His father, Immanuel (born 1800), went to a technical school and became an inventor just as Sweden began to industrialize. By his middle twenties, Immanuel Nobel had patented a planing machine, a press with ten rollers, and a rotary machine. But nothing worked out. The year Alfred was born, a fire put the father into bankruptcy. He experimented with India rubber for surgical uses, and invented a barge; it sank. He invented a floating backpack for soldiers; the army was not interested.

Since 1800 there had been many schemes to cut a canal across the Isthmus of Suez. Another surfaced in the 1830s, and this one indirectly gave birth to the invention of dynamite and Alfred Nobel's fortune. Gunpowder was then the only means of blasting out the millions of tons of earth that had to be removed. But it was highly ineffective. This set Immanuel — who, like his sons, always thought big — to thinking about explosives. He taught himself a little chemistry and built a workshop, and in 1837 succeeded in making some chemicals explode. But they also blew up the workshop and alarmed the neighbors, and the authorities forbade further work. Heavily in debt, he left his family in Sweden and went off to Russia to begin again.

This was a common move for a Swede at that time. Through the seventeenth century, Sweden and Russia had been rivals as the two great powers in the north of Europe (the wars continued to the early 1800s, when Russia seized Finland from Sweden). When Peter the Great built the fortress in Saint Petersburg, his prize new city, he faced the cannon toward Sweden. The famous equestrian statue of the Bronze Horseman in Saint Petersburg grinds a snake, symbolizing Sweden, under its hooves. But Russia lagged behind Sweden industrially and technically, and foreign experts were needed. One was John Paul Jones, who served Catherine the Great as Kontradmiral Pavel Ivanovich Jones.[2]

In Finland and then Russia, Immanuel kept up his explosives work, successfully inventing an underwater mine. With Russian military backing, he opened a factory in Saint Petersburg to produce mines, cannon shells, mortars, and machinery to make wheels. This "Michelin of his time," as someone called him, expanded into steam engines, iron piping, steam hammers weighing several tons, even window sashes and central heating systems for houses; his own house had the first in Russia. The factory was called Colonel Ogarev's and Mr. Nobel's Chartered Mechanical Wheel Factory and Pig Iron Foundry. Ogarev had earlier hired the American engineer George Washington Whistler — the painter's father — to build Russia's first important railroad.

In 1842 Immanuel was prosperous enough to bring his family to Saint Petersburg. In Sweden, Alfred had attended school only a year, but was privately tutored. He was quick at languages, soon fluent in French, German, Russian, but especially in English: as an adolescent he fell in love with Shelley's poetry and wrote skillful if imitative poems in English throughout his life. He also studied chemistry, mostly on his own. His two older brothers, Ludwig and Robert, went to work in their father's Russian factory. Alfred, aged seventeen, was sent on a long visit (1850–52) to the United States to work with the famous Swedish engineer Ericsson, already planning armored vessels like the *Monitor* of Civil War fame — perhaps an idea borrowed from Immanuel Nobel.

Alfred returned to Saint Petersburg, just in time to take part in his family's boom in munitions work. Russia's designs on Turkey were raising war tensions in Britain and France, and the czar wanted to be independent of European war supplies. The Nobel factories thus kept enlarging until they were gigantic by nineteenth-century Russian standards, employing a thousand workers — almost all untrained and also not very reliable: all were searched on leaving the premises. When the Crimean War broke out in 1854, Immanuel's underwater mines helped keep the British fleet away from the naval fortress at Kronstadt, and his shells, mortars, and wheel machinery fed the Russian army.

But the Russians lost the war, and the czar decided that Russia should no longer depend on home-grown industries. Immanuel Nobel abruptly had all his military contracts canceled and went bankrupt again, and in 1859 the family returned to Sweden to start over. Immanuel was almost sixty.

The decline of the father and ascent of the sons began. The older sons took over the business, and soon headed back for Finland and eventually Russia to try for another fortune. They made projectiles, cannon, rifles. Then in 1873 they saw the enormous oil deposits of Baku lying unexploited. They moved in.

Meanwhile Alfred, restless to be on his own, moved to Paris. He had become an inventor himself; his first patent was for a gas meter. That he switched to explosives was mainly due to his father's new obsession. Immanuel had failed at inventing a self-propelled torpedo, and even speculated about training seals to carry explosives. But nitroglycerine had become Immanuel's new passion.

An Italian chemist had created nitroglycerine in 1847, then given it up as too dangerously unstable. No one could find a way to handle it safely. Immanuel nonetheless managed to interest the Swedish military in this powerful explosive. Uncontrolled, however, it was useless. Alfred, the chemist, was asked by his brothers to work on the problem, and thus stumbled into his great career.

Alfred worked from 1859 to 1863 before he found a partial answer: soaking nitroglycerine in a granular powder added considerable force to the explosion. But this didn't much decrease the danger of using it. In 1865, however, Alfred made his first major discovery. He invented the detonator.

An explosives authority has described the detonator as "certainly the greatest discovery ever made in both the principle and practice of explosives. On it the whole modern practice of blasting has been built."[3] Indeed, the atomic and hydrogen bombs use the same detonator principle, which is that a small bit of one explosive can ignite another. A tiny amount of mercury fulminate, acting as the firing cap for nitroglycerine, made that dangerously volatile chemical relatively safe to use. Nobel took out the Swedish patent, quickly followed by others in England, Belgium, France, and Finland.

But the personal cost was high. Alfred's many failures on the way to his discovery had been mocked by his father and older brothers. When triumph did come, the father insulted Alfred by declaring he had had the successful idea first. Even worse, in 1864 the youngest son, Emil, died at twenty-one in a nitroglycerine explosion. Soon after, the father had a severe stroke. He finally recovered enough to keep busy with various schemes. Worried about Swedish emigration to the United States, he tried to invent new manufacturing opportunities to keep Swedish workers at home. To this end, he invented plywood — which, ironically, became a popular industry in the United States. Immanuel died in 1872.

Alfred set up a factory in Hamburg to manufacture his new invention, and it gained worldwide sales. But nitroglycerine remained unpredictable and its users often handled it recklessly, with disastrous results. In 1865 a salesman managed to pulverize a building in New York City, injuring eighteen. The next month, in Bremerhaven, twenty-eight were killed and more than two hundred wounded. Another grisly explosion occured in Sydney, Australia. In 1866 Nobel arrived in New York — with twelve cases of nitroglycerine! — to oversee his New York Blasting Oil Company, only to receive news of another catastrophe in San Francisco, with a dozen or more dead. Other explosions soon left more dead or wounded in California and Liverpool. Nobel transferred control of his U.S. interests to the U.S. Blasting Oil Company, keeping one-quarter of the shares. Europe, with wars threatening, was more promising territory anyway, and governments there were less stringent. In the Prussian-Austrian war of 1866, Nobel made a handsome profit. Soon he was in England, demonstrating the advantages of his nitroglycerine for mining and engineering.

In 1866 came Nobel's greatest invention: dynamite. That year he discovered how liquid nitroglycerine, when absorbed in kieselguhr (a kind of silicified earth formable into a paste), could be shaped into sticks safe to handle. By the middle of the nineteenth century, public works were expanding on an unparalleled scale: mining, harbors, road and bridge building, dam construction, railways, great canals such as the Suez (opened in 1869), and military works. Much of this crucially depended on the new dynamite's power to move tons of earth, tunnel through mountains, dislodge or pulverize huge rocks.

Nobel assiduously patented his dynamite throughout Europe and in America, although nitroglycerine was not protected by patents there. Only eight years after his first patent, he had also built fifteen dynamite factories, crisscrossing Europe and the United States. There were factories in Hamburg and Cologne and Prague, in New York and San Francisco, in Norway, Sweden, Finland, Scotland, France, Spain, Switzerland, Italy, Portugal, and Hungary. Russia was hard to crack, since dynamite might help terrorists make bombs to assassinate the czar and other notables. In 1870, during the Franco-Prussian War, Nobel supplied dynamite to both sides. The British Dynamite Company was set up in Scotland in 1871, half its capital owned by Nobel, the largest dynamite firm in Europe.

Nobel still had two important and immensely profitable inventions ahead of him. In 1875 he lowered the freezing point of nitroglycerine and thus produced "blasting gelatine," opening a wide variety of new engineering and military uses. In 1887 he patented a smokeless-powder propellant called ballistite, an invention said to have most influenced all weapons design from the 1890s to 1914.[4]

To his final days, Nobel worked to improve and diversify his inventions and holdings. But he also tried his hand at other things: cannon borings more resistant to wear and tear, and an aerial projectile that could be used for war or rescue work.[5] In the 1870s he patented an automatic brake, a boiler that wouldn't explode under pressure, and a method of casting iron. Late in life he sought substitutes for rubber and leather from nitrocellulose, and ways of manufacturing artificial silk.

In 1875 Nobel lived in Paris — or, more accurately, kept a home there between his endless business travels. But troubles arose. His French company, the Société Centrale de Dynamite, had been involved in a Suez Canal scandal, and though Nobel did not manage or own this company, he was famous or notorious enough to become the storm center. A few years later, after an arms sale to Italy aroused angry French press and parliamentary denunciations, Nobel was accused of being a foreign spy — his laboratory was near the government one — and of doing illegal experiments. His laboratory was searched by the police and padlocked. Nobel thereupon migrated in 1890 and set up a home and laboratory in San Remo on the Italian Riviera.

His last years were not quiet. His giant French company failed. Nobel, as a member of the board, could by French law be held responsible to the full extent of his fortune and thus wiped out. He reorganized the company with great energy and came out whole. A legal battle dragged on with two British inventors whom he had trusted but who now claimed they had independently invented Nobel's ballistite under the name of cordite. The British court gave the two Britons only a token victory, but Nobel was embittered. Friends, he complained, are "found only among dogs, whom we feed with the flesh of others, and amongst worms, whom we feed with our own. A grateful belly and a grateful heart are twins."[6] He vented his feelings in a satire called *The Bacillus Patent*.

Just past sixty, his health began to fail. Rheumatism was the least of it, heart trouble the worst. He was ordered to slow down, but kept on working and visiting his far-flung companies as before. He invested in the Swedish Bofors factory and built a large laboratory there with the latest equipment. He helped finance a dirigible balloon expedition to the North Pole headed by a Swedish explorer. The balloon vanished in the Arctic; remains were discovered in 1929.

As his health got worse, Nobel started writing curious things. One was a drama called *Nemesis* about the Renaissance nobleman Cenci who forced his daughter into incest. Nobel's poetic hero, Shelley, had of course written on the same theme in *The Cenci*. Nobel had not written any poetry since the 1870s, and then in his fluent and forceful English; this play was done in Swedish, which by now he wrote in a stilted manner. After Nobel died, the family tried to have all hectographed copies destroyed, but three copies survived.

Then came a massive cerebral hemorrhage which, as so often, reduced its sufferer to his childhood language, Swedish. His French and Italian nurses understood nothing he said. On 10 December 1896 Alfred Nobel died. No member of the family was present; his older brothers had died before him, Robert only a few months earlier, in July 1896, Ludwig in 1888, his mother in 1889. Nor were any friends present. But there is no evidence that Nobel ever had a single close friend.

The Vagabond and Wayward Millionaire

During the early 1870s, when Nobel was in his prime, an English business associate described him this way:

> He was of average height, with a slender stooping figure. He wore his beard, whiskers and mustache untrimmed. His eyes which were small and of light gray color were full of vivacity, and his face, especially when engaged in a conversation, betokened great intelligence.[7]

One of his personal assistants gave a rather different look:

> Nobel gave the impression of being somewhat nervous. His movements were lively, his gait somewhat mincing, his facial expression

very changeable, as was his conversational style, often spiced with
odd remarks and strange ideas. At times these remarks seemed
almost absurd and appeared deliberately intended to shock old
fogies. To his Swedish fellow-countrymen, unaccustomed to his
light, French-inspired way of talking, he often seemed a bit bewildering, to say the least.[8]

The inner man was elusive: shy, lonely, never allowing anyone
close to him, ironic, moodily changeable, in part a Nordic Shelley,
in part a master of vituperation who would wickedly tongue-lash
associates in public. A razor-sharp businessman indeed, but also
aloof, keeping all his employees at a great distance. In contrast, his
richer brother Ludwig's home was right by his Russian factory and
he spent off-hours with his engineers, foremen, and draftsmen.[9]
Ludwig, this report goes on, was not typical of the Swedish disin-
terest in human beings — the once-popular reason for "why every
second Swede is an engineer." But Alfred, obviously, fit that stereo-
type in several ways.

Insofar as Nobel had any home, it was in Paris. Victor Hugo, in
fact, may have been the one to label him the "millionaire
vagabond." He bought a mansion and had it decorated, but typically refused to state any preference for color or style. He added on
a private laboratory. The house became the stopping-off headquar-
ters of his complex business interests, the center of a vast correspondence in most European languages.

Nobel never married, and biographers know of his interest in
only two women. In 1876 Bertha Kinsky, of an Austrian aristocratic
family, adventurously answered one of Nobel's advertisements for a
private secretary to work for a "wealthy, highly educated, elderly
gentleman" — he was then forty-three. She was thirty-three, spoke
several languages, and was highly cultivated. They seem to have
found each other immediately attractive and sympathetic. She very
soon confided her story to him. She had had many suitors, some too
old or too young or too wild or tame or otherwise unsuitable. Once,
when he found her in despair and weeping, Nobel was moved
enough to present her with the manuscript of a hundred-page
"philosophic poem" written in English, which seems to have been
an outpouring of his most private feelings. That so secretive a man
would let anyone see such a poem is remarkable; that he let Bertha
read it so soon after meeting suggests he must have been more than

half in love with the lovely, restless, independent-minded Bertha: a mirror of himself in many ways.

But before anything could develop, before she even took up her secretarial duties, Bertha ran off to marry the son of a noble Viennese family. When she wrote Nobel the news, she was Bertha von Suttner. He kept contact with her, and when peace later became her crusade, Bertha no doubt persuaded him to add a peace prize to his will.

The same year, perhaps on the rebound, he met another woman during a trip to Vienna. She differed from Bertha in every way. Sofie Hess was an eighteen-year-old clerk in a florist's shop. She was pretty and vulgar and a little stupid, kind-hearted but bored except when talking about herself or gossiping about others. But he was somehow enchanted and bought her an expensive bracelet. He began seeing her whenever in Vienna, and set her up in an apartment. In one way their liaison was banal: the older rich man keeping a young mistress with whom he shared a bed and little else. Nobel wrote her continually but was too guarded to reveal much of himself to someone like Sofie. He called her "dear child," signed himself Brummbär (growling bear — her nickname for him), was avuncular, promised her presents and trips if she was "a good girl." He moved her into a Paris apartment. And he actually took her to Stockholm to meet his mother, which miraculously went off fairly well. But she was too immature; he shied from marriage or the personal intimacy and confidences she wanted.

Still, it went on for fifteen years, before ending oddly. He bought her a villa in Ischl, and she began declaring that she was Nobel's wife. As surprised acquaintances reported this news, Nobel grew more embarrassed. In 1891 the final break came. Sofie announced she was pregnant, not by Nobel but a Hungarian cavalry officer, who had not however proposed marriage. Nobel generously set her up with a comfortable annuity. The cavalry officer, by army code, was obliged to marry Sofie, but the scandal also forced him to resign his commission. He became a champagne salesman and, immediately after the marriage ceremony, vanished — or almost: he started writing Nobel for money, in vain. Contemporary Viennese gossip provided an alternative story: that the child was Alfred's and the cavalry officer only a decoy.[10]

Nobel seemed most to have loved his inventions and businesses. He was a prodigious, incessant, and single-minded worker who

wandered Europe endlessly, watching over the making of his products, expanding and consolidating his interests, fending off competitors. He also preferred to work from the outside rather than within.
When inspecting one of his many firms, he always did so unobtru-
sively; he was said to enter even his own laboratory by the rear door.
He chose never to personally own or manage any of the factories that
manufactured his inventions. He held the patents and some of the
shares, but the factories were all locally owned and managed. This
sometimes caused two Nobel firms to compete ruthlessly in the
same market, even issuing counterinjunctions against each other.

Nobel stood aside: when the German Nobel company started
exporting to Britain, Nobel thought the best strategy was for the
British company to strike back by exporting to Germany.[11]
Although on the board and a large shareholder of each of his companies, he had no authority to give orders. Yet it was the Nobel name
that made the companies rich. This ambiguous role apparently
suited Nobel. He was after all wealthy enough to remedy the situation at any time, simply by retaining the majority of shares in any of
the companies. He chose not to do so.

This way of being in but never quite of the great companies built
from his inventions, of having it always both ways at once by never
committing himself wholly, extended to every side of his life. "I
wish I could produce a substance of such frightful efficacy for whole-
sale devastation that wars should thereby become altogether impossible," he said. But then, with equal conviction, he told an assistant,
"Well, it is fiendish things we are working on, but they are so interesting as purely technical problems and . . . clear of all financial and
commercial considerations, that they are doubly fascinating."[12]

Nobel once toyed with buying a Stockholm newspaper, but
denied that it was because he wanted influence. He wrote:

> If I owned a newspaper, I would oppose my own interests. It is one
> of my peculiarities never to consider my private interests. My policy
> as a publisher would be: work against armaments and such medieval
> remnants.[13]

If armaments must be made, he went on, then each nation should
make its own. This was the same man who insisted on the right to
sell his weapons to all buyers, and fought legal battles when a
client-nation tried to deny him sales to a military rival.

In the same way, though he was perhaps the prototype of the international capitalist of the later nineteenth century, he was in but not quite of this group. It is striking that, like Nobel, so many of these were born in the 1830s: Rockefeller, Carnegie, Hill, Harriman, Gould, Pullman, J. P. Morgan Sr., and Nobel's two older brothers, Ludwig and Robert, those Rockefellers of the North. Depending on one's criteria, these men were either captains of industry or mere predatory capitalists. But there was another contemporary group, variously known as Merchants of Death or armaments titans: Krupp, Škoda, Vickers, the French Schneiders, the older Morgan, the Rothschilds, Bismarck's banker Bleichröder.

Nobel was a charter member of both groups, self-made millionaires who became colossi of profits from wars and industrialization. He was probably the first to invent the great monopolistic trust and holding company of the modern kind: family-owned firms were still the norm in Britain and France, and the Germans hadn't yet organized into cartels, only "profit-pooling" alliances.[14] Again, Nobel deliberately stood apart from those otherwise like him.

Certainly he could be as sharp and ruthless a competitor as any when necessary. His biographer Halasz noted how Nobel hastened to patent his inventions even before they were perfected.[15] Yet something in Nobel did not always find it necessary to dominate. The simplest evidence, as noted, is that he could easily have become far richer and more powerful by owning the companies exploiting his name. Few of those named above would have hesitated to do so. Nobel, however, had a fatal gift of introspection, of mordant self-observation, which would have crimped the relentless trajectory of a Rockefeller or a Krupp. Nobel once disapprovingly said of an overeager associate, "Nothing is sacred to him except his own interest."

Not that such views kept Nobel himself from selling his explosives to all buyers indiscriminately. But it slowed him, turned him inward in an unusual, tormented way, making him doubt anything but brainpower, especially his own. He sold to both sides in a war, but could never say with Basil Zaharoff, the later notorious munitions king, "I made wars so that I could sell to both sides." Perhaps Nobel at heart really was an idealist, as his Swedish defenders like to insist: a sort of high-minded sheep — or only half-wolf — among the wolves he did business with. Perhaps his dividedness reflected the melancholia he often complained of, and the sardonic tone that sometimes stung others.

Whatever the reason, it is surely difficult to imagine a Rocke-feller or Krupp sitting like Nobel in his lonely Paris mansion read-ing history, classics, and Shelley and Byron. J. P. Morgan collected rare books, not to read but as beautiful artifacts. Between selling and improving his explosives, Nobel frequented "advanced" intel-lectual salons in Paris, talking of radical politics or the latest work of Zola or Maupassant. Would Morgan or the others take time from their busy schedules to attend a dinner, as Nobel did, in order to meet a poet like Victor Hugo? Or periodically take to writing poetry, drama, and novels?

The Will

Nowhere is Nobel's inclination to have it both ways more apparent than in his will. Most of Nobel's biographers feel that he was greatly influenced by his brother Ludwig's death — or, rather, the inaccu-rate obituaries that followed it. Some of the press mistakenly thought it was Alfred who had died, and he had the strange experi-ence of reading his own obituaries, many of which were hardly flat-tering. He was scathingly described as a war profiteer who became rich by inventing new ways to kill and maim people. He may have written a will in 1889, but it does not survive. His 1893 will gives part of his estate for scientific discoveries and an award for peace. Literature was not mentioned. In the 1895 and final will, all these came to share equally. He rewrote his earlier wills to vindicate his life: his riches would now go to benefit humankind.

Some questions arise immediately. Especially in light of his shock from the mistaken obituaries upon Ludwig's death, why didn't Nobel set up prizes while he lived? He was of course rich enough to have done so. "Surplus wealth," said Andrew Carnegie in 1889, "is a sacred trust which its possessor is bound to administer in his lifetime for the good of the community," and also: "The man who dies . . . rich dies disgraced." Carnegie, at least partly prompted by Nobel's will, established the Carnegie Trusts in 1900.

But Nobel, "the man nobody knew," characteristically also chose to become the philanthropist nobody knew. By arranging to be posthumously generous, he once again avoided any public intrusion into his privacy. His will nowhere directs that his prizes be named after him. Perhaps, as Elisabeth Crawford suggests, entrusting the prizes to Swedish institutions increased the distance between himself and those he helped.[16] He had always detested celebrity. To a Swedish publisher who simply wanted to publish his picture in a book about famous Swedes, Nobel not only refused but tartly added: "I am not aware that I have deserved fame, and I take no pleasure in its clatter." To a requested donation for a proposed memorial to Pasteur: "I am sure Pasteur would like to send all such manifestations to the devil, and that he loathes advertising his name."[17] Nobel apparently valued only two honors given him: election to the Royal Society and to the Swedish Academy of Sciences, which earlier awarded him its Letterstedt Medal for his detonator invention.

There is no question here of hypocrisy or false modesty, rather something in Nobel that, while intent on reaping the world's riches, also distrusted the value of all worldly things. To his nephew's request for biographical information, he replied sardonically:

> Alfred Nobel: his miserable half-life should have been terminated at birth by a humane doctor, as he drew his first howling breath. . . . One and only one wish: not to be buried alive. Greatest sin: that he does not worship Mammon.[18]

The same nephew wanted Nobel to have his portrait painted, and was once more turned down. Nobel claimed he was too old and hadn't enough vanity to want his "hog-bristle beard" immortalized. Besides, what could a portrait show him that he did not already know about himself, nakedly and painfully? "I am afflicted with a proclivity for self-criticism whereby every blemish is revealed in all its unredeemed ugliness."[19] But his famous will is in fact a kind of self-portrait for the world to see, where his inner tensions are turned outward into criteria of what he thought meaningful in life.

The Laureate as "Expert"

Many philanthropists hope to improve social conditions; scientific and literary societies usually honor great individual achievements. Nobel coupled these. His prizes go to individuals, who form an elite to benefit society. He distrusted politics and movements, even the companies that sustained his fortune. He trusted only certain individuals.

The word "expert" perhaps best captures Nobel's aim here. The term came into wide use by mid-nineteenth century, reflecting the new prestige of scientists, engineers, inventors, and Captains of Industry. Indeed, in the 1880s, a rage began for what would later be called technocracy, where industrial managers and technical workers saved society — from itself — by controlling and developing it "rationally." Edward Bellamy's 1888 novel *Looking Backward 2000–1887* promoted such ideas; it sold a million copies in ten years and was translated into a dozen languages. Nobel read Bellamy both with sympathy and in a cross-grained way: reverence about "cooperative production" and political "corporationism" did not escape his scepticism about any such schemes.

Nobel's laureates in one way reflect his lifelong fascination with Shelley. Nobel's scientists, writers, and peace workers lack the prophetic grandeur of the Shelleyan prophets, whose true benefactors of humanity are the "unacknowledged legislators" of the world: Plato, Moses, Jesus, Newton, Shakespeare. But the purpose is akin. If great prophets are not possible in bleak modern times, the "expert" will have to do. Nobel, himself the expert inventor of dynamite, probably included himself among these. At least he would honor those after him.

Nobel's "expert" makes the fundamental discoveries and helps create the new morality. Dynamite and ballistite may help abolish war, but that is up to the politicians. (Like the Nobel expert, the atom-bomb scientists built the terrible weapon but let political leaders decide whether to use it.) This possibility seems to have depressed Nobel's hope for progress. In his 1893 will, Nobel inserted the following telling restriction: that his will and the prizes perhaps should be canceled in thirty years, for "if in thirty years it is not possible to reform the present system, we shall unavoidably fall back into barbarism."[20] Partly he meant the unlikelihood of preventing war, partly that of reforming modern democracy. He luckily removed this proviso in his final will.

Nobel's perspective here shows most clearly in his many literary efforts. One is titled *In Lightest Africa*. The wordplay, of course, is on "darkest Africa": much of Africa was still unexplored by Europeans in the later nineteenth century. Nobel's subject, however, is obviously modern Europe. He means to strike at Europe's pride in its all-conquering Enlightenment, embodied in its proud bourgeois success.

In Lightest Africa is a fable of politics, ancient and modern. One main character is Avenir ("the future"), a very progressive democrat. The other is the "I" of the narrative, who favors the sternest, least democratic regimes of the past. Avenir, scorning the past, dismisses as atrocious the three historical forms of government: absolute monarchy, constitutional monarchy, and democracy. Government by heredity is absurd; constitutional monarchy is impotent; democracy is run by those who talk best, the orators and lawyers.

When the reactionary "I" urges a return to autocratic powers — ancient Rome was the only happy regime in history — Avenir naturally disagrees. He proposes instead to preserve democracy by giving the democratic president dictatorial powers in war; in peacetime, however, the president's powers will be fixed by prefects or governors. In fact, Avenir's prefects seem to have only one main duty: to elect the wisest, most dispassionate, hence most efficient leader possible.

Nobel is clearly both of the above characters. He sometimes called himself a socialist, but not the sort who yearned for a "mechanical barrack life." Nobel's kind of "socialist" is the independent, detached individual who saves others by resisting the tide of popular democratic tyranny.

> In former days governments used to be more narrow-minded and aggressive than their subjects; but nowadays it seems as though the governments were endeavoring to tranquillize the idiotic passions of a public roused by pernicious newspapers.[21]

Nobel could find no course of action worth taking. No wonder he gave his fortune to reward individuals, not institutions. Institutions, as Shelley had said, are shaped in the image of great individuals. And yet, Nobel did after all entrust the awarding of his prizes to Swedish institutions. He thus bequeathed his enigmas to posterity. In that one respect, at least, Nobel's prizes have surely succeeded.

2

The Nobel Prize
Invents Itself

In 1897 more than a hundred newspapers from Europe to Asia carried the news that the "dynamite king" had left his fortune to set up prizes.[1]

The public wasn't the only surprised party. So were Nobel's Swedish relatives, who had practically been cut out of the inheritance. No family member was appointed an executor, but the executors named were also caught unawares. They were Ragnar Sohlman and Rudolf Lilljeqvist, two Swedish engineers — Nobel trusted only his own sort — who had no legal experience. However clever and precise Nobel was in his laboratories and business dealings, he had managed to write a will that was a masterpiece of legal ambiguities, vagueness, and omissions.

His earlier will of 1893 was also written without any legal advice, and showed it. This left one-fifth of his estate to friends and relatives. Another seventeen percent was to be divided among the Swedish Club in Paris, a peace society in Vienna run by Bertha von Suttner, the Stockholm Högskola (="Hochschule"=advanced technical institute, like MIT), and the Karolinska Medical Institute in Stockholm for awards in physiology or medicine. The remainder went to the Swedish Academy of Sciences for prizes for intellectual discoveries left unspecified, and for a peace prize. No prize for literature was mentioned.

Nobel's final will, written in Swedish, after listing some small personal legacies, consists of only one long paragraph:

With the residue of my convertible estate I hereby direct my executors to proceed as follows: They shall convert my said residue of property into money, which they shall then invest in safe securities; the capital thus secured shall constitute a fund, the interest accruing from which shall be annually awarded in prizes to those persons who shall have contributed most materially to benefit mankind during the year immediately preceding. The said interest shall be divided into five equal shares, to be apportioned as follows: one share to the person who shall have made the most important discovery or invention in the domain of Physics; one share to the person who shall have made the most important Chemical discovery or improvement; one share to the person who shall have made the most important discovery in the domain of Physiology or Medicine; one share to the person who shall have produced in the field of Literature the most distinguished work of an idealistic tendency; and finally, one share to the person who shall have most or best promoted the Fraternity of Nations and the Abolishment or Diminution of Standing Armies and the Promotion and Increase of Peace Congresses. The prizes for Physics and Chemistry shall be awarded by the Swedish Academy of Sciences; the one for Physiology or Medicine by the Karolinska Medical Institute in Stockholm; the prize for Literature by the Academy in Stockholm and that for Peace by a Committee of five persons to be selected by the Norwegian Storting. I declare it to be my express desire that, in the awarding of prizes, no consideration whatsoever be paid to the nationality of the candidates, that is to say, that the most deserving be awarded the prize, whether of Scandinavian origin or not.

The brevity and ambiguities of this testament, disposing in so few words of so huge a fortune for such a variety of prizes, took its executors, and the academies and the Swedish government as well, five years to turn into a workable institution.

First, why only these five fields? Nobel's exclusion of mathematics has prompted some legends: for example, that Nobel planned to set up a mathematics prize but could not abide Mittag-Leffler, a leading Swedish mathematician of his time; or, more titillatingly, that Mittag-Leffler had stolen a woman from Nobel. A likelier, if less exciting, reason is that Nobel the inventor did not see pure mathematics as of practical benefit to mankind. Literature passed this test, at least since Nobel was himself something of a writer. The peace prize is described wholly in terms of its benefits.

The 1895 testament drastically cut the specific gifts to friends and relatives to only one-thirtieth of the assets. The previous bequests to the Högskola and the Viennese peace society were dropped. Literature was included for the first time. Instead of the earlier vague phrase about "intellectual discoveries," physics and chemistry were now specified. As Ragnar Sohlman commented, the 1893 wording was so loose that the "science" award could have meant almost anything. The new will shifted the peace prize from the Swedish Academy of Sciences, surely not competent to judge such a field, to the Norwegian parliament. But why did Nobel consider that small and remote institution competent to evaluate the complexities of international peace and war?

The largest dilemma was that Nobel had left his estate to a "foundation" that did not yet exist. How can one legally have a nonexistent legatee? This peculiar problem might have been solved if the three Swedish academies plus the Norwegian parliament had quickly agreed to form a foundation to administer the prizes. In fact it took two years of endless debating before these groups agreed to accept Nobel's assignment. Meanwhile, wrangling of other kinds broke out in public and private over who would get what of the huge estate.

At his death in 1896, Nobel's fortune, spread over ninety-three factories in nine countries, amounted to more than 33 million kronor (about $9 million in 1900 terms).[2] For a more concrete sense of the size of Nobel's generosity, Elisabeth Crawford set each prize, worth 200,000 kronor or $54,000 in 1900 value, at about "thirty times the annual salary of a university professor or two hundred times that of a skilled worker in the construction industry." Just one year's interest from Nobel's fortune equaled almost the entire annual budget of Uppsala University, Sweden's oldest and greatest university. A single Nobel Prize was equivalent to a decade's awards by the French Academy of Sciences, famous for its wealth.[3]

The line of claimants to the inheritance became a long one: Nobel's relatives; the several Swedish academies; the Swedish government, which at the time included the Norwegian parliament; and, not least, the French government. Indeed, the whole case, from start to end, needs not a historian but a novelist like Balzac, someone who can sympathetically but satirically render the allure of riches, the towering avarice of relatives, the intrigues of lawyers, the obsessions and fantasies of scholars and intellectuals, and the ambitions of politicians.

To begin with the central question, was Nobel a legal resident of France or of Sweden? Certainly he was not a citizen of either nation in any usual sense. He had been born in Sweden, but visited it only briefly after age nine. He had never paid the Swedish taxes that constituted customary proof of being a Swedish subject. He had lived in France almost thirty years, but had never applied for French rights or citizenship.

The question of Nobel's residency was crucial. If a resident of France, his estate was liable to heavy French death duties which could swallow up much of the bequest. Swedish law was far more lenient. Further, if Nobel should be declared to have been a French resident, his relatives believed they had a better chance of invalidating the will and the prizes. The executors wanted Swedish courts to adjudicate the will. But how to get Nobel declared a resident of Sweden, when he had scarcely lived there?

A strategy emerged, cobbled together by the executors and their Swedish advisers, with help from the Swedish government. It was decided that Nobel must have considered himself Swedish: he had written his will in Swedish, appointed Swedish executors, and designated Swedish academies to implement his will. He had invested in Sweden's Bofors plant and spoken of living near there. And hadn't the French government itself forced Nobel to emigrate to Italy?

This was flimsy. But the threatened lawsuit by Nobel's relatives lost steam when Alfred's nephew Emanuel — the son of Ludwig Nobel of the Baku oil riches — insisted on honoring his uncle's wishes to the full. Emanuel was the most influential member of the "Russian" Nobels, but his motive was more than piety to his uncle. Alfred, with his brothers dead, had come to hold the controlling shares in the Nobel Brothers Naphtha Company in Baku. Emanuel wanted that control. The pro-Sweden contingent made sure of Emanuel's support simply by selling him the shares at a bargain price.

The Swedish relatives battled on, helped by Swedish newspapers opposed to the will. It was claimed, for example, that Nobel had proved himself unpatriotic by giving the peace prize to the Norwegian parliament. Also that his lavishing riches on individuals was immoral, when masses of Swedes were impoverished and hungry.

The most promising argument struck at the heart of the will: that the prizes were impossible to award, since the academies would never accept the assignment.

It looked for a while as if this would be true. Even if only one of the academies refused, the Nobel Foundation could not be established. The will would thus have no legatee and could be declared void. Nobel had set down no alternatives.

Each of the academies had quite legitimate doubts. Awarding valuable annual and international prizes in science, literature, and peace was no easy task. The fields were dauntingly broad but also extremely diverse and specialized; the technical, aesthetic, moral, and political issues were complex. The judges might have to spend endless time learning about subjects outside their own training or interest. They would have to find knowledgeable nominators from across the world, evaluators, advisers, translators, and consultants. All this inevitably interrupted their own work, and was costly as well. But Nobel's will said nothing about compensating the judges or their advisers and staff for such labors and sacrifices.

According to the will, prizes were to be awarded each year for important discoveries, but what if no worthy candidates were found? The discoveries should be "recent": how recent was "recent"? Suppose that the experimental proof of a theory came decades later: did the theory still count as "recent"? How could one compare "discoveries" with "inventions": if Newton deserved the prize for discovering gravity, did the inventors of the gravity-defying airplane also deserve it? How, anyway, did one decide if a discovery or invention was of "benefit to mankind" when many obviously had harmful as well as beneficial possibilities? (This may have helped kill the Wright brothers' chances: airplanes weren't safe.)

Nor did the academies have any precedent to help them.[4] Such valuable prizes for such a range of serious contributions had never before existed. The different Nobel organizations perforce invented what they needed as they went along, often quite differently interpreting the Founder's will and its cryptic wording.

While the Swedish institutions delayed, the will remained in legal peril. Yet Nobel's will was doubtless saved precisely because he had selected those particular academies. That brought the Swedish government into the matter. In 1897 the attorney-general of Sweden was directed to help keep the will under Swedish jurisdiction.

This was an extraordinary legal step, since it made the state a semi-official adviser to Nobel's executors and their lawyers. Clearly, Nobel's prizes were of unique benefit to Sweden. For the public good, therefore, Nobel's relatives had to be sacrificed. They finally received only a fraction of what they wanted.[5] The intervention of the Swedish state may also have helped persuade the French courts that Nobel was a legal resident of Sweden.

The academies remained the last obstacle. By 1897 three of the four groups involved had agreed: the Norwegian parliament, the Swedish Academy, and the Karolinska Institute. The Academy of Sciences was the holdout.

In part, the academies all balked because they hoped for a larger share of Nobel's assets. One must imagine the effect on low-paid professors who for the first time in their lives saw a mountain of wealth almost in reach. These underpaid scholars can hardly be blamed for wanting to cash in on the bountiful estate that requested their services and respectability. They also began to glimpse how much work and responsibility was being asked of them.

The academies therefore demanded that sufficient money be set aside to cover committees' expenses and honoraria. Some envisioned being paid double their annual salary. The Statutes finally set the compensation to be apportioned to each committee at one-quarter of the worth of the prize — a handsome return, since it added about one-third to a professor's annual salary.[6]

The scholars, as they gazed at Nobel's hoard of riches, also saw ample funds there for splendid laboratories, libraries, and lavish offices. They were dazzled by rosy hopes of a Nobel Institute for each of the five fields, each with its own director, staff, and assistants, or perhaps one grand institute to house all the fields under one roof. These costly projects could be funded from prizes not awarded or by cutting the amount of prize money. None of their grand plans came to be.

The special character of the Swedish intellectual community inevitably shaped the meaning and direction of the Nobel Prizes.

In 1900 Sweden had five million people, a tenth the population of Germany, France, Britain, or Austria. Its days as a great military and political power on the northern rim of Europe, able to challenge Russia, had ended a century before. It had been modernizing its industry through the nineteenth century but, as the steady emigration of skilled workers like the Nobels or the famous engineer John Ericsson suggests, economic conditions at home could be bleak. From 1850, tens of thousands of Swedes emigrated to the United States, and this soared after the ruinous famine of 1867.

In culture and science, Sweden exhibited all the symptoms of a small country with large, intimidating neighbors. The Swedish academies and universities reflected this acutely. The country had a few internationally famous writers like Strindberg, while Germany, France, Britain, and Austria each seemed to have a score of them. And compared with the many great scientists, universities, and laboratories in larger European countries, Swedish science lagged far behind.

Nobel's will sent an earthquake through the Swedish intellectual and academic world. Suddenly they were placed on an international stage, asked to take charge of the most valuable awards in modern times. That kind of publicity and pressure can magnify every crack and strength, and Sweden's smallness intensified this. In such close national quarters, disagreements of principle or opinion could often turn bitterly personal. These flared up continually, not only in the five years it took to hammer out the Nobel Foundation, but to this day.

In 1900, how competent were the Swedish academies and Norwegian parliament to award Nobel's prizes? The brief answer must be: not very.

First, the literature prize. The Swedish Academy was at the time moribund. Its permanent director, Carl Wirsen, a sternly moral character, has been called "an implacable opponent" of new directions in Swedish and Scandinavian writing. Since this meant "implacably opposing" such great writers as Ibsen, Tolstoy, and Zola, one can only say that his moral fervor skewed his critical taste. Nobel's adjective "idealistic" for prizeworthy writing suited Wirsen's every bias (see the chapter on the literature prize).

As for the science prizes, the Royal Swedish Academy of Sciences, which was to award the physics and chemistry prizes, was the oldest and most eminent in Sweden, but spent much of its energies on matters like agriculture, ironwork, weather services, and museum-keeping. Its largest membership sections, about fifteen each, were in zoology, botany, and medicine and surgery. Physics had just two members. Chemistry had twelve, but only because it was combined with meteorology. Science was seen as valuable mainly for technological progress, such as electric power, paper mills, and steel mills.[7]

For Nobel Prize purposes, of course, what mattered was the quality of the physicists and chemists in the academy. Expectedly, these came primarily from Uppsala University and the Högskola, schools frequently at loggerheads. Uppsala proudly dated back to 1477 and was located about as far from Stockholm as Oxford from London. Its counterimage was the Högskola, the technical institute established only in 1878. Set deliberately in Stockholm, the Högskola aggressively set out to reform the stagnancy of Swedish science, whose stronghold it located in Uppsala's "old guard." On its side, Uppsala saw the Högskola as an upstart, lacking true scientific thoroughness and solidity.[8] The outspoken, aggressive, and annoyingly famous Arrhenius particularly galled some at Uppsala. In 1900 the Högskola was not even permitted to grant any degrees. The school was in fact a daringly successful experiment in adult education: the faculty ran it and allowed unusually open admission to students.

Uppsala's physics department stressed precision measurement and instrumentation at the expense of theoretical physics — this during the decades when Maxwell, Boltzmann, Helmholtz, and others were laying the basis of a rigorous mathematical refashioning of all physics. In 1900 Uppsala finally established a lone chair for theoretical physics, but put it outside the physics department and kept it isolated. Not that it mattered: the theorist appointed, Lundquist, was mediocre; he held the position for the next thirty years but never served on the Nobel physics committee.

The Högskola's faculty included such internationally known figures as Svante Arrhenius, probably Sweden's foremost physicist and chemist, the physicist Otto Petterson, and Mittag-Leffler, the country's most influential mathematician. Arrhenius was a close collaborator of prominent researchers in thermodynamics like van't Hoff and Ostwald, and was esteemed by rising physicists like Max Planck and Walther Nernst — all four of them future Nobelists, like Arrhenius himself. Arrhenius especially attracted foreign postdoctoral students, always a measure of a scientist's reputation among colleagues abroad. Mittag-Leffler had contacts with most of the eminent European mathematicians.

Chemistry at Uppsala, in contrast to its physics, had kept in closer touch with developments on the Continent. But in physical chemistry, which was innovatively linking physics and chemistry, the Högskola was far ahead: Arrhenius was famed in just that field. Members of both faculties of course belonged to the Academy of Sciences. There, elections occurred only when a "chair" fell vacant, usually by death. Arrhenius was elected a member only in 1901, over much opposition; Ivar Fredholm, who held no academic post in 1900 but was Sweden's best mathematician, was not elected until 1914.

Before Nobel's will, this scarcely mattered: the academy's functions were advisory and honorary. But the chance to award the rich and prestigious Nobel Prizes introduced something worth fighting over. The Academy of Sciences, after all, had the final vote on all science prizes, and also selected the committees that made the initial choices. Whether Uppsala or the Högskola dominated a physics or chemistry committee now involved power, status at home and abroad, and intellectual principle.

In the early years of the awards, Uppsala had more votes in both the physics and chemistry committees than the Högskola, yet did not entirely control the decisions. Arrhenius was the kingpin here. As one of Europe's leading new physical chemists, he had a world reputation in both fields and knew how to use it politically. He was a power on the physics committee, but also on the chemistry committee where he held no seat. His influence was clear. Two of the first three prizes in chemistry went for physical chemistry, to van't Hoff and Arrhenius himself. But Arrhenius also championed the new theories of the atom emerging in the sensational discoveries of Röntgen's X-rays, the radioactivity findings of Becquerel and the Curies, and J. J. Thomson's discovery of the electron. Four of the first six prizes in physics went to this area. Arrhenius will appear again in these pages.

The medicine prizes, selected by the Karolinska Institute, were less fractious. The institute had been set up in 1810, when surgeons were needed to cope with the slaughter in the Napoleonic Wars, and became the preeminent Scandinavian medical school. But except for physiology, it is doubtful whether the Karolinska in 1900 was prepared to evaluate the daunting range of medical discoveries and specialized developments then appearing.

Nobel's designation of the Norwegian parliament to set up a committee to award an international peace prize stirred belligerent Swedish nationalism. Less populous and with many fewer resources,

Norway was inevitably dominated by Sweden — then forced to become part of Sweden in 1815, though it kept its own parliament. Swedes often accused Norway of being a separatist hotbed; indeed, Norwegian independence finally came in 1905. Because of his will, Alfred Nobel was posthumously accused of fomenting this separatism and betraying a lack of patriotism to his homeland. Some have more plausibly suggested that Nobel hoped to cement Swedish-Norwegian relations.[9] He could hardly have chosen the Norwegian parliament because of a demonstrated capacity to deal with peace issues or international arbitrations on war or such matters. It had no such experience.

Nobel's will first shook the Swedish intellectual establishment, then began to benefit it. Great prizes like Nobel's confer as much prestige on the donors as on the recipients. For Sweden to be the supreme arbiter of the world's richest and most famous awards was a national glory, if a reflected one. Certainly, this helped push the academies to take on the assignment. Sweden's small population and intellectual compactness also helped considerably. The academies were all in Stockholm, a very small city compared with London or Paris. Everyone in Stockholm cultural circles knew each other. Social, professional, and above all governmental pressure could be a strong lever. One might say that the Nobel Prizes forced the Swedes to swim or sink together.

Once having agreed to the assignments, at least the scientific academies were soon forced to improve and reform themselves. Even the literature jury had to contemplate change, though at a snail's pace. After all, when the committees sought out eminent foreign colleagues as nominators, they came under the close scrutiny of those colleagues. Nothing perhaps is so helpful in combating provincial complacency and lagging standards. The Swedish intellectual community had to live up to the Nobel Prizes. Staying abreast of developments abroad necessarily brought them into close contact with foreign scholars and researchers, and the benefit was mutual. The distinguished foreigners became nominators and often laureates as well; in return, they elected deserving Swedish colleagues to memberships in their own most distinguished societies. Inside information about who was likely to win a prize flowed out to friends and confidants. Foreign colleagues and hopeful candidates became frequent visitors to Sweden, and returned invitations. The latest scientific information, the lifeblood of research progress, arrived quickly in Sweden. Good prizes, of Nobel status and monetary value, make good neighbors, to paraphrase Robert Frost.

In 1898, two years after Nobel's death, agreement was reached on all sides, at last setting up the Nobel Foundation as legal legatee. In 1900 its Code of Statutes was published, signed by King Oscar of Sweden. It codified the general regulations and clarified some blurred matters: no posthumous awards were allowed; no self-nominations were permitted; except for the peace prize, nominated work had to be already published, thus forestalling claims for unfinished or unknown work; committee members could include foreigners; no protest could be lodged; and all minutes and records remained sealed.

The Nobel Institution

As finally arranged, the Nobel institution looks and works as follows:

The Nobel Foundation (Nobelstiftelsen) is the overall administrative and governing body but has no role in choosing laureates. It manages the investments, adjudicates the Statutes, arranges the ceremony, and coordinates everything. Its offices are in a regal building across from the Royal Library in Stockholm.

The money: This all-important item in the Nobel's scheme of things is managed by several bankers, the only members of the Foundation who do not also belong to one of the academies. The Foundation does not make public its specific investments, but a general picture has emerged. Until about 1945 the Nobel funds were generally invested in government bonds. Since then, the funds have been diversified in real estate, shares, and fixed returns. About half is invested in corporations, many in the U.S. or multinational. Any politically controversial investments are not divulged. The Nobel's wealth is taken for granted. But another once-wealthy Swedish foundation, the Wenner-Gren, well known for its support of anthropology and the social sciences, went bankrupt.

The Foundation oversees Nobel Prize activities in four sections:

1. The Swedish Academy (for literature)
2. The Nobel Assembly of the Karolinska Institute (for medicine and physiology)
3. The Royal Swedish Academy of Sciences (for physics, chemistry, and — since 1968 — economics)
4. The Nobel Committee of the Norwegian Storting (for the peace award)

The Swedish academies grant membership by election. For Nobel purposes, they each appoint a committee of five of their members to gather the nominations and evaluate them. Because they choose the nominators and consultants and do the first sifting, the committees are the cockpit of power. Their members, in the early days, often served long terms. Svante Manne Arrhenius was on the physics committee from 1900 to 1927, Karl Siegbahn from 1923 to 1963, though terms on science committees are now limited to nine or twelve years. The poet Erik Karlfeldt joined the literature committee in 1907, became permanent secretary of the Swedish Academy in 1912, and remained a committee member until his death in 1931. All three became laureates, Karlfeldt exceptionally after his death. Recently, most of the literary committee members have been rotated every few years.

Each committee chooses its own nominators. The permanent ones are Swedish members of the Swedish Academy, the Royal Academy of Sciences, and the Karolinska. All previous laureates can nominate, as can most of the Scandinavian professors of science or literature. The temporary nominators, chosen from various faculties around the world, are changed every two years or so.

A few individuals, usually laureates, become very frequent nominators. In physics up to 1937, half of the 1,345 nominations were made by just fifty-four nominators — and one-quarter of that half from just seventeen nominators.[10] On the other hand, more than two hundred nominators submitted just one name during their tenure. Einstein submitted almost as many nominations for the peace prize as for physics. But Harold Urey (U.S., 1934 chemistry prize) is said to have helped choose sixteen other science laureates since 1934.

Nominations are due by February first. Each committee typically receives hundreds of them. Some carry weight, some are clearly negligible, some are frivolous or crackpot (including those who nominate themselves or send gifts). From February to the middle of summer, the serious nominations — many are repeat nominations, often over several years or even decades — are evaluated and argued out. Then the committee's recommendation is passed to the parent academy for the final say. In October the awards are made public.

For the literature prize, the committee's proposals go directly to the entire Swedish Academy of eighteen members. In the sciences, the process adds a step. The physics committee submits its decision first to the physics section of the Academy of Sciences. The outcome of that vote is then passed to the full membership of the academy for approval in plenary session. The process is similar for the other science prizes. Though there are rare exceptions, the committee's choice is usually ratified.

The Peace Prize Statutes of 1901 had to be rewritten in 1905, when Norway became independent of Sweden. But the essentials did not change: the peace committee is still selected by the Norwegian parliament, and thereafter functions as an independent body which does not submit its decisions to the parliament or the Nobel Foundation for approval.

The economics prize is more of a special case. It was established in 1968 by the Central Bank of Sweden, and a committee of the Academy of Sciences evaluates nominees and chooses the laureates.

Nominators have never ruled the committees. Even juggernaut efforts to gain a prize for a candidate often failed entirely. Supporters of the great French mathematician and physicist Henri Poincaré (1854–1912) besieged the physics committee with thirty-four nominations in the single year 1910. No one before or perhaps since ever amassed so many nominations in one year — Einstein had only fourteen the year he won. Still the committee rejected Poincaré. The man they wanted, the Swedish physicist Ångström, died prematurely, but even that didn't help Poincaré's chances. The prize went to the Dutch physicist Johannes van der Waals.

Informal connections also bulk important. Swedish committee members inevitably build up friendships and contacts abroad. Information constantly moves along this network in the form of serious evaluations, casual gossip, tips, complaints, advice. Without this living net, the Nobel committees would be out of touch with the current realities. Of course it works both ways: the Nobel committees, though sworn to secrecy, can and do provide friends with privileged information about who is high on the list and who is not. As Crawford says,

> The ability to exchange gossip about Nobel secrets knowledgeably is probably a better criterion of membership in the international scientific elite than many of the elite structures studied by sociologists.[11]

This is probably just as true in literature and peace.

Pistols and Negotiables

Aside from the settling of the will, there was still the matter of getting Nobel's fortune to safekeeping. This included some adventurous moments. The two executors had to liquidate all his securities and reinvest them safely. That first meant collecting the securities from several Paris banks and Nobel's Paris house and putting them in three large strongboxes at the Comptoir National d'Escompte, to be sent from there to a safe place for liquidation.

Some of the securities were to be sent to London, some to Sweden. The Rothschild firm agreed to insure them during delivery, but not beyond two and a half million francs per day. So each day the executors personally carried two and one-half million francs' worth of securities from the Comptoir d'Escompte to the Swedish consul general's office. It took more than a week. Each day the securities were carefully listed, tied in bundles, wrapped, and sealed. What happened next is told by Ragnar Sohlman, one of the executors:

> Since the actual transfers to and from the Consulate involved certain risks of hold-ups and robberies, special precautions were taken and exercised to avoid attention. . . . after the [day's securities] had been packed in a suitcase, we took an ordinary horsecab to the Consulate-General. With a loaded revolver in my hand, I sat in the cab prepared to defend the suitcase in case a collision with another carriage had been arranged — at that time a not unusual occurrence in Paris.[12]

Sohlman then did the second part of the transfer, to the railroad station where the documents would embark for Sweden, in the same way — also with loaded revolver in hand. The securities were negotiable if stolen, or they might have been destroyed. In either case, they would have lost their value. If either of those calamities had happened, there would have been no assets for Nobel's will to pass on.

And, of course, no Nobel Prizes.

3

The Nobel Prize
in Literature

For a portrait of what the Nobel Prize in Literature is not, one can't do better than Irving Wallace's novel *The Prize*. Published in 1962, it quickly became a best-seller and a hit movie, and no wonder, considering its sensational plot. The young, "lanky" author is dead drunk when he learns he has won the Nobel Prize. Embittered since his wife died, and a romantic rebel against social convention, he very reluctantly agrees to accept the award: he can use the money. But winning the Nobel Prize is the least of his triumphs in the book. In Stockholm he falls in love, plunges into a wildly complicated spy chase in which he single-handedly unravels a plot to abduct a science laureate to the Soviet Union, and solves everything just as the stately Nobel ceremony itself gets under way. Even aside from such a farrago, the writer-hero is much too young to have won a literature Nobel — by the time they are chosen, most literary laureates are too old to chase anyone. But then, *The Prize* paints the Nobel ceremony and literature laureates as the exciting things that thrillers and Hollywood wish they were.

Some offended mutterings arose about Wallace's preposterous sensationalizing of the exalted Nobel ceremony. Certainly, no very wild things seem to happen there. The acme of exciting behavior was probably reached by the Norwegian novelist Knut Hamsun, who won the 1920 prize. Hamsun started drinking riotously the night of the ceremony, pulled the whiskers of an "elderly Nobel committee man," and then snapped his finger against the corset of his fellow Norwegian laureate Sigrid Undset (literature, 1928) and cried, "It sounds like a bell buoy!"[1]

If the Nobel in literature is not exactly a thriller like Wallace's novel, it might however be compared to a ghost story. At least, as the king bestows the medals, a great ghost compounded of all the great writers ignored by the Nobel haunts the festivities. No prizes went to Tolstoy or Ibsen or Joyce or Virginia Woolf or Rilke, to Wallace Stevens or Vladimir Nabokov or Paul Celan. To exclude such figures is like a Nobel Prize in Physics that passed over Einstein, Bohr, Heisenberg, and Feynman, just to start.

Indeed, the world's most prestigious literary award has become widely seen as a political one — a peace prize in literary disguise. For the Nobel judges, it is charged, art and social reform are inseparable. Writers indifferent to moral uplift like Nabokov imperil their chances. An exception or two, such as Samuel Beckett in 1969, proves the rule. Writers of political taste disapproved by Nobel judges certainly risk being blackballed, as seems to have happened to Bertolt Brecht, André Malraux, Ezra Pound, and Jorge Luis Borges.

The Nobel Literary Museum

Reading through the Nobel list across the century is a curious experience: one is apt to think more about those absent than present. From 1901 to 1945, the list is depressing. Of the forty laureates in that period (awards were omitted in some years), only Kipling, Hamsun, Yeats, Shaw, Mann, and Pirandello have held stature. Hauptmann and Maeterlinck were once esteemed. The others are largely unread or unreadable, such as Sully Prudhomme, José Echegaray and Frédéric Mistral, Henryk Sienkiewicz, Selma Lagerlöf, Paul Heyse, Romain Rolland, Verner von Heidenstam, Gjellerup and Pontoppidan, Carl Spitteler, the philosopher Rudolf Eucken (so forgotten that even philosophers are usually surprised he was a philosopher), Anatole France, Jacinto Benavente, Władyslaw Reymont, Grazia Deledda, Erik Karlfeldt, John Galsworthy, Ivan Bunin, Pearl Buck, Frans Sillanpää, J. V. Jensen.

In that same period, the Nobel judges ignored or rejected all of the following (a deep breath is advised before reading): Leo Tolstoy, Emile Zola, Mark Twain, Henry James, Henrik Ibsen, August

Strindberg, Henry Adams, Thomas Hardy, Machado de Assis, Pérez Galdós, Joseph Conrad — and this is only the generation bridging 1900.

It takes a heroic blindness to miss everyone in so illustrious a list. But the Nobel committee managed to do as poorly in the next generation as well, missing or rejecting writers as towering as the century provides: Marcel Proust, Rilke, Joyce, Virginia Woolf, Gertrude Stein, Theodore Dreiser, D. H. Lawrence, Karel Čapek, Jaroslav Hašek, Willa Cather, Hugo von Hofmannsthal, Chaim Bialik, Miguel de Unamuno, George Santayana, José Ortega y Gasset, Alfred Döblin, Stefan George, Robert Musil, Karl Kraus, Arno Schmidt, H. G. Wells, Andrei Bely, Aleksandr Blok, Georges Bernanos, Fernando Pessoa, César Vallejo.[2]

After 1945 the Nobel committee began a sort of reparations campaign to honor neglected modernist pioneers. At long last, T. S. Eliot, Hemingway, François Mauriac, Juan Ramón Jiménez, and Boris Pasternak became laureates. Since about 1970 the prizes began to catch up with writers whose careers were still flourishing: Samuel Beckett, Pablo Neruda, Saul Bellow, Toni Morrison, Naguib Mahfouz, Derek Walcott, Seamus Heaney.

But again, great ghosts haunt the list. Since 1945 the Nobel Prize has denied (to list only the departed) Colette, Robert Frost, Wallace Stevens, W. H. Auden, William Carlos Williams, Anna Akhmatova, Hermann Broch, Bertolt Brecht, Giuseppe Ungaretti, Louis-Ferdinand Céline, Evelyn Waugh, Gunnar Ekelöf, Luis Cernuda, Hugh MacDiarmid, Ignazio Silone, Marguerite Yourcenar, Raymond Queneau, André Malraux, René Char, Yannis Ritsos, Jorge Luis Borges, Paul Celan, Witold Gombrowicz, Philip Larkin, Jean Genet, Italo Calvino, Alberto Moravia, Thomas Bernhard, Eugène Ionesco, Primo Levi, Danilo Kiš.

"Old Age Pension Prizes"

When pioneers like T. S. Eliot or André Gide or Hemingway began to receive prizes, most were so famous that their prize seemed only an anticlimax. These and others were usually long past their productive years. Eliot wryly described the prize as a nail in an author's coffin. The critic Herbert Howarth put it as gravely: the Nobel prize is like "a deathmask on fulfilled grandeur."

But long-delayed prizes continue: the Spanish novelist Camilo José Cela was at last honored in 1989 at age 73, almost fifty years after the innovative work that won him the prize. Of laureates since 1984, the Czech poet Jaroslav Seifert was 83 years old when honored, the French writer Claude Simon 72, the Egyptian novelist Naguib Mahfouz 77, the Mexican poet Octavio Paz 76, the Polish poet Wisława Szymborska 73, the Portuguese novelist José Saramago 75. When the Northern Irish poet Seamus Heaney was honored at 56, he could seem positively boyish by comparison. The youngest laureate ever was Kipling back in 1907— at age forty-two.

Such long delays allow the Nobel judges to have their cake and eat it too, avoiding controversy yet claiming to honor boldness. Eliot in the 1920s and 1930s was a rebellious sort the Nobel then spurned. But by 1948 he had become venerable and mainstream, and his prize could seem an appeal to tradition against some of the new rebels — say, the French dramatist Jean Genet, whose plays mockingly pulled down all respectable social and sexual values, and who was never Nobelized.

Long delays have made laureates of some who happened to outlive their unhonored contemporaries, and thereby became stand-ins for them. Anders Österling, the permanent secretary of the Swedish Academy from 1941 to 1970, is supposed to have admitted that the Nobel Prize given to the Russian novelist Bunin in 1933 was "to pay off our consciences on Chekhov and Tolstoy."[3] The Nobel citation for Juan Ramón Jiménez (1956) says:

> This year's laureate is the last survivor of the famous Generation of 1898. . . . When the Swedish Academy renders homage to Juan Ramón Jiménez, it renders homage to an entire epoch in the glorious Spanish literature.

This generous homage to a past generation was in fact caused by earlier Nobel neglect of a group of writers who in 1898 set out to revive Spanish writing, Antonio and Manuel Machado, Ramón del Valle-Inclán, Miguel de Unamuno, the Nicaraguan Rubén Darío (then living in Spain), and Jiménez among them. Jiménez is an excellent poet. But making him a stand-in for a neglected generation renders his own honor ambiguous. Did he deserve the honor on his own, or because the others died ignored and he happened to live so long? He was seventy-five when honored.

The citation for the Greek George Seferis (Nobel 1963) says: "Now that Palamas and Sikelianos are dead, Seferis is today the representative Hellenic poet." Palamas lived until 1943, Sikelianos to 1951, and Kazantzakis to 1957, yet none was honored. To the living belong the spoils, when the Nobel feels it is time to reward a Greek poet?

Paul Valéry's Nobel Prize was delayed so often that his death "regretfully" intervened in 1945. The next French poet honored was Saint-John Perse (1960). But would Perse have won if Valéry hadn't died "too soon"? The citation to Perse tactfully did not mention Valéry explicitly but surely invoked that poet by its praise of Perse's "rhetorical tradition inherited from the classics." And here is the German-Swiss novelist-poet Hermann Hesse (1946), another stand-in. The citation: "Since the death of Rilke and [Stefan] George, he has been the foremost German poet of our time." In short, if either Rilke or George were then alive, Hesse would not have become the laureate. The Spanish poet Vicente Aleixandre (Nobel 1977) was similarly the proxy for the dead Lorca, Jorge Guillén, Rafael Alberti, and Luis Cernuda.

Faulkner's citation suggests that his prize was partly meant to ease the Nobel conscience for neglecting Joyce. "Side by side with Joyce — and perhaps even more so — Faulkner is the great experimentalist among twentieth-century novelists." (The *great* experimentalist? One wonders if the Nobel judges had taken a look at *Finnegans Wake*.) Beckett's prize in 1969 may also have been a gesture toward Joyce, who was Beckett's mentor.

Part of the reason for honoring Joseph Brodsky, the Russian émigré to the U.S., was as a stand-in for an entire generation ignored by Nobel judges — the great line of Russian poets from Aleksandr Blok to Osip Mandelstam, Marina Tsvetaeva, and especially Anna Akhmatova. Brodsky was Akhmatova's favorite young poet. Else why a prize so young, at age forty-seven, and soon?

As the list of laureates makes clear, the Nobel Prize in Literature is still far from being the global award it claims to be. Its prizes have repeatedly gone to writing in a few major European languages, primarily English, French, German, Spanish — not to mention fourteen prizes in the Scandinavian languages, one-seventh of all awarded. Literature in India has been honored only once — Tagore in 1913, which was really another prize in English, since it was awarded on the basis of a translation. No Chinese writer has ever won the prize, though two Japanese writers have become laureates, by the luck of superb translations. Arabic, which spans the world and has a rich literary tradition, won its first and only prize in 1988 (the Egyptian novelist Mahfouz). Nothing in the Bantu languages, or Turkish, or the Malayan group.

Is it possible that no Chinese writer has ever measured up to Nobel standards? And none in India since 1911? That only one writer in Arabic can be found? One can easily imagine that so great a Hebrew poet as Chaim Bialik (died 1934) was invisible to Stockholm. The fact is that the Swedish Academy lacks the linguistic competence needed for a truly international jury, which is not surprising. Perhaps only three or four of the greatest universities in the world have such resources. Unprepared to read fluently and directly in major and populous languages such as Chinese, Arabic, or Hindi, not to mention minor ones, the Nobel committee is overly dependent on translations, whose occurrence and quality are notoriously capricious. One would assume that Nobel judges would all be fluent readers of French. But it has been claimed that the French novelist Claude Simon's Nobel award (1985) gained immeasurably from a Swedish translation of all his work just before his prize.[4] And that the French poet Saint-John Perse won his prize only because of the Swedish diplomat Dag Hammarskjöld's enormous influence and tireless promoting.

The Nobel Prizes in science and peace are true international awards; the literature prize is not. Unless it soon moves beyond its familiar linguistic horizons, it may end up a glorified Pulitzer Prize. It treads a fine line here. If it dutifully starts distributing the prize around the globe, it can become less a literary than an international goodwill prize.

The Nobel seems at least to be trying to close the gender gap. In almost a century, only nine women have been literary laureates: six in the first ninety years, but three since 1991 (Gordimer, Morrison, Szymborska).

The Nobel Replies to Its Critics

The Nobel literary jury has ringed itself with four main lines of defense.[5] A favorite official plea is that if Conrad and Joyce were bypassed, this was unfortunately because they were "never nominated." The official history of the Nobel literary awards trots out this bureaucratic disclaimer quite often, as if the rules regrettably tied their hands. But of course the Nobel committee itself selected those very nominators who, while ignoring a Joseph Conrad, did nominate Pierre Loti, Emile Faguet, Paul Bourget, Gaspar Núñez de Arce, Ramón Menéndez Pidal, Upton Sinclair, or Margaret Mitchell. Even if its nominators were so undiscerning, members of the Swedish Academy and its committee can enter nominations. If they chose not to do that, the fault is their own.[6]

Another favored argument, also wearisomely bureaucratic, takes the form "died too soon before could be properly evaluated." Frequently cited instances are C. P. Cavafy, Rainer Maria Rilke, Virginia Woolf, James Joyce, D. H. Lawrence, and Franz Kafka. Certainly, discovering the Alexandrian poet Cavafy (d. 1933) or Kafka or Anton Chekhov would have been a miraculous long shot: Cavafy and Kafka published very little before their early deaths; Chekhov died in 1904.

Neglect of others is not so easily explained away. True, Rilke died in 1926, only three years after writing his masterpieces, the *Duino Elegies* and *Sonnets to Orpheus*. But those poems, great as they were, were only the capstone of a brilliant career. Since 1899 his published work had given him outstanding claim as one of the greatest poets in the German language. Yeats, who came to greatness around 1910, won in 1923 — why not Rilke about the same time? Many critics have suggested that Yeats's award was politically motivated: Ireland had just become independent. But Rilke, born in Prague, wandered restlessly and had no nation, thus no Nobel "identity" or support from a national academy or critics.

D. H. Lawrence died in 1930, but had an international reputation by the mid-1920s. Joyce and Woolf died in 1941, both recognized as masters.[7] Proust is more problematic. He published the first volume of his great work, *À la recherche du temps perdu*, in 1913, and the second and third parts in 1919 and 1921. In 1920 he won the prestigious Prix Goncourt. Why was the Nobel committee in doubt that Proust was a deserving choice, when many international observers very early on thought him the greatest living novelist? True, he died only three years after finishing his great cycle. But this masterpiece had been available for nine years before he died, and the Nobel judges needed only nine years to honor Sienkiewicz for his *Quo Vadis* — "displacing Tolstoy," claimed a Nobel evaluator — and only three to make Pearl Buck a laureate.

An unspoken implication here is that the Nobel Prize in Literature cannot rush into things like lesser prizes, as the Prix Goncourt did in crowning Proust. The supreme international dignity and status of the Nobel, its great renown and prestige, require doing nothing precipitate. Alas, this lofty principle, useful against a Woolf or Joyce, has also been passed over at will, as with Buck, Sinclair Lewis, Joseph Brodsky, or Gabriel García Márquez.

A third defense often raised is related to the limitations of committees. Nobel defenders, with suitable murmurings of regret after the fact, acknowledge that certain kinds of writers (Tolstoy, Ibsen) were simply not acceptable to certain committees, especially during the first half of the century. This bias went under the rubric of "idealism"; we shall return to it shortly because it remains a major factor.

The final line of defense is to admit that mistakes have been made, but insist that the record on the whole is quite good. Thus, in the official history of the prizes, Anders Österling of the Swedish Academy begins roundly conceding the mistakes: "It is not to be denied that the history of the Nobel Prizes in Literature is also a history of inexpiable sins of omission." This is strong language. Yet loyal committeeman Österling immediately paints the brighter side:

> But even so, it may perhaps be said that the mistakes have been comparatively few, that no truly unworthy candidate has been crowned, and that if allowances are made for legitimate criticism, the results have reasonably matched the requirements and difficulties of an almost paradoxical assignment.[8]

This last statement of course expiates the "inexpiable" omission of Tolstoy, Rilke, and all the rest. After all, if the mistakes have been few, if no truly unworthy candidate has been crowned, and "if allowances are made for legitimate criticism" (whatever that may mean), who has any reason to complain?

For the moment, let us consider the optimistic side. Surely, if Czesław Miłosz, Saul Bellow, Toni Morrison, and Günter Grass have become laureates, the Nobel must be making progress. Better late than never. However hesitantly, the award has also begun to move beyond Europe with an occasional award to the Mideast, Japan, Africa. This sort of piecemeal improvement encourages some to believe that one or another remedy will cure the Nobel of its lapses. Let the judges embrace new stirrings. Let them become fluent in Chinese or Estonian. Let them not play so many safe bets among the unobjectionably good but do as the Swedish statesman Dag Hammarskjöld was said to urge, when protesting awards to the superfamous such as Hemingway or Churchill: "Oh — if once we could show a touch of daring!"[9]

Yet this sort of progress is at best only patchwork. Two main obstacles are the heavy moralistic-political emphasis and the committee system.

The Nobel Committee as Boyg

In Ibsen's *Peer Gynt* there is an all-devouring, formless monster called the Boyg. The Danish critic Georg Brandes (1842–1927) interpreted this as "the Spirit of Compromise."[10] The world of course leans on committees to arrive at a working consensus — which means being willing to cooperate and compromise. Safe choices are apt to be preferred to the trouble-making sort. The Nobel Prize is the work of committees. But a committee is a poor way to evaluate literature.

Nobel's will did not set up a committee to sift and nominate laureates. That was done by the Nobel Statutes of 1900. Practicality was and remains the reason. World literature — and the Nobel claims to deal with nothing less — is fragmented into hundreds of languages and diverse nations. There is so much of it, and so indigenous, that only a committee with a huge network of specialists can possibly cope with it, even in the most limited way. Literary "experts" — scholars, linguists, critics, historians, librarians — are required. As noted, luckily for the new Nobel literary committee of 1901, literature was then becoming institutionalized and professionalized as never before in history. This is why professors dominate the Nobel's nominators and judges; they already know how to work inside a bureaucracy.

Practicality is also the answer when the Nobel jury is reproached — continually — for having ignored this or that eminent writer. It responds, fairly, that there are too many worthy writers for any annual prize to honor. The official solution to this dilemma has been set forth recently by the chair of the literature committee, Kjell Espmark: What the Swedish Academy "cannot afford is giving [the] Nobel's laurels to a minor talent." One might counter that what the Nobel really cannot afford is giving its laurels to any but writers of the caliber of Tolstoy, Joyce, or Woolf. This is said not to be feasible. The Nobel jury receives two hundred nominations a year from respected nominators; these must be closely evaluated by committee members and their far-flung network of advisers; thick reports must be assembled to guide the academy's decisions. Doubtless some writers are "great" and some only "good." But any committee or academy member who claims to know who the geniuses are will only set off a long wrangle. Better to wait twenty or thirty years to learn who is worthy. As for "greatness," leave that to posterity.

The difficulty of getting agreement about how to rank contemporary writing is at least one reason why every account of the Nobel jury reports their often bitter electioneering. Some writers — the great poet Pablo Neruda, for example — openly campaign for a prize, thus creating factions on the jury. Even without this, the Swedish Academy and its committee seem to indulge in constant infighting. Some publish public denunciations of fellow members.[11] Others confide to journalists their contempt for their colleagues: one described the present permanent secretary, Sture Allen, as "an intellectual accountant" and as someone "who doesn't even read."[12] But of course the committee system itself, with its outlying bureaucracy of academic consultants and nominators long experienced in partisan maneuvers, is apt for intrigue.

Meanwhile, everyone realizes that a compromise must somehow be cobbled together in a few months so that the next prize can be announced by October. The committee and academy count up individual preferences and prejudices, and the majority wins. The decision is always presented to the public as a unanimous choice.

Using such a commmittee process is outlandish only for the literature award. Committees work quite well for the sciences. Robert Oppenheimer once wrote that "there is something inherently comforting about a panel of experts" because slanted and merely personal ideas can be corrected.[13] For science, yes: the best experts there must approve the work or else it is stillborn. But superior literary prizes are harder to choose than science prizes. Science speaks a common language around the globe, and is a cumulative, collective enterprise; theories can often be tested quickly by rigorous experiments. Literary works stand on their own. Comparisons are anyone's right and gamble.

The Swedish Academy is a self-perpetuating enclave: it elects its own successors and, like other bureaucracies, tends to preserve its character, including its fractious nature. Discussions and negotiations are secret and sealed, to ensure freedom of decision, but of course such secrecy also insulates it from outside criticism. As noted, a member cannot resign but can stop attending meetings and can refuse to vote. In 1989 two of the academy's members withdrew, protesting the body's refusal to denounce Iran's death sentence on Salman Rushdie. At present, three or perhaps four members of the academy are boycotting votes. This can produce very narrow margins, since twelve votes of the eighteen-member academy are needed to award a prize.

Certainly, the Nobel committees have changed character over the years. Espmark, who has documented this in detail, is sharp with critics of the Nobel system who make sweeping charges about the defects of the awards while not being "historical" about how each particular committee "had its special character and its own criteria."[14] The German naturalistic playwright Gerhart Hauptmann was thus anathema to the first committee but acceptable to the new one in 1912. That new committee sought the "great style," with Goethe's example of high classicism and universal appeal in mind. After 1945 there came another shift, honoring neglected modernist "pioneers." From about the 1970s a "pragmatic" attitude has prevailed.

Espmark's behind-the-scenes explanation is, however, beside the point. As the American critic Herbert Howarth has put it,

> As soon as one asks about a prize-man not "Was he the best man?" but "Why did the judges select him?" one is likely to perceive he was chosen for reasonable reasons; and one reports these; and in so doing willy-nilly defends the good instead of demanding the best.[15]

That is a succinct indictment of the committee system. Why certain judges did not choose Rilke or Joyce has the same sort of interest, finally, as an insider's details on how a political campaign was run. It can be absorbing, but what really matters is only that, for example, a Lincoln was elected or not. The rest is details for the archivist to pick over.

Yet the literature committee has undoubtedly improved, and the literature prize has become much more consistently a "literary" prize. The old bogey of "idealism" has been tamed if not altogether exorcized. But this change happened also because recent committees are in a luckier historical position than earlier ones. The recent sustained improvement of the prizes begins just after the once baffling "experimentalism" of early modernism — *Ulysses, The Waves, The Castle, Duino Elegies* — finally filtered into broad literary usage and also became familiar to a wide readership. The early moderns — "difficult" or "immoral" or "inaccessible" — were the ones who frightened the literary judges for more than half of the twentieth century. Nobel laureates in the last three decades obviously owe a diffuse and incalculable artistic debt to those forerunners — and also the Nobel's new welcome mat. The Nobel judges have become more open; so has everyone else. Late-twentieth-century writing does not bristle with the old shock and strangeness because it does not need to. That necessary battle was fought and won earlier. The Nobel committee presents its 1969 award to Samuel Beckett as a breakthrough. But the breakthrough for Beckett's own innovations was prepared decades before. Thus his *Waiting for Godot* and other plays, and even his novels, have enjoyed popular success as no early avant-gardist's did.

Are there any alternatives to the present committee system? Espmark complains that the nomination of *Gone with the Wind* showed up "a weak aspect of whole selection system," by which he means "the significant degree of incompetence" among nominators.[16] It is misleading to narrow that problem to *Gone with the Wind*. Nominators are usually as incompetent when it comes to *Mrs. Dalloway* or *Mother Courage*. Faced with the strangeness and newness that great writing often involves, the Nobel's eminent professors and critics are quite as fallible as the rest of us. Each year the Nobel jury faces a challenge that very few minds in history have been able to solve, and then only erratically: to know which literary works truly surpass others now, and will continue to stay alive for generations to come. In short, to predict how posterity will think, fifty or a hundred years from now. Each year's Nobel literary award is just such a gamble on the future. The Nobel's task is not to decide that the old Eliot was a great poet — everyone knew he was — but to have decided the younger Eliot was. Otherwise the Nobels degenerate into "old age pensions" or honorary degrees.

But literary reputations are among the riskiest businesses known. Kipling's stature sank for years, but now keeps rising fitfully. Sinclair Lewis — peculiarly hailed by the Nobel citation as an American "humorist" — and his once-shocking *Babbitt* and other novels have largely vanished from the minds even of Americans. Eliot and Hemingway do not rate as the colossi they once seemed; the stock has already fallen on Solzhenitsyn, even as he continues to publish.

The predictive gift is the rarest sort of critical intelligence. It has little to do with being a great scholar or critic or writer. Extraordinarily few have shown genius in the stock market of fame. In the English-speaking world, Ezra Pound is perhaps the best known. He had an uncanny eye for what was new, superb, and lasting. He proved it with his prescient judgments on the as yet unknown Robert Frost and James Joyce, the still obscure T. S. Eliot, the not yet famous Ernest Hemingway, and with his quick appreciation of Yeats's new style of poetry from 1910. No matter that Pound was wildly unbalanced about fascism and uneven in his own poetry. He would have made the perfect scout for the Nobel literary committee. Eliot and Hemingway could have been honored in midcareer, and Joyce, Frost, and Gertrude Stein made laureates as they deserved, to the future glory of the Nobel Prizes. Prophetic readers like Pound can recognize genius when they see it, light-years ahead of the rest.

Except that no Nobel committee could tolerate any such archspirit of the anti-Boyg.[17]

The Iron Corset of Idealism

Here is the other main stumbling block. Alfred Nobel's will contained only the following terse criterion for the literary award: it "should go to the person who shall have produced in the field of Literature the most distinguished work of an idealistic tendency." This sentence has bedeviled the prize. Should the award go to a specific work, or to an author's lifetime achievement? Honoring only works done "in the preceding year," as the will earlier and broadly stated, would have hamstrung the literary awards intolerably. The Nobel jury has mainly honored a writer's lifetime work, but occasionally a specific work has been singled out for the award (Thomas Mann's *Buddenbrooks*, John Galsworthy's *Forsyte Saga*).

The prickliest part was the phrase "of an idealistic tendency." Surely Nobel meant high-minded moral goodness? A minority view, however, startlingly maintained the opposite. The prominent Swedish mathematician Mittag-Leffler, who had known Alfred Nobel, claimed that the inventor intended "idealism" to mean a sceptical, even satirical attitude to religion, royalty, marriage, and the social order in general. Or so he was reported as saying by the aforementioned Danish critic Georg Brandes, one of the great early champions of Nietzsche, and himself a nominee for a Nobel.[18]

Many of Nobel's own writings are indeed sceptical and caustic — his play *Nemesis*, written only a year before he died, or the satirical *In Lightest Africa* and *The Bacillus Patent*. And he could be strangely ironic, as in his plan to set up that lavish mansion where prospective suicides could die amid luxury, rather than drown in the cold, filthy Seine. To Österling, Nobel's literary tone recalled Strindberg's mordant attacks.[19] That was strong backing for "idealism" as an ironically subversive force.

But can a grand international prize be devoted to subversive irony of this sort? And backed, no less, by a solemn academic institution and the Swedish government itself? It is unthinkable. The opposite and respectable view prevailed. Österling inadvertently describes how this was managed. While conceding that Nobel himself frequently spoke as if "an enemy of all religious faith, [even] an out-and-out atheist," Österling nonetheless pronounces this "so-called atheism . . . in reality . . . very close to Platonism and Christianity."[20] As shall be seen, this conversion of nay-saying into an optimistic and reassuring "idealism" threads decisively through all Nobel literature prizes to the present.

The first champion of such a view, the iron force in the first Nobel jury from 1901 to 1912, was Carl afWirsen (the prefix *af* denotes nobility in Sweden). Born in 1842, he was permanent secretary, or director, of the Swedish Academy from 1901 until his death in 1912. This moribund academy included no critic of real power and one minor poet, Carl Snoilsky (1841–1903), who wrote in the Swedish neoromantic manner of the 1860s. Ibsen and Strindberg, who could have revitalized things, had long before been blackballed. The rest of the first Nobel committee chosen by the academy in 1901 included Elias Tegner, orientalist (1841–1903); Carl Nyblom, Uppsala literature professor (1832–1907); and Carl Odhner, historian (1836–1904).

As their birth dates suggest, these judges were elderly Victorians who showed it. So were the rest of the eighteen members of the

Swedish Academy. Assigning them the Nobel Prize in Literature was quixotic. As twentieth-century literature entered its first great period of innovative achievement, it was disinherited by the Nobel jury set up to honor it. As one late-nineteenth-century observer put it, the guardians of Swedish culture were like "elderly men . . . who after a particularly refined dinner with a plenitude of wines, are discussing religion and the affairs of state over their glasses of arrak punch."[21] Strindberg, in his *New Realm* of 1884, pilloried the hypocrisies and pettinesses of Swedish culture that Wirsen embodied. Nor did Strindberg spare the Swedish Academy's eighteen "immortals" who thought of themselves as carrying on the traditions of the Académie Française, their "foster-parent" institution. Strindberg lived to 1912 but of course never won the Nobel Prize.

Wirsen was wonderfully unequipped to lead the Nobel assignment. Even back in 1889, he despised what he saw as a perverse new literature flooding the world. As chair of the Nobel jury, Wirsen used "idealism" — reactionary, respectful of State and Church and Society — as a stick to beat off Emile Zola as "lurid" and "spiritless and often grossly cynical." Ibsen, the greatest dramatist of the nineteenth century, was evaluated as "totally atheistic and, in ethical-sexual questions, highly adventurous in outlook." Hardy was unacceptable because his God "lacks any sense of justice or mercy."[22]

It was especially Tolstoy, widely and rightly admired as the greatest living writer, who put the committee in a terrible fix. Blessedly for the committee, a technicality saved them in 1901. Tolstoy had not been "duly nominated" that year. The very first Nobel Prize in Literature, in 1901, went to Sully Prudhomme, suggesting that he was the world's foremost living poet. He was in fact as forgettable a poet as can be found in the Nobel's long list of mediocrities. His poetry was of the mid-nineteenth-century French Parnassian sort, sculpted in line, refined in taste, quite vacant — or, as the Nobel citation chose to put it, "noble, melancholy, and thoughtful." When he became the laureate at age sixty-two, his productive years were long past. He was, however, a member of the Académie Française, strongly supported by that parent organization of the Swedish Academy, and thus a reassuringly respectable choice: no wild writers need apply.

Tolstoy's exclusion caused forty-two Swedish writers, artists, and critics to protest. The Nobel committee evaluated Tolstoy's work as containing "ghastly naturalistic descriptions" and "negative asceticism" and abhorrent religious, fatalist, and anarchist sympathies. But in 1902, again blessedly for the Nobel committee, Tolstoy declared himself happy not to receive such a valuable prize, since "money brings nothing but evil."[23] Saved from the terrible fate of honoring Tolstoy, the Nobel committee instead made a laureate of the German Theodor Mommsen, whose monumental history of ancient Rome dated all the way back to 1845–56, with a last volume in 1885. Mommsen was then eighty-five years old, and his work was hardly "recent" or of surpassing literary merit.[24] No matter: however aged and dormant, Mommsen rescued the Nobel committee from having to honor the "morbid" Emile Zola or his ilk.

In 1903 another crisis arose. The Norwegian Ibsen, greatest dramatist of the past century, was now a candidate. But, subverter of authority and champion of individual freedom, he was all too unacceptable to the Nobel jury. They found a proxy in another Norwegian dramatist, Bjørnstjerne Bjørnson.

In recent years Nobel officials have impatiently insisted that "idealism" is a dead and discarded issue. Now only the "best" writing is what matters.[25] Espmark declares that idealism of the "patently uplifting variety" is no longer a Nobel requirement, that only literary "integrity" matters, whether corrosive or uplifting. He cites prizes to Samuel Beckett and Camilo José Cela as honoring those who "uncompromisingly" depict the "human predicament." The American critic Alexander Coleman once wrote that "it would be easy to say that that Academy does anything it wishes, wrapping itself in the flag of idealism only at the hour of the ceremony." But, he went on, it has in fact always endorsed such idealism. (He also suggested that, as there used to be Kremlinologists, so there should be Nobelologists, who could divine the hidden tendencies of this secretive organization.)[26]

Certainly, the issue is not dead. When the Polish poet Wisława Szymborska won in 1996, the *TLS* reviewer still felt obliged to insist she had won for merit, not "for being a moral comforter to humanity, nor for being a literary activist indicating what the correct lines or parties are."[27]

The Nobel literary judges are doubtless sick of the issue. In 1997, indeed, it seems that their collective gorge rose and they provocatively chose Dario Fo, who is an actor, stand-up comedian, performance artist — almost almost anything but a writer in the sense of Yeats or Mann. After that, who could dare call the Swedish Academy old-fashioned?

But not much has really changed. In 1901 the Nobel citation lauded its very first laureate, the French poet Sully Prudhomme, for tirelessly seeking

> evidence of man's supernatural destiny in the moral realm, in the voice of conscience, and in the lofty and undeniable prescriptions of duty. From this point of view, Sully Prudhomme represents better than most writers what the testator called an "idealistic" spirit in literature.

Ninety years after Sully Prudhomme, the 1991 Nobel award went to the South African novelist Nadine Gordimer, praised in the Nobel citation for "her involvement on behalf of literature and free speech in a police state where censorship and persecution of books and people exist." This is still the Nobel idealism of 1901, only now politicized and liberal rather than spiritualized and conservative. In 1986 Wole Soyinka of Nigeria ended his Nobel lecture with these words: "The prize is the consequent enthronement of its complement: universal suffrage — and peace."

But as in Sully Prudhomme's case, high ethics or worthy politics do not make anyone's writing better or worse. Gordimer is a good novelist, yet one cannot forget — nor does the Nobel citation let us — that she was also a leading white South African activist against apartheid. While any comparison here will seem invidious, unavoidably, it may be said that Doris Lessing, also a white African but long removed to Europe and not such an activist, has thus far been passed over for a prize — although Gordimer has arguably never written a novel to match Lessing's brilliant, disturbing *The Golden Notebook*.

Kjell Espmark complains that such remarks are typical of the "armchair politicizing" surrounding Nobel literature prizes. But the cause lies not in the armchair critic but in the Nobel citations themselves. A sceptical reader is urged to read through the last century's citations for proof. In 1967, for example, the Guatemalan novelist Miguel Angel Asturias was praised for protesting against imperialism, tyranny, slavery, and injustice, and his citation concluded: "This was indeed what Alfred Nobel hoped to promote by his Prizes." His fellow Caribbean, V. S. Naipaul, though a more powerful writer, continues to be ignored, likely because of his scathing portraits of the Third World.

Now as then, too, the Nobel citations tend to nudge writers into an "affirming" mode. One recalls how Nobel's own "out-and-out atheism" somehow emerged "Christian." Did T. S. Eliot wince when his citation rephrased his idea of tradition to harmonize with Nobel sentiments? "The existing monuments of literature form an idealistic order . . ." was not quite what Eliot meant.

Some laureates have resisted Nobel uplift. The fastidious French poet-diplomat Saint-John Perse (Nobel 1960), after being lauded for exalting "man's creative powers," uncompromisingly concluded his acceptance speech by saying, "It is enough for the poet to be the bad conscience of his age." The most eloquent rejection of the Nobel's hectoring came from the Northern Irish poet Seamus Heaney. In 1995 he was honored for his remarkable poetry but also and inevitably "for concerning himself with analysis of the violence in Northern Ireland." Heaney's own views, however, indicted the Nobel's motives here. Poetry, he wrote, offers an alternative to reality

> which has a liberating and verifying effect upon the individual spirit, and yet I can see how such a function would be deemed insufficient by a political activist. . . . Engaged parties are not going to be grateful for a mere image — no matter how inventive or original — of the field of force of which they are a part. They will always want the redress of poetry to be an exercise of leverage on behalf of their own point of view; they will require the entire weight of the thing to come down on their side of the scales.[28]

Reading through the citations, indeed, one sometimes wonders if the Nobel judges recognized who or what they were honoring. In 1923 an earlier Irish poet, William Butler Yeats, became the laureate. Only two years before, he had published "The Second Coming," with its unforgettable vision of the nightmare settling on modern civilization. This apocalyptic vision is the voice of the devil's advocate condemning the Nobel's usual optimistic and middle-of-the-road view. Was the Nobel committee listening? One doubts it, since their citation for Yeats praised him as if he were still the dreamy Celtic Twilight poet of 1900. The citation incredibly described Yeats's 1910 volume *The Green Helmet* — where he began his "passionate syntax" to handle prosaic themes and responsibilities — as "a merrily heroic myth of a peculiarly primitive wildness."[29]

Such idealistic uplift and call for social betterment explain much about the Nobel choices that is otherwise mystifying. The prize to Pearl Buck in 1938 suggests she swept the Nobel judges off their feet.[30] Her famous trilogy on China, including *The Good Earth*, came out between 1931 and 1935. Three short years later, she was a Nobel Prize winner. The Nobel literary judges have rarely moved so fast. To honor her, the Nobel committee had to ignore Dreiser (whose *An American Tragedy* came out in 1925), Fitzgerald (*The Great Gatsby*, 1926, and *Tender Is the Night*, 1934), Hemingway (*The Sun Also Rises*, 1926, and *A Farewell to Arms*, 1929), and John Dos Passos, whose great trilogy *U.S.A.* (completed 1936) made the young Jean-Paul Sartre call him the greatest writer in the world. However exaggerated that was, Dos Passos deserved a Nobel Prize for his work through the 1920s and 1930s. On literary merit, the choice of Buck was dubious. But her Nobel citation sings a paean to her sympathy with the plight and dignity of Chinese peasants. Buck built "idealistic" international bridges between East and West in *The Good Earth* and sequels which became famed best-sellers through the world. Buck's heart was in the right place, though her prose remained as flat as ever, with the moral complexities flattened as well. Still, worrying about her literary merit may be irrelevant. In the official Nobel history, Österling astonishingly says that the "decisive factor in the Academy's judgment" was her "incomparable" biographies of her parents, both missionaries in China.[31]

Is it only coincidence that the last two prizes to Americans writing in English have gone to Saul Bellow and Toni Morrison? Bellow is "Jewish-American," and Morrison "African-American," and both can therefore stand as "minority" writers. One can scarcely believe that the Nobel judges chose such extraordinary writers even partly on so narrow a basis. And yet, the American laureate preceding them was John Steinbeck (1962), famous for his *Grapes of Wrath* set in the 1930s Depression. His selection as a Nobelist puzzled many American readers, since he was preferred over Robert Frost, W. H. Auden, Wallace Stevens, Marianne Moore, William Carlos Williams, John Dos Passos, and others. It puzzled Steinbeck as well. The suspicion that this was yet another politicized prize gained credence with a report from a Swedish source that the Nobel judges saw Steinbeck's award in 1962 "at least in part, as a social gesture in support of the tormented South. As if Americans would easily make the connection between the 'okie' of the Thirties and the Negro of the Sixties!"[32]

Modernism at Arm's Length

Herbert Howarth has astutely summed up the situation of the Nobel Prize in Literature:

> The Nobel's penitent longing for a better world will be answered whenever the Academy gives the Prize not to the best-wishing maker but to the best maker — even if the best maker appears to wish ill.[33]

But the Nobel has tended to shun writing of a modernist sort as too "difficult" or "morbid" or "inaccessible," or simply ignore it. The first Nobel Prize in 1901 came as the Dreyfus Affair split France for decades to come. That was a tiny but apt prelude to twentieth-century world wars, totalitarianism, and other nightmares. To many, human history has sometimes seemed to be radically disconnecting from its past and anchor. "Man is falling toward an X," Nietzsche said.

The Nobel's shying from literature too intimate with the dangers and extremism of our age shows in the number of awards to less disturbing writers. Up to 1945, the Nobel judges awarded nineteen prizes to fiction writers. Eleven of those went to the "saga" genre, mostly many-volume renderings of rural or folk and traditional ways of life, vanishing or vanished — which spoke not only *of* an earlier era, but *like* one. Of course, some saga laureates far transcend this genre, such as Halldór Laxness of Iceland (1955). Still, the Nobel committees favored the way the saga practitioners usually held at a safe distance the anarchic modern world so intimately linked to the city, the new unrooted intelligentsia, the energies of revolution and change. They were also accessible to a popular audience. There has always been a populist streak in the Nobel literary jury.[34]

Saga prizes began as early as 1905 with the prize to Sienkiewicz, author of *Quo Vadis*. In 1908 Lagerlöf became a laureate for her *Gösta Berling's Saga*. In 1915 the indefatigable Romain Rolland won the

Nobel for his *Jean-Christophe* (1903–12), which runs to ten volumes. Modernist literature was already on the scene in force — Pound and Wyndham Lewis's *Blast* of 1914, or the Italian Futurists of 1909 who sang of "glorifying war . . . the only hygiene of the world." Rolland instead preached being a "good European" via art — his French hero Jean-Christophe was captivated by German music. In 1917 two Danish novelists shared the prize: Henrik Pontoppidan and Karl Gjellerup. The Nobel's wish to award "neutral" prizes during the war made this possible. Any other reason for choosing Gjellerup remains a mystery. Pontoppidan however was in the saga line, with his eight-volume *Lykke-Per* (Lucky Peter, 1898–1904) and his five-volume *De Dödes Rige* (The Realm of the Dead, 1912–16).

The only other novelists honored up to this point had been Kipling (1907), Hamsun (1920), and Anatole France (1921). In 1924, however, the prizes reverted to saga writers with the Polish Reymont (Conrad, unhonored, died that year), and the 1928 winner was the Norwegian Sigrid Undset, whose *Kristin Lavransdattar* is set in fourteenth-century Norway. One may add the Italian Grazia Deledda (1926), who explored the life of Sardinian peasants. Perhaps also Thomas Mann in 1929. His 1900 novel *Buddenbrooks*, his closest approach to the saga genre up to the time of his award, was singled out in the Nobel citation, which passed over his 1926 masterpiece *The Magic Mountain*, a portrayal of modern diseased civilization, in a single phrase. In the 1930s three of the four fiction prizes again went to saga writers. John Galsworthy won in 1932 for his *Forsyte Saga*. If his subject was the gentry rather than the folk, the results could be as deadening. Someone has noted that Galsworthy's popularity abroad came from his portraying the English precisely as foreigners liked to imagine them. In 1937 the prizewinner was the Frenchman Roger Martin du Gard, whose best-known novel, still worth reading if one can persevere, is *Les Thibault* (1922–40), another many-volume, closely realistic chronicle, this time about the tensions and crises of a pre-1914 bourgeois family. He is an impressive writer, perhaps lacking only that final carrying surge of poetic verve or imaginative daring that lifts such writing above its steady level. In 1938 came Pearl Buck with her trilogy saga about China. In 1944 the prize went to J. V. Jensen of Denmark, whose six-volume saga moves with evolution from the great apes to early human history. After John Steinbeck came the Australian Patrick White (1973) for his masterpieces *The*

Tree of Man and *Voss*, though White surmounts any genre, as does Faulkner — who indeed did write a full-fledged saga, which perhaps influenced the Nobel judges to honor him in 1949.

Other laureate practitioners of the saga genre are Ivo Andrič (1961) and Mikhail Sholokhov (1965). Their work falls in the period when the Nobel Prizes collided with the Cold War, and needs looking at now.

Political Pressures from Within and Without

The Swedish Academy bristles at any suggestion that its awards have been influenced by politics. But as Henry Thoreau (pre-Nobel) once wrote: "Some circumstantial evidence is very strong — as when you find a trout in the milk." And some large trout swim in the milky Nobel record. In 1912 the Catalan writer Angel Guimera was denied a prize lest honoring him offend the Spanish government. Spain had conquered Catalonia centuries before, but memories are long there. The Nobel committee justified this rejection as "promoting peace."[35]

From the 1920s, some writers went right (D. H. Lawrence, Yeats, Pound, Hamsun), some left (Brecht, Aragon, Sartre, Auden). Some were card-carrying members for longer or shorter periods (Neruda in the Communist Party, Pirandello in the Fascist); some became totalitarian propagandists (Pound, or the Soviet poet Mayakovsky). T. S. Eliot was on the right, Hemingway on the left.

Intentionally or not, the Nobel by long delays diluted such contentious disputes into its own softer idealism. By honoring Eliot and Hemingway only after 1948 — after the Spanish Civil War and the defeat of fascism — the Nobel could present them as elder statesmen in a "republic of letters," with their earlier energizing differences covered over by ceremonial plaudits.

At the height of the Cold War, from about 1950 to 1970, the Nobel jury found itself dogged by politics as never before. The media, East and West, were eager to turn Nobel awards into simulacra of Big Power hostility or detente. The Swedish Academy could have tried to finesse this by choosing laureates as far as possible from Cold War partisanship. Instead they bravely plunged in, and did well in resisting outside censorship. But they indulged in some political censoring of their own.

First, the outside pressures. The most sensational disputes about Nobel neutrality involved the Soviet Union. Take the following chronology of prizes during the Cold War:

1955 Halldór Laxness

1956 Bertolt Brecht dies (never a laureate)

1957 Camus

1958 Pasternak

1961 Andrič

1964 Sartre

1965 Sholokhov

1967 Anna Akhmatova dies (never a laureate)

1970 Solzhenitsyn

1971 Neruda

1972 Böll

Laxness, the Icelandic novelist, won the first Nobel involving the Cold War. He had long championed the Stalinist regime; the Soviets were gratified. Almost immediately after, however, came three prizes in a row applauded by the anti-Soviet bloc. Camus eloquently opposed Soviet repressive policies and totalitarian premises, and was accused by Communists of winning the prize because he was a lackey of capitalism. Pasternak won the first literature prize ever awarded to a Soviet citizen, mainly for his novel *Doctor Zhivago*, but he had published this novel in the West without permission, and the regime denounced its new laureate as a Judas, "a foreign stain on our socialist country," and a traitor. The Soviet authorities refused to let Pasternak go to Stockholm to receive his prize. Nor did the 1961 award to the Yugoslavian novelist Ivo Andrič please Moscow: Yugoslavia was then led by Marshal Tito, who had broken free of the Soviet empire and remained defiant of the Kremlin.

Only a few years later, as if in reverse, three Nobel Prizes in four years went to Soviets or their apologists. This about-face suggested to many that the Nobel committee was making amends to Moscow, especially for the Pasternak offense. When Sartre was awarded the

prize in 1964 he was the most powerful intellectual in France —
probably in the world — defending Soviet policies or the allegedly
higher virtues of totalitarianism. Sartre however declined the prize,
the first to do so voluntarily since Tolstoy in 1902. The Swedish
Academy, grown wiser since the Tolstoy fiasco, refused to withdraw
his award. Some suggested that Sartre was in a pique because his
rival Camus had won first. Sartre's own explanation was that he
never accepted public honors; only an unaffiliated writer could
speak freely about politics. Accepting the Nobel Prize, he claimed,
turned one into a spokesman for that institution. Speaking of himself in the third person, he said that "Jean-Paul Sartre, Nobel Prize
winner" would thenceforth be appended to every statement he
made; "he is in a way inevitably coopted by simply being crowned.
It's a way of saying, Finally he's on our side."[36] For the same reason,
Sartre claimed he would never accept a Lenin Prize, although he
declared his sympathies lay entirely with the Soviet Union versus
the West, and the Nobel Prize, "objectively speaking," lined up
against the Soviet Union. It was after all "an honor restricted to
Western writers and Eastern rebels."[37] By such a rebel he meant
Pasternak, and regretted that Sholokhov was not honored before
Pasternak.

Indeed, right after Sartre, Sholokhov became the laureate. His
famous The Quiet Don (1927–32) is a saga of the sort long beloved by
Nobel committees. Sholokhov was also the "good" Soviet writer.[38]
He had denounced the award to Pasternak (in later years he
recanted this), and the Soviet leaders permitted him to accept his
Nobel in person. Then in 1967 the Guatemalan Asturias won;
highly sympathetic to the Soviet Union, he had spent much of his
life fighting Latin-American dictators and U.S. greed: his "banana
trilogy" attacks the rapacity of the United Fruit Company, at its
peak in the 1920s.

In 1970, however, the Nobel made a laureate of Solzhenitsyn, the
great scourge of the Soviet regime. He had been imprisoned in
labor camps and "internal exile" from 1945 to 1956 on trumped-up
charges; these experiences launched his epochal history of the
Gulag, the huge invisible Soviet prison system. During the "thaw"
initiated by Khrushchev in 1965, Solzhenitsyn published The First
Circle (1968) and The Cancer Ward (1968–69), both cited by the
Nobel judges. He had also become a leader of public protest against
the regime. The Soviet authorities derided his prize as "political

enmity" or worse. Espmark reports that the Nobel jury refused a request by the Swedish Foreign Office to drop the prize to Solzhenitsyn.[39] Solzhenitsyn declined to leave the USSR to accept his prize, lest the Soviet leaders refuse to let him return.

Then, one year after Solzhenitsyn, another possible flip-flop: the Chilean poet Pablo Neruda took the prize. He had served long years as a loyal Stalinist, in and out of Russia. Was this prize an effort to soothe Soviet resentment about Solzhenitsyn?

The Cold War staggered on, but from 1971 the prizes no longer ricocheted back and forth. After Solzhenitsyn it was seventeen years before another Russian writer won the prize — and he was then living in exile: Joseph Brodsky (1987). Later prizes went to several who had lived under Soviet oppression: Miłosz of Poland (1980), Jaroslav Seifert of Czechoslovakia (1984), and the Polish poet Wisława Szymborska (1996). The poet and critic Octavio Paz and the novelist Carlos Fuentes had long been the leading Mexican candidates for the Nobel award. For years, they had also been political opponents — Fuentes on the Marxist side, Paz against. Paz won the 1995 Nobel Prize. In 1989 the Soviet Union itself collapsed, and Cold War prizes with it.

The Nobel, the Stalin, and the "Hitler" Prize

Among the laureates just named, several of the Stalinist defenders had accepted Stalin Prizes. Why was a Stalin Prize acceptable to Nobel judges when a "Hitler Prize" would not be? (No Hitler Prize actually existed; it is meant to indicate those who might have accepted such an honor had it been available.)

That question cannot be lightly dismissed. The Stalin and Lenin Prizes, after all, honored a tyranny which lasted much longer than Hitler's and outmatched him in numbers of innocent victims. The Nobel committee's response to this was peculiar, to say the least. When Laxness was honored in 1955, he had accepted the Stalin Prize only two years before, although much was known by then about Stalinist terror and murder. Yet to go by his Nobel citation, the jury's main concern was only whether Communism had diminished his art. In his 1963 autobiography, *Skalditimi*, Laxness caused an uproar among his former ideological allies by denouncing Soviet Communism.

Neruda received a Lenin Peace Prize in 1950, and a Stalin Peace Prize in 1953. In 1954 this very great poet actually fawned on Stalin as "the high noon, the fulfillment of men and peoples."[40] Neruda hungrily sought the Nobel Prize, but was balked by the Swedish poet Gunnar Ekelöf, a member of the Nobel committee. Ekelöf suspected that Neruda had been involved in Trotsky's murder in Mexico in 1940; Neruda had been a Chilean diplomat in Mexico at the time.[41] Ekelöf died in 1968, and three years later Neruda was the laureate. In his *Memoirs* of 1963, Neruda recanted his Stalinism, though not his Communism. But the poems honored by the Nobel Prize had been written in his Stalinist years. Once more, the Nobel judges worried only whether Neruda's art had been compromised. So too with Asturias, who had accepted a Lenin Peace Prize in 1966, the year before he won the Nobel award.

The Nobel committee was not so lenient to writers on the right. As Dag Hammarskjöld in 1959 explained to Pär Lagerkvist (the 1951 Nobelist) about his objections to a prize for Ezra Pound:

> I have no objection to a Nobel Prize being given to an author who is mentally unbalanced. . . . But Pound [fell] victim to anti-Semitism. . . . such a "subhuman" reaction ought to exclude the possibility of a prize intended to lay weight on the "idealistic tendency." . . . I do not know exactly what the words "idealistic tendency" mean, but at least I do know what is diametrically opposed to what they can reasonably be assumed to signify.[42]

Racism is a horror. But if, as Hammarskjöld says, some acts are so foul that they should preclude any Nobel award at all, one can only ask again: why is killing people for belonging to the "wrong" race worse than killing them in gulags for belonging to the "wrong" class? The victims are both as dead, the motives are both as subhuman.

In 1979 Karl Vennberg, a Swedish critic, challenged the Nobel's claim that it judged literature apart from politics. If so, he asked, why didn't the academy award Ezra Pound a prize? "The private politics of an author amount after all to an aberration that dies with his historical epoch."[43] Even vehement Marxists no longer condemn the "reactionary" Balzac. A member of the Swedish Academy, Artur Lundkvist, disagreed with Vennberg: "the limited merits" of Pound's work could not make up for his "shameful outpourings of psychopathic hatred and evil."[44] Did Lundkvist mean that a less limited writer than Pound, but also a fascist, could be awarded the prize? He did not clarify this delicate point.

But there was such a writer. Lundkvist lumped the French novelist Céline with Pound as too limited in achievement, and too shamefully full of hatred, to be prizeworthy. Céline was the pen name of Louis-Ferdinand Destouches (1894–1961), a physician who worked selflessly for the desperately poor. From 1938 he also published tracts filled with ravening hatred of Jews — Pound's is feeble by comparison. But Céline was a writer whose "aberrations" did not diminish his work any more than Stalinism did Neruda's. One of the powerfully disturbing writers of our age, he deserved the Nobel Prize for his *Journey to the End of the Night* (1932) and *Death on the Installment Plan* (1936). Reading those novels, even now, one can feel the world's pious verities trembling beneath one's feet, and see how a rising hatred might well bring down the temples — as almost happened. In the fateful 1930s, the decade of Céline's horrific visions, the Nobel laureates included the tepid Galsworthy, Bunin, Pearl Buck, Frans Sillanpää, and J. V. Jensen.[45]

The Nobel judges have waged a Cold War of their own against other writers whose politics displeased them. Jorge Luis Borges, the Argentine poet, fictionist, and essayist, utterly deserved a prize but never won. A Nobel judge, Artur Lundkvist again, said he would blackball Borges because he accepted an honor from the dictator Pinochet. Lundkvist said he much admired and even had translated Borges, but "his political blunders, this time in a fascist direction . . . make him in my opinion unsuitable on ethical and human grounds for a Nobel Prize."[46] Borges was as far from being fascist as was Churchill. But neither the greatness nor the uniqueness of Borges's art could override this political veto. André Malraux felt he was also vetoed as too conservative (a Gaullist!) by the Stockholm judges.

The most telling case is not of a conservative but of a Communist: Bertolt Brecht, the famed author of *Mother Courage, The Threepenny Opera, Galileo,* and many other great plays from 1922 to his death in 1956. Brecht was clearly blackballed for political reasons. There was no other possible reason to delay or reject him. From the 1930s, Brecht was as great a dramatist as Europe produced, and one of Germany's best poets as well. Few writers deserved the prize more than he did. But he died unhonored — first nominated only in the year of his death, according to Espmark. Why nominated so very late? In his case, the judges did not "need more time for evaluation," as they often say. Espmark merely notes that Brecht's "tendentious" Communism kept him from being honored earlier. As an ideologue, he was of course tendentious: so are all ideologues. But that cannot be said about his dramas, which generously enlarge the meaning and mystery of life.

As for "benefit to mankind," as Nobel set forth in his will, why wasn't Arthur Koestler made a laureate, at least for *Darkness at Noon* (1940)? That novel helped shift European history from darkness at a crucial moment, circa 1948. Of how many poems or novels in any century can that be said? And the Nobel Prize, as seen, has singled out certain works as deserving the prize.

Sadly, one cannot say that the Nobel committee or the Swedish Academy has always been willing to fight very hard to back up its liberal or idealistic aims. In 1989 two members of the academy — Kerstin Ekman and Lars Gyllensten, publicly resigned, charging that the academy would not openly support the Anglo-Indian Salman Rushdie against the Iranian call for his assassination. Rushdie is not a laureate; if he were, that title might help protect him. But not necessarily. The Nigerian dramatist Wole Soyinka (Nobel 1986) was imprisoned in his homeland by the military junta from 1967 to 1969 and forcibly exiled in 1983. Despite his prize — or, more likely, because of the international attention it attracts — he has again been in exile since 1994; in early 1997 the regime charged him with treason, which carried the death penalty.

Soyinka's award points up how reluctantly the Nobel Prize guardians have moved outside the orbit of Europe and European languages. This is true not only of Asian nations and languages but of those on the margin of Europe itself, such as Greece, which won its first prize only in 1963, to the poet George Seferis. Israel and Egypt are Mediterranean countries, only a skip away from Greece — but the Hebrew and Arabic languages can seem light-years away. Still, Israeli literature won its first award as early as 1966, to the novelist Shmuel Y. Agnon, who wrote in Hebrew. Part of the reason was that he shared the prize with the Jewish poet Nelly Sachs, who wrote in German. Sachs, born and raised in Germany, fled to Sweden in 1940. After the Holocaust was revealed, her poems caught fire for a memorable decade or so. She can be haunting to the bone but also repetitive; Stephen Spender said that all her poems seem the same poem. Agnon is the greater writer. Why did they share the prize? According to the Nobel citation, because they shared a "kinship":

> to honor two writers who, although they write in different languages, are united in a spiritual kinship and complement each other in a superb effort to present the cultural heritage of the Jewish people through the written word.

By having them share a prize, the American critic Theodore Ziolkowski commented,

> the Swedish Academy has succeeded in making itself ridiculous and in reducing the Nobel Prize to a farce, so blatantly tactical, so palpably non-literary are the reasons for its choice.[47]

"It would have been more honest," he concludes, if Sachs had been given the 1966 peace prize, and Agnon the literary award alone. He adds that though Sachs wrote in German, her award was as much another prize for Swedish literature, since she had had no connection with Germany or its writing for thirty years. But others have claimed that, far from having no connection with Germany, her poems had a too intimate connection which the Germans sought to evade: the death camps. Her major book of poems is titled *The Chimneys*. It has been plausibly argued that Sachs's prize was prompted by West Germany's wish in the 1960s for reconciliation with the Jews. Several high German prizes went to her just before the Nobel. But the distinguished German-Jewish poet Hilde Domin claimed that by thus locking Sachs into being "a poet of the Holocaust," the Germans could ignore her role in German writing and the German past. This freed the Germans "from the obligation to live with such poems." Certainly the strain wracked Nelly Sachs. She spent three years in a mental asylum, suffering from persecution mania. Her Nobel Prize came in the middle of this siege. She died in 1970.[48]

If non-European languages like Hebrew or Arabic can handicap a writer, being without a nation has excluded some from any consideration. Exile is not the issue here, but that small nations can be swallowed up by their neighbors and disappear. Up to the collapse of the Soviet empire, for example, no Latvian or Lithuanian as such could ever win an award; they did not even exist: they were all "Soviet" writers.

The far-ranging effects of a Nobel award in this context have been sharply noted by Czesław Miłosz, the Polish poet and 1980 Nobelist. Until recently, he said in 1983, the literary map of Europe had several blank spots. England, France, Germany, and Italy were distinct. So too Spain, Portugal, Holland, Belgium, and Scandinavia. Moscow and Russia bulked large to the east. But for Eastern Europeans like Ukrainians and others, the "white spaces" could easily have borne the old inscription found on medieval maps: *Ubi leones* (Here be lions). That blank space included cities like Prague ("mentioned sometimes because of Kafka"), Warsaw, Budapest, and Belgrade. The effect of this kind of literary map is by no means negligible, said Miłosz:

> The images preserved by a cultural elite undoubtedly also have political significance as they influence the decisions of the groups that govern, and it is no wonder that the statesmen who signed the Yalta agreement so easily wrote off a hundred million Europeans from those blank areas.[49]

Miłosz refers, of course, to how Churchill and Roosevelt ceded Eastern Europe to Stalin in 1945. Would a less provincial and parochial Nobel attitude to Eastern European writing have made a difference at the time of Yalta? Miłosz suggests yes, and his point cannot easily be set aside. Because of prizes to writers like García Márquez, Octavio Paz, Miguel Angel Asturias, and Pablo Neruda, Latin America is no longer one of the blank places in world consciousness. The effect of a Nobel award can be incalculably important.

A Handful of Poets, and Fewer Playwrights

Since 1901 the Nobel literary awards display a curious statistic. Although laureates have often crossed genres, generally fiction writers have won almost three times as often as poets, and eight times more often than dramatists. Up to 1999, of ninety-six laureates — there were no awards in some years — poets have won twenty-six whole prizes and shared six more times. Dramatists have won seven whole and three or four shared prizes; the rest are almost all fiction writers. The above number does not include writers who also wrote poems but were more famous in other genres, such as Kipling or

Beckett. Why this disbalance? One can hardly conclude that our century has been so lacking in worthy poets and dramatists.

Poetry competes with fiction under two obvious handicaps. Great modern poetry often has seemed "obscure" to general readers and the Nobel committee alike. As late as 1960, the citation for the French symbolist poet Saint-John Perse apologized for his "difficulty," by which time such modernism was an undergraduate school subject. And of course, fiction "travels" much better in translation than poetry. It would be interesting to know what languages the Nobel committee of 2000 read fluently in the original.

Since the Nobel judges depend so heavily on translations of verse, poets from minor European languages are at a disadvantage — if the Polish Szymborska had not been available in German and Swedish translations, would she ever have won? — and those from non-European languages all the more so. Nobel officials often point to the Indian laureate Tagore (1913) as an example of an early non-Western poet on their list. Unfortunately, although Tagore did write originally in Bengali, he won the Nobel Prize because of his English translation of the collection *Gitanjali* (Song Offerings). This once roused great enthusiasm in the West as an expression of Indian wisdom, and still has many admirers. It reads like a late-Victorian effusion edged with vague melancholy: "This frail vessel thou emptiest again and again, and fillest it ever with fresh life." A Nobel committee member, Verner von Heidenstam, a later laureate, claimed that just as knowing only a selection of Goethe's poems would convince us of his greatness, so too with Tagore. Reading some of Goethe in the original German, if you know German, and deciding he is a great poet is one thing. To read Tagore only in an English translation and conclude he must be a great Bengali poet is fatuous. And of course the Nobel judges could not read Bengali.[50]

If the Nobel has heavily favored fiction over poetry, it has almost disinherited drama. Its eight awards (shared or whole) are: Bjørnson (1903), Maeterlinck (1911), Hauptmann (1912), Shaw (1925), Pirandello (1934), O'Neill (1936), then a fifty-year wait until Wole Soyinka (1983) and, after another decade, Dario Fo (1997).

But one can argue that the twentieth century was a great age of drama: Ibsen, Strindberg, Chekhov, Claudel, John Millington Synge, Sean O'Casey, Brecht, Brian Friel, John Osborne, Harold Pinter, Athol Fugard, Ugo Betti, Giraudoux, Jean Anouilh, Fernando Arrabal, Eugène Ionesco, Tennessee Williams, Edward Albee, Friedrich

Dürrenmatt, Max Frisch, Peter Weiss, Vaclav Havel, Michel de Ghelderode, Peter Barnes, Tom Stoppard.

Some reasons for ignoring Chekhov, Strindberg, and Brecht have been mentioned. As for the mighty Ibsen, the Nobel committee derailed his nomination in 1903 by selecting Bjørnstjerne Bjørnson, inferior but more gratifyingly "idealistic." The committee resorted to some astonishing arguments to justify barring Ibsen. One was that "the genius of Ibsen had unquestionably burnt out."[51] Between 1892 and 1899, Ibsen had merely written *The Master Builder, John Gabriel Borkman*, and *When We Dead Awaken!* A historian of Swedish literature has remarked that Bjørnson would still be one of Norway's national heroes if he had never published a line — as a supreme orator, political influence, and publicist. Wirsen's citation did not fail to mention that Bjørnson had written the Norwegian national anthem. Ibsen himself said that Bjørnson's life was his best work. Of course, Bjørnson's choice effectively put Ibsen out of the running, since Scandinavians could not be honored too frequently. Ibsen died in 1906. Once that happened, however, the worry about too quickly honoring another Scandinavian quickly faded. Only three years later, in 1909, the Swedish novelist Selma Lagerlöf was made a laureate.

Paul Claudel, perhaps the greatest French dramatist of this century, did his major work before 1920. The Nobel committee thus had ample time to come to know his work before he died in 1955. In 1926 he was a candidate for the prize. The evaluation praised the richness of his work and style but, with the usual Nobel nervousness about any "difficult" writing, worried about joining "this strangely esoteric poetry with the publicity of the Nobel Prize." Espmark sums up the objections: "unnaturalness" and "unreality" versus "immediate" accessibility. Claudel was passed over. In 1937 Claudel was again rejected as too "difficult." Österling, the permanent secretary of the Swedish Academy in the year before Claudel's death, called him "France's leading poet"[52] but complained that, in the dramas, the religious symbolism stifled the aesthetic side. W. H. Auden wrote that Time worships language and

> Will pardon Paul Claudel,
> Pardons him for writing well.

The Nobel jury apparently could not accept posterity's strange excuse. Claudel was vetoed.

In 1997 the prize went to the Italian Dario Fo, whom many consider not a dramatist but a writer of scripts for his own performances. He is a vivid and popular actor of farce and satire, aimed mostly at political but also at other targets — the Vatican, anti-abortion, graft, genetic engineering. In each performance he improvises at will, so that his scripts are never quite available in permanent form, but remain prompt-books. He is the first post-modern "playwright" — or performance artist — in the Nobel list. One remembers that Charlie Chaplin was once nominated for the literature prize, since he too wrote his own scripts, but was rejected as not truly a dramatist. Yet Chaplin's films now exist in more permanent form than Fo's scripts.[53]

Philosophy and History

History entered the Nobel literary canon with the 1902 award to the German historian Mommsen. Only one other award to a historian — Churchill in 1953 — has ever been given. Philosophy arrived when Eucken of Germany won the 1908 prize. After a two-decade pause, the French philosopher Henri Bergson was honored in 1927. A quarter century later, in 1950, came the British philosopher Bertrand Russell. Jean-Paul Sartre was honored both as writer and philosopher in 1964.

Trying to discover a pattern or principle in these prizes is hopeless. Committee quirks seem the only explanation. Eucken was a last-ditch compromise candidate when the judges deadlocked over Swinburne and Lagerlöf.[54] Bergson was a candidate from 1915, but his militant French patriotism kept him from being honored during the war. A magnificent stylist, he was the most popular philosopher in France; savants and society hostesses and Proust attended his lectures. Whatever else, the Nobel conservatives saw him as a staunch opponent of the materialists. Not least, Bergson brought to Stockholm the prestige of the French intellectual world and the Académie Française.

But the American philosophers William James (d. 1910) and George Santayana (d. 1952) were as fine stylists as Bergson, and his intellectual peers. Santayana should have been a candidate from 1920 on, but there is no sign he was ever nominated. The American Henry Adams (d. 1918), who wrote *Mont-Saint-Michel and Chartres* as well as *The Education of Henry Adams*, and some first-rate American history, was ignored. The Spanish philosopher and cultural critic José Ortega y Gasset (d. 1955) deserved a prize, but he too may never have been nominated. Though Benedetto Croce was a candidate and strongly recommended, the Italian was rejected in 1933 perhaps because the judges were then disinclined to move away from strictly literary fields. The Spaniard Unamuno was rejected in 1935 as too "abstract," which may surprise anyone who has read his *Tragic View of Life* (1913) or his *Meditations on Don Quixote* (1914). J. G. Frazer, author of *The Golden Bough* in 1915, was rejected because his work was "too old." Freud, a master of German style, was set aside as having "a sick and distorted imagination"[55] and as really belonging in the field of medicine, where he was also denied a prize.

Bertrand Russell began as a philosopher of mathematical logic as forbiddingly technical as possible. But he then shifted to intellectual popularizations of any subject under the sun — science, history, psychology, pedagogy, political thought. Like George Bernard Shaw, Russell turned into a long-lived and revered perpetual enfant terrible; his Nobel chances were certainly helped by his receiving the prestigious British Order of Merit the year before. He was surely a lucid philosophic expositor, but even the Nobel judges could hardly believe that amounted to great literature.

Mommsen was eighty-five when named a laureate, a living monument of historical scholarship. Churchill himself was a living monument of history. His six-volume *The Second World War*, published from 1948 to 1954, provided a "literary" reason for making him a laureate, but the Nobel jury suggests it was thinking as much or more of his oratory during World War II.[56]

Nobel Identities: Language and Nation

Nobel laureates have always been identified by nation. But with the literary prizes, language provides a more accurate reckoning. Nations divide, redivide, and sometimes vanish. A laureate's nation is not always easy to determine. Languages are stabler. Czesław Miłosz, the poet and Nobel laureate who writes in Polish, was born and raised in Lithuania, which together with part of Poland was then under Russian rule. Miłosz has lived many decades in America, but the Poles rightly count him as one of their own, as Russians do the émigré poet Joseph Brodsky, an American resident to his death. Languages ignore all such political happenstance. Isaac Bashevis Singer is part of Yiddish writing, for which there has never been, and now will never be, a nation.

The Nobel Prize in Literature has of course mostly honored the major European nations. But being a Great Power does not guarantee success. Germany did moderately well until 1929, when Thomas Mann took the prize, but has had only two prizes since then, spaced almost thirty years apart: to Heinrich Böll in 1972, and to Günter Grass in 1999. But though a nation may not do well, its language can. Although Germany has earned only seven prizes, the German language also lives in Austria, Switzerland, and here and there in Central Europe; Kafka and Rilke, both from Prague, wrote in German. The German language has a total of eleven laureates, including two from Switzerland plus the German-writing Canetti and also counting Nelly Sachs. Spain has won only five awards, but Spanish-language Nobels have mounted up impressively: Spain after all colonized a continent. Of the thirteen nations in South America, nine speak Spanish, as do all countries in Central America; Brazil, with no winners, uses Portuguese. There are now five Latin-American laureates, all but one in the last third of the century.

English has spread even further. Prizes here now dominate the Nobel list — twenty-one awards, including writers from Great Britain, the U.S., Ireland, Australia, South Africa, Nigeria, and the West Indies.

France, with a very high total of eleven up to 1965, has had only one prize in the last thirty years. Italy has won six, Poland four, and a handful of others one or two.

Scandinavian nations have had the extraordinarily high total of fourteen laureates. But the Swedish Academy's generosity to its own and neighboring writers has ceased, at least for the moment: the last Scandinavian laureates were in 1974. One of the Scandinavian prizes was to the Finnish novelist Sillanpää; Finland is a Scandinavian nation but Finnish isn't a kindred language, which shows how complicated counting Nobels by nations can get.

Nobels in English

Laureates from Great Britain and Ireland

1907 Rudyard Kipling, fiction

1923 William Butler Yeats, poetry (Irish Free State)

1925 George Bernard Shaw, drama

1932 John Galsworthy, fiction

1948 T. S. Eliot, poetry

1950 Bertrand Russell, philosophy

1953 Winston Churchill, history

1969 Samuel Beckett, fiction and drama (Irish-French)

1983 William Golding, fiction

1995 Seamus Heaney, poetry

As a representation of Great Britain's best writing in the twentieth century, this list is of course absurd, and the Nobel judges realize it.[57] Without the Irish component of Yeats, Shaw, Heaney, and Beckett and the Anglo-American Eliot, the English fiction list shrinks to Kipling, Galsworthy, and Golding: not brilliant. The Nobel jury, at least, has not been able to find any native English, or Scottish or Welsh, writers of true distinction.

Instead of the undistinguished Galsworthy, a more competent Nobel jury would have chosen Virginia Woolf, James Joyce, Joseph Conrad, D. H. Lawrence, Sean O'Casey, or E. M. Forster. As noted, Golding's merits were so disputable that a Swedish Academy member, in a rare breach of Nobel secrecy, publicly dismissed him as a nonentity. Among his contemporaries, the Nobel jury could have honored Evelyn Waugh, Anthony Powell, Philip Larkin, Graham Greene, Anthony Burgess, Hugh MacDiarmid, or Doris Lessing.

Early unsuccessful British candidates included the philosopher Herbert Spencer, too "agnostic"; George Meredith, too "often artificial and febrile"; and Thomas Hardy, vetoed for his unGodly novels — his present high status as a poet came after his death in 1928. There was also the Victorian poet Algernon Swinburne, whose best work by 1901 lay more than thirty years back. He lost out in an inimitable Nobel comedy. Swinburne's perverse, sometimes sadistic touches ("O lips full of lust and laughter, / Curled snakes that are fed from my breast, / Bite hard . . .") and his pagan anti-Christianity had often shocked his Victorian readers, and he also once sang songs of revolution. The reactionary Wirsen nonetheless enthusiastically backed him for an award. He blamed Swinburne's excesses on the wicked Baudelaire's influence; he was also pleased that the old Swinburne, come to his senses, now censured libidinous poets like Whitman and stoutly championed monarchy. But Swinburne lost out in 1908 and died soon after.

Some of those passed over by the Nobel judges could comprise a Great Books collection:

> **Joseph Conrad:** Conrad desperately hoped to win the award, always anxious about his reputation and always in financial straits until the last few years of his life. He had high claims as the world's finest sea writer, but also for such novels as *Lord Jim* (1900), *Heart of Darkness* (1902), and the extraordinary sequence of political novels *Nostromo* (1904), *The Secret Agent* (1907), and *Under Western Eyes* (1911). Conrad, never very practical, pinned his hopes for a Nobel Prize on his novel *The Rescue* (1919–20), not one of his best. But the 1919 prize went to the Swiss poet Carl Spitteler. Conrad hoped that after the 1923 prize to Yeats, a novelist would be chosen next — perhaps Conrad himself. In 1924 it was indeed a novelist, and a Polish one — Władysław Reymont. Conrad died that same year. Espmark claims that Conrad had never been nominated for the Nobel award from Britain or the U.S.,[58] though he later adds that "not a single legitimate proposal" was made. This is cryptic: had Conrad been nominated or not? Conrad's reputation was high not only in Britain and the U.S. but in France. A simpler reason doubtless kept Conrad from a prize. If the Nobel jury could not see the Yeats of 1923 except in terms of his Celtic Twilight self of 1900, what could they make of a Pole writing exotic English about terrorists and nihilists, as in *Under Western Eyes* and *The Secret Agent*, or strange and sinister colonialists as in *Heart of Darkness*? T. S. Eliot quoted from Conrad, unidentified as from a classic, in his *The Waste Land* and "The Hollow Men" of the early 1920s; but the Nobel judges at that time also found Eliot indigestible.

D. H. Lawrence: Lawrence's "international breakthrough" occurred in the 1920s, Espmark concedes, but Lawrence died in 1930, "too soon to be evaluated." Lawrence had by then written *Sons and Lovers* (1913), *The Rainbow* (1915) and *Women in Love* (1921), *The Plumed Serpent* (1926), and *Lady Chatterley's Lover* (1928), as well as much powerful short fiction. But it is useless to repeat that the Nobel jury needed only three years to honor Pearl Buck, less than ten for others like Sinclair Lewis or Sienkiewicz. Espmark broaches the real reason Lawrence was never honored: it was unlikely that the Swedish Academy of those days "would have been capable of realizing the importance of this controversial figure." In short, Lawrence would never have won a prize no matter how long that hostile jury "evaluated" his works.

Virginia Woolf: If they ever read her, the Nobel judges might have wondered if Woolf's lyrically allusive *Mrs. Dalloway* (1925) and *To the Lighthouse* (1927), not to mention the dazzling poetic formalisms of *The Waves* (1931) and *The Years* (1937), were in fact novels at all. In Nobel view, she was all those things they disliked and feared — "difficult," "eccentric," "exclusive," their code words for a writer without popular appeal.

James Joyce: As usual, we are told that Joyce was never nominated. In 1923 Desmond Fitzgerald, a minister of the new Irish Free State, wrote Joyce that Ireland should propose him for a Nobel prize. Joyce commented that such a move not only would not get him the prize but would probably get Fitzgerald sacked.[59]

Defending the Nobel jury, Espmark claims that Joyce's "stature was not properly recognized even in the English-speaking world." This is limp. Ulysses was published in 1922, and within ten years, discerning and influential critics — T. S. Eliot, Pound, Edmund Wilson, Ernst Robert Curtius, and others of that rank — "properly" recognized him as one of the world's greatest living novelists. Espmark concedes this by saying that Joyce would doubtless have been honored as a "pioneer" like Eliot in 1948 if he had only lived until the post-war years. But Joyce died in 1941. In 1947 or so, he would have been worthy of a prize, but not six years before? The Nobel litany of "died too soon" thus really seems to mean "didn't live long enough for us."

Laureates from the United States

1930 Sinclair Lewis, fiction

1936 Eugene O'Neill, drama

1938 Pearl Buck, fiction

1949 William Faulkner, fiction

1954 Ernest Hemingway, fiction

1962 John Steinbeck, fiction

1976 Saul Bellow, fiction

1978 Isaac Bashevis Singer, fiction in Yiddish (resident in the U.S. when awarded prize)

1980 Czesław Miłosz, poetry in Polish (resident in the U.S. when awarded prize)

1987 Joseph Brodsky, poetry in Russian (resident in the U.S. when awarded prize)

1993 Toni Morrison, fiction

As a record of great American writing, this is as peculiar as that of Britain. First, the Nobel Prize ignored giants such as Twain (d. 1910, apparently never considered) and Henry James. In 1911 Edith Wharton, Edmund Gosse, and William Dean Howells began a campaign to get James the Nobel award. He deserved it, was ill, and badly needed the money. They did all the right things: they gathered eminent supporters; they had impressive letters sent to the Nobel committees spelling out James's towering position as an Anglo-American novelist. It had no effect. The Nobel jury read the letters but, as James's biographer Leon Edel puts it,

> the Northern judges of the world's literature had not read James. They had not read about him in the newspapers; he was intensely private. Moreover, they tended to be influenced by the degree to which foreign writers were popular in other countries than their own and the extent to which they were translated. James had been very little translated. He considered himself — and most translators agree — untranslatable.[60]

The evaluators of James, as Espmark reports them, admit he had fine style, but with wondrous blindness claimed his novels were too often only "conversation and situation novels," and he "lacks concentration." *The Wings of the Dove* had "an improbable and odious subject."[61]

After no prizes at all to Americans until 1930, three came in quick succession to Lewis, O'Neill, and Buck. Was the Nobel committee trying to make up for past neglect? Perhaps they were truly smitten by what seemed fresh new voices. But Sinclair Lewis has faded dramatically. It is difficult now to recapture the excitement of Lewis's early novels, each a devastating satirical blow at American complacency: *Main Street* (1920), *Babbitt* (1922), *Arrowsmith* (1925), *Elmer Gantry* (1927). He was the deadly deflater of twenties boosterism and American brashness. His satire had a photographic perfection in which every fatuous flaw in the target loomed up at one. But when the provincialism and hectic phoniness of the 1920s gave way to the deeper problems of the Depression, he seemed at sea. He lived to 1951 and turned out novels regularly, often best-sellers, too often bloated and formulaic.

Why was Lewis chosen as the first American Nobelist? The Nobel committee claimed he was beginning a new national literature. Having earlier passed over Twain and James, they now managed to ignore other new makers of American writing far more important than Lewis. In fiction alone, there was F. Scott Fitzgerald, Ernest Hemingway, Willa Cather, and Theodore Dreiser. In his Nobel acceptance speech, Lewis honorably and generously suggested that Dreiser was more deserving of the Nobel award: "more than any other man" he was the real pioneer, "marching alone, usually unappreciated, often hated," but "he cleared the trail from Victorian . . . timidity and gentility." A better description of exactly the sort of writer the Nobel juries of that time would never honor could hardly be given.

Faulkner's award was one of the Nobel's finest moments: they actually picked a writer who had been dismissed in the United States and Britain as perverse, grotesque, impenetrable, or a mere regionalist, and most of his books were out of print. The *New York Times* derided his prize: "Incest and rape may be common in Faulkner's Jefferson, Mississippi, but they are not elsewhere in the United States." As for Hemingway, he was one of the world's supercelebrities when he won the prize, but though he was only fifty-five, his career was essentially over. The Swedish Academy praised *The Old Man and the Sea* (1952) as a masterpiece and a sign of Hemingway's regenerated powers; it was neither. Then came John Steinbeck, described by the Nobel citation as embracing all America in his sympathy for its mountains and coasts, its oppressed and misfits and ordinary folk — the citation in its turn embracing all of Steinbeck by devoting a paragraph of praise even to *Travels with Charley* (1962), Steinbeck's book about touring the country with his dog in a truck named Rosinante. Far more gifted than Pearl Buck, Steinbeck is however also her closest relative on the Nobel's American list.

The prizes to Saul Bellow and Toni Morrison have rightly received wide approval. Bellow, with Beckett, is the greatest comic novelist on the Nobel list; Faulkner is a contender. Another supreme comic master unjustly denied a Nobel Prize was Vladimir Nabokov (1899–1977). Perhaps the Nobel committee, blinking like a mole at too much sunlight, judged *Lolita* (1955) obscene, *Pale Fire* (1962) too eccentric, and the enchanting *Pnin* (1957) too slight.

A real test of the Nobel's maturity, openness, literary wisdom, and determination to honor genius would have been a prize to Gertrude Stein. Her novel *Three Lives* (1903) has lost none of its audacity and freshness (in both senses); nor has *Tender Buttons* (1915) or *The Making of Americans* (1925) or *Operas and Plays* (1937). But for such a "difficult" and "eccentric" writer, her chances were zero. She died in 1946.

To date, American laureates have all been fiction writers, with O'Neill the only dramatist. No American poet has ever been honored. Worthy candidates have hardly been lacking. By the 1920s, an American renaissance in poetry was spilling over: Robert Frost, Wallace Stevens, Marianne Moore, Hart Crane, William Carlos Williams, Ezra Pound, to name only the most prominent. If a Nobel Prize is ever given to an American poet, the future poet-Nobelist is going to have to contend with these potent ghosts, and the comparisons will likely not be polite.

Why no American poets? The Swedish judges patently lacked a sense of what was new and good in American poetry. And the Nobel's disdain for "difficult" writing put most of the above poets out of court automatically — except Robert Frost. Up to the late 1950s, Frost was still widely seen in the United States as the homespun philosopher of rural New England folkways; the sense of his darkly ironic, even nihilistic side spread slowly. He was America's most popular poet of the time. He wrote always in disciplined meter and style, and could never be accused of formal eccentricity. Indeed, if any poet seemed ideal for the Nobel Prize in the Swedish Academy's own terms, it was Frost. Why then did he never win? Our cicerone to the Nobel committee, Espmark, notes without further explanation that the Swedish statesman Dag Hammarskjöld thought Frost lost out to Hemingway for "political" reasons.[62]

Frost lived until 1963, Stevens to 1955, Williams to 1963, Moore to 1972.

The one "American" poet who came close was W. H. Auden, who died in 1973. Here arises another nationality tangle: Auden had lived in the United States for thirty years, and became a citizen; if Eliot was counted English, didn't Auden count as American? In 1965 the two leading candidates apparently were Auden and Sartre. Sartre was deemed the philosophy pioneer, Auden the literary innovator. Sartre won; Auden's best work was thought "too far back in time." In 1967 Auden came up again with Miguel Angel Asturias of Guatemala and Graham Greene as his rivals. But now Auden was set aside by a Nobel swing of mood against honoring too well-known writers: why bother to celebrate the celebrated? The same argument obviously worked against Greene; Asturias won.

English-Language Laureates from Elsewhere

1973 Patrick White, fiction (Australia)

1986 Wole Soyinka, drama (Nigeria)

1991 Nadine Gordimer, fiction (South Africa)

1992 Derek Walcott, poetry (West Indies)

Patrick White (1912–1990) dominated Australian writing in his lifetime and still does. His is no provincial reputation; White is properly seen as one of the great writers of the twentieth century in any language. Soyinka and Gordimer are two from a vast continent of important writers, as yet scarcely noticed by the Nobel committee. Soyinka is a major dramatist, Gordimer a distinguished novelist. But prizes to African writing in English could as rightly have gone to the Nigerian novelists Chinua Achebe (b. 1930) and Amos Tutuola (b. 1922), the Ghanaian poet Kofi Awoonor (b. 1935), the Kenyan novelist Ngugi wa Thiong'o (b. 1938), J. M. Coetzee (b. 1940) of South Africa. Or the major poets Léopold Sédar Senghor or Aimé Césaire, who wrote in French. There may also be worthy prize candidates who write in native African languages or in Portuguese. Walcott's poetry focuses on his West Indian roots, but he draws eclectically from European and American modernism, Greek myth, and much else. V. S. Naipaul is from Trinidad but, as earlier noted, has been passed over by Stockholm.

Nobels in French

Laureates from France

1901   Sully Prudhomme, poetry

1904   Frédéric Mistral, poetry (shared with Echegaray of Spain)

1915   Romain Rolland, fiction

1921   Anatole France, fiction

1927   Henri Bergson, philosophy

1937   Roger Martin du Gard, fiction

1947   André Gide, fiction

1952   François Mauriac, fiction

1957   Albert Camus, fiction

1960   Saint-John Perse, poetry

1964   Jean-Paul Sartre, philosophy and fiction

1985   Claude Simon, fiction

Anatole France used to be thought a sceptical Epicurean, Martin du Gard an epic novelist of the bourgeois, Gide an intellectual in the guise of novelist, Mauriac a novelist of Catholic guilt on the rack. Their reputations have faded, Mauriac's perhaps the least.

Albert Camus was the first laureate (1957) from the World War II generation. He wrote existential philosophy in *The Rebel* (1951), and novels of the "absurd" with classic control: *The Stranger* (1942), *The Plague* (1947), *The Fall* (1956). Camus agonized over his award. He thought André Malraux more deserving; and he worried that all his writing from then on — he was only forty-four when he became a laureate — would have to live up to his Nobel reputation. His prestige as a Nobelist and his Algerian birth made him a large political target during the Algerian crisis exploding at that time. But three years later, in 1960, Camus was dead in a car accident.

His onetime existentialist ally and then political opponent was Jean-Paul Sartre, the combative lion of that generation of French intellectuals. But after Sartre's refusal of the 1964 prize, no French writer won for twenty years. Many French saw this as the Swedes' revenge. Others pointed out that Beckett's prize in 1969 was half for writing in French. In 1985 the novelist Claude Simon finally brought France a "full" laureate. A candidate since the 1960s, heavily influenced by Faulkner, Simon's stylistic explorations or obsessions make him one of the few strenuously avant-garde prose writers on the Nobel list.

Among the excluded:

André Malraux: The omission of Malraux (1901–1976) is one of the Nobel's great lapses. He began as a novelist and in midcareer moved into art history, with his famous *Voices of Silence* (1951) and *The Imaginary Museum* (1953), and other works including innovative biography and autobiography. In 1969, after Camus and Sartre had become laureates, many expected Malraux finally to win. He had long been a prominent candidate. But Beckett was chosen instead as the French representative. Malraux believed that the Swedish Academy refused to honor him because they considered Gaullism to be semifascist; Malraux served as a minister under de Gaulle. The Nobel's explanation, according to Espmark, was that Churchill's Nobel Prize, given when he was prime minister, raised charges of political favoritism. Since then, the Swedish Academy chose to honor no writer holding political office. This is supposedly why Léopold Sédar Senghor, president of the Republic of Senegal from 1960, was not honored. But Senghor stepped down in 1980. And why, when de Gaulle was out of office and Malraux not a minister, wasn't he honored then? One is forced to conclude Malraux was right: the Nobel jury's politics vetoed not his work but his Gaullism.

Colette: Sidonie Gabrielle Colette (1873–1954) was so brilliantly the writer of sensuous life, landscape, longing and love, that she was also often confined to a narrow and quintessentially feminine carnality. For the same reason, she has been charged with being trapped in the fin-de-siècle, in the demimonde, in childhood memory and adolescence wakening to sexuality and life. Yet she was a writer of overwhelming natural power, perfect instinct, and inexhaustible vitality. Colette still seems to await adequate appreciation. But after novels like *Chéri* (1920) and memoirs like *Sido* (1929), and her prolific output before and after, she should have been honored in the later 1930s, when she easily outclassed the Italian Grazia Deledda or the Danish J. V. Jensen, to mention no others.

Paul Valéry: Scheduled to be the laureate for 1945, Valéry died in July of that year. The Nobel jury had awarded a posthumous prize in 1931 to the Swedish poet and member of the Swedish Academy Erik Karlfeldt, but decided against this with Valéry, probably since there were many protests that Valéry should have been honored a decade or so before. Valéry's selection was meant as a sign that the Nobel had somewhat abandoned its resistance to "difficult" modernist poetry. A new committee had been appointed, the same that soon honored Faulkner; the next poet selected, Eliot in 1948, was in Valéry's symbolist tradition, as was Perse in 1960, and both were also used to pay homage to Valéry.[63]

Of the three poets among French laureates, only Perse has great distinction, the two others being Sully Prudhomme and Frédéric Mistral. But there has been a crowd of superb poets in French: Louis Aragon, Blaise Cendrars, René Char, Henri Michaux, Pierre Reverdy, Francis Ponge, Yves Bonnefoy, Mohammed Dib, Aimé Césaire.

And why did Marguerite Yourcenar never receive a Nobel?

Nobels in German

Though the few Nobel awards here suggest otherwise, twentieth-century writing in German has been one of modern literature's richest areas, as well as one of the richest mixes of participating nationalities. Poets included Rilke from Prague, Hofmannsthal from Vienna, Paul Celan from Romania, Stefan George and Arno Holz and Peter Huchel from Germany, Carl Spitteler from Switzerland. In fiction and drama, Thomas Mann, Günter Grass, Heinrich Böll, and Bertolt Brecht from Germany; Kafka from Prague; Hermann Broch, Robert Musil, Thomas Bernhard, and the satirist Karl Kraus from Austria; Hermann Hesse and the dramatists Max Frisch and Friedrich Dürrenmatt from Switzerland. With all this talent, the Nobel has netted seven Germans, two Swiss, and two émigré writers. Of these probably only Thomas Mann is of undoubted first rank. How, even in the erratic history of Nobel committees, could so many have been missed by so few?

Laureates from Germany

1902	Theodor Mommsen, history
1908	Rudolf Eucken, philosophy
1910	Paul Heyse, poetry
1912	Gerhart Hauptmann, drama
1929	Thomas Mann, fiction
1972	Heinrich Böll, fiction
1999	Günter Grass, fiction

Laureates from Switzerland

| 1919 | Carl Spitteler, poetry |
| 1946 | Hermann Hesse, fiction |

Other German-Language Laureates

| 1966 | Nelly Sachs, poetry (Sweden) |
| 1981 | Elias Canetti, fiction (Bulgaria-Austria-Britain) |

Germany's Nobel list is perhaps the strangest of any major European country: four to 1912, then only three in almost ninety years following. Hauptmann, Spitteler, and Heyse were a generation older than Thomas Mann. But Mann's generation is the one strikingly missing from the Nobel awards. Mann (born 1875) was almost an exact contemporary of Rilke (b. 1875), Kafka (b. 1883), Hofmannsthal (b. 1874), Musil (b. 1880), Karl Kraus (b. 1874), Broch (b. 1886), Alfred Döblin (b. 1878). The Nobel judges missed them all. Kafka published too little. The others had the bad luck, with the Nobel in mind, to come to maturity from around 1900 to about 1940 — true even of Brecht, born 1898, because of his precocity — when the Nobel strongly disdained modernism.

They also came from unlucky lands: Germany and Austria with their wars and Nazi interregnum, or Central Europe with its contentious small nations and minorities — Czechs, Slovaks, Serbs, Bosnians, Croatians, Poles, Romanians, Bulgarians, Hungarians — often swallowed up by powerful neighbors or thrust into precarious, short-lived independence. Small, fractured, inwardly clashing nations scarcely provide the sort of prestigious nominations and organizational support possible in France or the U.S. In this Mitteleuropa, even becoming visible through translation was difficult, since it was often a point of honor not to know a major language like German or Russian.

Remarkably, there is as yet no Austrian laureate, unless one counts the émigré Canetti.[64] Yet Vienna, in concentration of genius, easily rivaled Paris before Hitler arrived in 1938. Perhaps these Central Europeans were too precocious about the tremors and disorientations of modernity — the Central Europeans knew disorder and fragmentation, as it were, in their bones and history, "along the blood," in a way not available to the French or British, or Swedes. The Nobel committee took fifty years or more to begin to catch up with them. And by then, the 1870s generation were dead or "too old" or still undiscovered. Robert Musil's great novel *The Man without Qualities* (written 1930–43), like those of the Austrian Joseph Roth (1894–1939), is only now coming into its own.

Of this lost generation, special mention must be made of Hermann Broch and Hugo von Hofmannsthal. Broch's epical, many-layered, prose-poetical *The Death of Virgil* (1945) puts him on the level of Proust, Mann, and Joyce. Thomas Mann and Einstein were among those nominating him for a Nobel Prize. The Nobel evaluator felt that *The Death of Virgil* lacked a wide following (true, but irrelevant) and that it mixed narrative, poetry, philosophy, and history to excess (how define "excess"?). Broch died in 1951. By the 1980s the Nobel jury was finally ready to cope with such writing and they chose the lesser Canetti. Hofmannsthal is best known as the librettist for Richard Strauss's operas, but as a poet and dramatist, and analyst of the disintegration of language, he has few superiors.

The novelist Günter Grass, Rabelaisian in energy and enormities, is also outspoken and truculent politically. In 1972, when the Nobel judges finally selected their first postwar German laureate, they passed over Grass — who by then had published *The Tin Drum, Cat and Mouse*, and *Dog Years* — and instead chose the excellent but also more respectable Heinrich Böll, who spoke for decent, middle-of-the-road Germans. Grass finally won in 1999, aged seventy-three.

Of recent writers, the poet Paul Celan is among the Nobel's most serious lapses. Celan was a Romanian Jew born in 1920, who survived the Holocaust, worked in Paris, and wrote poetry in German. Any discussion of modern writing must soon move him into the forefront. His subject was the Holocaust and in his style — the chopped syntax, the words burdened with silences and derailments — that horrifying experience leaks through like blood at every point. But he committed suicide in 1970, aged fifty, while the Nobel evaluators were still cautiously deciding if he measured up to Nobel standards. Was he perhaps not old enough for a prize? One wonders if the Russian poet Brodsky, honored so young and quickly, was another of the Nobel's stand-ins here.

Nobels in Scandinavia

Scandinavian Laureates

1903   Bjørnstjerne Bjørnson (Norway)

1909   Selma Lagerlöf (Sweden)

1916   Carl Verner von Heidenstam (Sweden)

1917   Karl Gjellerup (Denmark); Henrik Pontoppidan (Denmark)

1920   Knut Hamsun (Norway)

1928   Sigrid Undset (Norway)

1931   Erik Karlfeldt (Sweden)

1939 Frans Sillanpää (Finland)

1944 Johannes V. Jensen (Denmark)

1951 Pär Lagerkvist (Sweden)

1955 Halldór Laxness (Iceland)

1974 Eyvind Johnson (Sweden); Harry Martinson (Sweden)

One may perhaps add Nelly Sachs, though she wrote in German and is considered above.

This is fourteen or perhaps fifteen Nobel Prizes to Scandinavian writers — against twelve for France and seven for Germany. One might thus assume we are dealing with a very major body of world writing. But only Hamsun's reputation, and recently Martinson's, has grown. Sillanpää is often said to have won because the Nobel wanted to reward Finland for its brave resistance to the Soviet Union in the 1939 war; Espmark refutes that, pointing out that the USSR attacked Finland on 14 December 1939, months after Sillanpää had been named. But wasn't the Soviet threat discernible months before? Harry Martinson's epic poem *Aniara* is a haunting masterpiece of humans leaving the earth as the space age begins; perhaps Martinson lacks the international fame he deserves because the list's general Scandinavian mediocrity makes him suspect.

It could have been a much more impressive list. To start, there were Ibsen, Strindberg, Georg Brandes, and Isak Dinesen. Was the superb Swedish poet Gunnar Ekelöf (1907–1968) omitted only because by then the list was already swollen with not-so-great Northern writers? And has the arresting Swedish poet Tomas Tranströmer been denied because adding another Swede might be too embarrassing now?

Nobels in Italy

Italian Laureates

1906 Giosuè Carducci, poetry

1926 Grazia Deledda, fiction

1934 Luigi Pirandello, drama

1959   Salvatore Quasimodo, poetry

1975   Eugenio Montale, poetry

1997   Dario Fo

As poet and critic, Carducci was a dominating figure in Italian literature in the last third of the nineteenth century. His is the aura of an emancipator. From midcentury, he challenged a decayed romanticism with an invigorating classicism, and at a time when Italy preferred even poor translations of mediocre French poetry or fiction to its own living best, he helped restore Italian writing to dignity in its homeland. This was the period of his great *Odi barbare* (1877–89), of many sonnets, and of poems celebrating Shelley, Rome, and Dante's church.

Grazia Deledda was self-educated and wrote against all the odds for a woman at that time in that place. Her Sardinian landscapes and peasants, the social world that seemed as fixed and archaic as the earth, are real yet not compelling. The Nobel committee of the 1920s, Espmark notes, considered her an example of the Goethean "great and noble simplicity" they had chosen as their model. One suspects this was another way for the Nobel to finesse the challenge of modern writing, the greatest of which did not meet, nor wish to, Goethean neoclassical standards.

Pirandello is still perhaps the most famous Italian writer of this century. He anticipated the modernist theater, experimental, existential, and absurd. Unfortunately, "Pirandello" too often narrows down to one or two of his plays, *Six Characters in Search of an Author* and *Right You Are, If You Think You Are.* He wrote more than forty plays, seven novels, a hundred-odd short stories, and a great weight of criticism and essays.

Salvatore Quasimodo's Nobel Prize before Montale's seems to have depended crucially on a brilliant English translation by the American poet and translator Allen Mandelbaum, which came out at the opportune moment. That Quasimodo wrote some lovely verses, says Ragusa,

> and that at a certain point he rejected the poetics of Hermeticism to turn to a more readily graspable diction seem insufficient reasons for the decision of the Nobel committee at the expense of alternate possibilities.[65]

Montale has great humanity. But the unanointed Giuseppe Ungaretti (1888–1970) was a greater poet, of such compact power that he can make all other poets garrulous.

Nobels in Russia/USSR

Russian Laureates

1933 Ivan Bunin, fiction

1958 Boris Pasternak, poetry and fiction

1965 Mikhail Sholokhov, fiction

1970 Aleksandr Solzhenitsyn, fiction

1987 Joseph Brodsky, poetry

Twentieth-century Russian literature has been extraordinarily rich, but almost three entire generations were murdered or had their careers chopped short by the Soviet regime, or emigrated — the young Nabokov, for example. In 1925 the Communist Party declared total censorship privilege over all art. In 1932 the Soviet Writers Union took over direct control of publishing and support. A short list with dates suggests how some of the greatest writers had no chance at a Nobel award:

Andrei Bely, fiction, 1880–1934 (remained in USSR; no important work after 1920s)

Aleksandr Blok, fiction, 1880–1921 (died from overwork)

Vladimir Mayakovsky, poetry, 1893–1930 (suicide)

Osip Mandelstam, poetry, 1891–1938 (died in prison camp)

Eugene Zamyatin, fiction, 1884–1937 (exiled in early 1930s)

Marina Tsvetaeva, poetry, 1892–1941 (suicide)

Isaac Babel, fiction, 1894–1941? (murdered in purges)

Mikhail Bulgakov, fiction, 1891–1940 (major work banned during life-time)

Anna Akhmatova, poetry, 1889–1966 (mostly unpublished from 1920s; publicly denounced 1946)

Of those who matured during and after the revolution, Boris Pasternak was the first of a meager handful to become a laureate. Pasternak's *Doctor Zhivago* is, however, often said to be rivaled or surpassed by Bulgakov's novel *The Master and Margarita*, allowed into print only sixteen years after the author died. Anna Akhmatova survived by the skin of her teeth, and from the 1950s gained international notice, but the Nobel jury let her die unhonored. It is one of the Stockholm mysteries. Isaiah Berlin, the famous Oxford don and Russia expert, visited her during the war and shortly after, and knew her great worth. Was he ever a Nobel nominator, and if not, why on earth not? There appears only one reason he might not have nominated her — that she might thereby suffer more official harassment. But if the Nobel jury were concerned about that, why then did they expose Pasternak to even worse possible harassment, since his "crime" of publishing a historical novel in the West about the Soviet world was more flagrant? Akhmatova is as great a loss to the list as anyone namable.

Ivan Bunin (Nobel 1933) survived by leaving the Soviet Union in 1920 and never returning. He kept writing in Russian, and happily was widely translated, by D. H. Lawrence among others. It is difficult to see Bunin as anything but a minor writer, but the Nobel citation, laying stress on his link with Russia before the Communists, and even bringing in Tolstoy, suggested Bunin was preserving the great pre-Bolshevik tradition. Even by the time of Bunin's award, however, Nabokov was often considered the best Russian émigré writer. It is known that Aleksandr Solzhenitsyn, for all his apparent distance from Nabokovian playfulness and dandyism, nominated him for the Nobel Prize. Nabokov never won — he seems to hold the record as the writer who should have won a Nobel in either or both of two different languages.

Nobels in Poland

Polish Laureates

1905 Henryk Sienkiewicz, fiction

1924 Władysław Reymont, fiction

1980 Czesław Miłosz, poetry

1996 Wisława Szymborska, poetry

Sienkiewicz's *Quo Vadis* appeared in 1896 and over the next few decades sold millions of copies. The Nobel judges have often been greatly impressed by the international popularity of a writer — it can seem a testimony of worth — and here was one indeed.

By the time Reymont's historical novels were honored, Polish writing was starting to remake itself into writing as vital as any in the world. In the 1920s new movements sprang up. Before and after the Second War there were such fiction writers, to mention only those best known in the West, as Tadeus Borowski, Witold Gombrowicz, Bruno Schulz, Jerzy Peterkiewicz, the science-fantasist Stanisław Lem — and such Yiddish writers as I. J. Singer, brother of the Nobelist I. B. Singer. Poets included Miłosz, Alexander Wat, and the slightly younger Zbigniew Herbert, Tadeus Resewicz, and Adam Mickiewicz. In the 1980s, the later Russian Nobelist Joseph Brodsky was not alone in saying that everyone should learn Polish because the century's most interesting poetry was being written in that language.

Miłosz came to maturity in the 1930s, in a Poland wracked between the Soviets and Nazis, and inwardly by its own many tensions; he witnessed firsthand the destruction of the Warsaw ghetto; in 1951, he went into exile. His poetry brims with extraordinary richness, an unsettling blend of generosity and bitterness, open to all experience. The next Polish laureate, in 1996, was another poet, Wisława Szymborska (b. 1923). Younger than Miłosz, she is little known in the West. She has been called one of the least prolific major poets of our time. No one else quite so casual and commanding comes to mind.

And should Isaac Bashevis Singer be added to the Polish list? The puzzling notion of nationality arises again. He lived in Poland, mainly Warsaw, until he was thirty-one, writing in Yiddish, publishing there his famous story "Satan in Goray." In 1935 he emigrated to the U.S., but he kept writing in Yiddish and setting his fiction most often in Poland. After James Joyce left Ireland, he kept writing about Dublin, and remained an Irish writer. So should Singer be listed among "Polish" writers?

Nobels in Spanish

Spanish-Language Laureates

1904   José Echegaray, drama, Spain

1922   Jacinto Benavente, drama, Spain

1945   Gabriela Mistral, poetry, Chile

1956   Juan Ramón Jiménez, poetry, Spain

1967   Miguel Angel Asturias, fiction, Guatemala

1971   Pablo Neruda, poetry, Chile

1977   Vicente Aleixandre, poetry, Spain

1982   Gabriel García Márquez, fiction, Colombia

1989   Camilo José Cela, fiction, Spain

1990   Octavio Paz, poetry, Mexico

The awards to Echegaray and Benavente, both deemed light-weight writers, roused scepticism and protests in Spain. No prizes thereafter for Spain for thirty years, until the award to Jiménez. He was famous in Spain for his *Platero y yo* (1917) and later symbolist poetry, but, as noted, his prize was partly to honor a generation passed over by the Nobel jury. So too with Aleixandre.

The opening of Latin America to the Nobel Prize was bound to cause disputes about awards. The continent seemed overflowing with talent. Was Gabriela Mistral really a more deserving poet than César Vallejo of Peru, or did she simply outlive him — he died in 1938, aged forty-six — and so be there when the Nobel jury decided it was time to honor the first South American?[66] Mistral's award also blocked one to the eminent Chilean poet Vicente Huidobro, whom many believe superior to Mistral. The prizes to Neruda, García Márquez (*One Hundred Years of Solitude*), and Octavio Paz seem universally approved.

Against Latin America's two fiction laureates, Spain has one: Camilo José Cela, who reinvigorated Spanish fiction after the Civil War, especially by his *The Hive* (1951), whose hero is Madrid itself, traversed by 116 characters. It remains a puzzle why the Nobel judges delayed Cela for more than forty years, or after such a delay, honored him.

Two Argentines were never honored, to the Nobel's impoverishment: Julio Cortázar (died 1984) and the incomparable Jorge Luis Borges (died 1986).

And not until 1998 was the first Portuguese laureate named: the novelist José Saramago, at age seventy-five.

Japanese Nobels

Laureates from Japan

1968 Yasunari Kawabata, fiction

1994 Kenzaburo Oe, fiction

Of all Asian nations, Japan alone has won two Nobels. The remarkable interest from the 1950s of English and French translators in Japanese literature helps account for this, as well as Japan's own determined effort to westernize itself. Its first great modern novelist, Natsume Soseki (1867–1916), studied in England from 1900 to 1902, and the influence of European writing showed in his work only a few years later. A great and subtle novelist, of undoubted Nobel caliber, he remained untranslated before his death.

In the decades after the Second World War, when enough translations were at hand, two writers attracting world attention were Jun'ichiro Tanizaki (1886–1965) and Yukio Mishima (1925–1970). Tanizaki's subjects were unpredictable and startling: *The Makioka Sisters* (1948) seemed to some Western readers as clinically obsessed with disease as Mann's *The Magic Mountain*. His novel of a man masochistically submitting to lovely women for a glimpse of higher beauty (*Diary of an Old Mad Man*) is at once bizarre and brilliantly perceptive. But he won no Nobel. Perhaps, as a critic of Japanese literature pointedly noted, "his resolutely aesthetic focus, meager in what might be called redeeming social values," greatly reduced his Nobel chances.[67] The flamboyant Mishima committed ritual suicide in 1970 when he was forty-five.

The first laureate was Kawabata. His prize raised two questions that emerge about every non-Western Nobel Prize. Are the Nobel jury drawn to works showing Western influence, since these can be compared more readily to what they know? Or the opposite: do they seek what seems to them unwesternized, exotic, "other," redolent of strangeness? Many Japanese deemed Kawabata's novels quite inwardly Japanese. To go by their citation, the Nobel judges must have thought so too. He was lauded "for his narrative mastery which with great sensibility expresses the essence of the Japanese mind," and he thus contributes to "spiritual bridge-building between East and West." Kawabata is assuredly a great writer, so far as one can tell from an English translation that must render experiences of a fragmented modern kind narrated in prose that often seems like haiku.

The second award went — almost thirty full years after Kawabata's — to Kenzaburo Oe. His story is unusual and moving. He began writing fiction after a son was born brain-damaged. The experiences of Hiroshima survivors affected Oe's decision here as well: writing was "a way of exorcism." The son, though remaining mentally handicapped, emerged as a remarkable composer; the father won the Nobel Prize. Oe says he was greatly influenced by fellow members of a writers' group he belonged to, including Kobo Abe, best known for *The Woman in the Dune,* and Masuji Ibuse, who wrote *Black Rain.* Both died before Oe became a laureate; in a sense, he is another stand-in. Since winning the prize — and with his son's success as a composer — Oe has decided to stop writing novels, and perhaps try a different literary form.

The Nobel "Out There"

Artur Lundkvist, a member of the Nobel jury, once bluntly commented that while the Swedish Academy is reproached for neglecting writing in Asian, African, and other regions,

> I doubt if there is very much to find there. It is a question of literatures that [he cites Japan as an exception], as far as can be judged, have not achieved the level of development (artistic, psychological, linguistic) that can make them truly significant outside their given context.

This was taken by many as arrogantly Eurocentric. But Lundkvist was raising a real if politically unpalatable possibility: "The Nobel

Prize is after all a Western institution and cannot reasonably be distributed on the basis of other than Western evaluations."[68]

The literature Nobel is rooted in the centrality of the book and writing. What happens when such a self-contained artifact doesn't matter? Or when literature exists in ritual or political contexts that baffle analysis in Western terms? Or if, even among people of the Book, taking up Western literary forms is to be resisted, as among Islamic fundamentalists, in the name of national or religious integrity? The conviction can arise, as Lundkvist attests, that there is little of worth to find "out there" — at least for the Nobel Prize as now known.

There are other mountainous problems. In countries as vast as China and India, the number of writers about whom even the best-informed Western expert knows essentially nothing is staggering. It would take a generation of monumental labor and endless computerizing simply to read, tabulate, and sort them out, to get the lay of the literary landscape and the start of a feel for its special topography — and we are not yet speaking of translating or critical evaluation with sufficient cultural and linguistic intimacy and sympathy. The languages of Indian literature include Hindi, Kashmiri, Punjabi, Gujarati, Marathi, Bengali, Maithili, Tamil, Assamese, among others; prosodies can vary dizzyingly, as do the assumptions underlying imagery and themes, variously springing from Hindu, Buddhist, and Islamic roots. The important African novelist Ngugi wa Thiong'o, after establishing a reputation with novels in English, began writing in Kikuyu, his native tongue.[69]

What to do? The Nobel committee, as befits a committee, has sought the help of other committees and organizations such as PEN groups, and meanwhile beefed up its own resources — in earlier times with an Arabic scholar and someone who could read Tagore in Bengali (but chose not to!) and more recently with an expert on modern Chinese literature along with a member who can read Russian. Other specialists have been consulted.[70]

But this is like pitting a few sandbags against a flooding Mississippi. The sheer diversity of languages in the world is overwhelming. One needs a small army of linguists just for India, another for Africa. And linguists are beside the point here anyway, since one needs literary critics gifted enough to spot the very best, and there have never been enough of those anywhere.

There is also the Nobel's constant fear of being labeled politically biased. Should the committee select some neglected language area and then systematically search for the "best" writer? No: "Doing so would amount to a politicization of the prize."[71] But the alternative is to wait until, somehow, a writer from a "remote" area becomes prominent enough to be nominated as a candidate.

Yet it needs no emphasizing that writers' contemporary reputations often owe as much to chance and manipulation as to merit. In the West, with its free competitive cultural and economic markets, much depends on skill at promotion and self-advertisement. Advertising money spent by publishers can grease the slide. But how does it work in Somalia, or Sri Lanka, or Syria, or Surinam? The media and universities there are often government-controlled; scholars and critics usually command little international clout; professional literary societies may not exist and individual scholars may be poorly informed; translations, if any, may be rare or amateurish.

It cannot be doubted that the Swedish Academy acutely understands the difficulties involved in all this as well as anyone. But to have a resident specialist in Chinese and the like will not help much. Even in France or the U.S., where the scrutiny and assessment of contemporary writing is incessantly done by hundreds of experts, there is not the slightest guarantee that such effort locates the best writers. What then are the chances in an India with its multitudinous languages and subcultures? Or in a small African nation?

Can anything help? At the end of almost a century of awarding prizes, the Nobel is still quite unadventurous in its move out into global literature. But perhaps it is not unadventurousness, after all. Perhaps a certain realism is setting in, now that the easier awards (i.e., major Western) have been made. Perhaps the committee will reorganize itself radically to cope with the strange swarming mass of literary and linguistic usages "out there." Perhaps it will redefine what it means by "literature." Or perhaps it will stand pat, and wait for arbitrary market and other chance forces to flush up an author from a distant land who then, willy-nilly, becomes a "major candidate." This hardly seems satisfactory, but radical surgery on the Nobel doesn't seem likely either. Perhaps its slogan should be the very last remark of Beckett's narrator in *The Unnamable:* "You must go on, I can't go on, I'll go on."

Finale

The Nobel Prize in Literature is bedeviled by its history. A physicist who nominated Einstein added the warning: imagine how the Nobel scientific list will look fifty years from now with Einstein missing. The Nobel Literature Prize demonstrates the truth of that remark. But the prize has indeed changed greatly and for the better. At least in the last three decades, the awards have kept a high level. If this can only continue for another thirty years or so, the weak laureates of the first half century will gradually be forgotten. It is a high-risk task, given the uncertain nature of literary reputations, to say nothing of the uncertain future of literature itself.

Long before the Nobel existed, Herman Melville worried this same problem. Melville of course lost his own readership with *Moby Dick*, and in our century would never have won a Nobel Prize (too obscure, misanthropic). Here he is prophetically taking up our concern. He is thinking not of glorified prizes but of the literary establishment that sets the taste for the public and the age. He is writing about Hawthorne, trying to persuade the reader to see how great Hawthorne is right now, and not to leave him hanging until "posterity" (or any Nobel authority) hands down a verdict:

> Give not over to future generations the glad duty of acknowledging him for what he is. Take that joy to yourself, in your own generation; and so shall he feel those grateful impulses on him, that may possibly prompt him to the full flower of some still greater achievement in your eyes. And by confessing him, you thereby confess others; you brace the whole brotherhood. For genius, all over the world, stands hand in hand, and one shock of recognition runs the whole circle round.

4

The Nobel Prize
and the Sciences

By choosing only "hard" sciences for awards, Alfred Nobel did his future prizes a supreme favor. Besides the remarkable advances in knowledge made by physics, chemistry, and medicine, these disciplines obviously exert enormous power over world affairs and human life. This combination has made them the keystone of the Nobel Prizes' fame and influence. If Alfred Nobel had chosen differently — say, anthropology and sociology — the Nobel Prizes as a whole might today be mainly of academic interest. Quantum theory and relativity, biochemistry and molecular biology are abstruse, but the power of their progeny — H-bombs, electronics, medical breakthroughs and cures — is misunderstood by none.

The field has obviously mushroomed.[1] Now, as specialties divide and subdivide, journals multiply until no scientist can keep up with the literature even of a subspecialty.[2] Experiments once done on a tabletop now need equipment so complex that, in a single experiment, more technicians are needed than there were once advanced experimenters in the world.

In the same period, new technology expanded the mass media from the telegraph to satellite communications. This in turn expanded the celebrity of modern scientists — and of the Nobel Prizes as well. In November 1895, Wilhelm Röntgen discovered X-rays and published a short account in December. In January 1896 he also became the first scientist to discover the power of the mass media. In that month, he mailed off his astonishing photographs to leading scientists and scientific societies around the world. In only two weeks, his discovery — especially the X-ray photograph of the bones in his wife's hand — was featured in newspapers around the world. In a month or so, doctors in far-off Dartmouth, New Hampshire, using X-ray photographs, set a boy's broken arm. Within a year, a thousand newspaper articles and fifty big and small books appeared.[3] "Never before had a scientific breakthrough caused such excitement in the popular press."[4] The discovery had everything: mysterious rays, a first, thrilling view directly into a living human body, and the promise of unimaginable medical benefits. The dangers were long unknown: to make the famous photograph, Frau Röntgen had exposed her hand to fifteen straight minutes of radiation. Röntgen detested the publicity. When he won the first Nobel Prize in Physics in 1901, he even refused to give the obligatory lecture.

Röntgen's success was pivotal in certain ways. First, in the 1890s, some physicists feared they had exhausted what could be discovered and now could only refine the measurements. But Röntgen's discovery, as the historian J. L. Heilbron points out, brought a sense that a new age was beginning.[5] Röntgen also helped change the public perception of "pure" science. Well into the twentieth century, the popular image of the "scientist" was still engineers, inventors, or practical healers — and why not? Electricity was newly lighting the world; the telegraph and telephone, the electric omnibus, and the subway were shrinking space and speeding up time. Icons like Nobel or Edison or Marconi (Marconi shared the Nobel Prize in 1909, but who remembers him for that?) embodied and enacted Progress. But a competing image had always existed in the form of the "pure" scientist, descending from Pythagoras to Newton to Einstein, a priestly genius remote from everyday life who conjured abstruse theories and experiments. With Röntgen and others, these began to draw new public attention. The Nobel Prize's decision to celebrate only pure science also helped the shift from mere technological success.[6] Indeed, the science prizes have not honored inventors, engineers, or medical clinicians, with a few exceptions to be noted.

The exalted image of the pure scientist — the Nobel image: brilliant, selfless, and truth-seeking[7] — has been attacked in recent decades from without and within. One subversion from within was *The Double Helix* (1968) by the Nobelist James D. Watson, codiscoverer of the DNA structure. A tell-all, it baldly flaunted scientists' itch for priority and particularly for the Nobel Prize. His memoir offended many, including his colaureate Francis Crick. But Leon Lederman, the witty American physicist and Nobelist, offered this advice to anyone shocked: "Yes, Virginia, scientists do love recognition, but only since Pythagoras."[8]

Even a generation earlier, no scientist of comparable rank would have dared publish such an irreverent and confessional memoir.[9] Things have changed. The quantum cosmologist Stephen Hawking (who has not yet won a Nobel Prize) once would be known only to a handful of specialists. But his great gifts, tied to a cruelly crippling disease, electronic voicebox, and wheelchair, excited public interest in his TV appearances and helped make him a media superstar. His *A Brief History of Time* became a best-seller. Only in this new climate can one find even the sober *New York Times* speaking so sceptically about Hawking. He may now be the most famous physicist in the world, said the *Times*, but thanks as much to his gifts as a "self-promoter" as to his genius as a physicist. Hawking has emphasized that he was born on the anniversary of Galileo's death; the *Times* wondered whether this was "a coincidence of great astrological significance," and noted that many of Hawking's colleagues were dumbfounded to see him described on the jacket of *A Brief History of Time* as the "most brilliant theoretical physicist since Einstein."[10]

The Nobel Prize, if inadvertently, has powerfully helped bring about the new sceptical view. The prizes certify who the "great" scientists are. But by thrusting the laureates into the public eye, they help strip away the aura of distance. As celebrities, the once priestly prizewinners are at the mercy of all the intrusions and distortions that media publicity can invent. The proprieties that once cloaked scientists have vanished along with Rutherford's wing collar. Einstein, the most famous, was also the most plagued. His great new fame in the early 1920s brought open anti-Semitic attacks, often from within the scientific community. In 1922 his decision to take a world cruise reflected his concern about possible attempts on his life[11] (he was awarded the Nobel Prize while away on that trip). When he came to New York on a visit in 1930, the *New York Times* reported, Einstein was asked

within one brief quarter of an hour, to define the fourth dimension in one word, state his theory of relativity in one sentence, give his views on prohibition, comment on politics and religion, and discuss the virtues of his violin.

Einstein's private comment was that "the reporters asked particularly inane questions, to which I replied with cheap jokes that were received with enthusiasm."[12] And there is no letup. The 1990s brought a fascination with the details of Einstein's once-forgotten first marriage, sometimes to argue in revisionist spirit that Einstein owed his early insights to his first wife, or else that he was far from being the kindly fellow the world thought him. In 1999 *Time* declared him the Man of the Century.

Still, if one wants lasting fame, it is wiser to be a great writer than a great scientist. Not even two Nobels will help. The biochemist Frederick Sanger has won two, in 1958 and 1980: how recognizable is his name, how familiar his great achievements? Except for an exalted Einstein, scientific laureates are far less famous in their time — and often after — than entertainers or politicians. Even the physicist Niels Bohr or the chemist Linus Pauling has never achieved popular renown of the kind once and still given an Edison. A brief quiz for well-informed general readers: Does the name Woodward, or Bardeen, ring any bells? (Both won Nobels in recent decades. Bardeen won two in physics; Woodward's early death cost him a sure repeat prize in chemistry.) What did the peerless Dirac do to deserve his towering reputation? If the questions can't be answered, that puts the reader in some eminent company. The physicist Abraham Pais wrote a biography of Niels Bohr[13] because "one of the best and best-known" American physicists had little idea of what Bohr had done — Bohr, who died as late as 1962 and was one of the supreme creators of twentieth-century quantum physics!

If the public does not remember or much care who did the fundamental work that created the cornucopia of modern energy, pharmaceuticals, inexpensive goods and communications, one might assume the case would be different inside science. But it is not really so.[14] The hard sciences look forward, not back. They are rightly called "self-erasing" disciplines: what matters to the working researcher is the state-of-the-art advance, not the history of the discipline. Most Nobel Prize winners, even the greatest, surprisingly soon dwindle into modifiers: the Lorentz transformation, the Grignard reagent, the Compton effect, Planck's constant.

The Nobel science prizes, with their bright focus on individual discoveries, may best fit a few loners like Einstein. "The concept of the single moment of discovery," says Peter Galison, "while perhaps valuable for prize committees and physics textbooks, corresponds to little or nothing in the historical record."[15] The heroic stance seems particularly out of date in the present era of Big Science, where key experiments require Frankenstein accelerators or expensive biological laboratories — and large teams of researchers. The old freedom to explore whatever seemed interesting also meant very little funding. Big Science has reversed these terms: now the funding can be lavish, but individual freedom is constrained.[16] In 1960 an important experiment could be done by two, four, or six people. In 1995 a German team found that quarks may contain particles inside them — a possibility that might force theorists to scrap many accepted ideas. The team consisted of 444 physicists. If this experiment is confirmed, up to three of its directors may become Nobelists; the other 441, 442, or 443 will not share the prize.

The Nobel Prize can also importantly sway a scientist's research goals by shifting funding. For a very recent instance, see the chapter on medicine for the 1997 Nobel Prize in Medicine to Stanley Prusiner. His Nobel-winning theory that proteins, not genetic factors, cause fatal epidemic diseases such as the widely publicized "mad cow" illness in Britain in the 1990s, remains highly controversial and disputed by distinguished colleagues in the field. They also charge that his prize has cut off funding to alternative theories.[17]

Priority: Scientific Anxiety and Glory

Scientists want to make discoveries and add to knowledge — but they also want do it first. Researchers thus rush their findings into print as quickly as possible, lest someone else beat them to it. As in horse races, this can be a matter of nose lengths, settled only by photo finishes. From 1850 to 1900, the number of professional physicists rose from about five hundred to a thousand. Yet Lord Kelvin, whose work was done from the 1840s to 1880, had at least thirty-two of his discoveries duplicated independently.[18] As the number of physicists rises to hundreds of thousands over a century, the chances for simultaneous discoveries naturally increase. Multiple discoveries are inevitable when ideas are in the air. Priority disputes often arise.

The importance of priority is unique to science. It doesn't worry artists. Peter Medawar (1960 Nobel Prize in Medicine) once wrote that "Richard Wagner would certainly not have spent twenty years on the *Ring* if he thought it at all possible for someone else to nip in ahead."[19] But such nipping-in constantly happens in science. Someone named Elisha Gray patented the telephone only two *hours* after Alexander Graham Bell; but the courts decided for Bell. Who knows of Gray now? In countless cases since then, X has just made a brilliant find, only to pick up the latest journal with Y's paper explaining the same problem. X's and Y's papers can even appear side by side in the same issue of the same journal, yet Y's was "received" earlier — if only by a week or a day — and Y gets priority. Publication gives public testimony of one's findings, but it also bears on being "first," since the journal prints the date when the paper was "received." This is indispensable, because of time delays between reception of the manuscript and its publication. Coming in first, even by what seems a hair, can bring scientific fame and Nobel glory to Y and oblivion to second-place X. In nutshell form: "Who was the second person to say $E=mc^2$?"[20]

The experimenter Ernest Rutherford, inexhaustibly self-confident and buoyant, nonetheless wrote to his wife in 1905, explaining why he had to delay a trip: "It is very important I should write it up as they are following my trail, and if I am to have a chance for a Nobel Prize in the next few years I must keep my work moving."[21] The great nineteenth-century neurologist Ramón y Cajal solved the same problem uniquely. Around 1887 he wrote so much that journals couldn't publish fast enough to ensure his priority; so he financed his own journal and sometimes wrote every article in it.[22]

Lust for Nobel awards scarcely explains this desire for priority. It is simply unreal to suppose that most scientists work so hard on knotty experiments and theories, and much grindingly routine work, for medals and renown. The actual work itself must provide the constant spur of interest, or no scientist would keep doing it. When the work loses its compelling interest, for whatever reason, most scientists or artists give it up — Shakespeare stopped writing plays.

Since science is a collective effort, the phenomenon of two or three or more people independently emerging with the same findings, and at practically the same time, is commonplace in the history of science. Newton and Leibniz quarreled about who first discovered the calculus. Charles Darwin had his essential findings in manuscript by 1842, but for fifteen years couldn't bring himself to publish. "I wish I could set less value on the bauble fame, either present or posthumous, than I do, but not, I think, to any extreme degree." But in 1858 Alfred Russell Wallace, then in Borneo, sent him a letter setting out the idea of evolution by natural selection; he did not know Darwin had been working for years on the same theory. Darwin was alarmed. "I rather hate the idea of writing for priority, yet I certainly should be vexed if anyone were to publish my doctrines before me." Darwin finally sent a copy of an 1844 manuscript to a friend to establish his claim: "Do not waste much time. It is miserable in me to care at all about priority." Wallace generously bowed out. Darwin of course got his deserved priority and remains a very great name. Who but historians now remember Alfred Russell Wallace?[23]

Why did Darwin want priority? It was, he said, "the ambition to be esteemed by my fellow-naturalists."[24] But it can also yield something better described as exaltation — an inner, not outer, glory.

Richard Feynman described such a moment as the peak of his scientific career. Only once in his life, he said, did he discover a law before anyone else. Soon he would publish and then everyone would also know. But for the moment he savored the exaltation of being the first and only person on the globe (and in history) to possess this particular insight into nature. Everything written about Feynman makes clear that he was competitive to the bone, but not for external awards. He knew his own superiority, and for him this meant living up to his own great gifts — which can stand as true for all worthy scientists, artists, and thinkers. Luis Alvarez (physics laureate, 1968) said that Fermi seemed modest and self-effacing, yet Alvarez was sure that if asked who was the best living physicist, Fermi "would have thought for perhaps half a minute and nominated himself. He knew exactly where he fit in the world of physics, and was honest enough to give the right answer."[25]

Feynman was equally honest about where he ranked. He once said that he didn't want to be remembered as just another physicist who had won the Nobel Prize. That was too ordinary a goal. He wanted an inner prize of a different sort. In 1947–48 he had begun to develop new insights that would soon make him famous, but he was discouraged and hesitant to publish. In 1949 he was at a confer-

ence where the physicist Murray Slotnick gave the results of a complex problem he had worked on for two years, including six months
of calculating. Robert Oppenheimer immediately criticized Slotnick's findings as wrong because of a theorem so new it had not
even been published. Slotnick was baffled how to reply. Angry at
Slotnick's embarrassment, Feynman that evening recalculated
Slotnick's results, using new methods he had been reluctant to
publish, and found they checked. The next morning, Slotnick was
amazed that Feynman had done in a few hours what had taken him
six months. Here is Feynman's report of how he felt:

> This is when I really knew I had something . . . that was the moment
> that I really knew that I had to publish — that I had gotten ahead of
> the world. . . . That was the fire. That was the moment when I got
> my Nobel prize, when Slotnick told me he had been working two
> years. When I got the real prize it was nothing, because I already
> knew I was a success.[26]

He had a moment brimming with the same exultation in 1957 when
he discovered a new explanation of the weak interaction force.[27]
Such forces are a key to the entire understanding of atomic matter.
Feynman was elated.

> It was the first time, and the only time, in my career that I knew a law
> of nature that nobody else knew. The other things I had done before
> were to take somebody else's theory and improve the method. . . . I
> thought of Dirac, who had his equation [of 1928] for a while — a new
> equation which told how an electron behaved — and I had this new
> equation for beta decay, which wasn't as vital as the Dirac equation,
> but it was good. It's the only time I ever discovered a new law.[28]

In fact, Feynman at first thought of rejecting his Nobel Prize in
1965. He disliked having even such a high honor forced on him:
couldn't they have asked first if he wanted it? In his Stockholm
speech, he reverted to that earlier exalted moment when he knew
he had first fulfilled his powers: "That was my moment of triumph
in which I realized I really had succeeded in working out something
worthwhile."

Feynman's inner elation recurs constantly in science, a singular
mixture of enormous and justified pride but also modesty, an inner
spur to high accomplishment. This is why many scientists say that

the Nobel Prize did not honor them for their best and most satisfying work.[29] When Linus Pauling won the 1954 chemistry prize, he was pleased but reserved: But for which of his several discoveries? he asked the reporter. When told it was for chemical bonding, Pauling finally broke into a smile.[30] Other laureates also count themselves the best judges of whether what they have done is worthy.

But few are selfless enough not also to crave priority. A rare instance was the Indian physicist Satyendra Bose (his name is perpetuated in the important Bose-Einstein statistics and the "messenger" particle named the boson). Bose apparently had the idea for electron "spin" a year before its "official" discovery in 1925. He talked to Einstein about it, he told a friend years later. The friend, amazed, asked Bose why he hadn't written to Einstein "claiming his priority." Einstein would surely have backed him up. Bose only said, "How does it matter who proposed it first? It has been found, hasn't it?"[31]

Bose was truly exceptional. There hardly appears to be a similar case.

Notes on How to Win the Nobel Prize in Science

First, come from or emigrate to the U.S., Britain, or Germany: they did and still do dominate the prizes. France, once high in laureates, has dropped off much in the last forty years; Sweden once had a disproportionately high number of laureates for its population, but that has apparently ended.

"Genius" ensures no Nobels. Many who had genius, such as Oppenheimer, never won; and many who hadn't, did win. Indeed, too much genius can delay the prize: your findings may puzzle the Nobel juries; Lars Onsager's fearsomely difficult mathematical chemistry brought a forty-year delay before he became a laureate in 1968.

Remember that the race to Stockholm is to the swift, and therefore also remember that the most prestigious elite schools are apt to get one started faster — if one can stand the pace and not lose self-confidence.

Do research on problems where Nobels are spinning off (reader: please recall that the goal here is the Nobel Prize, not Truth). To do first-class work, you have to know where the research frontier is, sometimes month by month, week by week, or even day by day. You have to be in the swim, and this can be done best at one of the laboratories or departments in an important speciality in the tight research world of international physics, chemistry, or medicine, where stimulating colleagues strike off suggestions that may exactly illuminate a puzzling problem, where competition is stiff and stiffening, where publications, conferences, visitors, preprints, and hallway gossip abound. James Watson and Francis Crick walked all unknowing into just such a lucky situation when they wound up in the same room at the Cavendish Laboratory at Cambridge University, and started talking. In physics, to have been a postdoctoral fellow in Copenhagen at Niels Bohr's Institute of Theoretical Physics anytime from the 1920s to 1940 was worth its weight in Nobel gold. Since World War II, the world has flocked to the U.S.

Great universities don't always command the scene. The physics Nobelists Clinton Davisson (1937), John Bardeen (1956), and Philip Anderson (1977) did their prizewinning work at Bell Laboratories.[32] (Bardeen's work for his second Nobel was done at the University of Illinois.) The IBM laboratory at Zurich won consecutive Nobels in 1986 and 1987 — a feat few universities have matched.[33]

Persistence counts enormously, but sometimes so does luck. Carl Anderson (physics, 1936) claimed he found the antielectron "by accident." Alexander Fleming (shared medicine prize, 1945) discovered penicillin in 1928 by happening to leave a culture of bacteria uncovered.

Find a mentor. They teach, inspire, suggest ideas, and provide clout to the Nobel committee. One can succeed without a mentor. Einstein had none, and other Nobelists have had uninfluential ones. But given a choice, try to get a world-beater. Rutherford was Niels Bohr's mentor, and Bohr was Heisenberg's. The young James Watson was lucky enough to have Salvador Luria as his mentor, which made him part of the small but enormously influential molecular biology group pioneered by Max Delbrück and Luria in the 1940s (all those mentioned won prizes). If all goes supremely well, hope that someone like the great physicist Ernest Rutherford will be your Nobel backer. In 1932 James Chadwick, one of Rutherford's protégés, discovered the neutron — which the Joliot-Curies in France had actually found first but not recognized. Rutherford was vehement. "I want Jimmy to have it — unshared!" But should the Joliots just be ignored? Rutherford, with all his shrewdness and confidence, roared back: "That boy? Let me tell you. Joliot's so brilliant that before this year is out, he'll discover something so new and remarkable that you'll be able to give him a prize for that!" Which happened precisely as Rutherford predicted.[34]

But a caveat: A great mentor can intimidate you, even when not being a mentor. James Franck shared the Nobel Prize in 1926 and was a professor at mighty Göttingen. In exile from Hitler, he spent 1935 working with Bohr in Copenhagen on a Rockefeller grant. Even a Nobel Prize winner could feel inhibited:

> I made some experiments. And when I told Bohr about it, then he said immediately what might be wrong, what might be right. And it was so quick that after a time I felt that I am unable to think at all . . . Bohr's genius was so superior. And one cannot help that one would get so strong inferiority complexes in the presence of such a genius that one becomes sterile. You see?[35]

None of this will do the job, of course, unless the Nobel committee is also persuaded. Though they work in secrecy, they usually follow the lead of the international scientific elite. But when that will happen is unknowable.

In the ancient Roman *cursus honorum*, gaining the supreme office of consul required holding a set list of lesser posts beforehand that tested and made one visible. Winning the Nobel Prize involves a similar process. Murray Gell-Mann, the quark theorist (Nobel 1969), had earlier won the Heinemann Prize of the American Physical Society in 1959, the E. O. Lawrence Memorial Award for Physics of the U.S. Atomic Energy Commission in 1966, the Franklin Institute's medal in 1967, the Carty Medal of the National Academy of Sciences in 1968. The Nobel judges see that the elite scientific community has come to recognize one of its best.

But since one never knows when the Nobel committee will decide to award you the prize, the final advice on how to win the award is: Live to a very old age. They may finally catch up with you.

5

The Nobel Prize
in Physics

Of all scientists in the twentieth century, physicists have reaped the most fame. In the popular view, scientific advance has generally been in the realm of physics: radioactivity, atom splitting and nuclear energy, space exploration and electronics, gigantic accelerators and brainy theorists. And physicists, in turn, have brought most fame to the Nobel Prize. Einstein's renown around 1920 was as the man who had "revolutionized the universe." Physicists became the wonder workers of the tiny atom, the curved reaches of space, and the way the universe perhaps began and will end in a Big Bang. In the last few decades, biochemists have begun to rival the physicists in celebrity, but that is another story.

"Physics"

The word is in quotation marks because, for its first seventy years, the Nobel Prize in Physics did not in fact represent the entire field of physics. Instead, the juries arbitrarily honored only particle physics, which of course treats the smallest dimensions (atomic or subatomic) of matter.

Physics also includes astrophysics, which studies the structure and laws of stars — galaxies or quasars — the largest objects in the universe, where gravitation reigns, where distances are too vast to measure, and where matter takes unearthly physical form. There is also geophysics, the physics of earth, its interior and surface, seismic, atmospheric, and meteorological forces, its magnetic and electrical fields. Both astrophysics and geophysics can rightly claim to have made discoveries as important as many Nobel awards.

Yet the Nobel has long chosen to ignore almost all of the world's greatest astrophysicists and geophysicists. Some of these astrophysicists include Edwin Hubble (U.S., 1889–1953), who discovered the expansion of the universe; Arthur Eddington (Britain, 1882–1944), who discovered the mass-luminosity law explaining the sun's interior and mass, and gave first confirmation of Einstein's general relativity theory; and H. N. Russell (U.S., 1877–1957), who contributed to stellar evolution and solar spectrum explanations. Geophysicists of Nobel caliber included Alfred Wegener (Germany, 1880–1930), who discoverered "continental drift" and early theorized about plate tectonics in 1912; Vilhelm Bjerknes (Norway, 1862–1915), who founded meterological dynamics; Beno Gutenberg (U.S., 1890–1960), who from 1913 made seismography of major importance in geophysics. Imagine the Nobel Physics Prize list without such names as Heisenberg or Fermi, and one can begin to glimpse the black hole that exists here.

In 1967 the Nobel jury began making belated gestures toward astrophysics, in the award to Hans Bethe (a particle physicist) for his 1938 explanation of the nuclear process in the sun (a twenty-nine-year delay). Four other shared prizes for astrophysics followed in the next thirty years. The first prize for work involving gravitation came as late as 1993, to Taylor and Hulse. Geophysics was first honored in 1947, with the prize to Appleton for discovering the ionosphere in 1924, but the next came only in 1970 to Hannes Alfvén for work on plasma, partly applicable to geophysics. All other prizes have gone to particle physics.

Some pertinent facts are provided by Elisabeth Crawford and Robert Marc Friedman, historians who have studied the early Nobel physics committees. The present account is indebted to both, though it diverges from their conclusions.[1]

In 1904 the physics section of the Academy of Sciences (when it expanded to ten members) was called Physics and Meteorology, a heading able to accommodate astrophysics, geophysics, physical chemistry, and much else. Thus, the American George E. Hale was early and often nominated. He was an astronomer and astrophysicist (following the old division: astronomy as a measuring science, astrophysics as a science of the structure of matter in space). For inventing the spectroheliograph (to photograph the sun at a specific wavelength), Hale was first proposed for the physics prize in 1909, then five more times before 1917. His candidacy was soon tied to that of Henri Deslandres, a French astrophysicist who had independently helped develop the spectroheliograph. The 1913 Nobel committee enthusiastically stated that their work "sooner or later — and rightly so — ought to come to be regarded as deserving of the Nobel physics prize."[2]

Then World War I broke out. Hale and Deslandres were set aside. When the war ended, Planck, Einstein, and Bohr were long overdue and took the prizes for 1918, 1921, and 1922. After that, the committee cast out astrophysics from physics.[3] A main reason was finances. One never thinks of the wealthy Nobel Prize as feeling any pinch, but after the First World War, Sweden as elsewhere in Europe saw runaway inflation wash away capital. Svante Arrhenius, the Nobel-winning physical chemist, in his pugnacious way declared the financial condition of the Academy of Sciences "quite terrible" and "quite hopeless."[4] Not quite: there was still enough money to fund the prizes at a respectable level, but not enough left over to build the various Nobel Institutes yearned for by Nobel judges for testing prize nominations and doing original research. Nor enough surplus to support Swedish research in all fields of physics.

Remarkably, Arrhenius began to argue that astrophysics was not part of physics. Astrophysics, he said, had in recent years come to include all of astronomy, and astrophysics therefore "should be identified with astronomy rather than as part of physics." This view, which would exclude Einstein's gravitation theory of 1916, was the more extraordinary in that Arrhenius had once strongly supported astrophysics and continued to pursue his own version of it. As Friedman notes, Arrhenius even tried to have the Statutes revised to exclude astrophysics, but was blocked.[5] The physics prizes could be narrowed to atomic physics in only two ways: change the Statutes legally and publicly, or use the committee and the Academy of Sciences to block unwanted astrophysicists and geophysicists. One was open and aboveboard, the other not. Legally revising the Statutes could cause international friction and unwanted publicity. The Nobel committee resorted to "packing" the Academy of Sciences with cooperative scientists, and used the committee to block nominations they disliked.

Fears were voiced that a prize to Hale and Deslandres could set off a flood of prizes to astrophysicists and geophysicists; atomic physics would thus obviously see a reduction in awards, funds, and prestige. By slicing away astrophysics and geophysics, atomic physics could prosper in Sweden. The 1923 Nobel Prize thus went not to Hale and Deslandres but to the American atomic experimenter Robert Millikan, who had received many fewer nominations that year.

Certainly, if Swedish scientists, facing financial stringencies, decided to make the prizes yield a certain return to help their own special work, that was a reasonable enough if unhappy decision. It could help keep Swedish physics in the international mainstream, and the Nobel Prizes surely benefited Swedish atomic science enormously in foreign honors, influence, and research opportunities.

But the issue is not only pragmatics. The physics jury made and kept their decision secret within the academy. They may well have resorted to leaking misleading stories to eminent foreign scientists about the situation.[6] Since they controlled the world's most prestigious prize in physics, they should also have felt honor-bound to announce publicly that they had redefined eligibility for the prizes. In atomic physics, at least, the record has indeed been generally superb. As the historian James MacLachlan puts it, the early physics committees themselves deserve a prize from physicists for coping with the confusing changes that occurred in that specialty.[7]

Reconnaissance

From 1901 to now, modern physics has been built by four generations of physicists.

The first generation was at strength from 1900 on. Here arrived Planck's quantum law, Einstein's special and general theories of relativity, the Curies and Rutherford on the phenomenon of radioactivity, Thomson's discovery that the atom contains an electron, and Rutherford's discovery that it also has a nucleus. Bohr gave the first quantum theory of the atom in 1913.

The second generation entered in 1925, precociously mature, and created the "new" quantum physics in the form we still know it. Wolfgang Pauli's exclusion principle of 1925 clarified how many electrons may occupy energy levels and why, shedding great light on atomic physics and also on chemistry. In 1925–26 Heisenberg and Schrödinger created quantum mechanics, and Heisenberg's uncertainty principle of 1927 set precise limits on observation and accuracy. Dirac's 1928 equation first explained the quantum electron in relativistic terms and predicted antimatter. With Fermi in the early 1930s, nuclear physics took off, and a start was made at explaining the three forces at work inside the atom.

The third generation began its work from 1947, with Feynman, Gell-Mann, Weinberg and Salam, Lee and Yang, Lederman and Lamb, Richter and Ting, among others. It resolved many of the problems left by its predecessors: a quantum field theory of electrodynamics (QED) was established; the basic forces in the atom were explained; a standard model of all particles was created; the nucleus was redescribed in terms of quarks. New specialities like superconductivity began to thrive.

The fourth generation, born after 1940, is now well on stage.

The basic questions of physics, of course, sprawl untidily across the generations. So do the Nobel Prizes: scientists who did their brilliant work as young men are most honored when gray-haired.

Physicists: Cats and Dogs

In textbooks and Nobel Prizes, physicists are either experimenters or theorists. Experimenters first won most fame and the early Nobels — the Curies, for example. But starting with Einstein around 1920, theorists became and remained far more famous and glamorous to the public. In the popular imagination but also often in physics itself, experimenters and theorists can seem almost two different species — different in temperament and tasks, and in permanent rivalry. One proof often cited is how very few physicists are equally good on both sides; Fermi (d. 1953) is among the last usually named. But now specialization is even more intense and narrowing. An experiment can take a year or four or five of continuous work, and especially when working in expensive giant labs, experimentalists can't easily drop a project or work on something else on the side. Theorists, who ride light, can switch more easily or even juggle several projects at the same time.

Myths abound here, with grains of truth scattered throughout. Experimenters need laboratories. Theorists (so the legend goes) need only paper and pen.[8] The legend even suggests that while theorists think deeply all the time, experimenters hardly ever do. Röntgen the experimenter, when asked how he came to discover X-rays, merely said: "I didn't think — I investigated."

In any case, someone may (or certainly should) have noticed that these two types resemble cats and dogs. They surely enjoy baiting each other. "Plumbers," some theorists call experimenters; "couldn't run a hamburger stand," said some experimenters of an egghead theorist like Oppenheimer. Experimenters, naturally, are the dogs — not clumsy (God forbid, in a laboratory) but noisy, buoyant, energetic, gregarious, and they run in packs. The archetype here is Ernest Rutherford, with his booming voice, boundless enthusiasm, and an uncanny feel for an experiment that could be important and how to do it. When he headed the famous Cavendish Laboratory, they hung TALK SOFTLY PLEASE signs all around, since noise disturbed the delicate instruments; also NO SMOKING signs.[9] Little good it did.

Rutherford's scornful fun of theorists never dimmed: "They play games with their symbols, but we in the Cavendish turn out real facts of nature."[10] Nowadays one can still get a whiff of the Rutherford archetype in the ebullient, wisecracking Leon Lederman (prize 1988), or the frenetic Carlo Rubbia (prize 1984), who besides being a brilliant experimenter seems something of a carnival barker and evangelist. Deftness and a supersharp nose for the profitable experiment are taken for granted.

The archetypal theorists, by comparison, seem like cats: loners, fastidious formalists, able to see in the conceptual dark, with ears that can pick up unheard-of ideas. Dirac had an inimitably theoretical way of thinking about anything. Of Dostoyevsky's *Crime and Punishment* he said: "It is nice, but in one of the chapters the author made a mistake. He describes the sun as rising twice in the same day."[11] Equally exemplary is the bongo-playing Richard Feynman, who may seem a dog among the theory cats; yet who but a theorist would go to a topless bar the better to write equations? It only proves that Feynman, like all cats, would have flunked out of obedience school. Or Robert Oppenheimer (never a Nobelist), who directed the largest scientific experiment in history — building the atom bomb, which involved thousands of workers and billions in funding. But like a theorist invented in heaven, he read Sanskrit and medieval French poetry for relaxation.

The 1925 generation of Heisenberg, Pauli, and Dirac helped mythify theoretical physicists as all young geniuses. The following verse is sometimes ascribed to Dirac:

> Age is, of course, a fever chill
> That every physicist must fear.
> He's better dead than living still
> When once he's past his thirtieth year.[12]

This dictum applies mainly to theorists, who work so much with mathematics. Mathematics has always been famous, along with music and chess, for its wealth of prodigies. Experimenters need more seasoning, experience, practical work — and, in the last forty years, lots of funding. Of course, all theorists do not achieve their feats so young. Einstein was 26 in his annus mirabilis of 1905, and James Watson helped find the double helix at 25, but Planck was 43 when he discovered the quantum law, and Schrödinger 37 with his wave equation; Dorothy Hodgkin was 46 when she laid clear the structure of vitamin B_{12}. In fact, the youngest Nobelists were experimenters: Lawrence Bragg at 25, and Carl Anderson at 31. The youngest theorists, each aged 31 when they became laureates, were Heisenberg, Dirac, and Tsung-Dao Lee.

In historical fact, the split between theorists and experimenters emerged only in the late nineteenth century. Before that, say around 1875, "theorist" was apt to mean someone who gave very exact measurements of experimental findings. But by 1900, mathematical physicists such as Poincaré, Planck, Boltzmann, and Lorentz had built a new kind of mathematical theory which led to the later triumphs associated with Einstein or Heisenberg. From the 1890s on, physicists had to absorb new methods: matrix algebra, vectors, linear integral equations, multiple algebras, group theory, tensors (useful to Einstein's general relativity), variational calculus, and the like. A mathematician is said to have remarked: "Physics has become too hard for the physicists." In 1915 Wilhelm Wien dared claim that the great theorists "have also been the greatest scientists," and he toasted "the now mighty theoretical physics."[13] Confident of the truth of his equations in 1915, Einstein launched his audacious vision of curved space; when an experiment "proved" him wrong, he loftily dismissed it as flawed; he was right. Yet in 1927 Lorentz, that prince of mathematical theorists, admitted despairing at how physics "had taken an enormous step down the road of abstraction."[14]

A majority of the early Nobel physics committees actively disliked highly mathematical physics, especially theory, and saw "measuring physics" as the very peak of achievement in the field, with high-precision measurements "the very root, the essential condition ... our only way to new discoveries."[15] This of course included astronomers, who were excluded in the 1923 Nobel putsch. It was no accident that the first two American laureates, Albert A. Michelson in 1907 and Robert Millikan in 1923, were very skilled "measuring" physicists. As the prize list shows, the early Nobel committees generally opposed or ignored theoretical physics. In this first generation, experimenters won four times as many prizes as theorists, and far more quickly. Every ten years or so, an award went to a theorist: Lorentz in 1902 (but he had to share with an experimenter), van der Waals in 1910 and Wien partly in 1911, Planck in 1918. A mob of experimenters, but hardly enough theorists for a tea party.[16]

"Experimenter" is a term that muddies the waters. Some experimenters primarily devise the equipment that other experimenters need. Here, prizes have gone to Ernest O. Lawrence (for the cyclotron), C. T. R. Wilson (the cloud chamber), Donald Glaser (the bubble chamber), Dennis Gabor (holography), Martin Ryle (radio astronomy), A. Schawlow and N. Bloembergen (laser spectroscopy), C. H. Townes, N. G. Basov, and A. M. Prokhorov (the maser and laser), Kai Siegbahn (X-ray spectroscopy), Ernst Ruska (electron microscope), G. Binnig and H. Rohrer (scanning tunneling microscope), Norman Ramsey (atomic clock improvement), H. Dehmelt and W. Paul ("ion trapping"), and W. Phillips, S. Chu, and C. Cohen-Tannoudji (laser cooling to "trap" atoms). Most of these have no major experiment to their credit — or perhaps one should count the devising of their equipment as itself a major experiment. The line is sometimes hard to draw.

Then there are the experimenters who make basic discoveries, and often on their own, sans theorists. Rutherford, the Curies, the Joliot-Curies, Lederman, Otto Stern, I. I. Rabi, Henry Kendall, Jerome Friedman, Richard Taylor, and others have turned up X-rays, the nucleus, the proton and neutron, radium and polonium, and particles like the upsilon, the muon, and the tau lepton.[17] Theorists have predicted the positron, the pi-meson, the neutrino, the antiproton, the omega minus, and parity violation — and experimenters have confirmed these.

Still, the famous names remain those of theorists. As Peter Galison notes, "Despite the slogan that science advances through experiments, virtually the entire literature of the history of science concerns theory."[18] From Einstein to Feynman or Stephen Hawking, these are the names that convey intellectual glamour to the public and the field itself. Michael Riordan, himself a quark experimenter, has protested that most accounts "have presented quarks as a profound theoretical triumph — as if they had sprung full-formed from the mind of man." In fact, "they were the mutual offspring of both theory and experiment."[19]

Such protests have changed little: theorists still command the glory. For one thing, theory "dates" more slowly than experiments. Rutherford did surpassingly great experimental work over three decades. Yet unlike the work of his contemporaries Planck and Einstein, Rutherford's seems historical now, if only because laboratory equipment changes so quickly and radically that even the most famous old experiments soon fade — "we don't do it that way anymore." Good theory, rooted in mathematics, is much less vulnerable to change, and the old equations are still mostly done the same way now, with updated notations.

Experimenters nonetheless hog the Nobel Prizes. Experiments also make front-page news much more quickly than theories do, especially abstruse theories. Moreover, while important experiments keep occurring and win Nobels, it has been argued that no really significant theory has emerged since 1980.[20] At least, few theorists have been honored.

Prizes to Experimenters (E) and Theorists (T)

	E	T
1901–1920	19	4
1921–1940	10	7
1941–1970	25	15
1971–2000	34	25

Note: 1921–40 includes belated prizes to Einstein and Bohr for work done a decade or two before. Between 1984 and 1998, only two theorists won prizes. Two theorists won in 1999.

The First Generation: 1901–1925

> **Soddy:** "Rutherford, this is transmutation."
> **Rutherford:** "For Mike's sake, Soddy, don't call it transmutation. They'll have our heads off as alchemists."
>
> *— on their discovery in 1902 that "permanent" elements transform into other elements*

Twentieth-century physics began about a decade before 1900, when matter was observed behaving as it never did in everyday life or as classical physics explained it. To begin with, the dimensions are unimaginably tiny. The atom's diameter is $1-2 \times 10^{-10}$ meters. The diameter of the nucleus is one hundred-thousandth that of the atom. If the atom were the size of a huge stadium, its nucleus would be no bigger than a grain of rice. The electron's "size" is 10^{-16} centimeters, or about one-thousandth that of a proton in the nucleus. Particles have been discovered whose lifetime is shorter than 10^{-24} seconds.[21]

The peculiarities revealed by the infinitesimal realm of the atom forced physicists to answer basic questions over again, almost from scratch: what is light, what is an atom — what indeed is matter? The early Nobel Prizes give a fair picture, along with some blots and smudges, of the new phenomena on the physicists' plate.

From Radioactivity and Electrons to the Quantum Atom

Radioactivity begins with Röntgen's discovery of X-rays in 1895 ("X" because the rays shot forth were a mystery). J. J. Thomson discovered the electron in 1897, proving that the atom was divisible. These seemingly separate discoveries soon converged.

Röntgen, the first physics laureate in 1901, was also the first of many Nobelists who achieve one high point but whose career is otherwise middling. Having made the discovery, he did little to further it. But Becquerel in 1896, investigating the new X-rays, found that photographic film in darkness was penetrated by rays spontaneously emitted from uranium. From 1898, the Curies found two new elements, radium and polonium, both radioactive. More important, they suggested that radioactivity wasn't caused by some external factor; it was a property of the atoms.

But Ernest Rutherford so dominated both atomic and radioactive research in the first third of the twentieth century that this "Newton of atomic physics" deserves a closer look before he dissolves into his discoveries.

He was probably the greatest experimental genius who ever lived, with Michael Faraday in the nineteenth century the only possible competitor. Born in New Zealand in 1871, he won a fellowship to Cambridge in 1895, and in 1898 took a chair at McGill University in Montreal. There he began sorting out radioactivity into alpha, beta, and gamma rays (1899–1900). With his collaborator Soddy, he discovered that certain elements transform radioactively into other elements. With that discovery, the elements forever lost their old ultimate status and unalterable identity. He won the 1908 Nobel Prize — but in chemistry, which surprised and amused him, since he was in the habit of making rude remarks about chemistry as only a sub-branch of physics. "All science is either physics or stamp-collecting." This was part of his unconquerable self-confidence and boisterousness.

A physicist who had been a friend of Rutherford for many years once remarked: "One can hardly speak of being friendly with a force of nature."[22] Indeed he was. In photographs, he stands taller and larger than his colleagues, legs spread powerfully, his large head and thick mustache held high. He seemed not to walk but stride, in person and in his work. Congratulated for his luck on riding a wave of successful experiments, he retorted, "Well, I made the wave, didn't I?" His disciples reported him loudly singing "Onward, Christian Soldiers" in the halls when work went well, and a "less holy tune" when otherwise.[23] He liked to act the uncultured fellow fresh from the farm, with back-slapping manners, surprising his stiff German colleagues.

But Pyotr Kapitsa, the Russian experimenter (and Nobelist, 1978) who was one of Rutherford's most brilliant and favorite students, saw beyond the booming exterior. Soon after meeting Rutherford, Kapitsa wrote home: "The Professor is a deceptive character. [The English] think he is a hearty colonial. Not so. He is a man of *immense temperament*. He is given to uncontrollable excitement. His moods fluctuate violently."[24]

In Montreal, then in Manchester from 1907, where he did his greatest work, and finally from 1919 to his death as director of the Cavendish Laboratory at Cambridge, he ran his laboratories as personal fiefs. But he had the great experimenter's uncanny sense of what would work successfully, and passed it on to his many assistants, whom he called his "boys." They kept turning into Nobel laureates: Bohr, Blackett, Walton, Chadwick, Cockcroft, Kapitsa.

After winning his own Nobel Prize in 1908, far from resting on his award, Rutherford went on to do the really important work of his career, some of it the most important physics of the century. In 1909, but published in 1911, he discovered the atom's nucleus. He was Bohr's mentor when the latter produced the first quantum theory of the atom in 1913 — though Rutherford of course never ceased dismissing theoretical physicists as misguided or a waste of time. About relativity he said, "Oh, that stuff. We never bother with that in our work." He was partly tweaking noses, partly saying that relativity wasn't much use in his own work. He himself, says Pais, did important theoretical physics when discovering the nucleus, and when first explaining half-life decay. In 1919 he also first "smashed" the atom, breaking off protons from the nucleus by bombardment — the first person to change one element into another — and did the experiment by himself, with one technician attending. He also predicted the neutron that Chadwick discovered in 1932.

Made a baron, Rutherford included a New Zealand Maori and a kiwi bird on his coat of arms, along with Hermes Trismegistus. He died at age sixty-six. Chadwick said that Rutherford had no cleverness, just greatness.[25]

Rutherford's Montreal collaborator, Frederick Soddy, discovered isotopes in 1913; in 1919 Francis Aston invented the mass spectroscope and found isotopes that were not radioactive. Soddy became a laureate in chemistry in 1921; Aston, also in chemistry, in 1922. Isotopes proved of central importance in understanding the atom and chemical elements, in medicine and nuclear fission. Soddy felt, with some justice, that the Nobel jury should have given him a share of Rutherford's prize in 1908. Rutherford must have felt the same: he nominated Soddy for the chemistry prize.

When J. J. Thomson discovered the electron inside the atom in 1897, there had been many near misses by others, generating disputes about priority. Everyone used the same apparatus — the cathode ray tube, a small vacuum tube filled with gas. When electricity was shot through it, X-rays and electrons could be generated.

Many experimenters found new phenomena, but either didn't realize they were new, or misunderstood the reason, or else couldn't get as rigorous measurements as Thomson.[26]

The first case of disputed priority in the Nobel physics list came as early as the 1905 Nobel Prize to Philipp Lenard, professor at Kiel. He had worked with cathode rays since the 1880s, yet managed to miss the discovery both of X-rays and the electron. But Lenard coveted priority. When Röntgen in 1895 discovered X-rays, Lenard promptly declared himself codiscoverer. He had certainly found rays passing beyond the tube, but Röntgen showed what these rays could do, and Lenard did not. Lenard nonetheless grandly complained: "If Röntgen was the midwife to the discovery of the X-rays, I was the mother." He had in fact only lent Röntgen a component of a cathode ray tube. When Thomson found the electron in 1897, Lenard claimed himself codiscoverer of that as well. If his peers did not accept his claims, at least Lenard's students had to: he used to interrogate them. "And who did this first?" "You did, Herr Professor." "Exactly right."[27] Still, he won the Nobel award the year before Thomson, for his discovery of the photoelectric effect in 1902. But he couldn't explain it. In 1905 the young Einstein gave the correct explanation, and in 1921 won his Nobel for it. Later, Lenard harangued against "Jewish" physics; under Hitler, Lenard became the Chief of Aryan Physics.

J. J. Thomson took the 1907 prize. It says much about the confused richness of the period that the discovery of the electron inside the atom did not convince some experts that atoms also existed — Ostwald, the 1909 chemistry laureate, was one longtime sceptic. Oddly, therefore, the atom's own existence was finally experimentally confirmed after the particle inside it, by Jean Perrin's studies of Brownian motion in 1908. In 1913 Perrin also established the existence of molecules. Indeed, he came near discovering the electron in 1895 as well. Perrin won the 1926 prize.[28]

In 1913 came Bohr's revolutionary model of the atom. Bohr described electrons "orbiting" Rutherford's nucleus, but according to quantum rules that allowed them to move only in fixed and discrete levels of energy. Bohr's model rescued Rutherford's atom from incoherency, since Rutherford couldn't explain why the electrons didn't eventually lose energy and drop into the nucleus, and gave the quantum theory its most crucial support yet. Bohr's theory proved itself able to calculate the binding energy between the electron and nucleus (the Rydberg constant), derive Planck's constant, and explain no more than the hydrogen atom. In 1914 further support came when James Franck and Gustav Hertz bombarded mercury atoms with electrons in gases and found that energy was absorbed and emitted only in quantized amounts, in line with Bohr's claim. Franck and Hertz shared the 1925 prize — just in time to lend support as well to the "new" quantum theory of Heisenberg, Pauli, et al.

As noted, inventions were given short shrift by the Nobel committee. Edison, the Wright brothers, Pupin (induction coils), and other inventors were nominated for the Nobel Prize. But only twice have "practical" inventions or technology, as against contributions to fundamental knowledge, been honored — and within a few years of each other. In 1909 Marconi and Karl Braun won the prize for improving radio transmission over long distances. Their work, from 1896 to 1901, depended on Maxwell's nineteenth-century theory that electromagnetic waves could travel through the atmosphere; Heinrich Hertz in 1888 actually transmitted such waves. The technology was thus well known. In the early 1890s, before Marconi, Rutherford had transmitted radio waves over a mile. Braun improved Marconi's equipment by inventing the crystal detector; all early radios were "crystal sets" until the vacuum tube, invented by the American Lee De Forest in 1906, became commercially viable in the 1920s. No Nobel for De Forest — but why wasn't the vacuum tube more important than the crystal detector? Marconi and Braun also patented their inventions and became rich before winning the Nobel Prize. Yet laureates were not supposed to profit excessively from their scientific work.

In 1912 the next "practical" physics prize — and last, thus far — went to Nils Dalén of Sweden for improving lighthouse power by using acetylene. He won on the basis of a single nomination. This remains the least impressive award in any science category. It seems to have happened because of the academy's deadlock over far more impressive candidates such as Planck.

Two other prizes kept X-rays on the Nobel list in this early period. In 1912 Max von Laue, an aristocratic young Prussian turned physicist, was the first to prove that X-rays had an extremely short wavelength — he used crystal grids to trace the path of the X-rays — and quickly won the 1914 prize. From 1912 to 1914, W. H. and

W. L. Bragg in England, father and son, turned Laue's method about and showed how crystalline structures could be accurately measured by using X-rays. When the Braggs shared the 1915 prize, the younger Bragg was only twenty-five — still the youngest ever in any field. X-ray crystallography has been indispensable since then; it played a key role in the discovery of the DNA structure in 1953.

How Einstein Won the Nobel (But Not for Relativity)

After the discovery of X-rays, electrons, radioactivity, and the atomic nucleus, even the best physicists were confused and confusing about how to explain things. In fact, Planck's quantum concept of 1900 and Einstein's special relativity of 1905 soon began to give deep coherence to the field, but Planck did not receive his Nobel award for nearly twenty years, and Einstein was delayed almost as long.

One would hardly have picked Max Planck (1858–1947) for taking the most revolutionary step in modern atomic physics. He looked the archexample of the German pedant: dry and stiff as a stick, a bald-skulled head with pince-nez spectacles clamped above a drooping mustache. No photograph ever seems to have caught him smiling. He downplayed his own bombshell insight, and it was Einstein who first pushed or perhaps even first recognized its revolutionary implications. Planck, though the Galileo of quantum physics, worried throughout his life about the dreadful break he had caused with classical physics and causality. Nonetheless, at age forty-two, he did make the break, did boldly plunge into unknown territory as other eminent physicists had not dared or been insightful enough to do. Both his conservatism and his radicalism reflect what everyone has said about Planck: he was a model of integrity. A very proper German professor he always remained, but a noble, generous, and humane spirit.

The best biography in English, by J. L. Heilbron in 1986, is aptly titled *The Dilemmas of an Upright Man*. German history put Planck on the rack. A dutiful patriot, Planck signed a manifesto defending German militarism in World War I; he was reviled by Allied supporters; his eldest son was killed in action. When the Hitler regime took power in 1933, he was (after Einstein) the most famous German scientist, the very pillar of respectability. In 1930 he had been named president of the prestigious Kaiser Wilhelm Society for scientific research. In that position, he was forced to preside over the persecution of his Jewish colleagues. Planck decided to remain in Germany despite the Nazis, and was among the very few to publicly protest anti-Semitic policies. In his official capacity as president of the Kaiser Wilhelm Society, he even said so to Hitler. Hitler exploded. Planck was silenced, and resigned his presidency in 1937. But his only other son took part in the conspiracy to kill Hitler, and was executed for it in 1944. Planck outlived Hitler; he died in 1947 at ninety.

So much has been written about Albert Einstein (1879–1955), the man and the myth, that only some sidelights bear notice. His status as an icon of saintly intellect has obscured his great wit and shrewdness. A "merry boy" is how a friend described the younger Einstein. Reputations never impressed him. On Freud: "The old one . . . saw keenly. He allowed himself to be lulled by no illusory consolations except an exaggerated confidence in his own ideas." On Princeton as he saw it when he moved there in 1933 (in a letter to Queen Elizabeth of Belgium): "a quaint ceremonious village of puny demigods on stilts."[29] He was a superb master of German prose, and could write with Goethean eloquence: "Die Natur verbirgt ihr Geheimnis durch die Erhabenheit ihres Wesens, aber nicht durch List" (Nature conceals her secret through her essential nobility, not out of cunning).

During World War I, living in Berlin, Einstein once told his friend Max Born that he could happily live without any possessions, or even friends. He had, he said, no binding ties to any nation, religion, or group. In later life, an exception emerged in his deepened sense of belonging to the Jewish people. But the inner distancing was always present, though he was famous for his Zionism and one-time pacifism, answering letters to schoolchildren about arithmetic, taking time to see visitors of all kinds, and donating his name to all sorts of worthy causes. After leaving Germany just before the Nazis had a chance to arrest or expel him, he never returned or forgave.

His extraordinary fame owes much to his willed inner isolation as well: more than any other major physicist since Newton, Einstein's was remarkably a one-man achievement. His general theory of relativity was completed in 1915, and the experimental confirmation in 1919 that space was "curved" as Einstein had predicted, made him overnight the most famous scientist of the century. But, as many have noted, he would still be one of the century's greatest physicists merely on the basis on his contributions to quantum physics — whose break with classical causality in the mid-1920s he deplored for the rest of his life.

He married twice, first in 1903 to Mileva Marić (1875–1948), a fellow student of physics, with whom he had three children. The first was Lieserl, about whom little is known. A son, Hans Albert (1904–1973), became a professor of electrical engineering at Berkeley. Another son, Eduard (1910–1965), was a bright student and musically talented, but developed schizophrenic symptoms after graduating from high school and was hospitalized most of his life. Einstein and Mileva divorced in 1919, after a long and bitter separation; he gave Mileva all the prize money from his 1921 award, and later that year he married a cousin. Einstein dropped hints that he had been unfaithful to his second wife on several occasions — a shock to those who see him only as marble.

Old, and knowing how unsuited he was for such a position, he declined the presidency of Israel offered him in 1952. Ben-Gurion is reported as saying, "My God, what if he accepts?" Einstein died of an aneurysm, after refusing an operation. "It is pointless to prolong life artifically. I have done my share, it is time to go. I will do it elegantly," he said.[30] A few days later, he did. The aftermath was scarcely elegant. His body was cremated, but his brain was put into formaldehyde as a precious specimen to help medical pathologists understand how "genius" is physically constructed. Its weight — 2.6 pounds — was disappointingly average. The brain, sliced into hundreds of tissues over the years, told the researchers nothing and in the 1980s ended up in Wichita, Kansas. In 1999, however, neurologists discovered that Einstein's brain had an enlarged inferior parietal lobe, which may be linked to visualizing and mathematical ability.[31] One wonders how Einstein would have reacted to the posthumous adventures of his brain. A simple man he was not.

It was as if the ground had been pulled from under one.

— *Einstein on Planck's quantum theory*[32]

We return to 1901.[33] Alfred Nobel's will and the Statutes of the Nobel Foundation mentioned only "discoveries" and "inventions," certainly not *revolutionary* discoveries. How could any prize-giving institution set up rules to deal with discoveries that reinvented the rules? In fact, there have probably been few true revolutions in physical theory. The eligible names since Newton seem to come down only to Faraday and James Clerk Maxwell in the mid-nineteenth century, and Planck and Einstein at the start of the twentieth.

Planck's quantum discovery began modestly as an answer to a specific problem called, for historical reasons, the "blackbody" problem, which involved the relation between temperature and wavelengths. As metal gets white-hot, it radiates wavelengths that are shorter and shorter. Some notable physicists could not find a way to account for the results. In December 1900, "in desperation," Planck tried an outrageous new approach. He threw out the sacred law of classical physics that energy flowed continuously, and assumed instead that it was discontinuous, moving in discrete or quantum bits (from the Latin *quantum:* howevermuch).

This approach gave a stunningly correct and precise solution. Soon after, Planck calculated a quantum constant, one of only a few such universal constants thus far known — the speed of light is another — which apparently remain true through all of nature. But such discontinuity violates our deepest experience and intuitive convictions. In the everyday world, you can drive at speeds of 3, 17, 32, or 90, or anything between; energy flow is continuous. In the subatomic domain, it is discontinuous and no in-between speeds exist. Hence the so-called quantum leap: you can drive only at certain unalterably fixed speeds, and never mind how you get from one speed to another.

One might think such a radical departure from all previous physics, and so experimentally successful, would cause a sensation. In fact, physicists — and Planck himself — saw it mainly as only an ingenious mathematical answer to an otherwise insoluble but localized problem. How could it pertain to other phenomena, all of which seemed to deny such discontinuity? The full implications emerged only later.

The meaning and use of Planck's discovery puzzled almost everyone, including Planck, because no context for his audacious solution existed. Making a discovery, as Abraham Pais put it, is by no means the same as understanding that discovery.[34] Einstein was the first to understand it, and with stunning success.

In contrast to Planck, who was unable or unwilling to develop his epochal law into a proper theory, the young Einstein was not at all shy about producing theories with daring implications and assumptions. In 1905, his annus mirabilis, came four path-breaking theories: on special relativity, the equivalence of mass and energy, the explanation of Brownian motion by molecular movement, and light-as-quanta. Relativity remains his most famous discovery. But while Planck's quantum formula exactly met all its experimental tests, Einstein's special relativity theory long lacked experimental confirmation.

It might be thought, therefore, that Einstein's special relativity theory would meet much resistance. After all, it dismissed the exalted nineteenth-century theory of the "aether" without deigning to discuss it; it revised fundamental notions of time and space laid down by Newton himself; it made the speed of light, the fastest speed possible, the invariant for any observer in physics. Moreover, his theory came into effect only when matter approached the speed of light. Experimental confirmation required the large accelerators that arrived in the 1930s and after. Yet Einstein's bold theory gained wide acceptance long before its confirmation.

For one thing, relativity — special, not general or gravitational — was a familiar topic. Eminent elders like Henri Poincaré of France and Hendrik Lorentz of Holland had made tries at such a theory shortly before Einstein. Einstein's better version quickly won over a distinguished band of admirers — the cautious Planck being the first among them. As editor of the esteemed German physics journal *Annalen der Physik*, Planck had accepted the young Einstein's first papers on special relativity. The very next year, 1906, Planck himself wrote the first paper ever on Einstein's theory, lectured on it in his important Berlin colloquium, and soon urged promising young faculty like the future Nobelist Max Born to study it. That kind of support drew in influential others. If anyone helped build Einstein's career, it was Planck. And if anyone built Planck's fame, it was Einstein. Planck's second greatest discovery — in J. L. Heilbron's phrase — was Einstein himself.

It can come as a distinct shock to anyone who has struggled to understand special relativity — via moving trains and different observers and the speed of light as measuring rod — to learn that Einstein did not think his relativity theories very revolutionary at all. In 1921, by which time he had both the special and gravitational theories under his belt, he described them as only the "natural completion of the work of Faraday, Maxwell and Lorentz."[35] But, he insisted, his light-quanta concept was "very revolutionary." Judging by the reaction of his colleagues, Einstein was right about both of these.

In 1905 Einstein took the first daring step toward turning the quantum concept into a theory. Contradicting the prevailing and venerable view that light was wavelike, he hypothesized instead that light consisted of discrete quanta. This forced the revolutionary implications of Planck's quantum concept into the open for the first time. At the end of the paper setting this forth, Einstein suggested how his hypothesis could also explain the photoelectric effect.[36]

Planck was distressed by Einstein's light-quanta hypothesis. Along with others, he clung to waves as the true description of light. The only prominent German physicist who supported Einstein by 1909 was Johannes Stark (Nobel 1919), an expert in wavelength determinations. But Planck and Wien argued with Stark and Göttingen's great teacher, Arnold Sommerfeld, scolded him, and the next year Stark dropped his support. Though the American Robert Millikan's two years of experiments (1912–14) had proved Einstein's equation right, Millikan had in fact set out to prove it wrong. Millikan doggedly asserted that "the physical theory behind it appears to be completely invalid" and claimed that Einstein probably didn't believe it himself.[37] As late as 1920, even Niels Bohr didn't entirely believe in light-quanta. Planck was disturbed by Einstein's bold extension of his concept. In 1913, in a letter nominating Einstein as a member of the Prussian Academy, Planck praised his younger colleague very highly, then added that his hypothesis of light-quanta should not be held against him: Einstein's penchant for new ideas involved taking risks.[38]

In 1911 Planck had also cast cold water on the first international conference planned to discuss quantum physics, the first of the famed Solvay Conferences. A year later Einstein wrote to a friend: "The more success the quantum theory has, the sillier it looks. How nonphysicists would scoff if they were able to follow the odd course of developments!"[39]

Niels Bohr's quantum atom model appeared in 1913, and none too soon, as we shall see. All this was directly involved in the Nobel Prizes of Planck and Einstein.

Because of the quantum revolution in 1925–26, Planck now of course is immortal. For long he was only another very eminent physicist, first nominated for the Nobel Prize in 1906,[40] and twice more in 1907, though his quantum discovery was was not emphasized. In 1908 he almost won. The committee voted him the prize, but in the full academy, which had final say, everything fell apart. Here scientists who weren't members of the physics committee or even physicists could maneuver for their own candidates. The eminent Swedish mathematician Fredholm, who had earlier supported Planck, now called his quantum law "hardly plausible." Two committee members reversed their vote. Others rejected honoring a theorist without also including an experimenter. Both Planck and Wilhelm Wien, the other leading candidate, ended out in the cold. The prize went to Gabriel Lippmann of France for improvement of color photography.[41]

From 1909 Planck often led in nominations, without winning. By 1916 Planck's concept had been successfully employed by Einstein, Bohr, Gustav Hertz and James Franck, Peter Debye, Max Born — all future Nobelists. Still the Nobel evaluators held that the quantum concept did not harmonize "with other seemingly well-established propositions in physics."[42] In 1918, however, it was clear that unless Planck were honored, awards could not go to Einstein or Bohr, to mention only two important figures waiting in the wings. In 1919 Planck finally won the Nobel Prize for the previous year, 1918. That cleared the way for Einstein.

Planck nominated Einstein for the 1919 prize, for general relativity, but in vain. The German experimenter Johannes Stark won that year. The chemistry prize in 1919 went to Fritz Haber. Stark was an anti-Semite, Haber was a Jew. Stark also resented the greater fame of Planck and Haber. They all appeared on the Stockholm stage side by side.

A legend still flourishes that Einstein was a misunderstood and neglected genius. In fact his career was an extraordinary success story. It did begin unimpressively. In 1902, a new Ph.D., he took a job as "provisional technical expert, third class" in the Bern patent office; only in 1906 was he promoted to second class. In 1907 he applied but was rejected for a position as Privatdozent at Bern University, an unsalaried, nontenured appointment: the instructor was paid fees according to how many students took the class. He tried again in 1908 and was accepted. That put him on the bottommost, least prestigious, and most precarious rung of the academic ladder.

Yet the very next year, when he was thirty, the University of Zurich offered him a position as associate professor for its first appointment in theoretical physics (he accepted). That same year Geneva awarded him an honorary degree. By 1911, then a full professor in Prague, he had become one of the youngest members of the still very small European top scientific elite, as the invitation to the 1911 Solvay Conference shows. In 1912 he was a full professor at his old university, the ETH in Zurich. In 1913 he reached the heights: full professor at the prestigious Prussian Academy in Berlin with no teaching duties. He was then just thirty-four. In the ultraconservative academic world of that time, with its strong anti-Semitism, Einstein's ascent was very rapid.

His fast-growing prominence was reflected in the frequency and quickness with which he was nominated for a Nobel Prize. The first nomination came as early as 1910. Again in 1912, for theoretical physics. Again in 1913, 1914, 1916, and so on to 1922 when he won the 1921 prize that had been "reserved" that year.

His distinction couldn't be denied, but the committee refused to honor either of his relativity theories. This stemmed, as regards his gravitational theory, not from the decision to eliminate awards for astrophysics — that came in 1923. The old Nobel bias against theoretical physics[43] was still a factor, and experimental confirmation of special relativity was also a problem. In 1919 the general relativity theory had seemed to receive confirmation when the astrophysicist Arthur Eddington made an expedition to an island off West Africa to take measurements during a total eclipse of the sun. His findings supported Einstein's prediction that the gravitational force of space would curve light in the vicinity of the sun. Eddington's report launched Einstein on his career as a world supercelebrity. But Eddington's measurements included a quite risky thirty-percent error factor. In 1920 Einstein was nominated for relativity by Lorentz, Bohr, Kamerlingh Onnes, Zeeman, and others; Arrhenius wrote a favorable evaluation. But the 1920 prize went to Charles Guillaume, a "measuring physicist" who improved measuring devices using alloys back in 1889. He directed the International Bureau of Weights and Measures at Sèvres for thirty years, and his prize is said to have been prompted by the Nobel committee's wish to please a dying colleague.

In 1921 nominations again came from Planck, from Eddington ("Einstein stands above his contemporaries even as Newton did"), from the famous French mathematician Jacques Hadamard. But Allvar Gullstrand of the committee (physiology prize, 1911, for geometry of optics) wrote a special report rejecting both of Einstein's relativity theories as unworthy of a Nobel award; he privately stated that Einstein should never win a prize.[44] The prize was "reserved" that year.

By 1922 Einstein had been nominated about fifty times. Most had urged his relativity theories for the Nobel; his other contributions, such as the quantum photoelectric effect or Brownian motion theory, were mentioned far less. Léon Brillouin of France wrote: "Imagine for a moment what the general opinion will be fifty years from now if Einstein's name does not appear on the list of Nobel laureates."[45] In 1922 C. W. Oseen, a theoretical physicist and once a student of Bohr's, wrote a shrewdly worded evaluation of Einstein that finally won him the prize. Since the Nobel's opposition to the relativity theories hadn't lessened, Oseen suggested honoring Einstein only for his light-quanta hypothesis explaining the photoelectric effect. After all, Millikan's experiments had already confirmed Einstein's theory here.

As Crawford and Friedman show, Oseen's divorcing of Einstein's "law" or equation from his "theory" became the key to Einstein's winning the prize. Oseen drafted a citation that read "for discovery of the law of the photoelectric effect, through which quantum theory received a new especially vigorous renewal." His earlier draft read "theory" instead of "law." Oseen also dropped the earlier wording "derived from the quantum theory." These shifts in wording were shrewd political moves: "law" was more acceptable than "theory" to the "measuring" physicists, and the new wording about quantum physics moved Einstein's achievement apart from Planck's. Oseen also was seeking a wording to help his former teacher Bohr win the 1922 prize. The maneuver worked: Einstein won the hitherto reserved 1921 Nobel Prize, and Bohr won for 1922.[46]

Thus, though Einstein did not win for his renowned relativity theories, he did win the Nobel Prize for what he considered his most revolutionary idea.

As a laureate, Einstein had the right thereafter to nominate. He submitted names mostly between 1923 and 1931.[47] Many other physicists nominated much more frequently. Perhaps Einstein's scepticism about claims for post-1925 quantum mechanics and his later absorption in unified theory made him feel unprepared or disinclined to judge new work; his last nominations, for Bothe and Pauli, referred to work from 1924 and 1925. But he kept nominating for the Nobel Peace Prize.

The Nobel Prize–winning work of Niels Bohr (1885–1962), done in 1913, was the epochal first theory of the atom on quantum principles. Its limitations as well as success led to the new quantum mechanics of 1925–26 and its regnancy to now.

Born of a Danish professor and a Jewish mother from a Danish banking family, Bohr grew up in patrician and privileged style. The year before he became the first Dane to win the Nobel Prize, the government built him an Institute of Theoretical Physics, to which flocked the cream of the world's physicists. Later he and his wife and large family were given the Carlsberg Palace as their home, courtesy of the state.

But what struck everyone about Bohr was his modesty. Einstein, who admired and loved Bohr, said, "He utters his opinions like one perpetually groping and never like one who believes himself in possession of definite truth." Bohr had a homely, heavy face, which in some photographs can fool one into thinking the man must be dull or oafish. He was anything but. To a friend, Einstein expressed gratitude that so great a genius as Bohr was alive in his time. Rutherford was as impressed by this archtheorist.

When the young Dutch physicist Abraham Pais went to study in Copenhagen in 1946, Bohr described himself as a "dilettante." Pais was staggered to hear this from so great a scientist, but Bohr was utterly serious: "He explained how he had to approach every new question from a starting point of total ignorance."[48]

Bohr was perhaps the greatest teacher and mentor in twentieth-century physics. Einstein was a natural loner: he worked by himself and preferred not to teach. Bohr taught endlessly, compulsively, joyously, and best of all in conversation. He was like a wizard to the brilliant young scientists of the 1920s and 1930s who collected around him in Copenhagen — later Nobel physicists such as Heisenberg and Pauli and Dirac, the Dutch physicists H. A. Kramers and Hendrik Casimir, the Nobelist Lev Landau and George Gamow from Russia, Nobel chemists such Linus Pauling and Harold Urey, and Max Delbrück of later molecular biology fame. Bohr took everyone walking, hiking, skiing, motorcycle riding — meanwhile always talking physics. When Erwin Schrödinger discovered his wave quantum theory in 1926, Bohr invited him to Copenhagen to discuss his interpretation, put him up at his house, and meanwhile conducted a running debate — it had begun in the railway station when Schrödinger first arrived — that never let up. Poor Schrödinger, not used to such intensity, took to bed exhausted. Werner Heisenberg, who was present, says that Mrs. Bohr kept bringing Schrödinger tea and cakes, while Bohr sat on the edge of the bed saying very sincerely to Schrödinger, "But surely you must realize that . . ."[49] Schrödinger himself was struck by how Bohr, despite all his renown, remained "rather shy and diffident, like a theology student."[50]

The Second Generation: 1925–1950

> Physics . . . is much too difficult for me and I wish I were a film comedian or something like that and that I had never heard anything about physics!
>
> — *Wolfgang Pauli, May 1925, just before the "new" quantum mechanics of Heisenberg and Schrödinger*[51]

In this period, quantum physics takes a first full grip on the Nobel Prizes and never lets go. The list here begins in the 1920s with a few retrospective awards, to Perrin, Wilson, Richardson. In the same decade, prizes for quantum contributions included Arthur Compton (1923), James Franck and Gustav Hertz (1925), and Louis de Broglie (1929). In the 1930s the trend grew stronger.

The end of Europe's dominance of physics and other science Nobel Prizes also arrived, with Enrico Fermi's award in 1938. After the Nobel ceremony, instead of returning to a fascist Italy which that year had adopted anti-Semitic laws, Fermi and his Jewish wife immediately left for the U.S. The Nazi destruction of German and then European science drove most of its best into exile. This migration of talent, and the emergence of several great American schools of physics in the 1930s, finally brought more Nobels to the U.S. than to the rest of the world combined.

This second generation doubtless gave rise to the myth that theoretical physicists are all youthful prodigies. In 1905 Einstein's feats at age 26 were in fact the exception; in the 1920s they began to seem the norm. The sardonic Pauli, himself one of them, called the new quantum mechanics *Knabenphysik* (boys' physics). Heisenberg and Pauli did their Nobel-winning work at ages 24 and 25, but Dirac was the most precocious. At 23 he independently clarified the mathematical meaning of Heisenberg's brand-new matrix mechanics. Dirac was an aging 26 when he introduced relativity into the theory of the quantum electron, plus the idea of antimatter. At 31 he had a Nobel Prize.

Leading Characters, Second Generation

In 1922 Göttingen invited Bohr to give a series of lectures on his atom theory, which caused such excitement it came to be called the Bohr Festival. Werner Heisenberg (1901–1976), then twenty years old and a graduate student, attended, and raised a point of argument that set Bohr, as usual, deeply thinking. Afterwards, the famous Bohr — it was the year of his Nobel — sought out the student, walking and talking, of course.[52] Heisenberg remembered this as the event that made physics come alive for him. Bohr spoke to the young student about the real problems facing physics at the moment, and somehow made him see what a true physical viewpoint as against merely mathematical meant. Bohr became his mentor, but World War II brought a sad break, never repaired.

If Bohr was homely and Max von Laue the perfect stiff Prussian — which in fact he was — Heisenberg resembled a healthy, naive farm boy which he was not: his father was a professor of Greek in Munich. Young Werner's absorption in theoretical physics almost made him fail his doctoral examinations. The committee included Wilhelm Wien (Nobelist 1911), who was irritated that Heisenberg had skipped his lab course. Wien decided to ask some practical questions which he had discussed in his course. What was the resolving power of a certain kind of telescope? Heisenberg couldn't answer. An easier question: How did a storage battery work? Again, unsatisfactory. Wien wanted to fail Heisenberg, but Sommerfeld talked him into graduating Heisenberg with a C grade.[53] It was a disastrous start for a German academic career. That was 1923, when Heisenberg was twenty-two. By 1925 Heisenberg had established quantum mechanics, and in 1927 the uncertainty principle. Nine years after almost flunking out, he won his Nobel Prize.

Bohr became Heisenberg's guide and gyroscope, intellectually and personally. In one archetypal story, Heisenberg launches another of his endless brilliant ideas at Bohr, whose answer always begins, "Yes, yes, Heisenberg, but . . ." Heisenberg's other pivot was his exact contemporary Wolfgang Pauli: they barraged each other with lengthy letters.

Bohr, Heisenberg, and Pauli made a perfect team in many ways: daring speculations matched with analytic rigor at every step, with no holds barred. They could operate no other way. But Heisenberg was more thin-skinned and less emotionally mature than the other two. Something of the delayed adolescent infected him. Even when doing his Ph.D., he had been an ardent member of a German youth movement resembling the famous Wandervogel groups, the sort that led many into early sympathy with Nazism or its atmosphere — young men heartily hiking and camping together, enjoying a sort of self-conscious primitivism and romanticized comradeship. A story told by Dirac is pertinent here. In 1929 Dirac and Heisenberg traveled together from San Francisco to Japan. They climbed a high tower to a platform at the top, which was encircled by a stone balustrade. Heisenberg climbed out on the balustrade, said Dirac, "and stood there, entirely unsupported, standing on about six inches square of stone-work. Quite undisturbed by the great height, he just surveyed the scenery. . . . I couldn't help feeling anxious. If a wind had come along then it might have had a tragic result."[54] But when Bohr argued in 1927 that Heisenberg's new uncertainty principle had some problems and publication should be delayed, Heisenberg burst into tears. Heisenberg published anyway.

This side of Heisenberg shaded into political ambiguities during the Hitler regime, which clouded the rest of his life. When Hitler came to power in 1933 and began to expel Jewish academics, Heisenberg's three closest associates were half-Jews (Bohr, Pauli) and a full Jew (Max Born, professor at Göttingen). Bohr and Pauli worked outside Germany. But Born was abruptly discharged from his professorship in 1933, the same year Heisenberg received his Nobel Prize, awarded for the preceding year. Heisenberg decided to remain in Germany.

During the war Heisenberg became the director of the German atom bomb project, Oppenheimer's counterpart. What Heisenberg did or didn't do between 1939 and 1945 remains unclear. Many have charged Heisenberg with trying desperately hard to make the bomb, so that Germany would not suffer humiliation or obliteration. Heisenberg said he knew his country did not have the resources to build it, but misled the authorities. In 1940 German troops occupied Denmark and incidentally took over control of Bohr's Institute. In 1942 Heisenberg made a brief visit to Copenhagen. His and Bohr's accounts of what they said then do not match. Heisenberg claims he tried to explain to Bohr that Germany would never make the bomb. Bohr's version differs; he surely did not try to persuade the Americans to abandon their bomb work on the basis of Heisenberg's claims about German incapacity.

Heisenberg did not have an easy time of it during the Nazi period. The effort to cleanse the German soul meant dismissing relativity, among much else, as "Jewish" physics. Heisenberg at first kept teaching it, but was denounced as a "white Jew." The compromise was to teach relativity but never mention Einstein, and not even call it relativity. Heisenberg defended himself against continuing attacks. At one point, he took the offensive and requested Heinrich Himmler, no less, to clear his name and honor. Heisenberg's parents and Himmler's had been acquaintances in Munich. Himmler had the pressure taken off Heisenberg. Himmler's mother, with weird naïveté, said about her monstrously murderous son, "Do you think, Mrs. Heisenberg, that my little Heinrich is not on the right path after all?"

After the war Heisenberg and Bohr patched up relations, but the old warmth and trust never rekindled. For all this, Heisenberg's scientific genius had the bold originality and penetrating insight one associates with an Einstein or a Bohr. The incomparable Dirac once paid him just such a tribute for clearing the path, as no one else could, for people like Dirac himself: "I do not think I would ever have made progress in studying atomic theory if it had not been for Heisenberg. I was so much attached to the Bohr orbits. It needed quite a different kind of intelligence to be able to break away from just building up theories in terms of Bohr orbits."[55]

Erwin Schrödinger (1887–1961) was the oldster among the prodigies. He was thirty-seven when he made his great contribution. His Ph.D. dated back to 1910 and he really belonged to the pre–World War I generation, a different world indeed from the troubled postwar 1920s of the others. Schrödinger always was something of an "old" Viennese, with a great personal charm, not to say ardor and sensuality, that one scarcely associates with Dirac, Pauli, or Heisenberg.

Schrödinger was good enough to advance steadily to a professorship, but with no truly outstanding achievement to his credit. Then, in middle age, lightning struck. In 1923 the French theorist de Broglie proposed that particles might act like waves. Einstein praised the insight, but it was still only a "qualitative" theory. In 1926 Schrödinger worked it all out rigorously. He had taken one of his young mistresses (he was married, but his love life was always complicated) on a Christmas vacation to the Alps. In such an unlikely situation for concentrated abstract thought, Schrödinger came up with the first of an extraordinary series of four papers that poured out in early 1926. They included his wave equation, one of the most famous equations in modern physics. It gives the "wave function" of the electron, later extended beyond electrons to protons, even quarks. Truly the golden all-purpose equation, it is probably the most-cited equation in the literature of modern physics.[56]

What happened after that bedeviled Schrödinger: he had really hoped to expel the quantum view of the atom, but found himself part of it. He spent the rest of his life in fierce opposition. He never made another discovery in any way comparable. He kept switching countries. He moved into the margins of many fields, in the center of none, writing on Greek philosophy, or on applying physics to biology; his book *What Is Life?* (1944) inspired many young scientists to shift into molecular biology, which led to the DNA discovery. Like Einstein, he took up the search for a grand unified theory. Once, he announced actually finding such a theory, but he did so directly to the press, bypassing scientific journals. Though they had been quite close, this was too much for Einstein, who thought poorly of the theory but especially of the unseemly publicity-hunting; he didn't write to Schrödinger for two years.

Perhaps Schrödinger achieved only one great triumph because he was interested in too many things, including women and love. He may have been more of a philosopher at heart than a physicist, and a romantic rebel. Dirac once described him arriving at an important conference encumbered with rucksacks and looking like a tramp. Max Born, who bluntly opposed his interpretations and argued with him for a lifetime, also called him the most interesting man he had ever met.

* * *

Paul Adrien Maurice Dirac (1902–1984), born in Britain, got his French names from his Swiss-French émigré father. Much of Dirac's unusual personality stems from his father's tyranny as well. The older Dirac insisted on speaking only French at meals; his English-born wife could not speak French, so she and two other Frenchless children ate in the kitchen. Père Dirac however thought his son should learn French, so Paul ate with him. Since he couldn't express himself in French, "it was better for me to stay silent than to talk in English. So I became very silent at that time — that started very early."[57] It lasted his whole life. Dirac did become fluent in French, and was a most elegant stylist in English, but he also became famous or notorious for his few words and unnerving reserve. His lack of normal social life as a child shows in one story. At a party, he watched Heisenberg dance with pretty girls. "Heisenberg, why do you dance?" "Well, they are nice girls," said Heisenberg. A few minutes later Dirac asked: "How do you know beforehand that the girls are nice?" On another occasion a French scientist came to see Dirac in England, and stumbled a long while in very broken English. Dirac listened politely but said nothing. One of Dirac's sisters came in and spoke in French, and Dirac answered in French. The Frenchman was furious. "Why didn't you tell me you spoke French?" Dirac: "You didn't ask me."[58] Dirac's manner obviously puzzled people. When he won the Nobel in 1933, a London paper headline called him THE GENIUS WHO FEARS ALL WOMEN, and inanely went on to describe Dirac as "shy as a gazelle and modest as a Victorian maid." He was none of these things.

He brought rare mathematical gifts to physics. The novelist C. P. Snow, who had studied with him, claimed Dirac was the only physicist who pure mathematicians think could have succeeded in their rarefied field. All theoretical physicists are more or less gifted in mathematics. But Bohr said that when the math got too abstract, he got lost.[59] Einstein used professional mathematicians as assistants; he was very talented, but that is far from being a "mathematician."

Dirac exceptionally would have excelled in either field. He once said, "A great deal of my work is just playing with equations and seeing what they give."[60] In 1925 Dirac read Heisenberg's first paper on his new quantum mechanics. It used the unfamiliar and awkward form of matrix mathematics, with the symbols arranged in a rectangular array. The twenty-three-year-old Dirac quickly restructured the equations in a different, clearer way. Max Born, professor at grand Göttingen, who had formalized Heisenberg's theory using conventional means, related how he felt on reading Dirac's unexpected paper:

> This was — I remember well — one of the greatest surprises of my scientific life. For the name Dirac was completely unknown to me, the author appeared to be a youngster, yet everything was perfect in its way and admirable.[61]

Another great contribution, in 1927, laid the first foundation of quantum electrodynamics. But his most famous came in 1928, when he discovered an equation still so essential and fertile that it is simply known as Dirac's equation. It was the first to meld relativity into the quantum theory of the electron, as Schrödinger's famous equation could not; it accounted for the recently discovered phenomenon of "spin"; it provided the right magnetic moment. On top of this, it was also the first theory in physics ever to predict a particle — and what a particle! It was the antielectron, an electron that is positively charged, and its detection in 1932 marked the first known existence of antimatter.[62]

In 1932 Dirac became the Lucasian Professor of Mathematics at Cambridge, a chair held by Newton and now by Stephen Hawking. In 1933 he shared the Nobel Prize with Schrödinger. Dirac at first wanted to refuse the prize, as too much distraction from his work. Rutherford counseled that a refusal would mean much more publicity and distraction. Dirac accepted, but refused to invite his father to the prize ceremony; he took his mother instead. As a laureate, Dirac thenceforth had the right to nominate at any time. His biographer Helge Kragh has written that, so far as he knew, Dirac never nominated anyone.[63]

Dirac remains the greatest modern physicist most devoted to mathematical beauty as the key to physical reality. But this has been emphasized so often that his extraordinary physical intuition is too often slighted.

With Enrico Fermi (1901–1954), the great second generation comes to an end, and a new begins. An exact contemporary of Pauli, Dirac, and Heisenberg, he was also a prodigy. But while their great achievements were in the mid-1920s, his came mainly in the early 1930s. The reason lay less in Fermi than in Italy. While Germany, Britain, and France by the 1920s had long and powerful scientific traditions, Italy did not, though it did have great and flourishing mathematicians. Indeed, Fermi established modern physics in his native land. Around him gathered a group of brilliant young physicists including Emilio Segrè (Nobelist 1959). They affectionately but seriously called Fermi the Pope, because he was seen to be infallible. His American colleagues later did the same, and for the same reason. He was rarely wrong and often startlingly prescient.

But coming from a country on the margins of first-class physics can mean no Bohrs or Rutherfords at hand to learn from. The young Fermi therefore went abroad, first to Göttingen. Somehow he didn't impress Born enough, or become part of the dazzling Heisenberg-Pauli-Bohr mix. For the only time in his life, Fermi may have wondered how good he was. Fortunately, he went to Leiden and talked to the Austrian-Dutch theorist Paul Ehrenfest. Ehrenfest (1880–1933) never won a Nobel or made a transcending discovery, but he was highly admired by Einstein and others not given to easy praise. Ehrenfest knew great quality when he saw it, and assured Fermi that he had it.

Fermi lived up to it. His younger colleague Segrè tells how the young Fermi once wrote a textbook, *Introduction to Atomic Physics*, without consulting any reference books, and writing the manuscript with a pencil that had no eraser. It was accepted and printed. This might seem bravado, but was really something else: Fermi's amazing lucidity. This was so true that a word has attached itself like an epithet to his name: Apollonian (as against Dionysian). He was always calm, self-possessed, clear-headed, clear-cut. When even the sanest others might be rattled a bit, Fermi became coolest and most concentrated. A famous story tells that in 1942, when Fermi supervised the first free nuclear reaction under the old stadium at the University of Chicago, some of the eminent scientists there feared a runaway chain reaction or other nasty surprises. Fermi, having started the reaction, made some mental calculations, reinserted the rods used to stop the reaction, and calmly marched everyone off to lunch. In due course, work resumed.

Fermi's self-control was legendary. Dying of cancer at fifty-three, he was visited by an old friend who asked, as one does, how the treatment was going. Fermi, cut off so young, might have indulged some anger or sorrow. He put it scientifically instead, citing the impossible odds against him. That was that.

Fermi won fame for neutron research, for the "Fermi-Dirac statistics" (discovered independently by each in 1926), and for discovering the weak force, a force in nature not known before. Physicists keep paying tribute to him. His name is memorialized in the Fermilab, fermions (a class of particles), the fermi (a unit of length), the Fermi level (measurement of energy in a solid), fermium (a radioactive element), the Fermi Prize, and perhaps others that have missed the eye.

The New Quantum Theory Is Born

No sooner had Planck, Einstein, and Bohr won their Nobel Prizes than their pioneering work was transformed, it seems in a twinkling, into the "old" quantum theory.

For one thing, as Pauli's lament in the epigraph on page 149 shows, quantum physics was becoming chaotic. Was matter particles or waves? In 1923 the American experimenter Arthur Compton at Chicago demonstrated that X-rays behaved like particles, not waves.[64] But that same year came a reversal seemingly arranged by the god of paradoxes. The French theorist Prince Louis de Broglie (the title dates from the eighteenth century; they had been dukes even longer) came up with one of those insights that make quantum physics a headache and delight. If, said de Broglie, light waves can act like particles — he was thinking of Einstein's light-quanta and Compton's confirmation of them — then perhaps particles can act like waves.

Dissatisfaction had also been growing with Bohr's 1913 model of the atom with its quantized electrons orbiting the nucleus. He had modeled the electron orbits on planetary orbits around the sun. Visually striking as this was — it remains the popular logo of the atom — no evidence for any such orbits existed; one imagined them only by analogy to the solar system. To the young Heisenberg this was unacceptable. The old days of mixing Newtonian and quantum rules on an ad hoc basis were to be cast out.

In 1925 Heisenberg, at age twenty-four, did just that: Anything unobservable, and thus imagined or taken on faith, had to go. Now we would rely only on what our instruments reported — our only eyes, after all, into the subatomic depths. To do this, Heisenberg improvised a novel if awkward mathematics, soon clarified as "matrix" by Max Born. The new theory excited but baffled many, but it could at least be applied to the hydrogen atom, the simplest one (only one electron, one proton).

Then six months later, in January 1926, Erwin Schrödinger's equally ambitious theory of wave mechanics appeared. Schrödinger dismissed particles and spoke rather of "matter waves" which surge, meld, and cancel each other, creating "wave packets" or nodes in which electrons both dwell and move and of which they are composed. This was exciting and also confusing. How can an electron spread like waves and still be a measurable entity? Where did these waves originate? Nonetheless, Schrödinger's equation likewise correctly applied to the hydrogen atom. And unlike Heisenberg's newfangled matrix mathematics, Schrödinger elegantly used differential equations, the kind all physicists were trained in.

These two theories were soon shown to be mathematically equivalent, though interpretatively at swords' point. Heisenberg hated Schrödinger's claim that electrons were actual waves: "gruesome" and "the more I ponder it, the more disgusting it seems." Schrödinger hated Heisenberg's use only of measurable observables: "I was discouraged if not repelled." In fact, they were personally friendly, and their disagreement was a war about truth. Heisenberg had really launched a Reformation to banish classical physics root and branch from the atomic realm. In turn, Schrödinger's Counter-Reformation sought to undo the "damn quantum jumps" and return to the "continuum" certainties of classical theory.

Alas for Schrödinger, he had hardly finished publishing his new theory when it was turned on its head. Wave mechanics, said Max Born, was not a description of matter itself as Schrödinger claimed, but only a mathematical way of showing where particles might be found — the "wave" gave a "distribution of probability," an averaging of chances for the appearance of an electron. Schrödinger protested, but instead of displacing the quantum theory, he found himself swallowed up by it. Schrödinger's ambitious theory was reduced to being only an equation — if the most valuable equation — in the enemy theory. Yet if anything holds quantum mechanics together mathematically, it is Schrödinger's jewel.

Oseen, the Nobel physics committee's main authority on theory, was unsympathetic to the new quantum theory. Unsurprisingly, the laureates from 1923 through 1928 were all experimenters — Millikan, Karl Manne Siegbahn, Franck and Hertz, Perrin, Compton and C. T. R. Wilson, Owen Richardson. De Broglie, the first "new" quantum theorist to become a laureate (1929), likely won because his theory had strong experimental support in 1927 from Davisson and G. P. Thomson, who shared the 1937 prize.

The nominations for Heisenberg and Schrödinger had begun arriving by 1926–27 and mounted each year. By 1930 the new quantum revolution could not be ignored. Still the 1930 award went to a non-quantum experimenter, C. V. Raman of India — the first physics laureate from outside the West. For 1931 and 1932 no Nobel Prizes in Physics were awarded; perhaps the committee was too confused or unwilling. By 1933 Heisenberg and Schrödinger had each been nominated twenty-five times. In that year, finally, the committee retroactively awarded the 1932 prize to Heisenberg for theory but also, soothing the experimental faction, for "discovering the allotropic forms of hydrogen," and Dirac and Schrödinger shared the 1933 prize.

Dirac's share of the Nobel Prize in 1933 was a near thing. From 1930 to 1933, Schrödinger and Heisenberg averaged about ten nominations per year; in 1933 Dirac had a bare two nominations.[65] The Nobel evaluator Oseen said that Dirac's work wasn't truly pioneering, that it depended crucially on Heisenberg's. Great figures such as Einstein, Bohr, Planck, Rutherford did not nominate Dirac either. Perhaps Dirac's spectacular prediction of antimatter violated their deep, settled intuitions about matter. If so, Dirac here replayed the role of the young Einstein of the once notorious light-quanta theory. Dirac himself delayed committing himself to the existence of antimatter. Contemporaries like Fermi and Wolfgang Pauli were sceptical. Then in September 1932 Carl Anderson discovered the antielectron. Even so, Dirac shared the 1933 Nobel Prize only because the full plenary session voted for him in a rare exercise of its power.

The next quantum-theorist laureate from the golden 1920s did not arrive until twelve years later, in 1945: Wolfgang Pauli, for his important exclusion principle of 1925.

Third and Fourth Generations: 1950 to Present

From 1950, the Nobel jury caught up with the past. Prizes for work done as much as fifty-three years before went to Max Born, Walther Bothe, and Ernst Ruska from pre-Hitler Germany; John Cockcroft, E. T. S. Walton, and Nevill Mott from Britain; Pavel Cherenkov, Igor Tamm, and Ilya Frank of the USSR; Eugene Wigner, Hans Bethe, John Van Vleck, S. Chandrasekhar, William Fowler, and Frederick Reines, all of the U.S. Some older work became prize-worthy because of new developments, as with Van Vleck and Wigner. And Chandrasekhar, Ruska, and Reines deserved awards long before.

It is unlikely that older work was honored because not enough Nobel-caliber new work was being done. In fact, much new and important work kept arriving. From 1950 to 1980 the forces at work inside the atom — strong, weak, and electromagnetic — were finally explained, and the latter two unified into the electroweak force: a first step, or maybe not, to a grand unified theory. Quantum electro-dynamics (QED) was solved or at least tamed. The baffling diversity of "matter" particles poured out by accelerators from around 1950 was sorted out by the quark theory from the late 1960s, and a stan-dard model of fundamental particles emerged. At the same time, new specialties became more prominent in the Nobel list, such as the astonishing phenomena of superconductivity and superfluidity.

Problems Old and Newly Solved

Rutherford began nuclear physics when he discovered the nucleus in 1909. He shot rays at atoms, expecting (or, cannily, perhaps not) that they would tear right through. In 1936 he reminisced:

> It was quite the most incredible event that has ever happened to me in my life. It was almost as incredible as if you fired a fifteen-inch shell at a piece of tissue paper and it came back and hit you.[66]

At every step since, the nucleus has revealed itself more complex than imagined.

Up to 1932, the atom seemed a simple contraption: in the nucleus was a proton (positively charged), around which swung an electron (negatively charged). By 1932 this family was twice as large and not so simple anymore. It had added the neutron, discovered in 1932 by Chadwick, plus that bizarre entity the antielectron, predicted by Dirac and found by Carl Anderson also in 1932. Plus that more bizarre entity the neutrino, postulated by Pauli in 1932. Plus the meson, predicted by Yukawa in 1936. For something as tiny as the atom, this was a population explosion.

Also in the 1930s, on top of this, came the stunning eruption of nuclear discoveries. The newly invented accelerators and other techniques helped probe the nucleus more subtly and powerfully. In 1934 the Joliot-Curies achieved artifical radioactivity by splitting the nucleus with helium nuclei, called alpha rays. The same year, Fermi found that "slow" neutron bombardment was more effective. (Neutrons are electrically neutral — whence their name — and can thus evade the electrical fences of the nucleus and split it; slow neutrons are more easily absorbed by the nucleus. Fermi "slowed" the neutrons by paraffin or water. He used a goldfish pond in Rome for some of these first experiments.) In 1939, Hahn and Meitner discovered fission.

Not as heroic as the mid-1920s, but heroic enough. Here is a short list of some major developments and prizes in the 1930s:

1931 Urey discovers "heavy hydrogen" isotope deuterium (prize in chemistry, 1934)

1932 Carl Anderson discovers antielectron, or positron (prize 1936)

Chadwick discovers neutron, second particle within nucleus (prize 1935)

Cockcroft and Walton first use accelerator to split nucleus (prize 1951)

E. O. Lawrence invents cyclotron accelerator (prize 1939)

1933 Fermi postulates beta decay, weak force in nucleus (no prize)

1934 Fermi uses "slow" neutrons to bombard nucleus (prize 1938)

Joliot-Curies achieve artificial radioactivity (prize in chemistry, 1935)

1935 Yukawa postulates strong force in nucleus, negotiated by new particle called "meson" (prize 1949)

1936 Carl Anderson discovers meson (no prize)

Eugene Wigner suggests short-range nuclear force binding protons and neutrons (prize 1963)

Niels Bohr creates liquid drop model of nucleus (no prize)

1937 I. I. Rabi achieves precise measuring of nuclear spin and magnetism by using radio-frequency signal to make atoms change their spin orientations (prize 1944)

1938 Hans Bethe describes nuclear reaction that produces energy in the sun (prize 1967)

1939 Otto Hahn bombards uranium nucleus to produce two nuclei with about one-half energy of original (prize in chemistry, 1944)

1940 McMillan, Abelson, and Seaborg, by bombardment, create transuranic element neptunium, then plutonium (prize in chemistry, 1951, for McMillan and Seaborg)

Without this immediate rich background, the nuclear ("atom") bomb could not have been made as quickly as 1945. Making the bomb did not earn or deserve a prize.

Three models of the nucleus have emerged. In 1936–37, Bohr proposed a model of a heavy and thus unstable nucleus: like a liquid drop, the nucleus bulges and may eventually rupture. This was important for the nuclear bomb but too static to explain excited movement up and down the energy levels. In 1948 Maria Goeppert Mayer and J. H. D. Jensen clarified things by independently proposing that, just as electrons cluster in energy levels around the nucleus, so the nucleus contains its own "orbital" system or shell formed by protons and neutrons. These are arranged by a series of numbers so remarkably spaced that they had long been called magic numbers.[67] From 1950 James Rainwater, and later Aage Bohr (Niels's son) and Ben Mottelson, produced a "collective" model, which combined the shell and liquid-drop models. They shared the 1975 Nobel Prize. The historian Kragh has noted that this was the last prize awarded to date in nuclear physics, so that the "classical era" of this field ended around 1960.[68]

By 1958, Rudolf Mössbauer found that if a photon is emitted from the nucleus, the nucleus recoils. By delicate spectroscopic instrumentation, Mössbauer moved two nuclear energy sources toward each other, changing the frequency of the emission, and was thereby able to measure changes in nuclear energy levels. Mössbauer shared the 1961 Nobel Prize with Robert Hofstadter of Stanford who, by measuring how electrons are deflected by the nucleus, fixed the shape, size, and density of the nucleus itself. In one of those astonishing feats now taken for granted, he measured the thickness of the outer surface of the nucleus (it is 2.44×10^{-13} cm) and suggested that the nuclear particles may have entities within them, a prophecy of quarks. All this seems light-years away from the solid, stolid "battleship" nucleus that Rutherford discovered in 1909.

Forces in the Atom

Atoms are so potent with forces that their cohesion can seem surprising. Two positive electrical charges, as is well known, repel each other: protons in the nucleus are positively charged and thus should tear away from each other, destroying the nucleus. Electrons, all negative, similarly should flee each other, disintegrating the atom and all matter, living and otherwise. In a different way, radioactive elements such as uranium can be violently unstable: their nuclei spontaneously decay, releasing intense radioactive particles.

Forces — many physicists now prefer the term "interactions" — inside the atom keep it from tearing apart. Up to 1932, only two forces were known: gravity and electromagnetism. Gravity is of course the most familiar force; its effect is "attractive" only, binding stars to galaxies, planets to suns, apples and moon and humans to earth. But on the subatomic level, its effect seems too slight to count. Electromagnetism is more anciently known — as in magnets, or how rubbed amber creates static. After the work of Faraday and Maxwell, it became clear that electricity and magnetism are aspects of the same phenomenon, and that light is an electromagnetic wave.

The other two forces in nature, first understood from the 1930s, operate within the atom's nucleus. The "strong" force keeps the nucleus inwardly stable, binding its components so tightly together that only the most intense bombardment can split them. The "weak" force, on the other hand, can be visualized somewhat as helping unstable elements get rid of excess energy, as in the spontaneous emission of rays from uranium. Fortunately, the strong force is much more powerful than the weak force. Inside the nucleus, at least, Might (the strong force) makes Right and promotes the general welfare and stability of all atoms.

These forces differ astonishingly in strength and range. The electromagnetic force is stronger than gravity by the staggering factor of 10 followed by forty zeroes. Inside the atom's nucleus, the strong force prevails, 137 times more powerful than the electromagnetic force. The weak force, meanwhile, is a trillion times weaker than the strong force. No one yet has any idea how to fit gravitation to quantum conditions. Indeed gravity, once the only force understood at all, has become the most mysterious of the forces, standing by itself.

The key to these forces — except gravity — was the discovery that nature has two species of particles. The "messenger" or interacting particles, such as the photon, create the forces binding together "building-block" particles, such as electrons and protons. Loosely put, the force carriers are now generally grouped as "bosons" and the bricks of matter as "fermions."

In 1927 Dirac set out to find a quantum version of electromagnetism, but progress came only by 1950. The weak force, suggested by Fermi in 1932, was balked until about 1980. Yukawa's 1935 prediction that the strong force within the nucleus was carried by a particle called the meson was not clarified until 1980.

QED: Maxwell Revisited

This was the first major success in particle physics after World War II. Richard Feynman once said that if anyone remembers the nineteenth century a few hundred years from now, it won't be for ephemeral events such as the American Civil War, but because James Clerk Maxwell lived then. Feynman may be right. Maxwell's theory (1865) showed, among other matters, that electricity and magnetism were aspects of each other, hence "electromagnetism"; showed that all frequencies across the spectrum including light were electromagnetic waves; and established the idea of a field that embraces and originates every particle of energy in it. Clearly enough, then, until a quantum theory of electrodynamics (QED) was available — and was as embracing as a field theory should be — a jagged hole gaped in the center of atomic physics.

But Maxwell's was a classical theory, pitched to the scale of the everyday world. Efforts to find a quantum version of this kept failing. The calculations stubbornly solved out to infinity, as if the electrons had infinite energy, which is plainly impossible. No one could resolve the difficulty, and in the 1930s this seemed to some great physicists — Dirac, Heisenberg, Pauli, Oppenheimer, Landau — a grim sign that quantum physics might never become coherent. Perhaps another revolution in quantum physics was required.[69]

After 1945, when physicists returned to their own work, QED became their first focus. Another Maxwell didn't emerge, but four semi-Maxwells did: Richard Feynman, Julian Schwinger, Shinichiro Tomonaga of Japan, and Freeman Dyson. The first three independently solved the major problems. Dyson indispensably showed the equivalence of these theories.

These new theories were triggered by an experimental finding in 1947 by Willis Lamb of Columbia. Many physicists place him among the very last, like Fermi, able to master the whole of physics as theorist and experimenter.[70] His experiment sent a deep shock through the physics community, since his numbers disagreed with Dirac's 1928 equation about the electron — and Dirac's equation was Scripture. Lamb's "shift" was between two energy levels in the hydrogen spectrum, where the Dirac equation said no shift occurred. Lamb found that Dirac was off by about 0.033 cm^{-1}.[71] This seemingly pedantic point was anything but: it implied that something was wrong with the accepted theory of the electron — and eventually suggested a solution.

A brief excursus can help see why electron theory is so central, and why Lamb's minute correction of Dirac mattered so much and so quickly won him a Nobel Prize — and Nobels later for Feynman, Schwinger, and Tomonaga. In the everyday world we see a stone or potato and know it has certain properties. On the quantum level, physicists must work in reverse, from the properties to the object. Try to imagine identifying something that can be a particle or wave, a point or smear; there is no "object" before us. Fortunately, some of its properties remain constant and can be measured. Thus, if certain measurements — of mass, orbital momentum, spin, magnetism — occur as specified, it must be an electron. Indeed, such measurements are what is *meant* by "electron." Like everything else in quantum physics, the electron packs surprises.

In the early 1990s, it was found that an electron's charge can be fractionalized, which was not fully accountable by any theory (see quantum Hall effect below).

All electrons are exactly identical. Precisely that bare sameness makes the electron measurable with hair-raising precision — in 1912 Robert Millikan pinned down its charge at $4.77 \pm 0.009 \times 10^{-10}$ electrostatic units, or 1.6×10^{-19} C. in current notation. The electron, coming so early, measured so exactly, and so clearly central to the workings of the atom, became the benchmark against which other particles were gauged.

A long string of Nobel Prizes honors the filling out of the portrait of the electron. By "orbiting" the nucleus, electrons become magnetized. In 1920 Otto Stern at Frankfurt first measured the electron's magnetic moment (a wonderful name for a perfume, said the physicist Jeremy Bernstein). Stern found that this magnetism obeyed quantum rules. In ordinary pocket compasses, magnetism can align north or south or any other direction, but under quantum conditions, it can align only one of two ways. Rabi extended this discovery and won the 1944 prize; Felix Bloch and Edward Purcell refined Rabi's approach and shared the 1952 prize.[72] In 1947 Polykarp Kusch, one of Rabi's team at Columbia, showed that Dirac's equation also didn't give a precise enough measurement of the electron's magnetic moment — another important clue for solving QED.[73]

But electrons also spin around themselves millions of times a second (imagine a furiously spinning top). "Spin" of this kind, intrinsic angular momentum, was discovered in 1925 by two young Dutch physicists, Samuel Goudsmit and George Uhlenbeck — who absolutely should have won a Nobel Prize but did not. An electron spins as it "orbits" the nucleus. Spin is always quantized: an electron's spin occurs only at fixed energy levels, expressed as multiples of rotational movement, by half-units: a particle's spin can be 1/2 or 3/2 or 1 or 0, and so on. But how can rotation be so neatly chopped up if the electron can also be a spreading wave, a fanned-out set of probabilities? Making sense of these confusions became urgent.

All this was known by the late 1920s. In 1928 Dirac did his amazing juggling act of mathematical virtuosity and physical intuition, with inimitable elegance. The Dirac equation brought together everything then known about the electron: its magnetic moment, its mass and charge and spin, its wave behavior, how special relativity was involved. It even explained the "fine structure" (lines close-spaced on the spectrum, reflecting transitions in energy levels). "Spin" and the rest weren't merely interesting phenomena out there, but now integral fingerprints of the electron. Everything seemed in place for a true quantum electrodynamic theory — except that the calculations kept solving out as infinities and stalling progress.

One large problem was the so-called self-energy of the electron considered as a point, a sober way of saying that the electron exists in a sea of virtual particles.[74] Under certain conditions, Dirac said in 1927, an infinite number of photons can be created and emitted. A month later, Heisenberg's uncertainty principle arrived, and opened this Pandora's box in reality. Where there is undetected matter, according to the uncertainty principle, there can also be undetected energy: particles can be so short-lived that they escape being observed or measured. Thus photons or electrons swarming energetically can number in the trillions, though unseen.

But now in 1947 Lamb had pinned more precise numbers to the entire problem. This made "renormalizing" possible. The solution, in broad, was to separate the electron's original self-energy from the virtual one it becomes swathed in, thus turning it "normal" again. Introducing a cutoff got rid of the infinities in the calculations while preserving the finite part. Lamb gave them the tiny handle they needed. Feynman invented a "space-time path" expressed in probabilities which explained the Lamb shift. Schwinger used a relativistic way of calculating the magnetic moments of electrons, using Kusch's new measurements, without flushing up the infinities.[75]

Once renormalized, QED's predictions proved accurate to an astonishing ten or eleven decimal places. It has been called the most successful precise theory in the history of physics. But was the "renormalizing" mainly a formalist sleight of hand? Feynman joked, or maybe not, that he and his colleagues had only "swept the problems under the rug." Dyson said that the QED theories of Feynman and Schwinger "were in essence nothing more than clarifications" of Dirac's 1928 equation; they left Dirac's basic concepts untouched "and added only new mathematical tricks."[76] Dirac remained suspicious. In 1984, the year he died, he declared that QED is not based on strict mathematics, but is "rather a set of rules."[77] For Dirac, this was a damning judgment.

Niels Bohr was also distrustful. Yuval Ne'eman, the Israeli particle physicist, said that Feynman, Schwinger, and Tomonaga could have won their prize many years before, but Bohr's negative attitude to renormalizing deterred the Nobel committee. Only after Bohr's death in 1962 did the prize arrive, in 1965.[78]

After his experiment, Lamb remembered, he woke the next day, thought about what he had done, and decided it was of Nobel quality. He was right. He shared the physics prize in 1955 with Polykarp Kusch.[79]

When Feynman, Schwinger, and Tomonaga shared the 1965 prize, Freeman Dyson was not included. He had shown that the three theories gave fundamentally the same results. The Nobel committee either thought this not crucial or else, since only three can share a prize, Dyson was odd man out. But the physicist Silvan Schweber argues that Dyson should have shared the Nobel Prize.

> Without minimizing in any way Tomonaga's accomplishments . . . the developments in the period 1947–50 would not have been substantially different without him, yet one cannot conceive of the subsequent developments without Dyson.[80]

The Strong Force

In 1929 the young Heisenberg visited Japan, and an even younger physicist named Hideki Yukawa heard him lecture. Yukawa was then twenty-two, one of a small group of Japanese physicists who in a few years brought that country from a backwater of physics into the front rank, in an extraordinary bootstrap operation.

In 1932 Heisenberg pictured the strong force as a messenger particle shuttling between proton and neutron, binding these nuclear particles together, like a ball thrown back and forth between players too swiftly to see. But no experimental evidence existed for any such strong force or messenger particles. Yukawa read Heisenberg's paper and was inspired, and by Fermi as well (see "weak force" below). He decided that the messenger particle must be large enough to influence the massive protons and neutrons, but also small and swift enough to bind them together — about ten times smaller than a proton and two hundred times larger than an electron, hence a "middle" or intermediate particle. It was finally named the meson, from Greek *mesos*, middle (Yukawa wanted to call it the U particle; Oppenheimer, mercifully ignored, suggested the "yukon").[81]

No particle of such size was known. Yukawa thought it might be found in the intense cosmic rays. "In the best of all possible worlds," wrote Jeremy Bernstein, "one might imagine that Yukawa's paper would have been widely read and . . . inspired a search in cosmic rays for his meson." Nothing like that happened. In 1936 the first meson was found "by accident" by Carl Anderson (the discoverer of the antielectron, also "by accident"!) who was investigating cosmic rays.[82]

For the next ten years — and with the war intervening — this meson was thought to confirm Yukawa's strong force theory. But experiments during World War II proved that Anderson's particular meson didn't interact with the nucleus. These experiments, amazingly, had been done in wartime Rome, with whatever equipment could be scrounged on the black market. The experimenters were O. Piccioni, M. Conversi, and E. Pancini, who published their findings in 1947.[83] But no prize for their important experiments — no one ever wins for proving wrong an unconfirmed theory.

Yukawa's idea was saved in 1947, when a team headed by Cecil Powell of Britain, using refined photographic emulsions, found another meson, the pi-meson. This truly was Yukawa's meson. Anderson's wrong one was renamed the mu-meson (pi-meson is now abbreviated to pion, mu-meson to muon). With this confirmation, Yukawa won the Nobel Prize in 1949, and Powell in 1950.[84]

When the quark theory emerged in the 1970s, the strong force would be seen in terms of the theory called quantum chromodynamics.

The Weak Force

Meanwhile, in 1933–34 Fermi proposed a theory of the weak force, to explain the beta rays of radioactivity.[85] It was his major triumph as a theoretical physicist. Because beta rays emitted by atoms contained electrons, many assumed that electrons must be part of the nucleus. Where else could they have come from? Fermi firmly disagreed: "Before beta emission happens, electrons do not exist in the nucleus; they acquire their existence just when they are emitted." Electrons were not originally in the nucleus because in "every transition from neutron to proton, an electron is created along with a neutrino."[86]

This was the Fermi style, lucidly explaining startling facts, and pragmatically insisting there was no point in asking where the electrons were before; they were nowhere.

It took fifty more years to understand what Fermi had started. The long effort to explain the weak force — from 1934 to 1983 — should dispel romantic notions that physics is usually done by geniuses in a blinding flash of inspiration. Between 1950 and 1972, Pais records, writings on the weak force included a thousand experimental articles, thirty-five hundred theoretical articles, and a hundred reviews, by authors from fifty countries.[87]

Fermi's theory also predicted that a "neutrino" was created along with the electron. The neutrino is a vivid example of how physicists mostly swim from one perplexity to another in hopes of occasionally finding a landing place. In 1931 Wolfgang Pauli thought up the neutrino to account for why energy was missing from the nucleus in beta decay. Better to posit an unknown particle than to give up the great law of the conservation of energy, as even Bohr was considering, as a way out of the puzzle.

Fermi, following Pauli, adopted the neutrino to explain where the extra energy went, also to keep the bank balance straight. Fermi invented the name. Pauli had called his gambit simply the "neutron"; but after Chadwick found a different neutron in 1932, Fermi renamed Pauli's creature the neutrino, or "little neutron" in Italian. The neutrino made great sense — except that this crucial proof of the weak force didn't exist outside theorists' imaginations. It is probably the most elusive particle known in the universe. It interacts so weakly with other matter that a billion billions of them constantly drift through the earth colliding with absolutely nothing at all, as if the earth simply weren't there.[88] This is because it has no "rest" mass or charge, though some recent experiments imply differently, and it travels forever at or near the speed of light, making it uncapturable by any energy, which would have to travel faster than light.

Only in 1956 did the Americans Frederick Reines and Clyde Cowan definitely capture the first one. They immediately sent a congratulatory telegram to Pauli, who had started it all twenty-five years before.[89]

In 1962 the American experimenters Lederman, Schwartz, and Steinberger found a second kind of neutrino by using ten tons of scrap battleship metal as forty-foot-thick buffers; for this and other work, Lederman and team shared the Nobel Prize in 1988. Their neutrino was called the electron neutrino. That of Reines-Cowan became the muon neutrino. Reines had to wait until 1995 for his prize, although he and Cowan had been the first to find any neutrino. Cowan unfortunately had died by then.

Electroweak: The First Unified Theory — and Symmetry

Grand unified theories, like the one Einstein labored on vainly for thirty years, are the Holy Grails of physicists. The electroweak, which joined the weak and electromagnetic forces, was the first successful step in that direction. The challenge in any unified theory is to meld things that seem unlike or even opposed. The electromagnetic force is so long-range it can cross the universe, and fades slowly; the weak force is so short-range that it stretches only across the atom's tiny nucleus, and extinguishes almost faster than numbers can count.[90] Nonetheless, by the 1970s the weak force and electromagnetic force at high energies were unified. They turned out to be two aspects of a single force, and thus could properly be explained only in terms of each other. This first unified quantum theory won a shared Nobel Prize in 1979 for Sheldon Glashow and Steven Weinberg of Harvard, and Abdus Salam of Pakistan but working in London. In 1984 two experimenters, Carlo Rubbia and Simon van der Meer, shared a prize for finding the evidence only the year before. But much else and many others made the unification possible, though few won Nobels for it.

This unified theory was a triumph for symmetry principles, a key concept of the last thirty years. A mirror's reflection is an obvious example: it reverses left and right, as when one holds a page up to the mirror, but "conserves" the same configurations despite the transformations. The transformations are thus equivalent to one another. When this is violated — because of magnetism, electrical influence, vibrational disturbance, or impact from another particle — physicists say the symmetry is "broken." A deviation from a supposed original symmetry has occurred. All existing matter, the theory goes, exists in one or other broken symmetry, but in an orderly way. Nature, so to say, enforces an asymmetrical choice. The physicist must then discover what force-field causes this. If unity once existed, maybe theories can reveal such unity in their equations — at least, so hope the grand unifiers.

The original symmetry is still there, but "hidden" by the asymmetric order that makes the once single force now look like two different and separate forces — as in the weak and the electromagnetic force. Sheldon Glashow around 1960, and then Steven Weinberg and Abdus Salam independently in 1967–68 predicted that the "spontaneous breaking" of the symmetry would produce two heavy "messenger" particles, called W and Z bosons. But how to combine massive bosons with the massless photon of electromagnetism in the weak force?

Once more the old bugbear of infinities, as in QED, practically killed the idea from 1967 until 1971. A very odd situation developed. As Crease and Mann put it:

> Weinberg and Salam asked the [physics] community to believe that the weak interactions were based on a Yang-Mills symmetry that had never been seen; that the force was carried by three vector bosons that had never been observed; that these bosons formed a family with the photon, and that the whole business could in some way be made renormalizable.[91]

Yet it all finally worked. A graduate student in Holland, Gerardus 't Hooft, showed how to renormalize the theory. As one physicist put it, "'t Hooft's kiss transformed Weinberg's frog into an enchanted prince."[92] The W and Z were eventually found by experiments in 1983. But five years before the confirming evidence was on hand, Salam, Weinberg, and Glashow had shared the 1979 prize for the electroweak theory. 'T Hooft and his professor-collaborator Martinus J. G. Veltman shared the 1999 prize.

The Nobel judges do not usually pass out medals before the confirming evidence is in. But the omens were very promising. The most important came in 1956: the discovery of "parity violation," achieved by the Chinese-American theorists Chen Ning Yang and Tsung-Dao Lee. In physics, one kind of parity refers to the mirror phenomena mentioned earlier. As a mirror treats left and right as interchangeable, so does nature. Parity is therefore "conserved." But in 1956, Lee and Yang found that parity conservation in the weak force had never been proved. Physicists had simply taken it as self-evident.[93] Experiments showed that parity was indeed violated in the weak force. Feynman had bet fifty to one against them, and Pauli was flabbergasted: "I cannot believe that God is a weak left-hander."[94] Lee and Yang shared the Nobel Prize for 1957. All the experimenters confirming the Lee-Yang prediction were ignored by the Nobel judges.[95] Six years later, in 1963, the Americans James Cronin and Val Fitch discovered other parity violations,[96] and shared the 1980 Nobel Prize.

Within a decade or so, the weak and electromagnetic forces were better understood: at low energies they acted differently, but at high energies they acted alike — and thus could be expected to use the same sort of interacting particles. Rubbia and team found these in 1983, after several near misses, much squabbling, and many invaluable theoretical leads, as we shall see.

Matter Particles: Accelerators and Other Weapons

From 1950, ultra-high-energy equipment joined the attack, and the accelerator age began in earnest, resulting in the discovery of a spate of new particles. One discovery can bring insight; a flood of them can bring too much glare. That happened now as new particles poured out in the hundreds — a "zoo," some called it. Sorting them out and sifting them down to three basic sorts has been the achievement of the quark theory. A "standard model" of all particles has also emerged.

Into the 1930s, great coups were still managed with casually makeshift equipment — some galvanometers, coils of wire, ammeters and voltmeters, storage batteries for power. But probing ever smaller particles or antimatter, virtual photons and the rest, requires energies that can smash particles together at controlled but violent speeds — energies that must equal or surpass the mass of the target particle.

In 1932 the first working accelerator was designed by the British experimenters Cockcroft and Walton (protégés of Rutherford, naturally). Their device accelerated hydrogen nuclei (protons) through an electric field of half a million volts, converting lithium and hydrogen into helium. They had split the atom by a high-energy device for the first time.[97] A few months later, at Berkeley, Ernest O. Lawrence's cyclotron — circular rather than straight-line — went into action. His first model was about four inches wide. Not long after, its magnet weighed eighty tons. He kept building new models, always larger and heavier. The results were spectacular in voltage and honors. Lawrence won his Nobel Prize in 1939; though with clear priority, Cockcroft and Walton had to wait until 1951.

Since then, accelerators have become fearfully expensive race-tracks, circular or straight — in 1983, Fermilab's ring was four miles in circumference — crammed with thousands of detectors, electronic, photographic, and otherwise, to record every instant of every experiment.[98]

The American Nobelist Leon Lederman, reviewing his unusually wide-ranging experimental career, gives a vivid sense of this:

> My own experimental work brought me to such accelerators as the Nevis Synchrocyclotron; the Cosmotron and Alternate Gradient Synchrotron at the Brookhaven National Laboratory; the Berkeley Bevatron and the Princeton-Penn Synchrotron; the SC, Proton Synchrotron and Intersecting Storage Ring machines at CERN; the Fermilab 400 GeV accelerator; and the electron-positron collider Cornell Electron Storage Rings at Cornell.

He also, of course, had to learn to use the many kinds of detectors involved: he

> ... began with Wilson cloud chambers, paused at photographic nuclear emulsions, exploited the advances of the diffusion cloud chamber, graduated to small arrays of scintillation counters, then spark chambers, lead-glass high-resolution Cerenkov counters, scintillation hodoscopes and eventually the increasingly complex arrays of multiwire proportional chamber, ring imaging and scintillators.[99]

Since Lawrence and Cockcroft and Walton, no other Nobels have been awarded for accelerator design. Yet six prizes have been bestowed on detector inventions, perhaps because detectors are designed by detectable individuals, while giant new accelerators just grow: Brookhaven near New York, Dubna in Russia, CERN near Geneva. By 1952 the Brookhaven machine reached more than three billion volts; in the 1980s the trillion-volt level was first reached by the Tevatron at Fermilab.

Early accelerators hurled a moving particle against a stationary one. But just as a head-on collision between two speeding cars smashes things apart more violently than when only one is moving, so with particles. The "collider" (or "storage-ring accelerator"), dominant since the 1960s, works on this principle. Protons, neutrinos, electrons, or any other particles usable as bullets are propelled against particles moving toward them at furious speeds.

Detectors at first were like other tabletop equipment. In 1913 Hans Geiger in Rutherford's lab, tired of counting scintillations by eye, invented his famous counter (no Nobel). In 1911 C. T. R. Wilson of Britain brought in the cloud chamber, a far better detector; ions speeding through a vaporous medium leave a trail that can be photographed. In 1927 Wilson shared the Nobel Prize.

For decades the cloud chamber was the mainstay of important experiments. P. M. S. Blackett of Britain improved it in 1932, and was cited partly for this in his 1948 Nobel Prize. "The most original and magnificent instrument in the history of research," Rutherford called it. But it was tricky to handle. "More biological than physical," said Lederman, "subject to poisons, track distortions"; Blackett said that "to make it work you had to spit on the wire on some Friday evening in Lent."[100]

High energies finally made it obsolete. Light traverses twelve inches in a billionth of a second, and can speed by a proton in less than a billionth of a billionth of a second. The sheer number of collisions that can take place is flabbergasting: one million per second is not unusual. All must be recorded, to be scanned by computers and the human eye.

In 1952 came the bubble chamber, soon honored with two separate and unshared Nobel Prizes. Donald Glaser of Michigan took the 1960 Nobel for the original design: in it, particles moving through hot ether under pressure leave a bubble trail. Luis Alvarez of Berkeley, a cyclotron veteran under Lawrence, became the 1968 Nobelist for greatly improving and enlarging the bubble chamber. Only ten years after Glaser's first model, the bubble chamber's volume swelled a million times. Ten years after that, it went up twelve million times at the CERN laboratory in the high-energy site named Gargamelle after Gargantua's mother.[101] In 1958 the Russian Pavel Cherenkov shared a Nobel, partly for designing an accurate high-speed particle counter. In the 1960s Georges Charpak of France invented the "wire chamber" detector, which became the detector of choice in experiments from 1970. A particle speeding through the chamber ionizes a gas which moves to wires connected to a computer system. The wire detector allows the computer to record and sift very accurately. Charpak's detector was crucial in finding the W and Z bosons of the electroweak theory. Charpak won the Nobel Prize, unshared, in 1992.

Quarks: Reclassifying Everything

The several hundred new particles churned out by the new accelerators ("particle factories") from the 1950s were quickly extinguished.[102] But even in their brief life spans, they showed quite varying properties. This allowed them to be grouped in ad hoc categories — hyperons, k-mesons, cascade particles, sigmas positive and negative, xis. Names were sometimes whimsically or desperately pasted on. For example, certain particles produced by the strong nuclear force strangely decayed a billion times slower than expected,[103] so they were simply called "strange," later a quark category.

Clearly, some grand new classificatory principle was needed akin to Mendeleev's periodic chart of the elements in the mid-nineteenth century. But what in these particles corresponded to Mendeleev's "elements"? A successful theory would be sure to harvest many Nobel Prizes.

The leader here was the American theorist Murray Gell-Mann. At twenty-four, in 1953, he developed a concept to explain "strangeness." In 1961 he began rearranging the whole spendthrift number of particles in terms of "internal symmetry." Yuval Ne'eman of Israel independently discovered the same scheme at the same time. Gell-Mann labeled his classification scheme the Eightfold Way, after one of Buddha's sayings.[104] Gell-Mann and Ne'eman predicted the omega-minus particle, previously unknown but identified in 1964 at Brookhaven Laboratory by a team of more than thirty physicists when one photograph out of 100,000 was found to contain it. No experimenter won a Nobel Prize for this discovery. With improved accelerators in 1984, the same experiment produced not one but 100,000 photographs of the omega-minus.[105]

Gell-Mann won the 1969 prize. Ne'eman was ignored.

In 1964 came quarks, introduced independently by Gell-Mann and George Zweig. Nature is (one hopes) simple. The quark theory has a similar thrust. It proposes that the many hundreds of particles making up the building blocks of matter sift down to just two fundamental particles — those like electrons, which have no internal structure, and those like protons, which have an internal structure of quarks. Neither Gell-Mann nor Zweig won a prize for quarks. Gell-Mann had just been honored, and the Nobel jury has not yet recognized Zweig's contribution as deserving enough.

Gell-Mann has always been playful with terminology, which is why his improvement on the Eightfold Way is called quarks. (Zweig called them aces.) Gell-Mann borrowed his term from Joyce's *Finnegans Wake* — indeed, *Finnegans Wake,* with its endlessly interbreeding puns, could have supplied much of the terminology of quantum physics if Gell-Mann had only been around in 1926 and seen Joyce's early drafts. Some of the terms that Gell-Mann and other quark theorists went on to invent — "flavors," "colors," "charm," "beauty" — are more charming and flavorful than helpful.

Quarks have never been individually seen. The very idea of a free quark seems self-contradictory. A paradoxical effect — the technical term is "asymptotic freedom" — keeps them imprisoned: the harder quarks strain to separate from each other, the less chance they have of doing so. It is a game that quarks can never win. The farther apart they get, the more energy they need to break free. But, as the energy stretches to breaking, it creates a pair of quarks and their antiquark partners; four quarks exist where one did before.

Bizarre as all this sounds and is, experiments proved that "pointlike" forces are inside the proton. Quarks also pair off. If there is an "up" quark, there has to be a "down." If a "charm" quark, then a "strange." If a "bottom" quark, then a "top." These names denote nothing physical. The full theory can seem like the medieval scheme of epicycles, with intricacies embroidered on intricacies.[106] There are "generations" or families of quarks, depending on the electric charge, how many protons and neutrons the nucleus contains, and the quark's heaviness.

The quark theory, as noted, also radically redescribed the strong force. Instead of Yukawa's meson, which glued proton and neutron together, there are now eight different kinds of "gluons" which (no surprise) glue the quarks together. In quark-talk, gluons have "color." This involves the esoteric concept that while other "messenger" particles like photons do not take on the qualities of the particles they mediate, the gluons do. The full explication of this intricate notion is contained in the quantum chromodynamics theory (QCD), modeled on QED. But there are dissenters here.[107]

The quark theory has shown predictive power. Five quarks have been confirmed, and probably a sixth as well. This is crucial since nature, according to quark theory, demands a pairing-off: there must a sixth or "top" quark to balance the fifth or "bottom" one. In 1994 a Fermilab team of 439 physicists found results that may turn out to be the top quark. It will have been quite a feat: the top quark's life span is a trillionth of a trillionth of a second.

Whoever wins the Nobel Prize for the top quark may be the last, unless, of course, more quarks or "flavors" are found. Physicists are divided about this.[108] There is a certain dissatisfied feeling that the "standard model" is too complicated, unbalanced, and even messy. Eighteen quarks — or thirty-six when one includes the antiquarks. Twelve leptons — particles that make up ordinary matter, such as electrons. Forces — weak, strong or nuclear, electromagnetic — transmitted by three vector bosons, the photon, and eight gluons. All this seems a bit untidy (nature should be simple). A team in 1995 found possible evidence of particles within quarks. In 1997 tantalizing reports came that "leptoquarks" might have been found. If so, this would be the first particle that was both a "matter" particle and a "messenger" particle — a hermaphroditic particle. If true, it might make the existing quark theory and the "standard model" almost instantly obsolete.

The quark theory has prospered in Stockholm — but not for theorists. Gell-Mann did not win in 1969 for quarks, which still were mainly seen as a mathematical device rather than a physical truth. A trail of other theorists have been passed over by the Nobel jury.[109]

Experimenters have done much better, with several awards, all to Americans. Samuel Ting at Brookhaven and Burton Richter at Stanford shared the 1976 Nobel for independently discovering the J/psi particle, one of the "charm" quarks. Leon Lederman shared the 1988 Nobel partly because he led a team at Fermilab that found a second neutrino in 1962. The 1990 prize was shared by Jerome Friedman, Henry Kendall, and Richard Taylor for experiments in 1967–73 verifying "pointlike" entities inside the nucleus, an important support for the quark theory.

Superconductivity, Superfluidity

Starting about 1950, the new field of condensed-matter physics has won several prizes. In contrast to particles, the focus here is on matter in the form of gas, liquid, amorphous solids, and plasma, and how they change into each other especially under the effect of extreme low temperatures.

Up to 1940 this was a sideshow, messy, even undignified. Pauli — who initiated the field in 1926 under its older name of solid-state physics — called it "dirt physics." This has changed dramatically in the last few decades; low-temperature physics is now a leading edge of physics, and the Nobels reflect this.

Consider that helium, the second simplest element, contains only 2 protons, 2 electrons, and 2 neutrons, and even a "massive" element like uranium has only 92 protons and 146 neutrons. But condensed matter casually includes entities that typically contain ten sextillion atoms or molecules. States of matter unknown before to particle physics have been revealed that — given the size of the phenomena studied — may even make possible a first quantum theory of both the unimaginably tiny and the everyday scale.

Condensed-matter physics has two singular branches. In the first, superconductivity, electrical resistance drops radically as low temperatures approach absolute zero. Even metal, freed of electrical resistance, can defy gravity and floats in the air. The experimenter who started all this was Heike Kamerlingh Onnes, a professor at Leiden in Holland. Kamerlingh Onnes made his breakthrough experiment in 1908 when he was fifty-three. A stout man with a bald head, walrus mustache, rosy cheeks, and a twinkle, he looked like a prosperous brewer. His laboratory was indeed jokingly called a brewery, with its tanks and pumps and cooling pipes and refrigeration.

He set out to push the temperature down the scale as far as possible toward absolute zero on the Kelvin scale. Centigrade and Fahrenheit can't measure this as conveniently, since their zero is perched midway between hot and cold. In the Kelvin scale, there is nothing below zero — you can only measure upwards. In 1908 Kamerlingh Onnes got down to 1.7 K, and became the first to liquefy helium. In 1909 he reached 1.38 K, and the next year 1.04 K. By 1999 experiments had reached 170 billionths of a degree above absolute zero.

In 1911 he discovered superconductivity when the electrical resistance of a wire of mercury, lead, and tin almost completely vanished. In 1913 he won a Nobel Prize. No existing theory could explain or had predicted his discovery; there were no landmarks. It clearly had no place in classical thermodynamics, and quantum theory offered no help at that time. In prequantum theories, metals that were good conductors of electricity were said to contain "free" electrons that carried the electrical charge. This had to be rethought in 1925, when Pauli's exclusion principle completely re-explained the arrangement of electrons in an atom. In his "housing plan," as Pauli called it, electrons must first fill up the lower energy levels before they can jump to a higher level. At very low temperatures, the lowest energy levels are filled, and the temperature is too low to energize any jumping to higher levels. The electrons that have not found a spot on an energy level are a "people without a homeland," as Arnold Sommerfeld vividly put it in 1927.[110] What happens to them?

Enter now the American theorist John Bardeen, the two-time laureate whose name is scarcely known to the public. He shared his first Nobel for the transistor, the first popular success of solid-state physics. In 1945, just out of the war, Bardeen hired on at Bell Telephone Laboratory. Bardeen, William Shockley, and Walter Brattain hoped to find a replacement for the vacuum tube — the old radio tube — that could more efficiently take in a weak signal and magnify it. Silicon, of which a transistor is made, is part of the solid-state family: it acts like an insulator at low temperatures and like a good conductor at high temperatures — but, neither one nor the other, it is thus a "semiconductor." In 1947 the transistor opened the floodgates to electronics miniaturization. In 1954 the computer industry started using silicon; in 1985, for the first time, one million components were printed on a single chip. Bardeen and his collaborators shared the Nobel Prize for 1956.[111]

By then Bardeen, having moved to the University of Illinois, was working on superconductivity with two other collaborators, Leon Cooper, a postdoc, and Robert Schrieffer, a graduate student. In its most simplified form, the Bardeen-Cooper-Schrieffer theory (BCS) starts with a latticelike structure, whose regularity makes analysis easier, as early X-ray researchers like Laue and the Braggs found out. Imagine further that the lattice, of some metal, is held together by atoms at each crossbar, but that the atoms have each lost one electron. Those free electrons, wandering about, compose a gas.

Since the lattice is positively charged and the electrons negatively, a tugging results, making the lattice vibrate, and this in turn affects other electrons — but always in pairs. This was Leon Cooper's discovery: superconductivity is accomplished not by single electrons but by these bound pairs. Now, when current is applied, these pairs begin to march in the current's direction, with their momentum overcoming all blockage.[112] The BCS theory was published in 1957; in 1972 Bardeen and Cooper and Schrieffer shared the Nobel Prize. Superconducting magnets soon appeared, on which the medical technique of MRI (magnetic resonance imaging) depends. So did the ambitious but canceled plan to build the $6 billion high-energy SSC, whose first *S* put superconducting right in front: the Superconducting Supercollider.

In the 1960s, Philip Anderson of Bell Labs and the British theorist Nevill Mott showed that free electrons in amorphous solids — matter that has a random arrangement of atoms; ordinary glass is a surprising example — can have fixed positions. They shared the 1977 Nobel Prize for opening up the field of magnetic and disordered solid-state systems. Their colaureate was John Van Vleck, an early theorist in this area.

Superfluidity, the other astonishing branch of condensed-matter physics, was discovered only in 1938, by the Russian experimenter Pyotr Kapitsa. Kapitsa had left Russia to become one of Rutherford's most prized assistants in the 1920s and 1930s. The Soviet government, anxious to have him back to build up Soviet physics, offered him a high position; to entice him further, they even offered to buy his Cambridge laboratory, lock stock and barrel, and ship it to Moscow. In 1935 Kapitsa accepted and returned — and was never allowed to leave.

In 1938 Kapitsa was trying to understand the results of some recent Dutch experiments; the Dutch long dominated low-temperature physics. Cooling liquid helium produced something strange. At 4.2 K, helium gas turned, as expected, into a boiling, seething liquid. Lower down, however, the boiling stopped, in a bizarre way: the helium became two different liquids at the same time, provisionally called Helium I over 2.2 K, and Helium II under 2.2 K. Another strange result: Helium II could conduct heat several hundred times better than the best metal conductors, such as copper.

Repeating the Dutch experiment, Kapitsa discovered superfluidity. He found that liquid helium, cooled almost to absolute zero and thus free of all friction, spontaneously slid up straight walls and moves effortlessly between what seemed impenetrably sealed layers. Clearly the helium had lost all viscosity — a liquid's inner resistance to movement (honey is famously viscous). Liquid helium has a viscosity only one ten-thousandth that of hydrogen gas. Yet, measured in the ordinary way, the helium's viscosity seemed normal.

The greatest theoretical physicist then in the USSR, and one of the greatest in the world, was Lev Landau. In the early 1930s he had studied with Bohr, Heisenberg, and Pauli, then returned to Kharkov to build a great school of physics. In 1937 Kapitsa brought him to Moscow. But under Stalin, the abnormal was the normal: in 1938 Landau was arrested as a German spy and spent a year in prison; Kapitsa protested directly to Stalin, and his prestige finally managed to get Landau released.[113] In 1945, after the U.S. developed the first atom bomb, Stalin placed Kapitsa himself under house arrest for eight years.

Out of prison, Landau took up the Helium II puzzle. The usual explanation for the two-helium mystery was that some atoms had a different quantum state than the rest and these composed Helium II. Landau more radically theorized that Helium I and II were the same. When heat was added, thermal energy passed through the cooled liquid helium in the form of quantum sound waves called "phonons," in analogy to the photons of electromagnetism, the oscillations that carry light. There are also "rotons," quantum rotation waves. Experiments below 1 K confirmed Landau's theory as the first adequate if partial explanation of superfluidity. It accounted for some known results, helped explain the viscosity puzzle, and predicted two different sound waves, one the conventional kind, the other a "temperature" wave.[114]

Landau won the 1962 Nobel Prize for his superfluidity theory, but never reached Stockholm. Earlier that same year he was critically injured in an automobile accident; he lived six more years, unable to work, and died in 1968, aged sixty-one. Kapitsa became a Nobel laureate in 1978 for his superfluidity discovery. David Lee, Douglas Osheroff, and Robert Richardson shared the 1996 prize for showing in 1971 that the helium isotope III had three distinct phases (of normal to superfluid) at 0.0027 K, 0.0021 K, and 0.0018 K.

In 1957 Richard Feynman beautifully described the fascination that superconductivity and superfluidity presented. They were "like two cities under siege . . . completely surrounded by knowledge, although they themselves remained isolated and unassailable."[115] Feynman himself soon admitted defeat. The seemingly simple question of how liquids, solids, and gases change into each other became unfathomably complex at very low temperatures. Two American theorists have made progress and won Nobel Prizes: Lars Onsager (chemistry, 1968) and Kenneth Wilson (physics, 1982).[116]

Experimenters in the field have also won prizes for work investigating three main phenomena. Tunneling is a startling effect in which a current passes phantomlike through a barrier because (per quantum mechanics) one can never predict exactly where an individual electron is. In practice, this means that at least some particles will appear on the other side of the barrier. In 1960 Ivar Giaever, working at a GE laboratory, found that superconducting electrons had enough extra energy to accomplish such tunneling. Around 1965 the Japanese physicist Leo Esaki, of IBM, demonstrated that a similar phenomenon existed with semiconducting "superlattices" — several lattices comprising one crystal. In 1962 the Welsh physicist Brian Josephson went further: he found that as the particles tunnel, they leave a magnetic trace which can be recorded and measured. The three men shared the 1973 prize.

Their work made possible the scanning tunneling microscope, which enables seeing surfaces one atom at a time, even down to a hundredth of an atom. Developed by Heinrich Rohrer and Gerd Binnig of IBM Zurich in 1978, it won them the Nobel Prize for 1986. The same laboratory also produced the 1987 physics colaureates Georg Bednorz and K. A. Müller. Instead of working down toward absolute zero, they worked back up: how far up the Kelvin scale from zero can one go before superconductivity disappears? This has immense consequences in the search for resistance-free "room-temperature" energy. They got near 35 K, something never done before, though since surpassed.[117]

The second phenomenon explored by experimenters is the quantum Hall effect, named after its American discoverer in 1879 and which, among other things, helps measure electrical resistance in semiconductors. In 1980 Klaus von Klitzing did an experiment with a silicon transistor, in which electrons were forced to move in two dimensions. Powerful magnetic fields were applied, and the temperature was lowered almost to absolute zero. The resistance dropped, then leveled off, then dropped again and leveled, and so on. The measurements exactly fitted the ratio of Planck's constant to the square of the electron's charge. Klitzing had found a precise new constant for electrical resistance. This was the "integral" Hall effect. But then a "fractionalized" quantum Hall effect was found by Horst Störmer, Daniel Tsui, and Robert Laughlin and won them the 1998 prize. Here matter behaved as never seen before: electrons became quantized as in Klitzing's experiment — but also as if their charge were only one-third or some other fraction of their normal charge. Quarks are fractionated this way, and speculation has arisen as to whether this discovery will eventually revise the current understanding of quarks, and the "standard model" of atomic particles with it.

Another area here involves "liquid crystals." Pierre de Gennes of France won the 1991 prize for explaining how molecules alter when about to solidify — among other things, their optical properties alter. He also elucidated how molten polymers can possibly flow. They do so, in his image, like slithering snakes.

Travails of Winning the Physics Prize

On Fast and Long-Delayed Prizes

Counting from when Nobel Prize–winning work was done to the year the physics prize was awarded — omitting work done before 1900 — among the shortest delays have been:

years	laureate	work	prize
1	Lee, Yang	1956	1957
	Rubbia, van der Meer	1983	1984
2	von Laue	1912	1914
	Karl M. Siegbahn	1922	1924
	Raman	1928	1930
	Richter, Ting	1974	1976
3	W. H. and W. L. Bragg	1912	1915
	Chadwick	1932	1935
	Powell	1947	1950
	Mössbauer	1958	1961
4	Compton	1923	1927
	Carl Anderson	1932	1936

years	laureate	work	prize
	Fermi	1934	1938
	Chamberlain, Segrè	1955	1959
5	Gell-Mann	1964	1969
	von Klitzing	1980	1985
	Binnig, Rohrer	1981	1986

Among the longest delays have been:

years	laureate	work	prize
17	Einstein	1905	1922, for 1921
19	Planck	1900	1919, for 1918
	Cockcroft, Walton	1932	1951
20	Pauli	1925	1945
21	Frank, Tamm	1937	1958
	Friedman, Kendall, Taylor	1969	1990
	Perl	1974	1995
22	Appleton	1925	1947
23	Cherenkov	1935	1958
25	Hess	1911	1936
26	Lederman, Schwartz, Steinberger	1962	1988
29	Born	1925	1954
	Bethe	1938	1967
30	Wigner	1933	1963
	Bothe	1924	1954
32	Alfvén	1935+	1970
34	Brockhouse, Shull	to 1960	1994
38	Ramsey	1951	1989
39	Reines	1956	1995
40	Kapitsa	1938	1978
45	Van Vleck	1932	1977
49	Chandrasekhar	1934	1983
53	Ruska	1933	1986

Experimenters have been the fastest winners, unsurprisingly, since experiments usually give quicker, more clear-cut results than theory. But both theorists and experimenters have been unaccountably kept waiting a long time.

Long delays can cause bitterness. When the Nobel finally changed its bias against astrophysics, the 1983 prize went to the eminent Subrahmanyan Chandrasekhar for work done almost fifty years before. He openly complained that this not only neglected his quite different and important work of the last half century, but now "the public views me in terms of the work done fifty years ago." Or consider Max Born, the great Göttingen physicist. When Heisenberg discovered his new quantum mechanics theory in 1925, it was Born who crucially clarified the mathematics of the theory, with help from his former student Pascual Jordan. Indeed, the new quantum mechanics was then called the Heisenberg-Born-Jordan theory (*die Dreimännerarbeit* or "three-man work"). Born also contributed the vital explanation of Schrödinger's wave function as probability waves — that is, the exact location of a particle can never be predicted, only its probability of being somewhere in the wave area. But Born was passed over. When Heisenberg in 1933 was awarded the prize, he wrote Born an embarrassed letter of apology and thanks, all the more embarrassed because Born, a Jew, had just been dismissed from his professorship by the Nazis. Chandrasekhar relates a haunting story of Born in 1933, the year Heisenberg and Dirac and Schrödinger all went to Stockholm. Heisenberg visited the Cavendish Laboratory to lecture. When those who had won Nobel Prizes walked in — Rutherford, Aston, Dirac, Heisenberg — everyone stood up and applauded. Chandrasekhar was sitting next to Born, who was in tears. "He said, 'I should be there, I should be there.'"[118] In 1954 Born finally got his Nobel Prize, twenty-two years after Heisenberg. It is one of the curses of a scientific reward system like the Nobel Prize that those who do not win can still be inside — yet never wholly inside — the charmed circle of the winners. Born was one of many who have felt such things deeply.

Losing out on a Nobel Prize can depress even those who seem buoyant as can be — the Berkeley experimenter Luis Alvarez, for example. In his autobiography, he recounts how he felt in 1960, when the news came that Donald Glaser had won the prize for his invention of the bubble chamber. It was unclear whether Glaser was sharing the prize. If so, Alvarez was the likeliest candidate, since he had made Glaser's invention decisively useful for high-energy experiments. But he was not named.

> None of my friends had felt up to the task of informing me that I had been considered by the Nobel committee and found wanting. That is something few physicists ever hear; nor have many seen that judgment reversed. I've enjoyed my life immensely, but I would not like to relive 1960.[119]

Alvarez was one of the fortunate few to have the judgment reversed: he won the prize unshared in 1968.

Arriving in a Crowd

In 1973 two experimental teams began work, one on the West Coast directed by Burton Richter at Stanford, and one on the East Coast directed by Samuel Ting at Brookhaven Laboratory. Each, unknown to the other, was chasing the same new particle. Using different methods, they thought they were seeking different things. The Ting team found a surprising peak of energy which indicated something new and interesting in sight. Ting cautiously checked and rechecked. By the end of October 1973, members of his team urged him to publish. Michael Riordan, who has richly chronicled these events, says that Ting kept delaying. On November fourth, the very experienced Austrian-American physicist Victor Weisskopf saw the data and "told him he was crazy not to publish immediately."[120] On November sixth, Ting finally began a draft of a paper.

Meanwhile, on November fourth, the Richter team at Stanford, having found the same surprising energy peak, were checking their data. Richter started writing a draft for publication. The news of the simultaneous research and discovery reached each coast in a haphazard way, was dismissed as a hoax, then was taken seriously. Riordan reports that Ting flew to Stanford to see Richter, and they had an "astonishing conversation."[121] Like tunnelers working from opposite sides and unaware of the other, they had run into each other. They had both discovered the J/psi particle ("J" because that was like the Chinese character for Ting's name, "psi" because

Richter wanted to call it that, so it was called both). The J/psi later turned out to be an as yet unknown quark, renamed "charm."

Ting and Richter shared the prize for 1976. But why did Ting delay so long that he lost sole priority? Riordan suggests that Ting almost lost everything through overambition. Early data convinced him that not only a new particle but perhaps a "whole family of new particles" was waiting to be discovered. That would of course be a "tremendous coup." Ting therefore held off publishing, though the single particle by itself was already worth a Nobel Prize. But publishing meant that other physicists could pick up the scent and perhaps beat Ting to his grander feat. Indeed, if Ting had delayed only a week longer, he might have lost all claim to priority.

Now let us see a reverse case, where publication for priority pushed greedily forward. Its history has been fully and vividly traced by Gary Taubes.[122] It features the Italian-American experimenter Carlo Rubbia, an irresistible force moving toward a Nobel. By 1982, CERN had two teams looking for the W and Z bosons predicted by Weinberg and Salam in their electroweak theory. Rubbia was in charge of a team called UA1, for Underground Area 1, with 135 physicists. Rubbia's coleader was the Dutchman Simon van der Meer, whose cooling technique made the experiment technically possible. But another team called UA2 were also hard at work, though only about half the size. When the UA1 accelerator began its tests in October 1982, confusing data showed up in the photographs. Rubbia became convinced that no W existed and toyed with writing a paper saying that Glashow, Weinberg, and Salam were wrong and hadn't deserved their prize in 1979. But, as Taubes notes, nobody ever won a Nobel Prize for proving something didn't exist or some theory was wrong. Rubbia knew that.

Then one photograph of a promising particle collision — physicists call it an "event" — appeared, the best candidate for a W thus far, though with certain faults. When team members urged more and better data, Rubbia argued that the discovery of the omega-minus particle back in 1964, which cinched the Nobel for its predictor, Gell-Mann, had also been a "one-event" discovery. Meanwhile, UA2 were gathering promising results, and might beat Rubbia's team to the goal.

The problem of publication now became serious, and devious. Rubbia told the leaders of the UA2 team that since both teams had apparently found the valuable W's, "they should think twice before publishing" for the sake of their reputations. Rubbia said he had therefore decided not to publish immediately. But the day before making this statement, Rubbia had actually delivered a first draft of his paper to the editor of *Physics Letters*, a European physics journal in Amsterdam, and promised the final draft quickly. His own UA1 team argued against rushing publication and recommended a few more weeks of checking. If they waited that long, Rubbia responded, "our priority claim would have gone to hell." A few days later Rubbia sent the final draft by hand-courier to the *Physics Letters* editor. Of the 135 physicists on the UA1 team, only a few read that final draft. Rubbia had given them two days to comment on it, then didn't wait for their comments.

UA2 meanwhile, unaware of Rubbia's action, wrote up their results, circulated the paper to all their sixty physicists, and gave them two weeks to comment. UA2's paper was finally published, but one month after Rubbia's. Rubbia had established his priority. Taubes reports that even two years later, many physicists assumed that UA1 had discovered the W particle three weeks before UA2, when in fact the discovery had been simultaneous.[123] CERN's director-general backed UA1 against UA2's protests.

When both teams moved on to try finding the Z boson, Rubbia's ruthless maneuvering happened all over again. UA2 found the particle first — and this time already had their paper written with blanks to insert the measurements found. But when, on the same day, the UA1 team found what seemed a Z, Rubbia telephoned CERN's director-general. Next morning, the director-general announced to the press — "on the strength of a phone call," as Taubes puts it — that the Z particle had been found by the UA1 team. Rubbia's ambition for a Nobel was hungrily matched by CERN's. Although CERN had the most powerful accelerator in Europe, it had not yet won a Nobel Prize in its twenty-five years of operation. Less than a year later, Carlo Rubbia and van der Meer shared the Nobel gold medal in Stockholm. The UA2 team were not mentioned.

In 1983, commenting on the Rubbia experiment reviewed above, and doubtless on his own experience ten years before, Samuel Ting said, "In physics there's no number two. Who will remember what UA2 has done? Nobody will remember UA2."[124]

By a Nose

Scientists continually miss discoveries worth a Nobel Prize. Luis Alvarez gives examples involving the discovery of nuclear fission by Hahn, Lise Meitner, and Fritz Strassmann. In 1939, when a young postdoc working at the Berkeley cyclotron, Alvarez read a newspaper report of the discovery to his graduate student, Phil Abelson, who was stunned: he saw he was within days of making the same discovery himself. Alvarez narrowly missed discovering fission in 1938: in an experiment on uranium radiation, he somehow blocked off rays and thus didn't notice fission fragments.

Even Fermi missed. While producing radioactivity from uranium, Fermi and colleagues got some strange data suggesting that a huge chunk might have been chopped out of the uranium nucleus — or, put differently, that uranium could decay into an element half its size. That violated all accepted theory. "Everyone knew" that the tiny helium nucleus was the largest bit that could be bombarded out of any atom. Fermi decided he had discovered the first known element beyond uranium in the periodic table, which would be number 93. A German chemist, Ida Noddack, said at the time that Fermi should have gone through all ninety-two elements in the periodic chart to see what had really happened. Fermi did not do this. But "no one took Noddack seriously."[125] Even Noddack didn't follow her own advice; if she had, says Luis Alvarez, she might have discovered fission three years before Hahn. When Fermi won the Nobel Prize in 1938, he was cited for demonstrating the existence of new radioactive elements heavier than uranium. But then Hahn's 1939 work that led to fission showed that Fermi had not discovered an element beyond uranium: no such natural element exists. Fermi had in fact discovered nuclear fission without realizing it. The Nobel lecture he had just delivered was wrong, and anyone less self-confident than Fermi would have squirmed. But he felt, rightly, that he had done quite enough otherwise to deserve the prize.[126]

Clouded Vision

As bad as being beaten to the post is running the wrong race — either not to notice what is staring you in the face, or to misinterpret it. Irène and Frédéric Joliot-Curie (she was Marie's daughter) did both of these.

In 1932 they explored what happened when a nucleus was bombarded with alpha rays. They concluded that gamma rays were ejecting protons from the nucleus, though they could not explain how the gamma rays could shoot out a sizable entity like a proton, almost two thousand times heavier than an electron. They published quickly, since many others were working on the same problem. This turned out to be a mistake. James Chadwick, a Rutherford protégé, read the Joliot-Curies' report and saw they had the right data but the wrong answer. Gamma rays had too little power to eject the big protons. There must be another particle in the nucleus with a mass approximately that of a proton. Chadwick thus discovered the neutron, and won the Nobel Prize in Physics in 1935.

That same year, on 2 August 1932, Carl Anderson of CalTech discovered the antielectron — the "positron," a positively charged electron that is its antimatter twin — confirming Dirac's prediction. This remains one of the important discoveries in the history of physics. Anderson won the 1936 Nobel Prize.

Except that Anderson didn't know at the time that he had confirmed Dirac's prediction, or that he had found a positron. He only knew it was a particle never seen before. In 1932 he published his findings, together with a photograph. P. M. S. Blackett and G. Occhialini, working at the Cavendish, realized that Anderson had found a positron. They knew because they had also found it in 1932 but, afraid of being wrong, had held off publishing, although Dirac himself helped interpret their photographs. "But nobody then took Dirac's theory seriously," said Blackett.[127] While they dithered, Anderson published and gained clear priority — and only then began reading Dirac's relevant papers. He always insisted he had found the positron "by accident."[128]

Meanwhile the Joliot-Curies, immediately after Anderson published, went through their cloud-chamber photographs of cosmic rays from the previous year and found some with exactly that same up-curving track Anderson stressed. But they hadn't noticed how unusual this was and had filed away the pictures.

In 1934 the Joliot-Curies finally came in first. They discovered artificial radioactivity. In this they barely nosed out Ernest O. Lawrence and his cyclotron staff at Berkeley. Lawrence's team could have discovered artificial radioactivity at least a year before, except that their Geiger counter shut down when their cyclotron did: thus the residual radioactivity wasn't recorded.[129] Nor were their Geiger counters good enough to separate the radioactivity emitted by the cyclotron from the "background" radioactivity that filled the whole laboratory.[130] The Joliot-Curies won the chemistry prize in 1935, the same year their rival Chadwick took the physics prize. In 1939 the Joliot-Curies learned they had just missed the discovery of fission as well.

Another way to lose is not to follow up leads relentlessly. In 1947 when Willis Lamb discovered the shift in spectral lines that led to QED renormalization, Victor Weisskopf had some bittersweet memories. He believed he could have made Lamb's discovery in 1936, again in 1939, and then a few years after that at MIT. But he was distracted into other areas.[131] So the crucial QED problem might have been resolved ten years earlier than it was — not to mention winning Weisskopf a Nobel Prize. He never did win one. An interviewer once asked him what he thought he had lacked.

> Persistence! I was much too interested in other things. I always say, you know, because I really believe it made me miss the Nobel Prize, that I think I'd gladly pay the Nobel Prize for having this general overview of physics which I have from those years. . . . I don't regret it at all.[132]

And here is Leon Lederman being rueful about not discovering (in 1967–68) the J/psi particle that won the Nobel for Ting and Richter in 1976. In inimitable Ledermanese, his feelings on first hearing the news in 1974:

> As a scientist, as a particle physicist, I was overjoyed at the break-through, a joy tinged, of course, with envy and even just a touch of murderous hatred for the discoverers. That's the normal reaction. But I had been there — Ting doing my experiment! True, the kind of chambers that made Ting's experiment sharp weren't available in 1967–68. Still, the old Brookhaven experiment had the ingredients of two Nobel Prizes — if we had had a more capable director and if Bjorken [a renowned theorist] had been at Columbia and if I had been slightly more intelligent.[133]

Yet another way to miss a Nobel award is to be ignored by the physics community. In 1946 George Gamow, the Russian physicist then teaching in the U.S., published some speculations on the Big Bang. In 1948 his doctoral student Ralph Alpher wrote a dissertation that first set forth the Big Bang theory in clear mathematical form and essential physics. Alpher's theory was published in 1948, with Gamow's collaboration. It raised much interest, but radio astronomy wasn't advanced enough to lend confirmation. Alpher kept publishing until 1955, then moved on to other things. In 1967 the American radio astronomers Arno Penzias and Robert Wilson detected cosmic radiation background, and the data confirmed Alpher's prediction. But Alpher's theory, despite his and Gamow's protests, was ignored. Penzias and Wilson, as well as some leading cosmologists, claimed they had not read Alpher's several papers or else had forgotten doing so. In 1978 Penzias and Wilson won shares of the Nobel Prize for their discovery. Alpher should have been included (Gamow died in 1968). His theory explained the Penzias-Wilson discovery, and had two decades' priority over later efforts. But Alpher was passed over in silence.[134] The cofounder of the Big Bang theory is not on the Nobel list.

Even if all else goes right, one can lose by not staying firmly enough in the mainstream so that others can follow what you are doing. A poignant example is E. C. G. Stueckelberg (1905–1984) of Switzerland, one of the most original but also exotic and eccentric physicists of modern times. He was the sort of aristocratic blue-blood one expects not in physics journals but only in the Almanach da Gotha — full name, Baron Ernst Carl Gerlach Stueckelberg von Breidenbach zu Breidenstein und Melsbach. He not only used his own unfamiliar mathematical notation but also published in obscure journals, two fatal strikes against winning a Nobel Prize. He independently theorized the "messenger" particle in 1934, a year before Yukawa, but on Pauli's bad advice, did not publish.[135] On QED he was years ahead of the rest. Between 1934 and 1938, and again in 1947, he published innovative papers, buried in peripheral journals. Victor Weisskopf, Pauli's assistant at the time, remembers that "had Pauli and I been capable of grasping his ideas, we might well have calculated the Lamb shift and the correction to the magnetic moment [by 1936]."[136]

His originality was finally noticed, though too late for Nobel recognition. Richard Feynman, shortly after sharing the 1965 prize for his part in the QED solution, was lecturing in Zurich, where Stueckelberg lived. Stueckelberg came to the lecture. Feynman was moved: "He did the work and walks alone toward the sunset, and here I am, covered in all the glory, which rightfully should be his!"[137]

Collaborator Problems

In a collaboration, how does one assign credit? In principle, and generally in practice, credit is assigned equally when the collaborators contribute equally. Or sometimes the collaboration clearly seems one person's show. But things don't always work out so clearly or fairly, and it falls to the Nobel judges — or the courts — to decide.

Occasionally a disappointed collaborator makes a public ruckus. Emilio Segrè and Owen Chamberlain won the 1959 Nobel Prize for discovering the antiproton in 1955. In 1972 they were sued "for theft of intellectual property" by the Italian physicist Oreste Piccioni, who charged that he had not been given proper credit in the discovery. A pivotal part of his claim was that the experiment measured how long particles took to move from one detector to another. Piccioni claimed he had worked out this method, and thus deserved credit. When the Segrè-Chamberlain team had its first successes in 1955, Piccioni said he complained to Ernest O. Lawrence, in charge of the laboratory, who allegedly warned him not to press charges or his career could be ruined. Piccioni's case was dismissed by the courts as brought too late.[138] The journal *Science*, reporting this case, also noted that in a poll of two hundred British scientists, more than a sixth suspected their ideas had been stolen by colleagues.[139]

The very next year, 1956, Piccioni and three collaborators discovered the antineutron. No prize for this. Too many people to honor? Had the earlier discovery of the antiproton made this discovery dispensable? Had Piccioni's earlier complaint damaged his Nobel chances?[140]

Poor Counsel from on High

In 1925 the young American Ralph Kronig derived a promising formula for "spin," hitherto undiscovered. Wolfgang Pauli, an imposing authority indeed, flatly told Kronig that his idea was impossible. Heisenberg was also sceptical. Kronig naturally didn't publish.[141]

Later that year in Leiden, two young Dutch physicists also thought of "spin." George Uhlenbeck and Samuel Goudsmit took their discovery to their professor, Paul Ehrenfest (one of Einstein's closest friends), who liked it. He suggested they show a copy of the paper to the grand old man of Dutch physics, H. A. Lorentz (Nobel 1902). Lorentz said the idea was impossible. Ehrenfest had apparently spotted the objections that Lorentz would raise, but had already sent the paper off anyway for publication. Thus Uhlenbeck and Goudsmit got full credit for discovering spin. "There is certainly no doubt," Uhlenbeck said, "that Kronig anticipated what was the main part of our ideas."[142] But Uhlenbeck and Goudsmit never won a Nobel Prize. Was it because the Nobel committee knew of Kronig's earlier idea? If so, why not honor all three? Goudsmit used to say that everyone always assumed he and Uhlenbeck had won a Nobel Prize.[143] Ironically, spin helped clinch confirmation of Pauli's exclusion principle of 1925, for which Pauli won the Nobel Prize in 1945.[144]

Knowing Too Much: The Hedgehog and the Fox

> I dare not publish anything about this idea and address myself confidentially to you, dear radioactive ones. . . .
>
> — *Pauli, hypothesizing the neutrino in a letter to friends (1930)*

The Greek epigram is: "The hedgehog knows one big thing; the fox knows many things." The British philosopher Isaiah Berlin used this to suggest the difference between monists and pluralists: Plato and Kafka are supposedly hedgehogs, Aristotle and Shakespeare are foxes. The epigram is appropriated here to point at physicists who dig in tenaciously, and those who roam widely.

Our examples are Wolfgang Pauli and Robert Oppenheimer, born four years apart (1900, 1904), both prodigies and later great figures in physics.

Wolfgang Pauli (d. 1958) was the most acute, learned, and sarcastic conscience of physics from the 1920s to the 1950s. A story often told about Pauli is how, as a very young student, he attended a lecture by the then world-famous Einstein, and made the comment "What Professor Einstein has said is not entirely stupid." And, doubly damning one theory: "That's not even wrong!" Any lecturer, famous or novice, might well dread propounding a new theory while Pauli — called the Scourge of the Lord for his penetrating criticisms — sat in the front row, ready to pounce on any mistake or unclarity, meanwhile regularly nodding his head. His nodding did not mean agreement. It seems to have been due to a nervous disorder.

Of all the famous physicists, he was the oddest looking. In photographs, his strange face leaps out from a crowd. "Levantine" is how he is usually described, with hooded and curiously slanted eyes, swarthy skin, thick squat figure — like a distant brainy relation of Peter Lorre. Heisenberg was his closest collaborator, Bohr was his mentor. That Pauli gravitated to the Danish rock of humility made sense. For all his biting comments, Pauli also had deep humility. It probably kept him from achieving more than he did.

At twenty-one he published a brilliant account of Einstein's general theory of relativity which the Master himself praised lavishly. Pauli retained the admiration of the physics community until his death. At twenty-five he made the discovery that still seems his greatest — the exclusion principle, whose importance for physics and all of chemistry can scarcely be overstated. Pauli found the law by which atoms fill up their energy shells or "orbits" with electrons. The result was an extraordinary clarification of the inner dynamics of an atom, and of the chemical table of elements. Pauli also postulated the neutrino between 1929 and 1931[145] to explain why energy was missing when electrons radiated. But, always a reluctant revolutionary, he did so privately. Fermi took up the idea a year or so later and developed it.

The physicist Abraham Pais recalls that in 1946 he had dinner with Pauli who, rhythmically rocking as usual in his strange way, complained that he had trouble finding a physics topic to work on. He fell silent and added, "Perhaps that is because I know too much."[146] He wasn't boasting, it was simply true. Knowing too much can sometimes handcuff one's inner freedom and originality. Richard Feynman studiously did not keep up with the flood of current literature, fearing it might stifle him. Feynman read the beginning of an article to see the direction, then set it aside to work the answer out for himself.

But Pauli read and understood and remembered everything. It made him cautious. Heisenberg, who was not afraid to go into print with less than final proof, lamented that Pauli held back many stimulating ideas because they were not impeccably done. Pauli contributed importantly to quantum field theory, conceived the neutrino, began solid-state physics, was a leader in meson theory. Yet he seemed to dissipate his creative energies in writing brilliant suggestions to everyone, offering insightful criticisms, and keeping in touch with all developments everywhere.

Oppenheimer went from Harvard summa cum laude to Rutherford at the Cavendish Laboratory, but switched to theoretical physics and took his doctorate with Born at Göttingen in 1927. He moved to Berkeley, where in the 1930s, according to the Nobelist Hans Bethe, he built up the greatest school of theoretical physics ever known in the United States. In the 1940s he directed the atom bomb project, and after the war became director of the Institute for Advanced Study in Princeton.

Though much too fastidious ever to say so, he also "knew too much." His ability to soak up the most difficult subjects with lightning quickness impressed everyone. Bethe says that his capacity to take in every detail of the labyrinthine work at Los Alamos — theoretic intricacies, engineering and equipment technology, experimental details in a dozen areas — was astonishing; no one else could possibly have done it. Rabi, who had studied abroad with Oppenheimer in the 1920s and knew him well the rest of his life, said that Oppenheimer plainly had the brightest, quickest mind he had ever seen. Thus the question always asked about Oppenheimer: How could someone that brilliant not win a Nobel Prize? Rabi's explanation was that Oppenheimer's mind was too quick and brilliant for his own good. It carried him dazzlingly from one topic to another, touching on everything but digging deeply into nothing. Rabi was slower but also more tenacious: he had the ability to sit on one problem for years, if necessary. Rabi won a Nobel Prize in 1944. Pauli, too perfectionist, and Oppenheimer, in thrall to his restless quick mind, became great critics of other people's ideas, rather than originators of their own.

Luis Alvarez however claims that Oppenheimer would finally have won a Nobel award if he had lived long enough. Alvarez points to two pioneering papers that Oppenheimer published in 1939, the first on neutron stars, the other on black holes. In the 1970s neutron stars (pulsars) were found and black holes were vigorously being sought, and the Nobel committee could have recognized Oppenheimer for his astrophysics.[147] Unfortunately, Oppenheimer died of cancer in 1967, aged sixty-three.

Before he became director at Los Alamos, Oppenheimer might also have won a Nobel Prize for solving the QED infinities mess. That was in 1938, when Oppenheimer was still at Berkeley. He and Felix Bloch had an idea about how to sort out finite and infinite energy. Instead of doing the calculations themselves (Oppenheimer was a notoriously poor calculator), they farmed the problem out to Sidney Dancoff, a mathematical physicist at the University of Illinois. According to Robert Serber, then a colleague of Oppenheimer, Dancoff botched the calculation but refused to correct the mistakes. Serber said that Oppenheimer afterward felt that Dancoff's stubbornness had cost him a Nobel award.[148]

Aftereffects of the Physics Prize

> My God! What happens now to the rest of my life?
>
> — *Tsung-Dao Lee, on winning at age thirty-one*[149]

Physics laureates, like all scientists, lament the drain on their time, energy, and patience by demands from the public, government, universities, colleagues, and cranks. Certainly such distractions cut into their research time and concentration. But it is unclear how much the Nobel award actually affects a physicist's creative work. By the time Einstein, Planck, Born, Yukawa, Lederman, and many others received the award, their most productive years were over. Some who received the award when young, like Marie Curie or William Lawrence Bragg, never again did work in any way as good. The American Ernest O. Lawrence invented the working cyclotron at age thirty-one and won the Nobel Prize in 1939. Up to then, he was a sort of human cyclotron of driving energy. But after winning the prize, not yet forty, his scientific productivity slackened off steadily. In such cases, was it because of distraction, or a natural winding down? Heisenberg, Pauli, and Dirac made many later brilliant contributions, but nothing like their early, Nobel Prize–winning work. Bohr, despite his wondrous ability to stimulate others, never produced anything comparable to his 1913 atomic theory. On the other side, Feynman and Gell-Mann remained impressively productive after their Nobelizing, as did Bethe. Bardeen won one prize in 1956 and another in 1972. And Rutherford beat everyone here.

The entire question is haunted by another: What in fact is important work? The last forty years of Chandrasekhar's research may have been, as he said, outside the mainstream of physics now. But when and if views shift, such work can turn out to be dead-center mainstream. In his last years, hunting the grand unified theory, Einstein joked about himself as only an old fossil. But his work here may turn out to be important in ways unimaginable now. After all, Einstein demonstrated just that when he brought the work of the obscure nineteenth-century non-Euclidean mathematician Bernhard Riemann to bear on the gravitational theory of the universe — and thus into the mainstream.

Perhaps the most unusual aftermath has been the post-Nobel career of Brian Josephson, of solid-state "tunneling" fame. He was thirty-three when he shared the 1973 Nobel. In the 1970s he became a disciple of the Maharishi Mahesh Yogi, guru of the Beatles, and sought to reconcile quantum physics with transcendental meditation. His former teacher and a Nobelist himself, Philip Anderson, was upset enough to publish an attack on Josephson's beliefs; Josephson replied that Anderson was caught in a "paradigm" that had outlived its usefulness.

Physics Super-Nobels

All Nobel Prizes are in principle equal, but — to adapt George Orwell — some are more equal than others. Einstein clearly towers over the rest, and then comes . . . dispute.

The television documentaries about Richard Feynman carried the subtitle "The Greatest Mind Since Einstein." Feynman was by then dead, else we might have been treated to one of his enlightening outbursts of outraged candor. He despised the game of trying to rank great physicists, much less venerating anyone, whether Einstein or his own special hero Dirac. But in 1963 Dirac rated Schrödinger close behind Heisenberg, though perhaps greater in "brain power" — "because Heisenberg was helped very much by experimental evidence, and Schrödinger just did it all out of his head."[150]

The brilliant Russian physicist Lev Landau (physics prize, 1962), who worked with Bohr and knew everyone else in the late 1920s and early 1930s before returning to the USSR, seriously tried to rank physicists. He used a logarithmic scale:

> This means that a physicist, say, of the second class has accomplished (precisely accomplished, we are dealing only with accomplishments) a tenth as much as a first-class physicist. On this scale, Einstein was of class one half, and Bohr, Schrödinger, Dirac, Heisenberg and a few others first class. Landau placed himself in a two and a half (i.e., only one hundredth of an Einstein!) and only some ten years ago, satisfied with some of his work . . . he stated that he worked his way up to second class.[151]

A most instructive story about the entire matter is related by the 1959 colaureate Emilio Segrè. He and Fermi, his friend and one-time teacher, once had a brief but resonating conversation:

> "Emilio, you could take all your work and exchange it for one paper of Dirac's and you would gain substantially in the trade," Fermi once said to me. I knew this to be true, of course, but I answered, "I agree, but you could likewise trade yours for one of Einstein's and come out ahead."

After a short pause, Fermi assented.[152]

6

The Nobel Prize in Chemistry

Worthy but Dull? Or Muddled but Central?

In 1929 the young British physicist P. A. M. Dirac, having written the first relativistic equation of the electron, was not presumptuous enough to claim that his equation explained all of physics; he merely claimed it explained all of chemistry.[1] Before him, the eminent nineteenth-century physicists Kelvin and Boltzmann suggested that chemistry could be reduced to "vortex atoms" or the kinetics of atoms. Many contemporary physicists still endorse such a view: chemistry is only applied quantum physics.[2]

It is striking that no one seems ready to make such imperious claims for chemistry. For biology or medicine, yes: the "human genome" project to map every last one of the millions of human genes is as grandiose as one could wish. But chemistry suffers a curious lack of glamour. Question: Can the reader name a single Nobelist in chemistry? Or a single important living chemist? Or any two from 1901? Some chemists themselves seem resigned to having their science seen as "worthy but dull."[3]

No chemist has the aura of a Newton, Darwin, or Einstein. Pasteur is perhaps the nearest claimant, but he is really a heroic figure of medicine. The American Linus Pauling (Nobel 1954) has good claim to being the greatest chemist of the twentieth century, but the general public probably knows him, if at all, not for his chemical bonding theory and other great discoveries but for his "peacenik" activities in the 1960s — he won a second Nobel Prize, in peace, in

1962 — or his crusade for vitamin C. Nor does chemistry seem to launch forth those epochal revolutionary ideas or discoveries associated with physics and medicine: antibiotics, transplants, relativity.

It is therefore wisest, says the historian of chemistry David Knight, to admit that chemistry has "its glorious future behind it." The nineteenth century was "probably the high point in the career of chemistry." But in the twentieth century, he says resignedly, chemistry became mainly a "service science."[4] Yet the opposite may in fact be the case. Biological research now is decisively biochemical and chemicophysical. Chemistry may thus be coming into ascendency at last.

The Beginnings

It took only twenty-five years for Planck's quantum concept of 1900 to dominate atomic physics. No such unification has happened in chemistry or appears likely. Molecules are bewilderingly more complex, multitudinous, and eccentrically behaved than the few, uniform particles of physics, though computers are helping to solve some of the problems, as are new mathematical procedures like fractals and chaos theory. But thus far, at least, a grand generalizing theoretical leap like Einstein's by a chemist is apt to end in a pratfall.

The Nobel Prizes in Chemistry cover a field that is rich, sprawling, and not a little untidy ("muddled, unfinished and inconclusive," as one of its admirers put it).[5] Its details are overwhelming. Chemistry takes up every kind of compound on earth and in space, liquid or gas or solid, living or inanimate. These millions of compounds and their ways of reacting with each other show dizzying variations in size, shape, behavior, and effects produced. Coping with such a prodigality of topics has bred more and more specialties, and kept the Nobel chemistry jury busy from its start.

In the nineteenth century, organic chemistry gained earliest success. It asked about the chemical structure of matter. But how various elements could join at all, much less to produce such different substances as blood, water, and coal, were at first bewildering problems. The chemist Friedrich Wöhler in 1830 famously compared organic chemistry in his time to a dark jungle. Around 1850, however, organic chemists had two great insights. First, that atoms of certain elements could join only with the atoms of certain other elements; it took more than seventy years for the quantum theory to explain why. Second, that carbon is found in all living things and easily combines with itself to form wondrously complex chains. With that, organic chemistry changed from an inchoate science of "life" into the science of carbon-based matter. Paths were thus cut through the jungle. The structural stick diagrams were invented that chemistry still uses today — those familiar formulae such as the six-sided benzene ring to which other atoms hook on. This was an extraordinary achievement. Modern physics simply adopted the existing symbolism of mathematics. Organic chemistry had to invent its own from scratch. If there were Nobel Prizes in 1860, how many awards would that feat be worth?

By 1901 organic chemistry dominated the field, but physical chemistry was a formidable new rival. It rose to prominence in the 1880s, pioneered by such early Nobelists as van't Hoff, Arrhenius, and Ostwald. This movement, disdaining its organic rivals as mere "descriptive" chemists, sought instead to apply the rigor of physics to chemical problems. More mundane things were also at stake: industrial and government funding and favor, and prestigious university positions; the first professorship of physical chemistry in the world was set up only in 1887 at Leipzig, with Ostwald appointed to it.[6]

The physical chemists had indeed grasped hold of a central problem that organic chemistry essentially ignored or couldn't handle: What actually happened in a chemical reaction? A reaction was after all not a static picture like one of organic chemistry's formalized stick diagrams. It involved change of all kinds. Energy was released in the form of heat, substances changed from solid to liquid or gaseous, new products were formed. Further, reactions could be made to go faster by using certain catalysts, or show unusual behavior with certain reagents or when an electric current was shot through the solution.

Biochemistry, the darling of the twentieth century, was the late developer among chemistry's major branches. Only from the 1920s did it truly gain a domain of its own — metabolism, enzymology, vitamins, hormones. This became "classical" biochemistry in the 1950s when the new molecular biology discovered the double helix and the wide-open horizon of genes.

Nobel Chemistry Prizes, 1901–1915, 1918–1945

In the Nobel's first fifteen years, organic chemistry — though the most prestigious and largest branch of chemistry — won just six times. Physical chemistry, much smaller and rather upstart, plucked off almost as many Nobels. One reason, at least, is that the physical chemists held power where it mattered, in the Stockholm Nobel chemistry committee.

The very first chemistry Nobel went to the Dutch physical chemist van't Hoff, symbolically anointing him the foremost chemist of his time — and physical chemistry the foremost branch. This choice came from political in-fighting on the Nobel committee. The first Nobel chemistry committee was comprised, with years served in parentheses, as follows:

Cleve, P. T. (1900–1905), Professor of Chemistry, Uppsala

Klason, P. (1900–1925), Professor of Chemistry and Chemical Technology, Royal Institute of Technology

Petterson, O. (1900–1912), Professor of Chemistry, Högskola

Soderbaum, H. G. (1900–1931), Professor of Agricultural Chemistry, Academy of Agriculture

Widman, O. (1900–1928), Professor of Chemistry, Uppsala

Hammarsten, O. (1905–1926), Professor of Physiological Chemistry, Uppsala (replaced Cleve)

Ekstrand, A. G. (1913–1924), civil servant, engineer (replaced Petterson)

These were all well-established chemists when appointed, and with their successors controlled the chemistry prize almost to 1930. The influential ones were Cleve, an inorganic chemist; Widman, an organic chemist; and Petterson, a physiological chemist. But the true mover and shaker isn't on this list: Svante Arrhenius, Sweden's most famous scientist and an internationally renowned physical chemist. He sat on the physics committee but also made nominations for the chemistry prize.[7] He and Petterson were allies: they had helped build the upstart Högskola technical school in Stockholm to challenge old Uppsala, and Petterson had strongly supported Arrhenius's electrolytic theory in its early controversial years. Arrhenius was all his life an embattled and battling figure. He stares out from the old photos, frock-coated, rotund, gold-chained, with something of the meaty face of a tough political boss. His fame rested on a theory first developed in his 1884 doctoral thesis, which the Uppsala chemistry department almost rejected. Arrhenius never forgot or forgave, or missed a chance to even the score. More-over, Arrhenius saw the concerns of radiochemistry as rightly allied more closely to physical than to organic chemistry; significantly, the physicists Marie Curie and Rutherford won prizes in chemistry.

It was therefore no accident that two of the first three Nobels in chemistry went to the physical chemists. Van't Hoff's major contri-bution, in 1884, was to help explain chemical reactions in solutions by analogy to the physical laws of gases. This clarified some of the complex dynamics involved. Unfortunately, salts and acids and alkalis didn't behave quite as van't Hoff predicted. Some other process was obviously involved in a reaction. It was electricity, as the young Arrhenius suggested in 1887: when salt, acids, and alkalis were put in a weak solution, they broke apart ("dissociated") and exhibited electrical as well as chemical properties — they became ions, negatively or positively charged. This plugged the hole in van't Hoff's theory, but itself raised much scepticism. Only far-sighted chemists were prepared to think of chemicals as involving electrical properties. This slowly began to change after 1897 with J. J. Thomson's discovery of the electron, the electrically charged particle inside the atom. But Arrhenius's theory had its own limita-tion: it applied only to weak solutions. It took forty more years before the Dutchman Peter Debye and the German Erich Hückel in 1923 explained how strong electrolytes behaved.[8]

The award of the first chemistry prize to van't Hoff drew a glee-ful letter from Ostwald to Arrhenius that same year:

> That van't Hoff has received the Nobel prize is a very good thing for physical chemistry in Germany; because now the organic chemists here are beginning to fear for their hegemony and try everywhere to repress us. So they have been offended that neither Baeyer nor Fis-cher were favored.[9]

This partisan spirit had a price. The award to van't Hoff meant passing over the greatest physical chemist then alive. He was Josiah Willard Gibbs, the American who had independently developed chemical thermodynamics between 1876 and 1878, almost a decade before van't Hoff. But he published in obscure American journals and remained generally unknown in Europe until the late 1880s. Still, van't Hoff, Arrhenius, and Ostwald knew his work well, since Ostwald had rediscovered him in the late 1880s, championed his views, and even translated him in 1892; a French translation followed in 1899. Gibbs quickly gained attention, and in 1901 won the prestigious Copley Medal of the Royal Society. Why then didn't Gibbs win the first Nobel Prize in Chemistry, since he had long priority over van't Hoff, and his theory went deeper in several ways? The official history of the Nobel Prizes says that he was never nominated.[10] Van't Hoff or Ostwald could of course have nominated him. But van't Hoff was the leading light of the new physical chemistry movement in Europe, while Gibbs, however distinguished, was not. Arrhenius had the influence and backed van't Hoff. By 1903 Gibbs was dead.

The first chemistry Nobels faced a long waiting list of eminent figures whose prizewinning work dated back from ten to thirty years. Of the first thirteen awards, only Rutherford's prizewinning work was done after 1901, and barely. It took fifteen years before the older eminences were given their due and the Nobel could finally turn to twentieth-century contributions. Organic and physical chemistry took the lion's share of prizes, but some of the lions were rather past their prime.

Not so the second laureate, in 1902. This was Emil Fischer, doubtless the greatest and most versatile organic chemist of his time, and before and long after. He tackled anything. The Nobel cited his work in purines and sugar, but he also analyzed complex sugars and the hydrocarbons (familiar to us as "saturated" and "unsaturated") and then, after winning his Nobel, went on almost single-handedly to establish the chemistry of proteins and their amino acids. Since proteins are so central to biology, Fischer thus stands as a founder of modern biochemistry. His virtuoso linking of eighteen amino acids into a near-protein wasn't outdone for forty years. Like Rutherford, Fischer easily deserved a second Nobel Prize. But in this period only Marie Curie managed that trick. Fischer's life ended tragically after his three sons were killed in the First World War; he committed suicide.

Having duly honored Fischer, the Nobel committee gave the 1903 prize to another physical chemist, Arrhenius himself. He had been nominated in 1901 in both physics and chemistry, but delayed partly because it could seem bad form and poor international relations for a Swede to take the first Nobel Prize in any field.[11]

In 1904 the prize paid its due to inorganic chemistry with an award to Britain's William Ramsay for his discoveries (1892–98) of new "noble" or inert elements — argon, krypton, and xenon. Then a clutch of older figures were honored. In 1905 the German chemist Adolf von Baeyer won at age seventy for his work on synthetic dyes, done thirty years before. Otto Wallach became a laureate in 1910 for classifying the hundreds of terpenes a quarter century before. Whatever the intrinsic importance of dyes and terpenes (which include perfumes), these were great, wide-ranging achievements, and the terpenes were among the first complex substances to be thoroughly analyzed. It needs remembering how new and uncertain organic chemistry was when Baeyer and Wallach began their careers.

Baeyer's Nobel symbolized something else. A chance discovery had launched organic chemistry into the role of privileged science for industry and government. In the 1850s Perkin in England, trying to produce quinine, did it wrong and quite accidentally found the first artificial dye, aniline purple. This synthetic dye was much cheaper, more vivid, and easier to use than natural ones, and British textile industries prospered. This also gave rise to the "mauve period" in European history; Perkin became so wealthy he retired at thirty-five. Baeyer, by far the better chemist, did the first synthesis — essentially a laboratory re-creation of a natural substance — of indigo dye, and Germany's textile and chemical industries soon rivaled or outdid Britain's. The dyes were the first of an endless line of synthetic industrial chemical products — celluloid, photographic film, plastics, artificial rubber, bakelite, rayon, and all the rest — none of which ever won anyone a Nobel award.

Other prizes honored narrower work. In 1906 Moissan became a laureate for isolating fluorine in 1886, the most reactive element then known. The colaureates in 1912 were the French chemists Grignard and Sabatier, who invented reagents that improved organic analysis — highly useful. In 1914 T. W. Richards of Harvard won for precise measurements of the atomic weights of elements. All this was the sort of clear-cut work that early Nobel science committees loved.

Of the early physical chemistry triumvirate, only Ostwald now remained without a Nobel. He was on the short list of candidates by

1904, but he was a problem. Certainly, his sheer productivity and energy were staggering: he wrote about forty-five books, five hundred articles and four thousand reviews, and edited six journals.[12] His writing was stimulating and well informed. Albert Einstein in 1901, then a new Ph.D. in Zurich, admired Ostwald, sent him a copy of his first published paper — no reply — and for a while may even have hoped to be invited to Leipzig as Ostwald's assistant.[13] But was Ostwald a first-rank researcher of Nobel caliber or only a superb publicist of chemistry? It seemed difficult even for his champions to specify one truly major new work that Ostwald had done.[14] He was also one of the last diehards to insist atoms had no physical reality. Ostwald's nomination was tabled, and the 1907 prize went instead to Eduard Buchner.

Buchner is the type of scientist whose long career produces a single highlight, though a grand one. Adolf von Baeyer is said to have commented on Buchner's discovery, "This will bring him fame, even though he has no chemical talent."[15] It did bring him fame. In 1897 Buchner caused dead cells of yeast to ferment after he added an enzyme. A century ago this was a startling discovery, and many disbelieved the finding, particularly since Buchner's experiment disproved the view that "life" activity was wholly contained in the cell. It also dismissed the revered but vague nineteenth-century theory of protoplasm, the "stuff of life."[16] Now enzymes were proven to be located outside the living cell — even the mighty Pasteur had claimed the opposite — and were thus available for separate laboratory analysis. The enzyme started its long career as an indispensable topic for the new militants who would soon be called biochemists.

In 1908 the prize went to the experimental physicist Ernest Rutherford — an unexpected award for a physicist who looked down on chemists! — for discovering that heavy complex elements like uranium spontaneously decayed until they reached lead, where the process stopped, since lead was not radioactive. This natural "alchemic" transmutation of elements into other elements permanently altered the understanding of chemistry.

Meanwhile, Ostwald lingered. In 1909 he finally conceded that atoms existed, else he might never have won a Nobel: it would have been distinctly odd to honor an antiatomist after Rutherford. In 1909 at last, with Arrhenius's maneuvering, Ostwald got his award. Then Marie Curie won her chemistry Nobel in 1911, for discovering the new elements polonium and radium, and for isolating radium back in 1898.

Two of the last three prizes before World War I went to great achievements. The 1913 award to Alfred Werner of Switzerland was for a seminal explanation of inorganic bonding (more later). The 1915 prize to the German Richard Willstätter, the leading organic chemist after Emil Fischer, was for innovative work in photosynthesis — how light can produce chemical change. Willstätter analyzed chlorophyll and discovered it was chemically related to hemoglobin. Why such seemingly unrelated things as plant pigment and human blood should have anything in common is one of the imaginative pleasures offered by chemistry. What indeed occurred in photosynthesis on the molecular level was partly explained in the 1940s by Melvin Calvin. Between 1982 and 1985, a more comprehensive explanation was developed by Hartmut Michel, Johann Deisenhofer, and Robert Huber, who shared the 1988 prize.[17]

Awards were canceled in 1916 and 1917 because of the First War. But in 1918, when the war ended, the German inorganic chemist Fritz Haber won the prize. This was probably the most controversial Nobel Prize ever awarded in science. Haber's ammonia process deserved honoring and had important agricultural benefits. But Haber also introduced the horror of poison gas into World War I, using basically the same process. Why the Nobel Foundation decided to honor him the very year the war ended, amid international acrimony gathered about Haber's name, needs further comment later.

The 1920 prize, on the other hand, concluded a long personal war. The Nobel winner was the physical chemist Walther Nernst, whose discovery in 1906 of the heat theorem, involving low temperatures and sometimes called the third law of thermodynamics, used quantum and statistical physics beyond the reach of van't Hoff and Arrhenius. But though Nernst had the most total nominations in chemistry from 1907 to 1914,[18] his Nobel award was delayed again and again. As the historian Elisabeth Crawford notes, Arrhenius was the main rock in the path. He and Nernst were willful personalities, once close friends, then antagonists. Nernst was the superior scientist, but Arrhenius had the votes. Arrhenius was still enough of a power to deliver the Nobel citation for Einstein's physics award in 1922.

There was another problem. Nernst had taken out a patent on an electric arc lamp he had invented, a rival to Edison's. He sold the patent rights to a German corporation for one million marks. In fact, Edison's invention worked better, and the Nernst lamp soon disappeared. But Nernst, no longer a modest-salaried professor but now a millionaire, lived like one and relished it too. He bought a string of expensive new automobiles and a hotel, opened a Cafe Nernst in Göttingen, and set up his family on a luxurious estate. He also enjoyed being considered a genius.

Nernst's patent raised an ethical problem. Personal profit from a discovery was nowhere explicitly prohibited in the Nobel regulations. But the assumption was that the prize money should go to help needy scientists do research; the "benefit of mankind" clause also seemed to argue against private enrichment. Nernst did put some of his new riches into research. But the issue has always been ambiguous. Marconi certainly profited handsomely from the "wireless" that won him a physics prize in 1909. So did Haber from his prizewinning ammonia process.[19]

From 1920 to 1940 the Nobel chemistry judges shed their first blessings on biochemistry and its hormones and enzymes, and on radiochemistry's isotopes. Meanwhile, the very basis of chemical bonding theory was being revolutionized by the quantum revolution, but the Nobel Prizes of the period — understandably, given the confusions of the time — looked away from that momentous fact.

First, enzymes and hormones. To say that an enzyme is a protein that catalyzes a biological process is like saying air is merely what we breathe. We can no more function without the astonishing variety of enzymatic action than we can without air. Hormones activate the specific reactions especially of growth and sexual development. In 1927, 1928, 1929, and 1930, Nobel Prizes went to research in bile acids, steroids, and enzyme-related compounds. Bile has the structure of a steroid, steroids are related to sex hormones, and hormones act in ways analogous to enzymes, which control metabolism. In 1937 and 1938, back-to-back awards went to research into vitamins, often the activators of enzymes, which brings us back to the work honored in 1927–30. To look ahead: hormone research has thrived in Nobel Prizes, unsurprisingly, since they control growth or organ activity — steroids, adrenaline, thyroid, ovary, testes, pancreas are involved.

The earlier awards in this field were in chemistry; thereafter they were awarded in medicine. The Mayo Clinic's Philip Hench and Edward Kendall shared the 1950 prize in medicine for developing cortisone, the first steroid drug. The American Earl Sutherland (prize in medicine, 1971) showed how hormonal activity works with the energy system of the body (ATP), and Alfred Gilman won a share of the 1994 prize in medicine for elaborating these findings into the discovery of "G-proteins." Roger Guillemin and Andrew Schally did early important syntheses of hormones, using Rosalyn Yalow's radioimmunoassay method; all three shared the 1977 prize in medicine. In 1982 Sune Bergström, John Vane, and Bengt Samuelsson became laureates for discovering the prostaglandins, which affect muscle and blood circulation.

From 1901 to 1930, six of nine Nobel Prizes for physical chemistry went for work on isotopes. In an isotope, different numbers of neutrons in the atomic nucleus can make the same element occur in slightly different forms. Successive awards in 1921 and 1922 went to the British chemist Frederick Soddy (Rutherford's collaborator in 1900), who discovered radioactive isotopes in 1913, and to Francis Aston for discovering nonradioactive isotopes by 1919 — and inventing mass spectroscopy to do it. Two more successive prizes went to the American Harold Urey in 1934 for discovering the "heavy hydrogen" isotope, and to the Joliot-Curies in 1935 for using particle bombardment to create isotopes that did not exist in nature. In 1943 the Hungarian chemist George de Hevesy won for his 1930 invention of the isotopic "tracer." The familiar barium enema gives the idea: living systems react to the element but not to the radioactivity — if in tolerable quantities — so the radioactivity allows the chemical reactions to be tracked. The Nobel immunologist Peter Medawar claimed that radioisotopic tracers are as important a revolution in biology as the microscope.[20]

Besides isotopes, other valuable separation techniques emerged at this time, all still in use. The ultracentrifuge separated out substances by high-speed whirling and won the 1926 prize for Theodor Svedberg of Sweden. Arne Tiselius (prize 1948), also of Sweden, refined this method to separate out the types of globulin or serum protein and to improve chromatography.[21] Chromatography itself was invented in 1906 by the Russian Mikhail Tsvett (1872–1920). Since different organic compounds adhere differently to a given substance, a mixture of pigments (for instance) may be separated by pouring it into a long tube of the substance; washed down, the components of the mixture form colored bands. But Tsvett wrote in Russian and his paper was ignored abroad: no Nobel for Tsvett. In 1944 A. J. P. Martin and R. L. M. Synge of Britain found a more refined method of the same principle; they took the 1952 Nobel. And in 1903 Richard Zsigmondy of Germany invented the ultramicroscope, which won him the 1925 prize.

Chemical advance is unimaginable without such improvements. But these new instruments also became weapons in what at the time was a bitter controversy in chemistry, with very important sequels. In the 1920s the German chemist Hermann Staudinger proposed that molecules could reach any size, however large — plastics and polymers are examples. The established view, however, was that no such giant molecules existed; only clusters of small ones. Svedberg's ultracentifuge confirmed Staudinger's view. But Staudinger was not awarded a prize until 1953 — the same year Watson and Crick discovered the structure of the macromolecule of DNA. Before and after this, the macromolecule flourished in the development of nylon, polythene, and refinements in "cracking" gasoline.

An invaluable technical advance was achieved in 1911 by Fritz Pregl of Austria. Up to about 1900, a researcher might need 0.20 grams to do an analysis. Tons of matter had to be processed to produce such a lump. Pregl managed to invent a balance that could measure as little as three milligrams. He became a laureate in 1923.

Quantum Chemistry: The Great Revolution Offstage

Meanwhile, a revolution had been proceeding in chemistry since about 1900, a fact underemphasized in the first half century of the Nobel Prize in Chemistry.

From Planck's quantum theory of 1900 to the new quantum mechanics of Heisenberg and Schrödinger in 1925–26, atomic physics became an ever more unified kingdom. In the 1920s, however, chemistry still resembled a far-flung empire, whose provinces spoke no truly common language or even held the same basic assumptions about their subject. There was no accepted capital: the provinces wrangled constantly over who should rule, and why.

Beyond specialist insularity, never to be underestimated, the problem was that organic chemists and biochemists needed to think like physical chemists, and vice versa. Neither was equipped to do that. It was physics that helped provide a common language and assumptions.

How and why atoms combine is, after all, the rock on which all chemistry is built. Atomic physics itself builds on the same rock. But where particle physicists seek to pulverize the atom to capture its inmost secrets, chemists wish to see how and why one atom combines with others to form the array of existing matter. The atom is the decisive pivot between physics and chemistry: swing into its innards, and you get particle physics; swing out from it toward other atoms forming molecules, and you get chemistry.

Mendeleev's famous periodic chart had been one of the greatest triumphs of classical chemistry. In 1869 he arranged all the known elements from lightest (hydrogen) to heaviest (then uranium) in such a way as to show that the properties of elements run in specific groups and keep repeating, hence the "periodic" table. There are ninety-two naturally occurring elements, and by about 1914, with Mendeleev as the guide, most had been found.

Then, soon after 1920, all these ninety or so elements, so diverse in makeup and properties, could be understood in terms of just the electron, proton, and neutron.

Chemistry's New Atoms — and How They Bonded

Bohr's 1913 quantum theory of the atom helped sweep away vague nineteenth-century ideas that when atoms combined — such as two atoms of hydrogen and one atom of oxygen to form water — it was done by "affinity" or some such reason. It was now seen that the electrons in the outermost orbit of the atom did the bonding.

There had been earlier moves. When J. J. Thomson discovered the electron in 1897, it set some chemists to rethinking chemical bonding. The first innovative theories of chemical bonding in the twentieth century issued from physical chemists such as Gilbert N. Lewis at Berkeley. Lewis had studied with Ostwald and Nernst. As early as 1902, he sketched out a theory of how atoms share paired electrons, pictured as two cubes with one common edge. In 1916 he developed a full-blown theory of this "covalent" bonding with a handy notation still used today. Surely, one would expect, Lewis must then have gone on to develop the implications of his new theory. He did nothing of the kind. He needed a theory of chemical bonding to further his work on reactions, he found it, and that was enough. He was, after all, a physical chemist. Having worked out the covalent theory, Lewis dropped the whole subject of structure and went back to his reactions. As the chemical historian John Servos pungently puts it,

> we should not be surprised. Lewis was little more interested in exploring the applications of his theory of the shared-pair bond in organic chemistry than searchers for spice were interested in the forests of America.[22]

Yet Lewis's fame today rests mainly on his bonding theory. He is also one of the great chemists who never won a Nobel Prize. Chemists found Lewis's theory of structure wonderfully illuminating. But when the new quantum mechanics of Heisenberg and Schrödinger appeared in 1925–26, the Lewis atoms were too static to represent the ultradynamic activity of quantum matter.[23] One of the new quantum chemical theorists, the American Nobelist Robert Mulliken, called Lewis's a "loafer electron" theory, where chemists "imagined the electrons sitting around on dry goods boxes at every corner, ready to shake hands with, or hold on to similar loafer electrons in other atoms."[24]

The effort to apply Schrödinger's quantum wave physics (1926) to chemical theory commanded great interest. Walter Heitler and Fritz London (no prizes) took a first step in 1927, explaining bonding on the basis of electron spin. As Schweber notes, this was quantum mechanics applied to chemistry. Linus Pauling and fellow American John Clarke Slater (no Nobel) created a truly quantum chemical theory, by way of the carbon tetrahedron.[25]

Pauling and Mulliken have emerged as the two great theorists of quantum chemical bonding. Both adapted Schrödinger's quantum wave theory to chemical bonding. In a memoir, Pauling described how confused theoretical chemists were at first:

> In 1925, I had accepted the idea that a covalent bond consists of a pair of electrons shared jointly by two atoms [i.e., the Lewis theory]. I had no sound theoretical basis, however, for any detailed consideration of chemical bonding. . . . I had no way of distinguishing

between the good ideas and poor ideas about the electronic structure of molecules. By 1935, however, I felt I had an essentially complete understanding of the nature of the chemical bond . . . developed in large part through the direct application of quantum mechanical principles to the problem of the electronic structure of molecules.[26]

In Pauling's "valence bond" theory, the "wave" that Schrödinger's equation described became a "cloud" of electrons. Almost at the same time, Mulliken developed an alternative theory that began not from the electron but from the molecular structure ("molecular orbital" bonding).[27]

Partly because mathematics' mighty usefulness to physics has never transferred to chemistry very clearly, it took until 1940 for Pauling's quantum bonding theory to begin to gain wide acceptance, and more than a decade longer for Mulliken's, which is now the dominant theory. The Nobel committee delayed twenty and thirty years respectively to honor this revolution. Pauling became a laureate in 1954 for his valence-bonding theory; Mulliken won in 1966. The 1954 prize to Pauling, only a year after the discovery of the double helix structure, which Pauling missed by a hair, symbolized the profound inner shift that chemistry had undergone. The old division into specialty rivalries began to seem increasingly pointless. This is perhaps why the 1981 prize went slightly more quickly to Roald Hoffmann for the molecular orbital theory of organic chemistry, which he formulated with the great synthesist Robert Woodward in the 1960s. Hoffmann instead shared the prize with Kenichi Fukui of Japan, who developed a related "frontier orbital" theory independently. The Woodward-Hoffmann rule has been called the most important theory developed in organic chemistry since the 1930s. It explains how a specific configuration, providing stability, will occur when bonding takes place in the right phase.

The picture that has emerged can be roughly summarized thus: Electrons group about an atom's nucleus in certain energy "orbitals." This is only a metaphor; a different metaphor might be energy shells like Chinese boxes. Simple atoms like hydrogen have one "orbital" of electrons, while more complex atoms like carbon have several. When electrons fill an atom's orbitals, it is most stable. If the outer orbitals is not filled, the atom seeks to lose or gain electrons to reach "saturation" and thus stability. From such considerations came a theory of chemical bonding that guides chemists today. From about 1970, chemistry textbooks have quickly introduced first-year students to the elements of quantum chemical bonding as basic terms of study. Contemporary chemistry reference works are also interwoven with physics.[28]

Atoms, via their outermost electrons, bond in three different ways. First, an electron is *transferred* from one atom to another. This is called an ionic bond. Salt is made this way: sodium donates an electron to chlorine, and then ions form which hold the two atoms together electrostatically. But such a grip is weak, which is why salt so easily breaks apart in water. Second, two atoms *share* a pair of electrons. This is a "covalent" bond, the primary kind in living matter. Since both atoms cling to the same pair of electrons, the bond is strong. In fact, a mere two-atom compound is extremely rare. Compounds usually involve a great many atoms clinging together as if with dozens of pairs of hands. Carbon normally has a five- or six-handed clutch, which makes it strong and versatile. Third, in metallic compounds — and here was the Nobelist Alfred Werner's great insight — a different kind of bonding occurs. Here each atom deposits its electrons around a central atom in a sort of "sea" or *communal swarm*. This helps explain why metals are malleable and can be bent or hammered without breaking or ripping apart. Thus a metal like bronze seems "immortal" compared to flesh.

But with clarity came new kinds of confusion. Atoms are very complex internally, and the molecules they form come in wildly varying shapes, sizes, and behaviors. In living or carbon-based compounds, an atom is specifically bonded to a nearby atom in a highly selective, quite finicky way: the energies of the atoms have to match precisely, the "fit" of properties and geometric shape must be exactly right. Compounds and molecules can twist, coil, pucker, flop, or spiral into helices. To make sense of this, chemists developed a geometry of molecular structure: electrons that join tend to repel each other since both are negative, and thus push the molecule or ion into different shapes — linear, bent, planar, tetrahedral. Moreover, electrons never move in neat orbits but "smear" into a sort of orbital cloud, best imaged as dumbbells or doughnuts tilted at various angles.

When sufficiently excited — when heat or some other form of energy is applied[29] — molecules will tumble and rotate, and also oscillate, meaning the bonds between the atoms keep stretching and contracting. An iodine molecule can rotate a million times a second, and the whole molecule may at the same time shift position. Its electrons may be leaping up and down the atom's energy levels according to quantum laws. A chemical reaction occurs if enough energy is at hand to break existing chemical bonds: the electron must absorb or lose enough energy to pass an energy barrier. Millions of such reactions take place simultaneously — and no molecule seems to act exactly like any other.

The Chemist's Turnabout

One must sympathize with the chemists and the Nobel chemistry jury of the time who were faced with all this. How can chemists keep track of this flying circus of acrobatic energy shifts, bondings, and reactions? Certainly no single existing approach sufficed.

Inside their separate enclaves, the different branches accomplished much. Yet the branches, as an historian remarks, made it almost a point of honor to remain ignorant of the others' work.[30] In 1904 the future Nobelist Otto Hahn, then a young organic chemist, was sent to Ramsay's laboratory in England mainly to learn English. Ramsay made him work on radioactive analysis, but the organic chemists on the faculty knew or cared little about this, so Hahn had to ask the physicists for help. By great good luck, Hahn moved on to Montreal to study with Rutherford. In 1907 he returned to Germany to work under Emil Fischer. Hahn recounts a colloquium with that superb organic chemist in which he vainly

> tried to convince Professor Emil Fischer that it was not the abominable smell of some organic compounds of sulfur by which the presence of minute quantities of certain substances was established, but that it was by means of alpha and beta rays that one could establish the presence of even smaller quantities, too small to be weighed.[31]

Still, unlike his colleagues, Fischer was curious enough about what he didn't know to employ Hahn. Organic chemists in general, however, stayed aloof until the 1930s or longer.

By the 1930s, the self-enclosed specialist was becoming an endangered species, despite many loud or proud denials. To do truly innovative work, chemists needed to move beyond their specialties. Classifying advances as organic, physical, and so on puts the cart before the horse. Disciplines, after all, do not drive science; certain fundamental questions drive the disciplines, as well as how one understands "structure" and "reactions."

At this point — and we are now at any time between 1900 and the mid-1930s — one can see something hopeful happening, time and again: organic and physical chemists studying the other specialty. Gilbert N. Lewis was an early example. Structure and reactions began to be two faces of the same coin.

The Russian physical chemist N. N. Semonov, who shared the 1956 chemistry Nobel with the British chemist Cyril Hinshelwood, voiced a general hope in his Nobel lecture that their joint work from the late 1920s "makes it possible to come nearer to the solution of a main problem in theoretical chemistry — the connection between reactivity and the structure of the particles entering the reaction." Reading this, it is hard to remember that Ostwald, at the turn of the century, was hoping to "purge" individual structure from chemical dynamics altogether.

As early as 1922 Gilbert Lewis, having done so much to turn physical chemistry's attention to structure, made a strong statement:

> The fact is that physical chemistry no longer exists. The men who have been called physical chemists have developed a large number of useful methods by which the concrete problems of inorganic chemistry, organic chemistry, biochemistry and technical chemistry may be attacked, and as the application of these methods grows more numerous, it becomes increasingly difficult to adhere to our older classification.[32]

The Nobel Prize — and Chemistry's Smells and Bubblings

To the physicists' claim (Dirac) that chemistry was now only a branch of physics, some eminent chemists responded by declaring physics entirely irrelevant to chemistry — and even passionately warned that, unless expelled, physics would be destructive as any parasite. And recall: these eminent chemists made nominations for the Nobel Prize. For them, the very spirit of physics was incompatible with chemistry. Some witty chemist put the whole problem most succinctly:

Q: What exactly is Chemistry?

A: At least to end with, it isn't Physics.

One can understand the complaint. Against the atomic physicists' few particles, the chemical world deals with some ninety-two natural elements, an ocean of compounds — at least eight million by the 1990s — bacteria and snapdragons, pigs and people.[33] The experimental physicist Leon Lederman wrote a book called *The God Particle*, about the final particle that may lead to a unified theory of all matter. It is hard to imagine a major chemist writing "The God Molecule." It would offend the very spirit of chemistry.

The problem is that molecules move, bulge and breathe, tumble and split, responding to electric, thermal, vibrational, and neighboring influences. And because chemistry's orderly yet motley realm has resisted stern mathematicizing, the sharp division between theorists and experimenters that one finds in physics does not really exist in chemistry.

In chemistry, indeed, rival theories can coexist without one or the other being cast out as wrong. In his Nobel lecture, Robert Mulliken mentioned that although his molecular orbital theory and Pauling's valence-bonding theory do not agree, they are yet valid alternatives to each other. "But why is not one right and the other wrong?" he asked, and went on to answer: "The explanation is, roughly, that both methods correspond only to approximate solutions of the complete equations which govern the behavior of molecules that contain more than one electron."

Chemists seem to remain resolutely eclectic, devoted both to "physical" rigor and to their beloved laboratory "stink" and all the muddling art it implies. David Knight speaks of every chemist's memory of

> the viscosity, mobility and viscidity of different liquids and the gritty, unctuous or glassy feel of solids; the indescribable but unforgettable smells of things . . . colors . . . tastes . . . bubblings, test-tubes becoming too hot to hold . . . sudden turbidities and precipitations.[34]

Linus Pauling, defending his "resonance" quantum theory of bonding, went on, almost as if he hadn't been a fiercely rigorous theorist, to speak warmly of "feeling":

The theory of resonance in chemistry is an essentially qualitative theory, which, like the classical structure theory, depends for its successful application largely upon a chemical feeling developed through practice.[35]

His peer in theoretic prowess, Mulliken, once said that "physicists are more concerned with fields of force and waves than with the individual personalities of molecules and matter." To hear such an enthusiast of quantum theory talk about the "personalities" of molecules is startling. He even added that "chemists love molecules, and get to know them individually." Can one imagine any physicist loving an electron?

One of the foremost new theoretical chemists, Roald Hoffmann (Nobel 1981), restates the eclectic credo of Pauling and Mulliken in a more contemporary idiom:

I think that in their richness and variety, molecules are to be compared with people. This is what I like about riding the subway in New York — the incredible range of ethnic types, physiognomy, clothes, and emotions. I see tired swarthy men, women with henna-dyed hair, people reading Korean and Russian newspapers, Caribbean blacks, a sleepy Indian girl. Angelic or rough, they're alive, and in their lives are a million novels. When I open a page of *Chemical Communications* or *Angewandte Chemie*, I get a similar feeling.[36]

After such statements, try imagining oneself a member of the Nobel chemistry committee, having to select this year's major achievement from among such a profligate diversity of topics.

The Godlike Organic Chemists and Their Syntheses

In the 1950s and 1960s organic synthesis achieved a brilliant number of structural successes. For more than a decade it soaked up Nobel awards, and deservedly so. Then, suddenly, this heroic way of doing organic chemistry, dating back a century, seemed over.

Whether there will be a Resurrection, and the once living brought back from the dead, is a question for religion, not chemistry. But a minor version of this problem arose early in the history of modern chemistry, and has had many sequels since. The

Swedish chemist Berzelius (1779–1848) had devised the chemical symbols, the first accurate list of atomic weights, and experiments confirming Dalton's theory that all elements must be made of distinct atoms. (He also coined the words "catalyst," "protein," and "isomer.")

Berzelius devoutly believed that an unbridgeable gulf separated life from nonlife. Life cannot issue from anything not living. Berzelius invented the terms organic and inorganic — organic matter could burn, proving it originated in living matter; inorganic stones or iron obviously were not combustible. But in 1828 one of his students, Friedrich Wöhler, synthesized urea that was in every way identical with the natural product — except that it had been produced in the laboratory from inorganic materials. Wöhler had simply heated ammonium cyanate, which Berzelius had to consider an inorganic substance. Berzelius stonewalled as long as he could, but chemists soon made other living compounds out of "dead" materials. The virus conjures up such a puzzle today: it seems exactly poised between being either the most active inanimate substance or the strangest living organism. In 1845 Kolbe produced acetic acid using its natural elements. Like Wöhler's, this was also "life created in a test tube," or what chemists call "synthesis": recreating in the laboratory a compound that is identical with one found in nature.

The high status of organic chemistry had always been linked to its synthesizing and analyzing prowess, since these provide a unique knowledge of structure. By 1900, as Brock notes, organic chemists like von Baeyer and Emil Fischer

> had made the art of structure determination and synthesis at one and the same time the most glamorous and prestigious, as well as tedious and plodding, areas of chemical research. The glamour and prestige were reflected year after year as Nobel prizes were awarded for what seemed incredible feats of synthesis and structure determination. The tedium and mechanically routine nature of much of this structural organic chemistry was reflected in the way generations of schoolchildren and university students were forced to learn ways of adding or subtracting [elements].[37]

Their Nobel Prizes were deserved. The daunting problems involved can hardly be overstated. In 1945 the British chemist

Frederick Sanger (Nobelist in chemistry, 1958 — and again in 1980) set out to synthesize the insulin hormone for the first time. The insulin hormone had first been isolated in 1922, but its structure remained unanalyzed. After eight years of unrelenting hard work, Sanger achieved the first complete analysis ever of a major protein molecule.

To suggest what Sanger faced, Isaac Asimov, a biochemist as well as a science-fantasist, did the following calculations:

> The number of possible arrangements in which 19 amino acids can be placed in a chain (even assuming that only one of each is used) comes to nearly 120 million billion. . . . When you have a protein of the size of serum albumin, composed of more than 500 amino acids, the number of possible arrangements comes out to something like . . . 1 followed by 600 zeroes. This is . . . far more than the number of subatomic particles in the entire known universe.[38]

Moreover, the arrangement of the sequence must be exact. Even one amino acid out of sequence will conjure up a different protein altogether.

Against such seemingly impossible odds, what first makes synthesis possible at all is "analysis" — the reverse of synthesis. Instead of building up a compound, one breaks it down into its components. This can be relatively simple, if the compound is simple. By the turn of the century Emil Fischer had solved the structure of cellulose — plants, trees, wood, and such, comprising one-half of all earthly organic matter — because it is built of a simple basic unit mechanically repeated thousands of times over. But with a complex substance, every weapon and ingenuity (and luck) must be mounted in siege. The chemist might start as Sanger did when he found the complete base sequence of the nucleic acids of a virus, and won his second Nobel in Chemistry, by chopping up the amino acid chain so as to learn where its links began and ended — and this was only an improved version of a method Emil Fischer could have used around 1900. Sanger found that, despite the dogma to the contrary, genes do overlap. These "coupling" units are identical and keep repeating, as when one builds a chain-link fence. To see what comes between, one can use certain reagents to distill away unwanted matter, or use chromatography where elements are separated by color differences, or even enzymes that selectively choose some portion of a compound and thus act as detectors. Sanger did all this and more.

But even if all the components in a compound are identified, the chemist still may be nowhere. Unfortunately, thousands of compounds have the same formula on paper, but are quite differently arranged in space. Chemists call these "isomers." So the chemist must work out the physical shape or conformation — no easy task. Some compounds or molecules contain thousands of atoms in every possible variety of twisting, bending, flexing, and curving, involving not only one chain of linked acids but two or three or more. Even in diagrams leaving out much detail, and helpfully highlighted by different colors, they look like gigantically tangled insane snarls that only God could untie.[39] Here X-ray crystallography has been of incalculable help. But this is also laborious, painstaking work. In X-ray diffraction, X-rays are shot through the atoms to project a pattern of regular marks on film. Chemists then work backwards, using the patterns to reconstruct the structure of the substance. This technique had its first successes with crystals around 1914.

But crystals are simple structures compared with organic molecules. Dorothy Hodgkin was the chemistry laureate in 1964 for her use of X-ray crystallography to analyze the structure of vitamin B_{12} and penicillin. In her own Nobel lecture, she described the tortuous complexities involved in the analysis of hemoglobin and myoglobin by the British laureate-chemists Max Perutz and John Kendrew:

> From a sufficient number of measurements, one can calculate directly the electron density and see the whole structure spread out before one's eyes. However, the feat involved in the calculations described was prodigious — tens of thousands of reflections from five or six crystals were measured to provide the electron-density distribution in myoglobin and hemoglobin.

And, Hodgkin added, even when all went perfectly, the answer only came "stepwise": having located some of the atoms, you had to begin anew, and so on again and again. Such a method provided crucial data that Crick and Watson used to discover the double helix model.

The feat of Perutz and Kendrew (shared Nobel in chemistry, 1962) was truly heroic. In the late 1930s Perutz took on the analysis of hemoglobin; ten years later Kendrew set to work on the related protein myoglobin. Besides an analysis, they wanted to achieve a three-dimensional model of their molecules. Proteins are giants among the molecules. The molecular weight — not an absolute weight, but how much a compound weighs relative to another — of a carbohydrate sugar can be around 200, and a fat around 800. Proteins can range from around 10,000 to 50 million in molecular weight. Hemoglobin, though enormous, is still small-sized in the protein realm, with a molecular weight of about 67,000; a single molecule contains "only" about 12,000 atoms. A molecule of myoglobin is even smaller, about 3,000 atoms. When finally analyzed, in 1959, hemoglobin proved to contain 2,932 atoms of carbon, 4,724 atoms of hydrogen, 828 of nitrogen, 8 of sulfur, 4 of iron (the "hemo" in the name refers to an iron-producing complex), and 840 atoms of oxygen. And "small" as myoglobin is, Kendrew's analysis required measuring the intensities of a quarter of a million X-ray reflections from 110 crystals.[40] Kendrew and Perutz nonetheless constructed a successful three-dimensional model, which meant solving the endlessly knotty conformation problems involved.

Although Sanger and Perutz and Kendrew used the new instrumentation available — the ultracentrifuge, infrared and ultraviolet spectroscopy, electrophoresis, isotopic tracers, chromatography — the basic methods involved were still reminiscent of the laborious methods of earlier decades. There were still two basic ways to synthesize: either slowly and laboriously building up a chain, link by link, one at a time, one after another; or putting together units of the chain, also slowly and laboriously, and then joining them. Hundreds, thousands of steps were involved. The whole process required endless washings to get rid of unwanted waste, but these also ran off much of the product sought.

In 1926 the American James B. Sumner first crystallized an enzyme and thereby proved once and for all that they were proteins, something as great a chemist as the German Willstätter had denied. In 1935 Wendell Stanley and John H. Northrop, also Americans, achieved the first crystallizing of a virus, a truly amazing feat, considering how little was then known about it. The three Americans shared the 1946 prize.

In the 1930s came the first synthesis of any vitamin (vitamin C) by Walter Haworth of Britain (Nobel 1937). The Swiss Karrer synthesized vitamin A in 1930 and B$_2$ in 1935. The German Richard Kuhn (Nobel 1938) independently showed carotenes were a precursor of vitamin A, synthesized B$_2$, and clarified its respiratory role.

In the 1950s came even greater masters of the art. The American chemist Vincent du Vigneaud (Nobel 1955) synthesized the first protein hormone (oxytocin) in 1953. He knew it had eight amino acids and beaded them together in the complex order of linkage he had theorized, and succeeded entirely.

Everyone's choice as the greatest synthesist ever is Robert B. Woodward. His brilliance was early recognized. Admitted to MIT at high-school age, he dropped out because he could learn faster alone. Readmitted and allowed to invent his own curriculum, he took his Ph.D. at twenty. At twenty-one he was on the Harvard faculty. His list of syntheses is unbeatable; no difficulty seemed to faze him. Woodward started in the 1940s with a synthesis of quinine, an enormously complex compound which had resisted a hundred years' effort to build it. He went on to synthesize cholesterol, cortisone, lanosterol, strychnine (devilishly intricate as well as poisonous), lysergic acid (the famous hallucinogen LSD), ergonovine, ellipticine, colchinine, aureomycin, and terramycin. He capped it all with the first full synthesis of chlorophyll.

And yet at least the heroic side of these enterprises vanished as suddenly as the horse-and-buggy gave way to the automobile. By 1970 the American Bruce Merrifield found a way to automatize synthesis of peptides, a short linkage of amino acids. Before this, William Stein and Stanford Moore of the Rockefeller Institute had taken thirty years to complete the first analysis of ribonuclease, an important and complex enzyme. That was in 1960, and they rightly shared the 1972 chemistry Nobel. No one thereafter repeated this feat — until Merrifield. In 1969, using his new method, he repeated Moore and Stein's thirty-year work, although synthesizing this enzyme required 369 reactions and 11,931 separate steps — and it took him only a few weeks.[41] His automated process also synthesized insulin, involving 5,000 operations, in less than a week.

The 1985 colaureates, Hauptman and Karle of the U.S., did something analogous for X-ray crystallography, but their 1950 method was long neglected as too mathematical and thus "unchemical." It is now widely used to quickly analyze molecular structure, especially to produce new drugs.

Elias Corey, the chemistry laureate for 1990, further simplified synthesis by what he called "retrosynthesis": he broke the compound down stage by stage, always making sure he could reverse each step. He thus found the rules for breaking apart compounds and rejoining them. Computerizing retrosynthesis speeds the process immensely, and Corey's computer program for this is now widely used.

Another use of the computer to map reactions was developed in the 1960s by the 1998 Nobelists, Walter Kohn and John Pople. Kohn's "density-functional theory" focuses on locating the average number of electrons in a specific molecule, rather than each individual one. Pople's method analyzes the properties and shape of molecules by computer; his computer program for this is popular.

New Reactions to New Reactions

To the 1950s, the study of reactions was like the late-nineteenth-century method: apply heat or other energy to compounds, and measure what resulted. Even when structural theory improved enough to help clarify the nature of reactions and vice versa, adequate instrumentation often wasn't available. In the 1950s, Manfred Eigen, Ronald Norrish, and George Porter developed methods allowing measurement of reactions occurring at a billionth of a second or less. (They shared the 1967 prize for their work.) Then came improvements such as those by Dudley Herschbach and Yuan Tseh Lee of the U.S., and John Polanyi of Canada, who shared the 1986 chemistry award. In the mid-1960s Herschbach brought into chemistry the kind of collisions that accelerators had introduced into physics. Instead of bombarding nuclei with particles, however, Herschbach bombarded molecules with molecules. He sent a beam of potassium smashing into a beam of carbon, hydrogen, and iodine molecules, hence the name "crossed molecular beams." Molecular collisions showed new phenomena and mechanisms such as energy "rebounds" and opened a new perspective on oscillations and rotations or tumbling, and "translational" energy where the molecule shifts position. Independently, Polanyi in 1968 found a different way called chemiluminescence to measure these same energies.

From the nineteenth century, reactions had been studied in terms of equilibrium. Put simply, all possible forces, energies, influ-

Alfred Nobel hated being photographed or painted because of what he called his "hog-bristle beard" and "unredeemed ugliness." Only a few photos exist, nearly all from his later years. *Courtesy of the Nobel Foundation.*

Albert Einstein's Nobel medal for physics, 1921. Germany jealously claimed him as a citizen, although he was, in fact, Swiss at the time of the awards. The Swedes artfully sidestepped a political dispute by presenting the medal to Einstein in his Berlin home. *Courtesy of the Albert Einstein Archives, the Jewish National and University Library, Hebrew University, Jerusalem.*

The awards to Einstein and Niels Bohr helped greatly in raising the prestige of the Nobel Prizes. Here, in Brussels in 1927, they are in typical form, Bohr talking intently while Einstein strides ahead confidently. They were warm lifelong friends. *Courtesy of Segrè Visual Archives, AIP.*

Only one year after Marie and Pierre Curie shared the 1903 physics prize, the two once-obscure physicists had become celebrities fashionable enough to be caricatured in London's *Vanity Fair.* *Courtesy of The Way We Were, www.waywewere.com.*

In Stockholm in 1933 are, from left, Werner Heisenberg's mother, Erwin Schrödinger's wife, Paul Dirac's mother, and the physicists themselves: Dirac, Heisenberg, and Schrödinger. Heisenberg's mother was recently widowed, while Dirac intensely disliked his own father and refused to invite him to the ceremony. Schrödinger brought his wife, although he had done his prizewinning work while on vacation with a mistress. *Courtesy of Segrè Visual Archives, AIP.*

The 1947 Shelter Island conferences. Three future Nobelists are pictured here: Willis Lamb, standing far left; Richard Feynman, seated at center of table, writing; and Julian Schwinger, standing second from right. Victor Weisskopf, standing third from left, was a near-miss Nobelist; George Uhlenbeck, fourth from left, should have won for discovering quantum spin in 1925. J. Robert Oppenheimer, sitting on edge of sofa at left, never won a prize. *Courtesy of National Academy of Sciences.*

Linus Pauling, here in his mid-eighties, won the chemistry prize in 1954 and the peace prize in 1962, and just missed discovering the double helix in 1953 and thus adding the medicine prize as well. *Courtesy of the Othmer Library of the Chemical Heritage Foundation.*

Robert B. Woodward, left, was the peerless wizard of organic chemical synthesis. He often returned to his lab after a dinner party and, loosening his tie, worked much of the night in his tuxedo. On the right, his Harvard colleague Bernhard Wittkop. *Courtesy of the Othmer Library of the Chemical Heritage Foundation.*

Otto Hahn's worktable on which nuclear fission was discovered in 1939. Adjoining, a 1980s "tokamak" for fusion plasma research, an example of the Big Science apparatus that became the norm in physics after 1950, especially in the case of gigantic accelerators. *Hahn table courtesy of the Deutsches Museum, Munich; tokamak courtesy of the British JET project.*

Frederick Banting, on the right, was a Canadian country doctor who rose swiftly and unexpectedly to Nobel fame. This photo was taken in 1922, when Banting, his student assistant Charles Best (on the left), and J. J. R. Macleod helped discover insulin. The dog in front was the first diabetic saved. The whole effort was Banting's very first experiment, and the next year he shared the Nobel Prize with Macleod. *Courtesy of the Banting House National Historic Site.*

The medicine award became more flexible in 1973 when it honored ethology, the scientific study of animals and birds in their natural conditions. Here Konrad Lorenz, one of the three colaureates, walks with young geese whose new-born eyes, opening on Lorenz, "imprinted" him as their "mother." *Courtesy the Archiv zur Geschichte der Max Planck-Gesellschaft Berlin-Dalhem.*

In 1986 the Swedish Post Office, in an example of the iconic status conferred by the prize, issued stamps honoring the peace prize winners. In the top row, Mother Teresa, Albert Luthuli of South Africa, and Bertha von Suttner; below, Martin Luther King Jr. and Carl von Ossietzky of Germany. *Courtesy of the Swedish Post Office.*

William Faulkner, receiving the 1949 prize, is a rare instance of the Nobel reviving a writer's reputation and career. Although probably the greatest American novelist of the twentieth century, most of his books were out of print when he received the prize. *Courtesy of UPI/Corbis–Bettmann.*

Above: The 1962 ceremony honors Francis Crick, James Watson, and Maurice Wilkins for discovering the double helix of DNA; Max Perutz and John Kendrew for pioneering protein analysis; and John Steinbeck for literature. Crick, Watson, Perutz, and Kendrew all did their prizewinning work at the Cavendish Laboratory in Cambridge. From left to right: Crick, Wilkins, Steinbeck, Watson, Perutz, and Kendrew. *Courtesy of Associated Press AP.*

Left: Dario Fo, the 1997 winner in literature, is more an actor than a writer and here "performs" his Nobel lecture. He remains one of the most puzzling and controversial literary laureates. *Courtesy of Associated Press POOL.*

ences in a reaction must finally balance out. As Gibbs noted in the 1870s, water provides a ready example: it can be frozen, then melted, then be turned to a gas, the gas can be liquefied, and so on. The Belgian physical chemist Ilya Prigogine, however, developed nonequilibrium systems — structures originally in "chaotic" form that nonetheless can self-organize themselves into orderly systems and become stabilized. Prigogine won the 1977 Nobel Prize, and helped spur interest in chaos theory.

Another long-familiar fact is that an enzyme performs only one specific task, so obviously it has to be able to recognize its select target from among the millions crowding any human being. But little was known about how such "molecular recognition" works. Donald Cram and C. J. Pedersen of the U.S. and Jean-Marie Lehn of France advanced a useful explanation. If one enjoys chemical detective stories with strange clues and crisscrossed plots, their research is thrilling. Enzymes of course select a specific organic target. In 1963, Pedersen found that enzymes unexpectedly select certain metal molecules as well, attaching only to special ions. But some metal ions, such as potassium and sodium, are involved in bodily and nerve processes. One puzzle was how those ions ever get out of the cell where they originate. The cell membrane is fatty, and the ions can't dissolve in fat. It turns out that a molecule called an ionophore can penetrate the cell membrane, and ionophores moreover display high selectivity for certain metal ions. Thus the ions "ride" the ionophores right through the cell membrane.

Now, a related thought: if certain ionophores-cum-ions can be used as antibiotics, and if one can bind ionophores to the metal ions artificially, a most useful pharmaceutical process might result, as well as much new insight into how molecular recognition works. Accomplishing this was tricky, to say the least, since "recognition" greatly depends on sensitivity to molecular shape.[42] The fit must be right. In 1894 Emil Fischer called it the lock-and-key pattern; as put later, enzymes seek exactly the right "substrate." Pedersen made molecules of a shape called crown ethers; Lehn built molecule traps for the ions called cryptands. Neither worked well enough. Cram found a better way called — the names begin to sound sinister — carcerands. For this "host-guest" process Cram, Lehn, and Pedersen shared the Nobel Chemistry Prize in 1987.

New achievement in inorganic chemistry began in the 1950s, partly sponsored by industrial demands. In 1938 Giulio Natta, trying to produce synthetic rubber, did research into polymers — molecules of long straight chains of repeated units. In 1953 Karl Ziegler of Germany found a way to catalyze these polymers more quickly, easily, and reliably. They shared the 1963 prize.

In 1973 Ernst Otto Fischer of Germany and Sir Geoffrey Wilkinson of Britain were made laureates for discovering the "sandwich" compound, an organometallic compound of great industrial value in preparing propene and ethene — flammable, colorless, gaseous hydrocarbons used for making other chemicals and plastics. In 1974 another prize in inorganic chemistry went to Paul Florey of the U.S., who showed that polymers have no definite length, but are composed of many macromolecules. He was able to establish the temperature at which specific properties or measurements of polymers can be determined. His findings helped improve, among other things, the elasticity of rubber. In 1994 the prize to George Olah of the U.S. was for discovering a "superacid" from the breakdown of carbon compounds, now much employed, for example, in manufacturing high-octane gasoline.

Poison Gas, the Atom Bomb, and the Nobel Prize

During the Great War, the Nobel Foundation canceled its awards in 1916 and 1917. The first prize given when peace came surprised many: it was, as noted, to the German chemist Fritz Haber. His Nobel Prize cited his discovery around 1908 of how to extract ammonia from nitrogen in the air. This discovery indeed had great benefit to mankind. As the world's population increased, the supply of nitrates for agriculture was decreasing. Soil became exhausted and needed revitalizing. Haber was honored for averting world starvation.

His prizewinning work had a dark side. If World War II was the physicists' war (the Bomb, radar), World War I was the chemists'. Haber's nitrates made possible not only fertilizers but explosives. Only months after the war broke out, Germany found itself running desperately short of nitrates for its munitions supplies. Chile had been the world's supplier, but the British navy cut Germany off from that source. Haber's artificial nitrate method certainly kept Germany in the war for years after it might otherwise have had to capitulate.

This, however, was not the reason Haber's Nobel Prize caused shock. It was because he had introduced poison gas into the war. He had set up the program, recruited other scientists, and devoted himself utterly to the project, as a staunch German patriot. He was not alone in this work. Other scientists who helped the gas warfare program, sometimes working directly for Haber, included the future Nobelists Nernst, Wieland, Hahn, Franck, and Hertz. None of these suffered the public opprobrium heaped on Haber. In 1968 when the University of Karlsruhe, where Haber once taught, celebrated his centenary, two students came forward bearing posters of protest: "Celebration for a Murderer"; "Haber: Father of Gas Warfare." In 1983 the German institute named in honor of Haber even attacked him in a pamphlet as the warmonger type leading to the Hiroshima atrocities.[43]

Haber's role during the war set off such an international uproar that he worried about being arrested at war's end and sentenced to death as a war criminal, a term coined later. Otto Hahn said that Haber

> toward the end of the war became very nervous about this and disappeared for a time. When I saw him he was wearing a beard in order to avoid being recognized instantly. But then, after the war, no steps were taken against him.[44]

All modern military technology of course derives from science, but poison gas seemed an especial perversion, a crossing of a line into the forbidden. The effect of the gas, even when not fatal, was particularly gruesome. Moreover, Germany had signed the Hague Conventions of 1899 and 1907 which banned poison gas in warfare — though such a weapon did not yet exist then, so the terms were vague.[45] What made the Germans ready to resort to poison gas was that their ammunition and food supplies were dwindling dangerously soon after the war began. They had hoped for a quick breakthrough and victory, but trench warfare threatened to stall them indefinitely. Gas seemed the only way to clear out the Allied trenches. So Haber went to work. He held the view that in peace a scientist belongs to the world; in war, to his nation. After all, Louis Pasteur, running for the French Senate in 1876, hadn't hesitated to use the slogan *Patrie et science*.

The first poison gas attack, in April 1915, was set off from five thousand canisters along several miles, and blew toward the French lines. The gas formed into a dense mist almost a thousand yards deep. The French, taken completely by surprise, suffered thousands of dead or seriously wounded — no very accurate figures are available from either side about numbers of gas victims in the war. Gas attacks seem to have been invariably terrible but also terribly confusing, sometimes damaging the attacker more than the enemy. At any rate, from poor planning, the German surprise attack got them no military advantage. A few months later, the Allies retaliated with their own gas attacks. Both sides used gas thereafter.

Haber undertook his ruthless task with patriotic fervor. Even in a very jingoistic age, he was a hypernationalist. When Haber recruited the young Otto Hahn in January 1915 to work on chlorine as a poison gas, Hahn balked because of the Hague agreement. Haber's main argument was that using gas would shorten the war and save lives. Alfred Nobel himself had of course gone further, suggesting that truly horrible weapons might end war altogether. But Haber, though one of Germany's most eminent chemists, and the man who kept Germany in the war with his nitrates, and a superpatriot, was also a Jew. In the gas war, he was at first made a sergeant, and later promoted only to captain. Haber's British counterpart, heading chemical warfare there, was a brigadier. Karlsruhe University had refused to promote Haber to full professor for many years because he was a Jew. Yet Haber spoke of anti-Semitism as a "privilege" — it stimulated Jews to work harder.[46] When Haber's colleague and future Nobelist Hermann Staudinger suggested that the Red Cross urge a ban on poison gas in future wars, Haber almost accused him of betrayal.[47]

He was bald, spectacled, plump, and could be deadly single-minded. But he could also be the liveliest of companions, a most amusing raconteur, a gifted improviser of light verse, a much sought-after friend and sometime colleague of Einstein, Planck, Born, and Willstätter. Haber's dedication to winning the war at any cost, however, had a high personal price. His wife is said to have asked him to give up the poison gas work, and he refused. She shot herself to death in 1915.

Because the Germans broke the Hague agreement first, no blame attached to any of the Allied poison gas scientists. Americans involved included James Bryant Conant, later president of Harvard, and the eminent G. N. Lewis. But since Haber was such a lightning rod for indignation, why did the Nobel chemistry judges honor him

as the first postwar laureate in chemistry? If international reconciliation was the Nobel's motive, it failed miserably: the choice of
Haber deepened Allied vindictiveness toward German scientists.

Haber's son suggests that the Nobel's own discussions about
Haber's prize were really a "curious mixture of ignorance and irrelevance."[48] The chemistry committee was divided about him. His
opponents argued that the Haber-Bosch ammonia process was still
secret, which violated Nobel statutes, and that this process also "had
prolonged the war." But the Nobel archives, says Haber's son, record
no criticism of chemical warfare itself. In 1918 the chemistry committee voted Haber down. In 1919 the same committee reversed itself
and unanimously awarded him the deferred prize. The historian
Elisabeth Crawford suggests that the Nobel committee would not
have honored Haber so soon after the war had there been much
international support for other candidates.[49] If so, the Allies by their
own factionalism awarded Haber at least this one victory.

The tensions involved were doubtless why Haber did not
receive his medal at the ceremony in 1919, as would have been normal, but only in June 1920. Even then, no member of the Swedish
royal family was present. The Nobel Foundation's citation says
only that the royal absence was due to the death of the crown
princess Margaret, and that the ceremony had been postponed to
1920 "for special reasons." Haber's war record and his Nobel Prize
must also have partly explained why, from 1915 to 1927, no German
chemist was nominated for a Nobel Prize by any Allied scientist.

Two other German laureates, first students and later colleagues
of Haber, were drawn into the Hitler war. These were Carl Bosch
and Friedrich Bergius, who shared the 1931 Nobel Chemistry
Prize. Bosch's share was for having made Haber's ammonia process
commercially possible back in 1910. Bosch did no poison gas work.
After Hitler came to power, Bosch was one of the few Nobelists
who remained in Germany; he succeeded Planck as director of the
Kaiser Wilhelm Institute in 1937, and died in 1940. In 1913 Bergius
had found a high-pressure means of increasing coal and gasoline
yield; this became practical in the 1920s, in time to prove most useful to the Nazi campaigns; it also produced ersatz food.

In hindsight, Haber's 1918 Nobel Prize is crowded with ironies.
Gas warfare apparently made little or no difference in the war. The
greatest irony attached to the British chemist who paralleled
Haber's achievement in producing artificial products for the British

war effort. This was Dr. Chaim Weizmann at Manchester, already the leading figure in world Zionism. As Jews, the ultra-assimilated Haber and the passionate Zionist Weizmann could not have been more unlike. Weizmann's great contribution to the British war effort was one reason for the famous Balfour Declaration of 1917, in which Britain promised a homeland in Palestine for world Jewry. In the 1920s, when Germany was suffering under the punitive and ruinous reparations and land seizures imposed on her by the Allies, the patriotic Haber spent his scientific energy on schemes to extract gold from the sea to pay the reparations — in vain.

The saddest irony came in 1933, when the Nazis took power. Haber as a Jew had to resign his post as director of the prestigious Kaiser Wilhelm Institute for Physical Chemistry and Electrochemistry. He went into exile — to Britain, where his old enemies gave him a friendly welcome. Weizmann tried to recruit him as a member of the new scientific institute being built in Rehovot in then Palestine, and Haber was strongly interested. But his heart weakened and he died in 1934.

Now, the Bomb. At the end of World War II, Otto Hahn won the Nobel in chemistry under the most curious circumstances ever. The award was made in 1945, retroactive to 1944. When the announcement was made, Hahn, aged sixty-six, was in a highly secret prison compound called Farm Hall in England, along with nine others including the Nobelists Max von Laue and Werner Heisenberg. Heisenberg and some of the others had key roles in the German nuclear bomb project. Hahn and von Laue had both refused to do scientific war work. Von Laue was openly anti-Nazi, and had resigned his Berlin professorship in 1943, at the height of the war, in protest. He stayed alive, apparently, because he was descended from one of the great Prussian military families, which still carried great influence in the German army.

The Allies put Hahn and the others under arrest partly to learn what they had done in the German atom bomb effort and to make sure they were not seized by the Russians. The detainees were permitted only strictly censored news, and their whereabouts were kept secret. Still, they were treated as eminent guests, though the British secretly taped their conversations; these were allowed to be printed in full only in 1993.[50]

The British intelligence officers occasionally gave thumbnail character sketches of their "guests." Hahn was described both as a man of the world "whose sense of humor and common sense has saved the day on many occasions" and as "unpopular with the younger members . . . who consider him dictatorial." The news of the American atom bomb attack on Hiroshima dumbfounded the German scientists, who could not believe the Americans had succeeded where they had failed. The British eavesdroppers reported that

> Hahn was completely shattered by the news and said he felt personally responsible for the deaths of hundreds of thousands of people, as it was his original discovery which had made the bomb possible. He told me he had originally contemplated suicide. . . . With the help of considerable alcoholic stimulant he was calmed down.[51]

Hahn was not immediately allowed to reply to the Nobel authorities, accepting the prize. The Allies did not want the world to know they were detaining this group.

While this was argued out, Hahn's fellow detainees arranged an impromptu celebration for him — surely the most unusual Nobel celebratory party ever held. A British liaison officer provided baked meats and drinks. According to the British eavesdroppers, the proceedings started badly when von Laue made a somewhat maudlin speech, referring among other matters to Hahn's wife, which brought Hahn to tears. Things cheered up when Heisenberg and the others gave comic parodies of absurdly sensational newspaper reports. One centered on the mysterious disappearance of "Hitler's atom expert" (i.e., Hahn), who was rumored to have escaped with Hitler in a U-boat or was reported seen in Tel Aviv. Another spoof compared Hahn to Goethe: one split hearts, the other atoms. In another, the amount of the Nobel Prize money was divided by the price of sugar, whose energy could be figured in terms of uranium, "though one can't eat uranium." Upshot: one kilo of sugar contains about 4,000 calories; the Nobel Prize is thus worth about 600 million calories. And finally, in true Germanic academic fashion, there was a student song — in a mix of German and English. Stanza one, as reported: "Detained since more than half a year / Are Hahn and we in Farm Hall here. / If one asks who's to blame / The answer is: Otto Hahn." And so on through fourteen more stanzas.

As in Haber's case, ironies abounded. In his memoirs Hahn reports that as the time for the Nobel announcement drew near, an article in the British *New Statesman and Nation* speculated that Hahn might possibly win prizes in both chemistry and peace, "since I had known the secret of how to make the atom bomb, but had not passed it to Hitler. What balderdash!"[52]

Several Nobel mysteries remain. When it awarded Hahn the prize, the Nobel chemistry committee seemed to have no idea where he was. Didn't that worry them? How did they know he was even alive? And what if Hahn were accused of war crimes? True, Hahn and Heisenberg and von Laue were extremely important scientists, about whom news would have probably leaked. But we do not know if the Nobel jury knew or even tried to find out where their absent new laureate was. Hahn certainly fretted that the Swedes would think him rude not to write accepting the award. He asked permission to go to Stockholm in person to receive his prize. This was rejected, but he was finally permitted to write in December declining, with no further explanation. A month later, on 3 January 1946, all ten detainees were allowed to return to Germany. Hahn went to Göttingen, to take up a position offered him by Max Planck as head of the Kaiser Wilhelm Institute, soon to be renamed the Max-Planck Institute.

Hahn certainly deserved his Nobel award. But his colleagues also deserved a share of the prize: the nuclear physicist Lise Meitner and the analytic chemist Fritz Strassmann. Hahn and Meitner had been an inseparable team for three decades, and Strassmann worked closely with them for the last decade or so. Because she was an Austrian Jew, Meitner fled to Sweden in late 1938 when Germany occupied Austria. She and Hahn kept in close and constant correspondence about every detail of the ongoing experiment. Hahn's view of Meitner's role wavered from wanting her name on the decisive paper to describing her after the war as only one among many who understood fission's potential. In his 1946 Nobel lecture he described Meitner and Strassmann as members of his team, but assigned them no credit as equal colleagues. Here the largest mystery lies with the chemistry committee and the Nobel Foundation. The Foundation had helped Meitner when she arrived in Sweden. She had been working in Sweden for at least five years when the Nobel committee voted. It remains unclear whether they ever consulted her about her part in the discovery.[53]

The Second Greatest Missing Chemistry Laureate

The Nobel chemistry judges began their work with two dismal failures. One has been noted: they failed to honor J. W. Gibbs before he died. A few years later they did the same with the great Russian chemist Dmitri Mendeleev, world famous for his indispensable periodic chart of elements. He published his final version of this in 1871. In 1905 and 1906 he was a leading candidate for the Nobel Prize, and the chemistry committee strongly backed him. But one member of the chemistry academy[54] argued that his discovery was too old and well known, and not justified as an exception by "renewed interest." This was odd, since Mendeleev's periodic chart was the basis of continued discoveries — and Nobel Prizes — up to the moment. In 1906 the inorganic chemist Henri Moissan won the prize by one vote over Mendeleev. The Nobel Foundation apparently felt it neither ironic nor unjust that Moissan was honored over Mendeleev for discovering the element fluorine precisely as predicted by Mendeleev. As is well known, Mendeleev had presciently left gaps in his chart where elements should exist, and the first chemistry committee devotedly honored all discoverers of such elements, not only Ramsay and Moissan but in 1911 Marie Curie, giving her a second Nobel, in chemistry this time, for her discovery of radium and polonium, again predicted by Mendeleev's work. Later discoverers of elements — rhenium in 1925, protactinium in 1917, hafnium in 1923 — got no prizes. Only the Americans McMillan and Seaborg were honored in 1951 for their group of artificially produced new elements.

Mendeleev's case is worth pausing on for the glimpse it gives into the often puzzling logic of Nobel juries. Why deny Mendeleev's work as too old, when Baeyer's work also dated from the 1870s? Baeyer's supporters argued that he had made continual contributions up to the time of his award. But Baeyer was also a towering figure in German chemistry, student of the great Kekulé and teacher of Emil Fischer. Mendeleev however was a Russian. In 1910, over in the physics committee, the Dutch physicist Johannes van der Waals was made a laureate for work on low temperatures that dated back to the 1870s; by 1910 his prizewinning work was nearly forty years old. But it had commanded renewed interest with the Dutch physicist Kamerlingh Onnes's low-temperature experiments from about 1908. A stronger argument along the same lines could have been advanced for Mendeleev anytime after J. J. Thomson's discovery of the electron — since that discovery enforced "renewed interest" in Mendeleev's periodic chart and its account of atoms and their weights.

Mendeleev's case also raised the problem of precedence: should the originator of an idea be honored before those who exploited it? This has always been a difficult question. But one committee complaint about Mendeleev was that the Italian chemist Cannizzaro (1826–1910), in his 1858 work on atomic weights, had made Mendeleev's chart possible. If so, why then not have Cannizzaro and Mendeleev share a prize? It would be interesting to know if that was ever considered. Or it may simply be that, at times like these, the Nobel award passeth understanding.

7

The Nobel Prize in Physiology or Medicine

Alfred Nobel's will set up a prize for discoveries in "Physiology or Medicine" — in that order. But few now are likely to be clear why he saw physiology as equivalent to medicine.

"Physiology"

From the middle of the nineteenth century, a revolutionary movement emerged called experimental medicine. In Alfred Nobel's time, this was what "physiology" meant — the effort to shift medical research from the doctor's clinic to the laboratory. "Physiologists" originally were low-status anatomists who taught in nineteenth-century medical schools. Rebelling against physicians' disdain or ignorance of a rigorous study of health and disease, they audaciously decided to refound their science.

In France, in the 1860s, the famous Claude Bernard saw medicine as stagnant and passive, bogged down in useless classifying. He called instead for an "experimental medicine":

> It is thus clear . . . that medicine is moving towards its definitive scientific path . . . gradually abandoning the realm of the [classificatory] systems in order to assume an increasingly analytical form . . . common to the experimental sciences.[1]

In Germany at the same time, a similar experimental psychology was launched, with battle cries of "psychophysics" and "physiological perception." One of the young rebels was Helmholtz, later the great physicist.

Alfred Nobel was a lifetime contemporary of the greatest figure here — Louis Pasteur (1822–1895), who was not a doctor but a chemist of medicine, out of whose experiments came revolutionary insights into bacteriology and immunology, and the demolition of the revered old idea of "spontaneous generation" of disease. He taught instead that germs, not some vague vitalist principle, caused illness. The triumphs of the microbe hunters' conquest of diphtheria, malaria, and other scourges emerged from his work. After Pasteur, not the prestigious physicians in their clinics but the humble chemists and anatomist-physiologists in the lab decided the direction of medical research. "Monsieur Pasteur, who is not even a doctor!" protested a professor of the Academy of Medicine in 1886.[2] True indeed; he was only Pasteur.

To understand the living body, the physiologists approached it as an experimental object. Some physicians saw this as a perversion of their aim of healing and feared that the "art" of medicine was being turned into a mechanico-reductive procedure.[3] The fight against vivisection began in the nineteenth century as part of this protest against the "perverse" attitude of the laboratory researchers.

Nobel was greatly interested in the new experimental physiology. He set up his own private laboratory in Paris and then Italy. He did experiments in blood transfusions, and kept up with developments elsewhere. In the 1890s he donated generously to Pavlov's laboratory in Russia. Physiologism also championed the belief in Progress through Science that was at the heart of so many of Nobel's deepest hopes.

Nobel selected the Karolinska Institute in Stockholm, a medical school and research center, to administer the medicine and physiology prize. That institute then decided that prizes should go only to fundamental research into human health. The Nobel Prize thus decisively linked medicine to the new laboratory research. At the time, it was a bold step. It also meant that clinical achievements could not win prizes. The early-twentieth-century pioneering American neurosurgeon Harvey Cushing, though often nominated, never received an award. Nor did Sigmund Freud, whose new psychoanalysis lacked any strict experimental confirmation.[4]

Indeed in 1895, when Nobel looked about at new medical innovations and insights, it could seem that progress was happening everywhere. By the end of the twentieth century, this could some-times seem an equivocal victory of the old physiological spirit, of patients kept alive by tubing and monitors in a hospital room jammed with all the inhuman equipment of a laboratory. Alfred Nobel died in 1896, when the curve of progress still seemed to be rising. Perhaps he was lucky not to die a century later. He was haunted his entire life by a fear of being buried alive.

Physiology won many Nobel Prizes through the 1930s, particu-larly in the anatomy of the nervous system, muscle, motor, and res-piratory mechanism. But even as it gathered prizes, it was dissolving into the specialties it had launched. A medical historian who was also a physiologist concluded in 1953 that physiology is "no longer a uniform and coherent field of investigation."[5] Perhaps the last prize to classical physiology was the 1963 award to John Eccles, Alan Hodgkin, and Andrew Huxley for, in the Nobel cita-tion, "eludicidating the unitary electrical events in the peripheral and central nervous system."

Nobel Medicine Prizes, 1901–1950

Up to midcentury, physiology was one of the two big winners. Bac-teriology was the other.

Physiology Nobels, 1901–1950
(year of prizewinning work in brackets)

1904 Ivan Pavlov [1890s], physiology of digestion

1906 Camillo Golgi [1873] and Santiago Ramón y Cajal [1887], both in neurology

1909 Emil Theodor Kocher [1890s], thyroid gland

1911 Allvar Gullstrand [1900s], dioptrics of the eye

1912 Alexis Carrel [1904–10], vascular suture, organ transplant

1914 Robert Bárány [c. 1910], ear physiology

1920 August Krogh [1916], capillary motor mechanism

1922 A. V. Hill [c. 1920] and Otto Meyerhof [1913–20], muscle oxidation

1923 Frederick Banting and J. J. R. Macleod [1922], insulin

1924 Willem Einthoven [1913], electrocardiogram

1931 Otto Warburg [1920s], respiratory enzyme action

1932 Charles Sherrington [1900s] and Edgar Adrian [1925], neurology

1934 George Minot, William Murphy, and George Whipple [c. 1926], liver therapy for anemia

1936 H. H. Dale [1929–36] and Otto Loewi [1921], nerve impulse transmission

1938 Corneille Heymans [1924–27], respiration mechanisms

1944 Joseph Erlanger and Herbert Gasser [1921–32], neurology

1949 Walter Hess [1925–40], interbrain as organizer of internal organ activity; António Egas Moniz [1936], lobotomy

Pavlov, the first physiologist to become a laureate, remains the most famous one, but his methods were too rigid to be truly representative of the field. His name is forever tied to the conditioned reflex, yet that theory largely postdated his Nobel award. Instead he won the prize for a theory of digestion that was apparently refuted even before Pavlov was Nobelized. In experiments in 1889, Pavlov restrung a dog's gullet so that food could not reach the stomach. But the gastric juices still ran. Why? Pavlov decided that the nerves in the dog's mouth stimulated the brain, and the brain commanded the digestive juices to run.

Unfortunately, when two English physiologists, E. H. Starling and W. M. Bayliss, repeated Pavlov's experiment in 1902, they found that a substance called secretin, an intestinal hormone, was setting the juices of the duodenum to work. In Saint Petersburg, Pavlov had their experiment repeated, and it turned out exactly as predicted. As an eyewitness later recounted, "Without a word Pavlov disappeared into his study. He returned in half an hour and said, 'Of course, they are right.'"[6] The pancreatic enzymes were not under neural control. Pavlov devoted himself thereafter to the conditioned reflex. In the Nobel lectures of 1904, neither he nor the Nobel citation referred to the refutation by Starling and Bayliss. One is tempted to think that the Nobel judges exhibited a conditioned reflex in honoring the famous Pavlov for a dubious discovery.[7]

Why didn't Starling and Bayliss at least share the prize with Pavlov? Their discovery was quickly and fully reported and confirmed before the Nobel award to Pavlov. But Starling and Bayliss deserved a Nobel Prize on their own for opening the field of endocrinology by their discovery of the hormone secretin in 1902. Starling invented the term hormone; adrenaline had been found earlier, but its general significance was not understood. According to the official Nobel history,[8] they were "found by the Nobel Committee examiner to deserve a prize" in 1913 and 1914. But the First World War interrupted, and Starling was not nominated again until 1926, when "the discovery was regarded as too old." This seems another instance of splintered reasoning in Stockholm, since other prizes in the same period went to work as old or older: see Golgi and Laveran below. And after the discovery of insulin (1921–22), which is a protein hormone, there was, as the Nobel Statutes allowed, "renewed interest" in hormones.

Early physiology made great advances in neurology. In 1887 the Spaniard Ramón y Cajal discovered the synapse (a name coined later), helped by work done by the Italian histologist Golgi in 1873. Both shared the 1906 Nobel Medicine Prize. Why, one wonders, wasn't Golgi's discovery "too old" by then?

By 1906, the English neurologist Charles Sherrington gave the first systematic account of the integrative action of the central nervous system. He distinguished between motor nerves and sensory nerves, traced the root of nerves in musculature, and investigated reflexes, inventing the famous "knee-jerk" reflex test.

Sherrington received 134 nominations from thirteen countries over thirty years. But his Nobel award was unaccountably delayed until 1932, when he was seventy-five. The Nobel history says that in 1910 the examiner advised delay, but then in 1912 and 1915 found Sherrington deserving. A member of the committee, however, raised the fantastical objection, which was taken seriously, that Sherrington's discoveries really had been anticipated — in 1826! The grounds of objection shifted as strangely after the First World War: Had Sherrington made a specific enough discovery? The same examiner who had been evaluating Sherrington so waveringly since 1910 finally retired in 1927.[9] Five years later, Sherrington finally became a laureate.

Physiology grew out of anatomical work, and long retained that orientation. Ramón y Cajal and Sherrington were virtuosos at laying bare microscopic nerve endings or cells. The process continued — but using electrical or chemical probes, more delicate than any scalpel — with Nobelists such as Edgar Adrian, H. H. Dale and Otto Loewi, Joseph Erlanger and Herbert Gasser. Others, like A. V. Hill, Otto Meyerhof, and Otto Warburg, used chemical probes. Banting and Macleod, in their insulin experiments, tied up ducts; Theodor Kocher surgically excised a thyroid gland in feathery slices to study the resulting changes.

Walter Hess (Nobel 1949) devised a "stereotaxic" scalpel to implant electrodes in the brain. Alexis Carrel (Nobel 1912) invented ingenious suturing techniques, which allowed vascular transplants. After his Nobel, Carrel kept a chicken heart alive — or at least pumping — for thirty-four years. In fact, it "outlived" him. The EKG (electrocardiogram) and EEG (electroencephalogram) were innovations in the physiological tradition. Alas, so were the brutal lobotomies of Egas Moniz (Nobel 1949).

But in the inevitable wars between the specialties, physiology began losing out to biochemistry.

Bacteriology Nobels, 1901–1952
(year of prizewinning work in brackets)

1901	Emil von Behring [1890], diptheria vaccine
1902	Ronald Ross [1897], malaria vector
1903	Niels Finsen [1893–94], lupus phototherapy
1905	Robert Koch [1880s–1890s], TB and anthrax vaccine
1907	Charles Laveran [1882], malaria research
1908	Elie Metchnikoff [1882], white corpuscles
	Paul Ehrlich [1890s], serum therapy
1913	Charles Richet [1901–3], antibody shock research
1919	Jules Bordet [1898–1906], immunity component
1926	Johannes Fibiger [1913], cancer therapy
1927	Julius Wagner-Jauregg [1917], malaria inoculation as cure for dementia paralytica

1928 Charles Nicolle [1902], typhus

1929 Christiaan Eijkman [1897], cause of beriberi

1939 Gerhard Domagk [1932], sulfa drugs

1945 Alexander Fleming [1928], Ernst Chain and Howard Florey [1938–41], penicillin

1948 Paul Müller [1939], DDT

1951 Max Theiler [1937], yellow fever

1952 Selman Waksman [1943], streptomycin

In the Nobel's first twenty years, excluding 1915 through 1918 because of war, bacteriology took half the prizes, and from 1921 to 1940, almost as many.

Pasteur found the parasite that was destroying the French silk industry and he found an inoculation against rabies and against anthrax. He died in 1895 and missed a certain Nobel award, but he caused a small flood of them later.

Heyday of the "Microbe Hunters"

From 1880 to about 1930, bacteriologists were the glamorous conquistadors of medicine; they traveled the globe in their white coats, carrying microscopes and test tubes intrepidly into jungles and epidemics, tracking down the bacterial enemies of humanity. That is how the popular imagination saw them; the reality was not much different.

The German bacteriologist Robert Koch began as a practicing physician in a small town. Outwardly stiff and guarded, he had an itch for adventure, longing to be an army doctor or a ship's physician. Despite his extreme nearsightedness, the Franco-Prussian War in 1870 gave him a chance for excitement; it also introduced him to epidemic cases of cholera and typhoid fever. When peace came, he shifted to bacteriology, certainly more adventurous than routine medical practice. He traveled to Egypt and India to conquer cholera. His discovery of the anthrax bacillus in 1876 was the first conclusive proof of Pasteur's germ theory. In 1882 he discovered the tubercle bacillus. Starting in 1897, he at last explained the dreaded bubonic plagues of the Middle Ages: the disease was transmitted by lice from infected rats. He also showed that sleeping sickness was transmitted by the tsetse fly. His "postulate" for proving that a microbe causes a disease means being able to isolate the microbe, use it to transmit the disease, then isolate it again.

This opened one of the modern ways of controlling epidemics: attack not the disease but the carrier. Wipe out the lice and flies, and the disease is ended. The life cycle of the carriers must thus be studied, and another new branch of bacteriology opened up. Koch, though the pioneer, won his prize only in 1905.

Another method was found by Paul Ehrlich, one of Koch's disciples: a direct attack by chemicals.[10] He conceived this in 1885 and developed it over the next fifteen years, with two years spent in Egypt recovering from TB — the microbe hunter hunted, this time. Ehrlich seemed ready to quarrel with anyone who did not obey his wishes to the letter. Still, this tyrant of the lab was clearly the coming man, and in 1896 he was made director of the State Institute for Serum Research and Control. Bacteriology, in short, had its distinct political and imperialist uses. Europeans needed protecting, but so did European colonies around the world.

Ehrlich found a new way to kill germs. He had stained bacteria cells so they could be seen with a microscope. He then asked, if bacteria would combine selectively with dyes, might they also combine with chemicals that would kill them? Such a substance bore the romantic name "magic bullet" — that is, a chemical that killed the germ without harming the human host. Ehrlich thus opened chemotherapy and the ever-continuing search for laboratory-produced drugs that directly attack pathogens. In the 1940s came sulfa drugs and antibiotics. Ehrlich's popular fame is from his cure for syphilis, the "magic bullet" salvarsan, but that came two years after his prize in 1908.

Emil von Behring, not Koch, won the first Nobel Prize in Medicine perhaps because diphtheria was then rightly feared by every child and parent in the world. Behring's inoculation method descended from a discovery by Edward Jenner in 1796: serum from an infection can protect humans against future infection. The second Nobel Prize involved the conquest of the colonial scourge malaria. Robert Ross, working as a government physician in India, found in 1897–98 that the anopheles mosquito carried the malarial parasite. Swamps were drained, mosquito netting was faithfully used, and the disease receded. In some of these cases, the Nobel medicine committee must have been greatly puzzled by what constituted a "discovery," since it awarded the 1907 Nobel Prize to the French military surgeon Charles Laveran, who in Algeria in 1880 isolated the parasite that Ross later saw was causing the disease. By then Laveran's work was almost thirty years old. Perhaps Laveran benefited from a chain reaction in favor of bacteriologists in the Nobel committee.[11]

The Russian chemist Metchnikoff's discovery of white corpuscles also dated back to the 1880s. By the time of his prize in 1908, shared with Ehrlich, he had been nominated every year from 1901. Metchnikoff is a good early example of an enduring type of Nobel candidate: a scientist who had a sizable achievement in the distant past but, aging, gives up research to administer a prestigious institute. He was Pasteur's hand-picked successor as director of the Pasteur Institute, and thus held a position of great influence with the Swedish Academy of Sciences. Figures like Metchnikoff are often nominated, carry weight, and can be hard to ignore. His life at times resembled a parody of the larger-than-life Russian: when young, after his wife died, he tried to kill himself but — odd for a chemist — he took too strong a dosage, couldn't keep it down, and survived. In later years he believed that the normal human life span was one hundred fifty years, and propagandized cultured milk as the royal way to such a long life. He himself died at seventy-one. His fame rests on the discovery of antibodies.

The 1913 prize went to Charles Richet of France for his discovery of anaphylaxis: a first dose of a vaccine may save, but a second dose can shock the system and cause its death. Richet's discovery in a way initiated the study of allergies, a word coined in 1906, and anaphylaxis remains topical, with allergic reactions a concern in the widespread use of antibiotics. Richet tried flying before the Wright brothers, saw two of his plays performed in Paris, and was a long-time president of the Society for Psychical Research. His Nobel seems almost a letdown.

Three more Nobels were still to come for bacteriology, but the line runs thin. The 1919 award to the Belgian Jules Bordet was for a reaction test that shows a disease is present. The famous Wassermann test for syphilis is based on it. Wassermann might well have shared or even carried off the award, but it was unthinkable: he was German and Richet was Belgian, and World War I had just ended.[12]

The final two Nobels for the older kind of bacteriology went in 1928 to the Frenchman Charles Nicolle for typhus research and in 1951 to the South African Max Theiler for yellow fever research. Both helped fight dread diseases, but they contributed little new in that each used basic methods by then decades old.

Bacteriology won such a wealth of prizes partly because the conquering of disease affects everyone. Partly, too, the Nobel medical committee then preferred its science with quick, clear-cut results, and not too theoretical. Early bacteriology, like early physiology, provided all this. Of course, microbe-hunting also had a glamour that commanded public interest (and self-interest) as few other scientific discoveries can. Finding the top quark may be a physics problem; finding a cure for cancer is everyone's problem. Koch and the rest were the forerunners of the researchers who mount "task forces" to find cures for polio, cancer, MS, AIDS, and other target diseases. Then as now, the Nobel judges, the public, industry, and government handsomely rewarded them. The non-Nobelist Jonas Salk is doubtless still a more familiar name than McClintock, Lipmann, or Medawar.

Vitamins, Hormones

The historian Robert Köhler remarks that "medical biochemists were rewarded for discovering a new vitamin or hormone, not for tackling large biological problems."[13] But vitamin and hormone research could hardly help but raise larger problems.

Vitamins were discovered in 1890 by the Dutch physician Christiaan Eijkman and partly confirmed by the British physiological chemist F. G. Hopkins. The Nobel awards here become a bit tangled.

We start with Eijkman who, after studying with the great Koch, then spent ten years in Java working on the deadly beriberi. He finally saw that it must be caused by diet. Husked rice gave beriberi to his experimental chickens; whole or unpolished rice did not. Eijkman decided the husk must contain something that countered a toxin in the rice. He had in fact discovered vitamin deficiency but didn't know it. Polishing the rice had created the deficiency.

It was Hopkins who wrongly got the main credit for explaining Eijkman's discovery. In 1912 he generalized Eijkman's and other clues into a theory of "accessory food factors" that the body requires, but could not identify the substance at issue. However, also in 1912, a Polish biologist named Casimir Funk found the entity in rice that cured beriberi. He named it vitamine, thinking it had something to do with amino acids, which it didn't. In the 1930s this was identified as vitamin B_1. But though Eijkman and Hopkins had not really proved the principle of vitamins and Hopkins's main findings lay in what he called "intermediary metabolism," Hopkins and Eijkman shared the 1929 prize in medicine; Funk was never made a laureate.

Biochemists are now celebrated. But Hopkins's career reminds one how discouraging the career of early biochemists could be, even the most prestigious. At the turn of the century, Hopkins was appointed the first lecturer in biochemistry at Cambridge, but the salary was so low he had to grub at teaching medical students for extra income and had little time for his own research. His laboratory was a depressing table set up in a cellar. In 1914, aged fifty-three, he was finally appointed to a professorship of biochemistry — but unendowed and without salary. Only in 1924 did a private donor, a hatmaker, make it possible for Hopkins to set up a proper laboratory. Hopkins made some important discoveries, though most of them seemed to issue from mistakes, and many of his prized theories turned out wrong. But he helped invent and build up modern biochemistry, especially in Britain. This small, lean, hollow-cheeked man, with drooping mustache and a courtesy that "was almost Chinese,"[14] deserved a Nobel for being a great teacher — except that no such category exists.

Biochemistry Ascendent

Like other scientific specialities, biochemistry arose out of diverse discoveries, in this case new techniques and enthusiasms in physiology, pharmacology, organic chemistry, and biology. Slowly it won a professional niche among, and often against, established specialties.[15]

Eduard Buchner's discovery that enzymes existed outside cells was a crucial start here. Further research into enzymes brought prizes from several directions, reflecting the central importance of the topic. Enzymes were puzzling precisely because, as is now known, they do so much: they are the most important agents of metabolism, ultimately involving all the chemical reactions of the living body. In 1904–5, the Briton Arthur Harden took a large step forward: he proved that an enzyme required another to complete its work, a removable part called the coenzyme. Harden shared the 1929 prize in chemistry with Hans von Euler-Chelpin of Sweden who in 1924–28 worked out the structure of the coenzyme for yeast. As the delay from 1904 to 1929 suggests, clarity about the remarkably complex enzyme was slow in coming.

As an example, the formidable German organic chemist Richard Willstätter (Nobel in chemistry, 1915) held that enzymes were not proteins, although neither he nor anyone else had been able to purify and isolate an enzyme. In 1926, however, the Cornell chemist James B. Sumner successfully crystallized an enzyme and also showed it was a protein — a great breakthrough. Sumner's finding was confirmed in the early 1930s when John Northrup of the Rockefeller Institute crystallized other enzymes, deploying a hundred reagents to do it. Sumner and Northrup shared part of the 1946 prize. Since the 1930s, several hundred enzymes have been crystallized. In 1931 the prize in medicine went to Otto Warburg of Germany, for discovering the respiratory enzyme that governs oxygen flow in cells, but also the first coenzyme. Warburg's Nobel Prize probably helped him survive protected through the entire Nazi period, although he was Jewish: Hitler was said to fear cancer, and hoped that the prizewinning Warburg would find a cure.

By the 1920s a new interdisciplinary specialty was clearly needed. Just then Providence — in the form of the Rockefeller Foundation — shifted its funding from medical to biomedical research and biochemistry, with the Rockefeller Institute in New York as home base. Similar steps were taken in Copenhagen, Cambridge, and the Kaiser Wilhelm Institute in Berlin. The metabolic pathways, the roles of hormones, vitamins, and amino acids began to be clarified.

Enzymes being agents of metabolism, that field blossomed into prizes in the 1940s and after. From the 1930s, the husband-wife team Gerty and Carl Cori showed how carbohydrates break down into lactic acid in muscle tissue: they shared part of the 1947 medicine prize. In 1937 Hans Krebs furthered the Cori findings by explaining how lactic acid itself is metabolized, a process known thereafter as the Krebs cycle. But how the cell gains the energy it releases into the body remained unclear until Fritz Lipmann gave a comprehensive explanation in his account of ATP (see page 264). Krebs and Lipmann shared the 1953 prize in medicine.

Biochemistry began another early line of successes in immunology. In 1902 Karl Landsteiner made the striking discovery that human blood types could be classified into four groups. Moreover, the groups included antibodies that could not attack their own group. He took the 1930 Nobel in Medicine for this. Why the delay from 1902 to 1930, since his discovery opened the way to blood transfusions as well as advances in immunology? Because transfusions required technological advances: a way to keep blood from coagulating, a way to save blood; experiments to see what was possible and how types were inherited. It was well into the 1920s before these and other questions began to be cleared up.

This body of work pointed to the possibility of transplants. In the 1930s the Australian immunologist Macfarlane Burnet raised the key question here: How can a living organism recognize toxins from its own body as against those introduced from outside? Burnet theorized that the body "tolerated" toxins it had known early in life. But could it develop artificial tolerance for new material introduced later? Burnet could not experimentally prove this. But Peter Medawar at Oxford did between 1947 and 1953. They shared the 1960 prize in medicine. Another prize in immunology went in 1980 to Jean Dausset, George Snell, and Baruj Benacerraf for clarifying "histocompatibility" complexes, crucial to transplants and antibody effectiveness. From 1955 to 1973 came the "clonal selection" theory of Niels Jerne: antibodies are produced when they attack or "bind" to an antigen; the body somehow recognizes this as valuable and clones that antibody in great quantities. In 1984 Jerne shared the medicine prize. In 1996 the Nobel in Medicine to Peter Doherty and Rolf Zinkernagel was for showing more clearly how "T-cells" — cytotoxic white blood cells — recognize the viral cells they attack. They found that two signals are involved: the T-cell has to recognize both the virus and the histocompatible protein of the body. The T-cells apparently have surface proteins as receptors.

In 1987 the laureate was Susumu Tonegawa, who explained the genetic basis for the astonishing diversity of antibodies. The 1990 prize to Joseph E. Murray and E. Donnall Thomas was, respectively, for the first kidney transplanted and the first bone marrow transplant between nontwins. When DNA arrived, immunology made other advances to be noted.

DNA and the Double Helix Onstage

Since the dramatic discovery in 1953 by Crick and Watson of its double helix structure, the genetic matter DNA (deoxyribonucleic acid) has became a public icon. Instant attention is commanded by any hint that a gene controlling a fearful disease has been found, or a murderer identified by a genetic "fingerprint," not to mention the possible test-tube alteration by cloning or genetic engineering of the entire human race. Molecular biology in turn has loosened into a catchphrase and broadened into a worldview.

The discipline emerged in the early 1940s as a motley, small, and self-elected group that set itself against the mainstream. It attracted and required a number of mavericks: chemists interested in physics or genetics like Linus Pauling, offbeat geneticists like Salvador Luria and James Watson, Edward Tatum and George Beadle, physicists interested in biology and genetics like Max Delbrück and Francis Crick, and a few X-ray crystallographers.

Genetics began modestly in 1866, when the Moravian monk Gregor Mendel patiently charted mutations in peas, and discovered heredity laws that implied the existence of genetic factors, later dubbed "genes." When his work was rediscovered, only in 1900, it excited much attention. Thomas Hunt Morgan, a young American zoologist — chemists and medical researchers didn't bother much with genetics until the 1940s — decided around 1908 to prove Mendel wrong. Instead, he proved him more right than ever. Morgan interbred fruit flies, which multiply fast and are easy to examine, and catalogued the endless mutations in eye color and wing shape. By 1911 he understood that cells contain chromosomes along which genes are arranged in definite positions. Morgan won the 1933 Nobel Prize in Medicine.

That Morgan's Nobel Prize was in medicine showed how much things had changed since he began research in 1908. At Columbia University, Morgan worked outside the medical school there. And why, in 1910, should any medical school be interested in breeding fruit flies? In 1928 Morgan moved to CalTech, which has no medical school. But the result was that, in 1953, it wasn't conventional biochemists who discovered the double helix, but the zoologist-geneticist Watson and the ex-physicist Crick.

A Map of Prizes Involving DNA
(years of prizewinning work in brackets)

1933 Thomas H. Morgan [from 1908], chromosome research

1946 Hermann J. Muller [1926], X-ray mutations

1958 George Beadle and Edward Tatum [1941], "one-gene-one-enzyme" link; Joshua Lederberg [1940s–52], bacteria's genes

1959 Severo Ochoa [1955], enzyme synthesis of RNA; Arthur Kornberg [1955–56], enzyme synthesis of DNA

1960 Macfarlane Burnet and Peter Medawar [1940–1950s], immunology and transplants

1962 Francis Crick, James D. Watson, and Maurice Wilkins [1953], structure of DNA

1965 François Jacob and Jacques Monod [1960s], genetic transfer

1966 Peyton Rous [1911], virus as cause of cancer

1968 Robert Holley, Har Gobind Khorana, and Marshall Nirenberg [early 1960s], genetic code

1969 Max Delbrück and Salvador Luria [1943], bacterial genetics; Alfred Hershey [1952], phage structure

1972 Gerald Edelman and Rodney Porter [1967], antibody structure

1974 Albert Claude and Christian de Duve [1940s], cell fractionation; George Palade [1960s], protein synthesis

1975 David Baltimore, Renato Dulbecco, and Howard Temin [1970], retrovirus

1976 Baruch Blumberg [1960s], hepatitis genetics; D. Carleton Gajdusek [1970], new infectious virus

1977 Roger Guillemin and Andrew Schally [1970s], brain aminohormonic production; Rosalyn Yalow [1959], radioimmune assay

1978 Werner Arber [1962], two-enzyme system and gene splicing; Daniel Nathans and Hamilton Smith [1971], restriction enzymes

1980 Baruj Benacerraf, Jean Dausset, and George Snell [1970s], immunological genetics

1983 Barbara McClintock [1950], movable genes

1984 Niels Jerne [1974], antibody recognition; Georges Köhler and César Milstein [1975], monoclonal antibodies

1985 Michael Brown and Joseph Goldstein [1970s–1980s], cholesterol genetics

1986 Stanley Cohen and Rita Levi-Montalcini [1980s], growth factors

1987 Susumu Tonegawa [1970s], genetics of antibody diversity

1988 James W. Black, Gertrude Elion, and George Hitchings [1970–1980s], DNA and blockage of cell replication

1989 J. Michael Bishop and Harold Varmus [1970s], retroviral oncogenes

1993 Phillip Sharp and Richard Roberts [1970s], "split genes"

1995 Edward Lewis, Christiane Nüsslein-Vollard, and Eric Wieschaus [1970–1980s], homeotic genes and human birth defects

To these must be added certain Nobels in chemistry related to genetics:

1946 James B. Sumner [1926], John H. Northrop and Wendell Stanley [1935], purification of enzyme and virus protein

1964 Dorothy Hodgkin [1957], X-ray techniques, clarifying molecular structure of vitamin B_{12}

1970 Luis Leloir [1959], sugar nucleotides

1980 Paul Berg [1956], recombinant DNA; Walter Gilbert [1977] and Frederick Sanger [1973], base sequence in nucleic acid

1982 Aaron Klug [1972–81], nucleoprotein complexes by electron microscopy

1987 Donald Cram, Jean-Marie Lehn, and Charles Pedersen [1970s], "host-guest" chemistry

1989 Sidney Altman and Thomas Cech [1980s], catalytic action of RNA

1993 Kary Mullis [1983], polymerase chain reaction; Michael Smith [1980s], site-directed mutagenesis to reprogram cell's DNA

Genetics Goes Molecular

Mutations were a puzzle: why and how did they happen? To say "genes" explained little. For long, genes were shadowy, perhaps even nonexistent things. At the genetic level, said Morgan in his 1933 Nobel lecture, "it doesn't make the slightest difference whether the gene is a hypothetical unit or a physical unit." They certainly were hard to pin down. During the First World War, some microorganisms were found that acted like viruses by parasitically devouring the bacterial host, but also mutated like genes. But genes weren't supposed to act like viruses.

One of these peculiar microorganisms was the bacteriophage, later famed in molecular biology. These strange viruslike genes caught the eye of the geneticist Hermann Muller, one of Morgan's first students, who in 1922 gave a remarkable prophecy. If genes and viruses were really different substances, said Muller, yet both subject to mutation, that would be a "curious coincidence indeed," raising the "possibility of two totally different kinds of life, working by different mechanisms." But suppose the virus and gene were the same or related: if so, that

> would give us an utterly new angle from which to attack the gene problem. They are filterable, to some extent isolable, can be handled in test-tubes. . . . It would be very rash to call these bodies genes, and yet at present we must confess that there is no distinction known between the genes and them. Hence we cannot categorically deny that perhaps we may be able to grind genes in a mortar and cook them in a beaker after all.

His next statement was a very bold one for a fruit fly experimenter at that time:

> Must we geneticists become bacteriologists, physiological chemists and physicists, simultaneously with being zoologists and botanists? Let us hope so.[16]

Muller then did what he preached. He literally took genetics to the molecular level of matter. In 1926 he sprayed his fruit flies with X-rays; mutations dramatically increased. Since X-rays penetrate the tiny ghostly reaches of matter, something was obviously happening to the genetic material in the cells on the microorganic level. Muller won the 1946 Nobel Prize in Medicine.

In the late 1930s a number of physicists took up biology because of genetics. At first sight, heredity and physics seem an odd couple. What have mutations in fruit fly wings to do with quantum physics? Muller's X-ray mutations were one such clue. A gene, after all, is an extraordinarily stable agent. It keeps replicating the same genetic message almost endlessly. Leaving aside the epochs of evolution, what else could mutate such a rock-steady form? Muller's high-energy X-rays had done it. That could set a physicist thinking about how to unsettle stable atom arrangements by energy levels high enough to excite electrons into different joinings. Perhaps the gene could be more directly explained by physics than by chemistry. After all, through the 1930s, as Max Delbrück later recalled, no one really was sure what a gene was at all, or how (or if) it differed from a phage or a protein.

> Genes at that time were algebraic units of the combinatorial science of genetics, and it was anything but clear that these units were mole-cules analyzable in terms of structural chemistry. They could have turned out to be submicroscopic steady state systems.[17]

Delbrück, from a grand German academic family, began as a theoretical physicist, a student of Niels Bohr. Bohr, who wondered about everything, wondered too if biology could provide new laws of physics. Delbrück found this suggestion irresistible, and shifted to biology. He published some speculations on the matter in 1935, shortly before he emigrated to the U.S.

In 1944 came a very influential book, hardly more than a hundred pages long: *What Is Life?* It was by Erwin Schrödinger, the famous quantum wave theorist (Nobel in Physics, 1933). Like Delbrück, he thought that the gene might be solved through physics, bypassing chemistry altogether. Schrödinger proposed that the gene, in its atomic arrangement, might embody a genetic "code-script," somewhat like a Morse code which "speaks" sentences through combinations of simple dots and dashes. Biologists and chemists had speculated on such codes, but Schrödinger's prestige and emphasis on physics made people listen. Among them were three young scientists who would later share a Nobel Prize for solving the structure of the gene: James Watson, Francis Crick, and Maurice Wilkins.[18]

In 1940 Delbrück started working on bacteriophages (phages, for short) with another émigré, the Italian chemist Salvador Luria. Phages made a fine experimental agent since they were amazingly quick breeders. In twenty minutes they could fill and then burst out of their host shell — the experimentalist hardly had to sit around waiting. The virus's primitive makeup, simply some protein and nucleic acid, also simplified lab techniques.

Delbrück and Luria — two "enemy aliens," as Delbrück put it — came up with an important discovery in 1943. In those days, Luria recalled, bacteriologists believed that bacteria "had no chromosomes and no genes." But if bacteria could mutate and become resistant to viruses, this dogma was wrong. Testing the idea was a problem. Alas, bacteria don't come singly, but in the millions. Finding "some" resistant ones is worse than hunting a needle in a haystack. In his memoirs,[19] Luria recalls how an idea struck him at a wartime college dance, while watching a slot machine. The machines occasionally came through with a big jackpot, but most of the time paid little if anything. If you tested bacteria, Luria thought, it would be like playing the slot machine at random: the odds were you'd come up with bacteria that hadn't developed resistance. But probability methods might show some clustering of resistant bacteria somewhere in the millions of bacteria, just as on a slot machine. Delbrück worked out the mathematics in a couple of weeks, and Luria's experiment panned out. They had proved that bacteria might be subject to mutation, which meant that bacteria evolved, and thus had genetic character. Delbrück and Luria shared the 1969 Nobel Prize in Medicine for their discovery, although their role as guiding spirits of the molecular movement was as important.

Genetics was now dramatically opened in a narrowed way at the molecular level, since a bacterium is ten thousand times smaller than a fruit fly.

But the physicists' hope to bypass chemistry was misplaced. Indeed, until the chemists cleared up a long-standing confusion, no real progress could be made by anyone. This roadblock was that until 1944 most biologists believed — wrongly, but understandably — that genes were made of proteins. Proteins with their twenty-odd amino acid components are large, complex, and versatile enough to handle life's many requirements. It turned out, however, that genes are composed of nucleic acids. The German physiologist Albrecht

Kossel had in fact demonstrated a link between nucleic acids and genes back in 1893 (he won the 1910 Nobel in Medicine).

Nucleic acid, however, long seemed a side issue. An important early researcher at the Rockefeller Institute who bore the improbable name of Phoebus Levene — he had been born in Russia as Fishel Levine, then Russianized Fishel to Fyodor, which he then Americanized, mistakenly, to Phoebus — was the first to show that nucleic acid was either RNA (ribonucleic acid) or DNA (deoxyribonucleic acid). Both contain, among other components, the sugar ribose plus carbohydrates; "deoxy" means the DNA lacks one oxygen atom in its sugar structure. This was in 1911. Despite his advance on Kossel, Levene won no Nobel award, probably because his model opened up few opportunities for further research. Discoveries like Levene's, however elegant, are stillborn unless they can be connected to other important findings (the fear of finding a lovely structure that led nowhere often haunted Crick and Watson). Levene was also the first to arrange nucleic acids in combinations or "bases" — a seminal idea, though his version was partly wrong because too mechanical.

In 1944, however, Oswald Avery of the Rockefeller Institute shifted the center of genetics. He proved that nucleic acid, not protein, composed the gene. One might think this would have caused a sensation. Alas, Avery was a poor salesman for his own discovery, fastidious and hypercautious, "almost neurotically reluctant to claim that DNA was genes and genes were simply DNA."[20] The opposition was anything but bowled over, and the Nobel jury missed him. Even inside the Rockefeller, prominent chemists still voted for protein as the genetic agent.[21] Avery's view gained wide acceptance only in 1952, when Alfred Hershey and Martha Chase proved him right. Hershey shared the 1969 medicine Nobel with Delbrück and Luria; Avery was ignored by the Nobel until he died in 1955, by which time his finding had been triumphantly confirmed by Watson and Crick's discovery in 1953, as well as by the Austrian émigré Erwin Chargaff's discovery in 1948 of nucleic pairing in DNA. But neither Chargaff nor Chase ever won a Nobel Prize either.

To be sure, Avery's chemical analysis was far from comprehending the actual structure of the gene molecule. One somehow needed to look directly through all the layering flesh and muscle, bone, tissue and cells, to see the shape and weave of the thing itself. The long-tested way of doing just this, at least indirectly, was

X-ray crystallography, which began before World War I with von Laue and then the Braggs, that fine father-and-son team. The son, later Sir Lawrence Bragg, eventually directed the Cavendish Laboratory at which Crick and Watson worked. X-rays have small enough wavelengths to slip through the tight bindings of matter and project themselves onto a screen beyond. Analyzing the resulting patterns, a concentric ring of reflections and shadows, the crystallographer can work backwards to reconstruct the structure that was X-rayed. By the 1940s, there was great expertise in this technique. This would provide the second clue for Watson and Crick.

A third clue came from Pauling, a master of interpreting crystallographic photographs, as of everything else in chemistry. He also liked to build models to work out actual physical details and problems. This is the reverse of the crystallographer's backwards-analyzing method: with models, a structure is built up "forwards," using prior knowledge of bond angles and lengths. In 1948, sick in bed on a visit to Oxford, Pauling began folding paper with a formula sketched on it, to see what the bonding lengths and angles would look like in three dimensions. Atoms bind by single or double bonds; double bonds enforce extra rigidity.[22] Where carbon atoms are double-bonded, the paper thus has to lie flat; where there are single bonds, the paper can be folded and twisted more flexibly. But all bends and twists have exactly to match the known bond lengths and angles.

Pauling had discovered the helix of genetics — almost. His model was of a single-stranded spiral, dubbed an alpha-helix. Others of course knew that molecules bend and twist and coil, but working out a model that matched the intricate data had defeated them, including a fiasco in 1950 by Bragg, Perutz, and Kendrew.[23] To say the least, Pauling's single helix greatly impressed Crick and Watson. But neither he nor they realized that Pauling should have proposed a double-helix model.

Toward the end of 1952, a few months before Crick and Watson made their breakthrough, the situation looked like this: It was finally known that nucleic acids, not protein, were the genetic agent. It was likely that the gene molecule had a spiral or helix structure — but no one was at all clear how many strands were involved, or how or whether they entwined, or whether the nucleic bases were on the outside or inside of the spirals.

Watson and Crick had learned from Pauling the use of models. They built them over and over again, always fruitlessly. It was like juggling with two or three balls too many. The geometry of these models more resembled Salvador Dalí's than Euclid's. Certain planes would intersect at right angles except for one of the angles, which could bend any which way.[24] The axis of the helices involved rotation in a strict but as yet unclear order.

Some expert X-ray crystallographers were at hand — Bragg himself, and Rosalind Franklin and Maurice Wilkins in London. Franklin and Wilkins were trying to solve the structure of DNA, but having little luck. In 1951 Watson and Crick first met. On 7 March 1953, they successfully solved the structure of the gene molecule, a double helix. In 1962, together with Wilkins, they were awarded the Nobel Prize in Medicine.

Watson and Crick on How to Win a Nobel in Medicine

When they first met, Watson was twenty-three and a brand-new Ph.D., while Crick at thirty-five was still a graduate student. That they became collaborators at all, that two such different people should have worked together so well and discovered what they did, ran against all the odds. But at every step, their careers bore out the conventional wisdom on how to succeed in science: be enormously gifted; get the best education, even if on-the-job training; find the right mentor and colleagues; do research in the right place at the right time, on a centrally important problem. Crick and Watson did all these things, haphazardly at times, dumb-luckily at other times, and with driving single-mindedness and genius when it most counted.

Watson was a boy Quiz Kid on the radio show, graduated from the University of Chicago at nineteen, and went to Indiana for graduate study in genetics because Hermann Muller taught there. But Muller's fruit fly mutations struck Watson as old-hat. Luckily, he chose Salvador Luria as his mentor, which brought Watson into the "phage" group around Delbrück, where molecular biology was percolating. Luria got him a fellowship to Copenhagen, but Watson was bored there. He had heard that "someone named Perutz" at Cambridge might be interested; this was of course the great — as yet un-Nobelized — biochemist. Luria sprung him from Copenhagen and off to Perutz. If true, it certainly proves something about having the right mentor behind you. Perutz, says Watson, accepted this beginner because Luria happened to run into John Kendrew, Perutz's coworker, at a U.S. conference and cozily arranged it. Watson went over to Cambridge and presented himself at Perutz's office. A man named Francis Crick was working in the same office.

Crick had graduated in 1938 from University College, London, and started graduate work there on "the dullest problem imaginable," the viscosity of water under pressure. He was thankful that in 1940 a German bomb destroyed his apparatus. After war service, to escape viscosity analysis, he settled on molecular biology, though he knew almost nothing about it, nor very much about biology or chemistry. But perhaps he could use his physics background there. He was then thirty-one, still lacking a doctorate: where did an aging student go to learn molecular biology in 1947? Regular chemistry or biology departments had scarcely heard of it or cared. He spent two unhappy years in a lab, and applied for another grant. The Cavendish Laboratory of Cambridge University, one of the world's most prestigious research institutes, planned a study of X-ray diffraction, headed by Max Perutz. Was Crick interested?

Crick knew very little about X-ray crystallography and was accepted essentially as a doctoral student who would work on protein structure, Perutz's own subject. Crick and Watson hit it off at once, sizing each other up as intellectual equals. Both, said Crick, had "a certain youthful arrogance, a ruthlessness, and an impatience with sloppy thinking."[25]

Strangely, until the last few months before the discovery, Watson and Crick never officially worked on DNA. They couldn't have done so, since the two official funded researchers were the crystallographers Rosalind Franklin and Maurice Wilkins in London. In their spare time, when Watson wasn't playing tennis, Crick and Watson talked, theorized, speculated, and made models using other people's data. They never did any experimental work on DNA. Wrote Crick:

> People often ask how long Jim and I worked on DNA. This rather depends on what one means by work. Over a period of two years, we often discussed the problem, either in the laboratory or in our daily lunchtime walk ... or at home. ... Sometimes, when the summer weather was particularly tempting, we would take the afternoon off and go punting up the river.[26]

Crick and Watson were impatient at the friction between Franklin and Wilkins, their slow progress and "pedestrian" methods. Crick and Watson knew Pauling's alpha-helix structure inside out, knew the constraints imposed by the interatomic distances and angles, and how postulating a helix narrowed the possibilities further. But Franklin and Wilkins didn't work that way.

Linus Pauling looms over Watson's memoir as the great rival for the prize. Pauling was an early member of the molecular biology movement and Watson hero-worshiped him. If Pauling took it into his head to try to solve the structure of DNA, Watson was sure he would quickly do it. The alpha-helix confirmed Watson's fears. "One could never be sure where Pauling would strike next." In 1952 Watson really started worrying. Pauling announced he would come to England, and while there visit King's College, London, where he would surely see Rosalind Franklin's X-ray photos, to which Watson and Crick had no access. Only later did Watson realize how valuable Franklin's data could have been to Pauling. With Pauling's expertise, that would be all he needed to solve the puzzle.

But Pauling was also then agitating against atomic weapons. The State Department revoked Pauling's passport as a suspected Communist sympathizer, and thus unknowingly handed the discovery to Crick and Watson. Still, in January 1953, Pauling announced a solution of the gene molecule structure, a three-stranded structure. As Watson and Crick examined it, they realized it was worse than wrong: amazingly, it seemed done by a poor chemist. Watson was surprised and delighted by Pauling's blunder. Pauling had obviously relied on poor X-ray photographs. Just then, Watson finally got to see — through Wilkins's subterfuge — a superb X-ray photograph that Franklin had taken. "My mouth fell open and my pulse began to race."[27] (Watson's memoir is usually far better written than that.) Still, Pauling remained a threat. Soon, chagrined, he would be working at DNA day and night, using better X-ray photos. "Then, in a week or two, at the most, Linus would have the structure."

Watson convinced Sir Lawrence Bragg that Pauling was close to the solution, and Bragg, who had been stingingly beaten out by Pauling before, didn't want a repeat. He gave Crick and Watson permission to work on DNA. In three months, they had the answer. Watson exulted: "I had probably beaten Pauling to the gate and . . . the answer would revolutionize biology. [I] would win the Nobel

Prize." Conjuring up Pauling as a rival doubtless energized Watson. Yet Pauling himself apparently did not know he was anyone's rival, or even that he was in a race.

Crick pondered what credit he and Watson deserved for the discovery. Certainly, though young and inexperienced and largely ignorant, they had picked the right problem and stuck to it. They were willing to work much harder than their rivals, prepared to invest endless time and energy studying genetics, biochemistry, chemistry, physical chemistry, and X-ray diffraction — plus countless hours collaborating, with its exhausting intellectual and personal demands. Franklin and Wilkins failed, Crick thought, because they grated on each other. Crick understood the value of a magical collaboration: "If Jim had been killed by a tennis ball," Crick said, he was "reasonably sure he would not have solved the problem alone, but who would?"[28] One suspects Pauling would very quickly have done so.

After the great discovery, there were no gala celebrations, no keys to the city, and no telegrams from Stockholm. Wilkins, Franklin, and Pauling, who were best informed, seemed delighted. Other knowledgeable colleagues allowed that the double helix model was "interesting." In 1953, few were utterly confident it was correct. The great German chemist and Nobelist Otto Warburg had not heard of the discovery even a year later.[29] Indeed, as Crick says soberly, not until 1980 was the double helix discovery finally proved beyond all cavil. So Crick didn't instantly go to a ceremony in Sweden — he went instead to the Brooklyn Polytechnic for a year's stay, meanwhile having at least gotten his doctorate. When he returned in 1954, aged thirty-eight, the Medical Research Council felt no obligation to tenure him. Only when he was almost forty and becoming internationally famous did tenure come. Indeed, when a TV film was released in April 1987 (Watson was played by Jeff Goldblum, Crick by Tom Pigott-Smith, Rosalind Franklin by Juliet Stevenson), Crick thought the ending especially absurd, with the two young discoverers bathed in congratulations and celebrations. "Indeed Jim and I were worried that it might all be wrong and we'd again made fools of ourselves."[30]

The Nobel Prize came in 1962. That Crick and Watson deserved it is obvious. True, one of Rosalind Franklin's X-ray photographs had helped greatly, but she was still foundering on the structural problems. Wilkins was in the same boat, and his crystallographic work wasn't up to Franklin's. Franklin died of cancer, aged thirty-eight, in 1958. But before that, in 1953, when Crick and Watson published their discovery in *Nature,* Franklin and Wilkins asked that their X-ray photographs be published at the same time. On that exceedingly slim basis, it seems, Wilkins was included in the Nobel award, an inclusion stage-managed by Bragg. As the scientist who had been a Nobel laureate longest as well as youngest ever, and as director of the great Cavendish, Bragg had enormous clout with the Nobel establishment. In 1960 he asked the Nobel chemistry committee to honor Crick, Watson, and Wilkins. He wrote Pauling a long letter asking his support, but Pauling replied that a prize to Watson and Crick was premature, and that Wilkins was wholly undeserving.[31]

Bragg tried again for the 1962 prizes, and this time succeeded. The historian Horace Freeland Judson, to whom he explained it, wrote:

> Wilkins, Bragg said, had been bitterly disappointed. "Because he'd been working at it for so long. And then, Perutz and I said, 'Wilkins must be in on this.' And they published their contributions jointly in *Nature.* And later on when it came to the Nobel Prize I put every ounce of weight I could, behind Wilkins getting it along with them. It was just frightfully bad luck, really."[32]

But if Bragg arranged the award for Wilkins, he also made it possible for Crick and Watson. The British-American physicist Freeman Dyson remembers that as a new student at Cambridge in 1946, he heard Bragg much cursed. Bragg had become director of the Cavendish Laboratory in 1938, only a year after Rutherford died. By 1946 the Cavendish had lost its world leadership in high-energy physics, and Bragg not only did nothing to stop it, he even encouraged it. Bragg had decided to make the Cavendish famous for something else. Dyson says:

> I decided I had nothing to learn from this bunch of clowns, and I came to America to be in a place where real physics was still being done. . . . Seven years later Bragg retired. . . . He left Cambridge a center of furious activity and first-class international standing in two fields of research which are probably at least as important as high-energy physics[:] radio astronomy and molecular biology. Neither of these sciences even had a name when Bragg was appointed in 1938.[33]

Bragg hired the as yet uneminent Max Perutz, who spent ten years doing an X-ray analysis of hemoglobin. And brought in as apprentices Crick and Watson.

Watson published *The Double Helix* in 1968.[34] Most scientific memoirs before had shied from anything intimate. The scientist spoke, rarely the private person. Watson's was different: a "tell-all." Its working title was *Honest Jim.* To many scientists, it displayed offensive vulgarity, bad manners, dubious history, and a violation of trust. Worse, as his colleague and Nobelist Max Perutz put it, was Watson's "shallow representation of research as a race for the Nobel Prize."[35] In a letter to Watson, Richard Feynman however expressed a different view: "That is how science is done. I recognize my own experiences with discovery beautifully (and perhaps for the first time!)."[36] The book leaned heavily on personalities, and some, like Rosalind Franklin, were treated cartoonishly. After Crick read a draft in 1967, he erupted and wrote Watson a furious six-page letter, with copies to Bragg and the president of Harvard, where Watson then taught. He charged that Watson had sensationalized their collaboration and their science, as if it were merely a lust for Nobel fame rather than hard intellectual work for the sake of understanding nature. Crick claims that Watson never once mentioned the Nobel Prize during their collaboration. They were too wrapped up in the problem and making sure they'd gotten it right. Harvard University Press withdrew from publishing *The Double Helix,* and Atheneum brought it out instead. The public ate it up; it sold a million copies and was translated into almost twenty languages. Crick's own more conventional memoir, *What Mad Pursuit,* was published only in 1988.

Rereading Watson's memoir now, one may wonder what the fuss was about. Gary Taubes's *Nobel Dreams,* for example, the blow-by-blow account of how Carlo Rubbia clawed his way to a physics Nobel, makes Watson's account seem quaintly reserved. But in 1968, Watson's account obviously hit the raw nerve of a forbidden topic. Wanting a Nobel Prize so hungrily was simply not to be admitted. To be publicly ungracious to one's predecessors and rivals was quite out of bounds, no matter what one said in private.

After his prize, Watson did little active research. He taught at Harvard and then became the full-time administrator of the Cold Spring Harbor Laboratory on Long Island, and for a while director of the Human Genome Project. Crick went on to some brilliant triumphs in DNA, especially its coding, then moved into neurobiology. Wilkins continued work on DNA and shifted to neurology.

DNA and the Nobels, Cont'd

The double helix only laid bare the structure of the gene molecule. No one yet knew how a gene encoded genetic information, how a gene conveyed its information to other cells, or the exceedingly diverse but specific pathways involved in all this. From about 1955, research clarified much, and the Nobels rained down.

DNA is a long, thin molecule, located inside the nucleus of a cell. Each gene has four molecules, which pair off — adenine and guanine, cytosine and thymine — and each gene has the same sugars and the same phosphate group.[37] A DNA molecule reproduces itself by an improbable piece of biological machinery. In the double helix mechanism, two strands of the gene face and tightly coil about each other. Their nucleic bases match strictly, like a twisted ladder at the ends of whose rungs nucleic acids are paired.[38] When DNA reproduces, the two strands pull apart a section at a time, move in opposite directions, and act as countertemplates for each other. In *E. coli*, the bacteria in the intestine, this can take about thirty minutes; in a human cell, sixteen hours or so.[39] When the cycle is complete, instead of the original double strand of one DNA molecule, there are now two. The new daughter strand passes into the nucleus of a new cell — the original cell splits into two.

A different process can ensue, by which DNA produces a copy of itself (RNA) in order to manufacture protein.

ATP

DNA is dormant and useless until an enzyme propels it into copying itself. But how the enzyme does this remained unknown until the late 1950s. Obviously, it had to possess a great store of energy, use it potently, and also be related to nucleic acid.

Here genetics caught up with earlier research. Molecular biology began with the gene, and later worried how it got the energy to operate. From 1937, the German-American biochemist Fritz Lipmann began from the other end, the cell's major energy source.

Energy must of course be provided to cells in a form they can use, or else life fails. In 1941 Lipmann identified the all-important go-between here: adenosine triphosphate (ATP). ATP is generated in the cell's cytoplasm: adenine is a family of carbon rings strung to a group of sugars from which extend a long string of phosphates. These phosphates, so to speak, ignite the sugars, setting off energy, as when a cell turns food into energy. Horace Freeland Judson, the historian of molecular biology, has aptly called this "the most magnificent achievement of late-classical biochemistry." But Lipmann shared the Nobel Prize for a different discovery. In 1945 he showed that ATP provides energy through coenzyme A. A coenzyme is a nonprotein molecule that "accepts" or "donates" what an enzyme needs to catalyze reactions. This was certainly a major finding, helping to clarify the entire metabolism of fats. But why did the Nobel jury pass over his greater discovery? Lipmann, in his otherwise reticent scientific autobiography, suggests that his "talk of energy-rich bonds aroused forceful, sometimes violent antagonism." Biochemists, in short, could understand that energy was needed to create chemical bonds, but not that energy could also derive from breaking those bonds. That opposition has long faded, but Lipmann remains far less famous than he deserves.

In 1957 Luis Leloir of Argentina discovered the coenzyme uridine triphosphate (UTP). This has an important role in carbohydrate metabolism, and is closely linked to ATP. Leloir won the 1970 chemistry prize, for which Argentina later put his portrait on a postage stamp. In 1992 another prize in medicine went to Edmond Fischer and Edwin Krebs of the U.S. for showing how another enzyme reacts with ATP to carry energy in genes, egg fertilization, and hormone mechanisms through the body. Related research on phosphate structures and cell energy won the 1994 prize in medicine for Alfred Gilman and Martin Rodbell.

From DNA to RNA, tRNA, mRNA, etc.

In 1955 the Spaniard Severo Ochoa isolated a bacterial enzyme that allowed him to recreate RNA in the laboratory. By so doing, he managed to decipher the code for eleven amino acids. Meanwhile, the American biochemist Arthur Kornberg, with Lipmann's findings also in mind, found a kind of enzyme — DNA polymerase — that allowed DNA molecules to be synthesized. DNA's self-copying works in an intriguing round-robin manner. The polymerase enzyme energizes the DNA molecule to provide templates, precisely so that this very enzyme can be produced, in order to make more templates. Ochoa and Kornberg shared the 1959 medicine Nobel. Kornberg had the wrong enzyme, but this was discovered only in 1970; one of those who corrected Kornberg's error was his son Thomas.

But to what end does DNA replicate itself? Simply to make protein in an existing cell. Crick said that DNA really has no other point. Protein is the substance of enzymes, the catalysts of all living change. Proteins also compose most of the living matter generated by these changes — brains, bird feathers, wood. The double helix structure is after all a simple repetitive spiral; but protein structure has no such neat repeating pattern. It can be labyrinthine, intractably eccentric, and selectively finicky. Protein can twist, coil, spiral singly or doubly or trebly, bend or fold in every possible combination. No theory can predict its manifold shapes. Chemistry here as elsewhere stays stubbornly empirical. This is no small problem.

The mechanisms at work involve a subtlety, precision, and imaginative freedom that biologists have only begun to sort out. Replication is how DNA reproduces itself, turning one double helix into two. Next comes transcription, by which the DNA information moves, via RNA, to the specific site where it fits and is needed. Finally, translation: the genetic information of the nucleic acids has to be translated into "language" that protein and its amino acids can understand.

DNA is often compared to a master blueprint. Except that here, the blueprint by itself has to manufacture the energy, parts, workers, and building site to turn the plans into actuality. Moreover, since the genetic process involves the creation of living matter, even a tiny error can be literally deadly.

DNA's large molecule houses the genes that shape each living thing. If the genes are damaged, life suffers abnormality, disease, or untimely death. If the DNA and its genes are destroyed, no life can be engendered. DNA thus remains inside the nucleus, the safest part of the cell. There it replicates itself, there it never leaves. How then does it send its information abroad?

The first part of the process is transcription: DNA transcribes its information onto RNA, a single-stranded molecule,[40] after which the RNA becomes DNA's messenger. RNA "peels off" and moves through openings in the nucleus wall into the outer regions of the cell called cytoplasm. This messenger-RNA (mRNA) transports the genetic information to the site where the protein will be made. Now another kind of RNA enters — transfer-RNA (tRNA) — which attaches amino acids to the mRNA, thereby producing proteins. But nothing in biology is simple, least of all its genetic side. Proteins and their amino acids can be arranged in sixty-four different combinations, and there is a specific transfer-RNA for each of these. Each of these, in turn, must find exactly the one messenger-RNA that matches. Here yet another sort of RNA enters the picture: ribosomal-RNA. In a famous old metaphor, some biological entities are built to fit as perfectly and specifically as lock and key, or else nothing happens. Ribosomes — the locks into which the transfer-RNA key can fit, to make protein — are minute cellular particles. For a sense of the complexities involved, consider that a tiny bacterial cell contains 15,000 ribosomes, a human cell about 150,000. How can any RNA messenger, moving randomly, bump into the exact matching site so that specific aminos can be turned into protein? When this happens and the protein is made, the RNA — having done its duty — perishes. If bees were the analogy here, RNA would be the drones. The precious DNA, in its nucleus stronghold, survives, like the queen bee.

The second step is translation: Each gene encodes one protein. Since genetic "language" is composed of bits of the sequences of nucleic or amino acids — which are different — nucleic and amino acids "speak" different languages. If you patiently bead together a specific number of amino acids in a specific sequence, you produce exactly this and not that kind of protein. One link misplaced, and you get a different protein. You have, as it were, mispronounced the language and been misunderstood. When that happens in a genetic system, mutations and abnormalities result.

So how can a message expressed in a sequence of nucleics be understood by a sequence of aminos? The solution has often been compared to the deciphering of the Rosetta Stone, where the Greek section helped decipher the cuneiform section. In the 1960s the American biochemist Marshall Nirenberg finally deciphered the genetic code. He began by synthesizing RNA that contained only one of the four possible nucleic bases. He mixed this with proteins, and out came only one amino acid. He thus had the first bit of needed information: a nucleic acid that signified only one kind of amino acid. Building on that, as cryptographers do, he eventually broke the entire code, and shared the 1968 Nobel award in medicine with Har Gobind Khorana and Robert Holley, who worked independently. The genetic code turned out like this: The triplet of the four bases of nucleic acid allow sixty-four permutations $(4 \times 4 \times 4 = 64)$, which cover all of the twenty amino acids. Some of these seemed at first to be nonsense or "junk," but now are seen as punctuation, signifiers of beginnings and endings, or involving other purposes.

All such clues are badly needed. The Human Genome Project is at work deciphering the code, which involves sequencing some three billion letters in the genetic blueprint. This figure, already overwhelming, is the more so when one considers that it all unfolds from what Peter Medawar called "the virtually inexhaustible combinational and permutational variety of the four different nucleotides out of which the molecule is compounded." He added that the combinational varieties of known human genes outnumber all the people who are alive today, have ever lived, or are likely ever to live.[41]

Immunology Again

"Classic" immunology (Burnet, Medawar) asked how a toxin excites an antibody. DNA immunology is more apt to ask: What information is conveyed that does this, and via what agencies? The new immunology is linked to molecular biology because information transferral is so important to both.

In 1952 Joshua Lederberg (1958 Nobel in Medicine) helped clarify both the DNA information process and the immunological one. As genes contain the information they need to reproduce, so antigens awaken or activate some "pre-existing potentiality in the responding cell."[42] Then in 1960, Jacques Monod and François Jacob of the Institut Pasteur theorized that a "messenger RNA" carried the genetic information a protein needed. They shared the 1965 Nobel.

The structure of antibodies became more clear in 1962 when Rodney Porter of Britain suggested a Y-shaped structure for the central antibody called gamma globulin. A few years later, in 1969, Gerald Edelman of the U.S. achieved an analysis of gamma globulin, the first analysis of the sequence of amino acids in a human antibody — 1,330 amino acids. Porter and Edelman shared the 1972 Nobel. By 1975 César Milstein of Argentina and Georges Köhler of Germany discovered how to combine an antibody with a cancerous cell to produce a single or "monoclonal" and specialized antibody. This helped in diagnosing and fighting viruses, tracing cancers, blood grouping, and finding vaccines. Milstein and Köhler shared the 1984 prize in medicine with Niels Jerne.

Prions

While genetics seemed to promise to explain all, two Nobel Prizes went to diverging discoveries. It began in 1957, when Carleton Gajdusek, a young American physician and researcher, went to New Guinea to investigate a peculiar neurological disease there. He found it was caused by cannibalism — specifically, the eating of human brains — and he suggested this was a cause of fatal illnesses named transmissible spongiform encephalopathies (TSE). Gajdusek, who won the 1976 prize for this work, found the unknown agent or agents were smaller than a virus, were invisible to sophisticated means of detection, and could resist heat and sterilization. He thought they might be viruses that matured very slowly.[43]

Gajdusek also thought that these agents did not contain DNA or RNA, as do all other viruses, parasites, and such infectious agents. The culprit seemed to be a new, previously unknown form of infection. What caused TSE seemed to be only protein. But how can protein reproduce itself by itself? Around 1968, Gajdusek suggested it reproduced not by genetic replication, but in crystallized form, as ice does. Neither he nor anyone else could confirm the theory, and Gajdusek refused to publish prematurely. But Stanley Prusiner, one of Gajdusek's collaborators, did publish in 1982, claiming discovery of a new biological principle and coining a name for the agents involved — prions (proteinaceous infectious particles). Richard Rhodes, in his account of this research, reports that

Prusiner's collaborator on the paper felt the evidence had been stretched, and withdrew. Prusiner thus became the sole author — a decisive point when it came to priority for the Nobel Prize. Eminent specialists in the field steadily insisted that Prusiner's claims were unsupported and exaggerated. The Nobel committee however sided with Prusiner. Rhodes says that Prusiner campaigned relentlessly, but that his 1997 prize may become a major embarrassment for the Nobel jury. The agent may yet turn out to be a virus. Meanwhile, however, there are complaints that the prize to Prusiner has had the effect of "choking off" funds needed for exploring any alternatives.[44]

The Virus and Cancer

From about 1910, virus and cancer study slowly began to link.

In 1926 a Nobel Prize in Medicine was actually awarded for solving the cause of cancer. The laureate so honored was the Danish researcher Johannes Fibiger. Around the turn of the century, cancer couldn't be reproduced in the laboratory on demand, and research thus suffered. In 1913 Fibiger thought he had found a method. Some of his laboratory rats had cancer of the stomach, and he found nematodes (roundworms) inside the cancers. Curious about how this had happened, Fibiger learned that his rats had come from a sugar refinery, and the refinery had many cockroaches. Perhaps the rats ate the roaches, and caught the cancer from the insects. He fed cockroaches to the rats, saw they developed stomach cancer, and convinced himself that he had found a link: the larvae of the roundworm parasite *Spiroptera neoplastica* in the roach carried the cancer to the rat. Fibiger did not claim that all cancer was caused by a worm, but more likely by some external cause which the worm aggravated. He was an esteemed, careful researcher, but in this case completely wrong. When his experiments were repeated in Japan, some rats developed benign tumors, probably because of vitamin-deficient diet.

Fibiger fell ill during the Nobel ceremonies in Stockholm, and died just over a month later — of cancer. He was sixty. He was also spared the embarrassment of the mistakes soon found in his "discovery."

*   *   *

At about the same time as Fibiger, an American researcher had a better insight: that a virus seemed to mutate like a gene. This emerged in 1909, when Peyton Rous, a young physician from Baltimore, had just begun doing research at the new Rockefeller Institute. A fowl breeder arrived with a sick Plymouth Rock hen, asking for medical help. Rous found it had a tumor. He mashed the tumor but couldn't capture the infectious agent in any filter; no one could, for a quarter of a century. By 1911 Rous decided his tumor-making chicken killer was that new and mysterious thing the virus, which had been discovered in 1892. Rous had of course stumbled onto the enormously important possibility that viruses somehow caused cancer. It had long been known that radiation can cause cell mutations and thus cancer — Marie Curie died this way. But no explanations existed, nor any way of capturing the infinitesimal virus. A bit of solid help finally came in 1935, when the American biochemist Wendell Stanley first crystallized a pure, concentrated virus, the tobacco mosaic virus. Stanley found it was a protein, and that its infectious power still existed after crystallization. In 1936 he further showed that the virus was composed of both proteins and nucleic acids.

In the 1930s, making such discoveries still resembled the sort of endless drudgery Marie Curie did in 1898. At the Rockefeller Institute where Stanley worked, he patiently grew Turkish tobacco leaves with just the right sort of infection. He pulped them into juice, by the pailful. He removed the juice, ran it through filters, and poured in chemical reagents, seeking a concentrated and purified substance.

> By age 31 (he had started the job at 28), he had reduced about a ton of tobacco plant to about a tablespoonful of infective crystals. As someone said afterwards, it was like capturing the flea in an elephant's ear by boiling down the elephant to a saucerful of caramel.[45]

Viruses are extraordinary creatures. They cannot replicate as genes or living things do. They are parasitic. They penetrate a host, using a protein sheath to deceive the host, and then insert their nucleic agents to create more viruses.

At the Rockefeller Institute, in the late 1930s, the Belgian émigré Albert Claude managed to extract ribonucleic acid (RNA) from a cancerous tumor and transplant it — where it also caused tumors.

This helped further to tie tumors to the virus. Claude shared the 1974 Nobel in Medicine with his colleague George Palade.

As Francis Crick enunciated it, the "central dogma" of genetics was: DNA makes RNA which makes protein. But the dogma also held that the process can't be reversed: proteins can't synthesize RNA, nor can RNA synthesize DNA. But by 1970 Crick was refuted. Howard Temin and his teacher Renato Dulbecco at Wisconsin, and independently David Baltimore, discovered the "retrovirus." This RNA virus is called reverse transcriptase because it surprisingly transcribes genetic messages back into DNA and thus becomes part of the original DNA chromosome.[46] This obviously causes disturbance of the normal gene's message and may cause cancer, AIDS, or hepatitis. In 1975 Temin, Dulbecco, and Baltimore shared the Nobel Prize in Medicine. The next year, J. Michael Bishop and Harold Varmus of the University of California explained the origin of the retrovirus.[47] They became laureates in 1989.

As for Peyton Rous, he had once given up hope of solving cancer, calling it "one of the last strongholds of metaphysics." But he went back to it as interest renewed in his early work. In 1966 he was finally made a laureate in medicine — then aged eighty-seven and still doing research! In retrospect, as Medawar declared, Rous "was the greatest experimental pathologist of his day."[48]

Did Anyone or Everyone Discover Insulin?

Until 1922 there was no cure for diabetes, nor any way to seriously alleviate its miseries — the wasting away of flesh, amputation of limbs, and early death. It was known that diabetes mellitus — there are other kinds — was linked to the pancreas and its metabolism. Laboratory researchers who cut out an animal's pancreas found that carbohydrates couldn't be absorbed; sugar poured into the blood and urine, and the animal soon died. A healthy pancreas, however, had some agent that allowed the sugars and their energy fuels to be absorbed harmlessly. The search to find this was intense, but to 1920, no one had succeeded.

In that year Frederick Banting, a Canadian physician, thought of a possible experiment. As Michael Bliss notes in his incisive account of this case, Banting was only a general practitioner, and a provincial one at that. He had no training in research. Even his medical education had been hastily completed in 1917 because of the war. His practice, in London, Ontario, was not very exciting and certainly not remunerative. When the idea for curing diabetes gripped him, he began to think of moving to Toronto to work in a well-equipped lab; escaping his dull medical practice was likely another incentive.

J. J. R. Macleod was professor of physiology at the University of Toronto and directed its physiology laboratory. Banting found Macleod aloof, Macleod found Banting raw and unequipped for experimental work. Yet by 1922 Banting's hope had come true: the pancreatic secretion called insulin had been found, and immediately improved, and was saving the lives of diabetes patients throughout the world. Up to then, treatment was ad hoc and desperate: sodium bicarbonate or even opium was administered; one French expert unfortunately advised eating great amounts of sugar, himself became a diabetic and died. A much favored method was the "starvation diet," meant to lower the intake of sugar. Often enough the strict dieting itself caused death by starvation, or "inanition."

The discovery of insulin swept all these helpless or harmful measures aside. Within a year, in 1923, Banting and Macleod shared the Nobel Prize in Medicine. If many collaborations — like Crick and Watson — work magically, this one showed how a successful collaboration can sometimes be done even at swords' point. The two men could hardly have been more different. Banting was a country doc with a face-splitting grin and the unmistakable air of hailing from the sticks. The urbane Macleod, born in Britain and with distinguished friends there, had an international reputation for work on the metabolism of carbohydrates. They came to hate each other quite soon.

At first, Macleod allowed Banting the use of the lab only for part of the summer, with a supply of dogs for experiments. He did give him an assistant, a senior undergraduate physiology student named Charles Best. Banting's idea was to tie off the duct leading to the pancreas, causing its degeneration, which would isolate the internal secretion of the pancreas for testing. Several researchers had earlier tried tying off the duct and atrophying the pancreas. But no one had searched for the valuable internal secretion in the atrophied pancreas. This may have been what interested Macleod in the country doctor's plan.

The research began unpromisingly. Macleod had to show Banting how to cut away a dog's pancreas. Banting and Best killed four dogs in their first try, and more soon went the same way. But by August, extracts from the excised pancreas began to show promising if erratic results. Enough progress had been made for Macleod to allow them to keep using the laboratory. Then J. B. Collip joined the team. He was a year younger than Banting, with a Ph.D. in biochemistry and a Rockefeller Travelling Fellowship. By December 1921 the extract was tried on the first human patient, a fourteen-year-old boy.[49] It failed. On 23 January 1922 they tried again, with great success — as Bliss says, "the first unambiguously successful clinical test" of insulin on a human diabetic. But not enough insulin extract could be made to meet the demand or even make adequate tests.

Meanwhile the team — if it could ever properly be called that — had long been fractious and became more so. Banting and Best paired off against Macleod and Collip. Banting began to think that Macleod was stealing his ideas. Collip and Macleod avoided the touchy Banting. Touchy, indeed. He was a poor public speaker, and at a Yale session on diabetes was so inept that Macleod stepped in to handle the questions. His polished manner infuriated Banting, particularly his way of referring to "our work": according to Banting, Macleod hadn't done a single experiment.

As a physician, Banting expected to be in charge of the first human patient treated; Macleod resisted this. Banting considered himself the rightful discoverer of insulin, and worried that Collip, who had found an improved form of the extract, was perhaps thinking of patenting it in his own name. An unusual formal agreement was drawn up forbidding any single member of the team to patent or divulge the extract without consultation with and consent of the others.[50] But could Collip or Macleod trust Banting not to try the extract on another patient? "Paranoia begat paranoia," Bliss comments.

The success of insulin caught North American attention, then European. Large pharmaceutical companies such as Lilly became interested. The 1920 winner of the Nobel Prize in Medicine, Professor August Krogh of Copenhagen, came to Toronto, talked to Banting and Macleod about the work, and went home hoping to use insulin in Scandinavia.[51]

The team's relations went from bad to worse. Banting and Best were not present when the grand announcement of the discovery was made in Washington, D.C., in May 1922. Partisans otherwise kept resentments stirring. When the distinguished physiologist Sir

William Bayliss of hormone fame, a friend of Macleod, wrote a hasty and uninformed article giving Macleod the credit for the discovery, Banting erupted; Macleod printed a guarded retraction granting Banting credit for at least the idea of tying off the pancreatic duct.

But, as Bliss vividly puts it, Banting became perfect press material:

> Banting's story was perfect: the wounded veteran, the failing small-city doctor, the great idea at night, nothing but discouragement from the establishment, only a young student helper, grinding poverty, imaginative experiments under the worst conditions — perhaps even having to steal dogs to keep going — and then brilliant spectacular success.[52]

If he was stumbling in speech and something of a bumpkin, this was ascribed to his "humble genius." He and Best dined with the Canadian prime minister. In May 1923 the Canadian government set up a Banting and Best Chair of Medical Research, to be held by Banting at a salary of $10,000 annually — a huge academic salary at the time.

Meanwhile, both Banting and Macleod were nominated separately for the Nobel Prize. The Nobel committee had trouble deciding the merits of the case; two evaluators finally agreed, with no great show of confidence, that Banting and Macleod should be honored. Another member objected to these evaluations as unprecedentedly full of hearsay evidence. But the source turned out to be Krogh, and his direct report from Toronto carried great weight. According to Bliss, Macleod told Krogh that Banting would have gone off on the wrong track without his advice.

Banting was so incensed by Macleod's being honored that he decided to refuse the prize. An older friend talked him out of it, pointing out that this was the first Nobel ever awarded Canada, and scientists should rise above personal differences. Banting gave in. But he announced that half his prize money would go to Best, his real "partner." A day or so later, Macleod announced that half his prize money would go to Collip. In 1923 in Stockholm, side by side, Macleod and Banting received their Nobel medals. Macleod left Canada in 1928 to become professor at Aberdeen in his native Scotland, and died in 1935. Charles Best replaced Banting as professor of physiology at Toronto. Banting worked on, vainly trying to find a cancer cure. He died in 1941.

Their quarrel lasted until their deaths, and then the Nobel Foundation kept it alive. Breaking their lofty silence about prize disputes, the Foundation claimed in 1962 that Macleod had wrongly been given a share of the prize: "he had taken no active part in the work, and in fact had been away when the decisive experiment was made." Best had deserved a share of the prize, but no one had nominated him.[53] Another historian of science has called Macleod "the only palpably undistinguished investigator in the whole list of laureates in science."[54]

Bliss, however, comes to a different conclusion. Banting and Best did not alone discover insulin, only part of it. They began the process. Collip, Macleod, and perhaps others made decisive contributions, nor did Banting's initial idea about duct ligation play an essential part in the discovery.

Even this is not the whole story. The Romanian Nicolas Paulesco in 1921 had published important articles on pancreatic extracts. But Banting and the others were working fast, and Paulesco never caught up. A scholarly article in 1971, however, claimed Paulesco as the true discoverer, and the Romanian Medical School in Bucharest agitated to have Paulesco honored. The Romanians accused Banting and Best of deliberately falsifying Paulesco's work (Bliss shows that Best only misread it, his French being elementary). They also hinted that Macleod got his share of the Nobel Prize because otherwise he would have exposed Banting's falsification of Paulesco. Paulesco had never been nominated for the prize, but Arne Tiselius, president of the Nobel Foundation and himself a Nobelist in chemistry, issued an apology to the Romanians in the name of the Nobel institution, and declared it his personal opinion that Paulesco had deserved the prize.[55] There were other claimants as well.

Insulin was clinically a triumph, but for a long time no one knew that it worked by making the body's cells increase the use of glucose. Insulin's structure also remained a mystery until Frederick Sanger, in the late 1950s in a brilliant synthesis, demonstrated its exact composition, winning the first of his two Nobel Prizes.

The Nobel for Not Discovering Streptomycin

In 1952 the Nobel Prize for Medicine was awarded to Selman Waksman for the discovery of streptomycin. This was the second famous antibiotic after penicillin, and particularly effective against tuberculosis. In his Nobel lecture, and in several books and articles, Waksman always presented himself as the sole discoverer.

But the facts, as recovered from the archives by Professor Milton Wainwright of the molecular biology faculty at Sheffield University in England,[56] show that Waksman was not the discoverer, probably not even the codiscoverer. That honor lay with Waksman's onetime doctoral student Albert Schatz. Neither the Nobel Foundation nor Waksman mentioned Schatz, nor do most of the histories of microbiology.

Waksman, born in 1888, had taught at Rutgers since 1925, and was a prominent scientist investigating humus, fungi, and other microbial agents in living soil that can provide antibiotics. In the 1930s Waksman's research here had gone so well that the Merck pharmaceutical company established fellowships in Waksman's laboratory. Rutgers and Waksman were to receive a royalty for any discovery; this was a common practice at the time.

Albert Schatz, born in 1920, returned from the U.S. Army in 1943 to finish his Ph.D. under Waksman. Working with physicians from the Mayo Clinic, Waksman by then sought an antibiotic useful against tuberculosis. Certain kinds of soil produce a funguslike bacteria that can cure certain diseases without harming the body. Back in 1916, Waksman thought he had found bacteria that would yield such an antibiotic, as later called. He was mistaken. Schatz found the correct one during 1943–44.

Because TB was so infectious, Schatz was assigned to an isolated basement room[57] where he produced two cultures of streptomycin. One came from a fellow graduate student named Doris Jones, who was trying to isolate antibiotics useful against chicken viruses. Those that didn't work in her experiment, she passed through the basement lab window to Schatz. In one of these "chicken throat strain" isolates, Schatz found streptomycin. Then he found another in soil, which generated larger amounts.

But who actually found it, Schatz or Waksman? The entire case, as Wainwright shows, turns on a small but crucial fact. If Jones passed the specimen directly to Schatz, Schatz was the discoverer. If she passed it to Waksman, who might then have first tested and screened the specimens, Waksman could rightly claim priority. Jones testified to Wainwright that she always passed the specimens directly to Schatz. Waksman himself confirmed this in a letter of

1946. At that time, priority didn't seem important. Indeed, the paper announcing the discovery was published in 1944, with the names of the researchers in the following order: Schatz, E. Bugie, and Waksman. Bugie, an assistant who checked on Schatz's work, later swore on oath to the U.S. Patent Office that she had no share in the discovery. Why Schatz's name came first figured in the later legal quarrels.

The legal tangle began when, in 1945, Schatz and Waksman filed a patent on streptomycin. It was granted in 1948, after necessary testing. They both signed a sworn affidavit that contained the statement "They verily believe themselves to be the original, first and joint inventors of an improvement in [streptomycin]."[58] They also made over the profits from the drug to the nonprofit Rutgers research facility.

Unknown to Schatz, Waksman received about $350,000 in royalties. Meanwhile, he had sent Schatz the trifling sum of $1,500, as if a gift, without mentioning the royalties he was receiving. Schatz put the $1,500 on his income tax as a gift; Waksman put it on his IRS statement as payment for work. Schatz wrote Waksman for clarification; he had heard that Waksman was claiming to be the sole discoverer. Waksman privately replied that he had indeed made the discovery by himself, and included Schatz only out of courtesy and friendship, the same explanation Waksman gave for why Schatz's name came first on the paper announcing the discovery — although every earlier paper where Waksman had made the discovery put his own name first.

Schatz filed suit to have his share in the discovery legally acknowledged, and his share in the profits recompensed. Waksman and Rutgers could do little but concede the case: Waksman's own sworn statements in the patent application admitted that Schatz was at least codiscoverer. They settled out of court. Schatz was acknowledged as codiscoverer and assigned three percent, against Waksman's lavish ten percent, of the royalties on streptomycin, which up to 1950 amounted to almost two and a half million dollars. Waksman donated part of the money to set up a research institute at Rutgers.

Wainwright documents the hostile reaction of the scientific community to Schatz's action. Waksman was a highly regarded, powerful scientist. When Waksman did not mention Schatz in his Nobel lecture in 1952, the president of Schatz's then college (the National

Agricultural College at Doylestown, Pennsylvania) complained to the Nobel committee. Their reply was as follows:

> It was generally regretted that part of the information in your letter had not been accessible to the members of the faculty, since it had not been published in any scientific journal. It may be of interest to you to know that numerous American colleagues . . . have suggested the name of Doctor Waksman, though none of them has proposed Doctor Schatz.[59]

In other words, those who nominated Waksman were either ignorant of the legal decision vindicating Schatz, or chose to ignore it. One must conclude it was the latter. In 1950, for example, two years before Waksman's Nobel award, the *New York Times* carried articles about Schatz's lawsuit against Waksman, and then a follow-up story on Schatz's winning the suit — with details of the monetary settlement involved.[60] That such a well-publicized case would not come to the attention of colleagues of Waksman is implausible. Nor could it be dismissed as gossip, since it was a matter of legal record. The senior scientists' old-boy network protected Waksman.

One may argue that Schatz should not have allowed Waksman to declare himself codiscoverer in the first place. This is unrealistic. Schatz was a brand-new Ph.D.; his formidable mentor professed great and paternal fondness for him. If Schatz had protested then and there that he was sole discoverer, he had no way of proving his case. Senior scientists would have rallied to Waksman. Schatz's entire career depended on good recommendations from Waksman, and both knew it.

That the Nobel committee was the unwitting instrument here does not add to its own glory or that of its nominators. Rutgers, however, finally honored Schatz, fifty years after the fact. In 1994 Schatz was awarded Rutgers' highest honor, the Rutgers Medal, as codiscoverer of streptomycin.[61]

EKG but Not EEG

In the 1880s, heart contractions were known to involve electrical changes, and electrodes were used to measure these. But clumsy instruments made measurement erratic and inaccurate. By 1901 the

Dutch physiologist Willem Einthoven solved the problem: he passed a conducting thread across a magnetic field, sensitive and stable enough to give reliable readings. The electrocardiogram, improved, is now in every clinic. Einthoven won the 1923 Nobel in Medicine.

In that same year in Jena, a German psychiatrist, Hans Berger, improved the electroencephalogram, which first measured electrical changes in the human brain. It had been done on a dog years earlier. The EEG has proved to be one of the most useful methods of studying the brain, and an indispensable method for diagnosing epilepsy. Berger also discovered the "alpha" and "beta" electrical brain rhythms.

Berger did not win a Nobel Prize. Perhaps he was never nominated. Certainly, he was a reclusive and secretive man. Far from worrying about rushing into print to establish his priority, Berger — after perfecting the EEG in 1925, often using his son's skull for experiments — published his findings only in 1929. For some years, the response was indifference or derogation. Few were ready to consider the brain so actively electrical. In 1937, however, he was honored for his discovery at a Paris symposium. He wept. "In Germany I am not so famous."[62] The Nobel Prizes in Medicine from 1940 to 1942 were canceled because of war. In 1941 Berger died.

Birds and Bees: Ethology

Modern medical research, as remarked, began when it moved from the clinic to the laboratory in the late nineteenth century. A century later, in 1973, the Nobel honored three scientists who moved out of the lab to study animals in their natural settings. Why a Nobel in Medicine for this? Certainly there is wide dissatisfaction with treating patients under artificial laboratory conditions. In a broader way, ethology helps break down the line separating human from animal health and illness: the similarities may have been overlooked to our cost.[63]

Karl von Frisch studied bees, Konrad Lorenz geese and dogs, and Niko Tinbergen the behavior of gulls, digger wasps, butterflies, and stickleback fish. They pioneered a new approach called ethology. Here is Tinbergen, speaking of Lorenz's work:

He studied animals for their own sake rather than as convenient subjects for controlled testing in severely restricted laboratory conditions. He restored the status of observation of complex events as a valid, respectable, in fact highly sophisticated part of scientific procedure. In the process he discovered many hitherto unrecognized principles.[64]

This description fits the work of all three laureates.

Frisch was the oldest, eighty-seven when made a laureate. He took a degree in medicine in his native Vienna but soon switched to zoology and studied perception in insects. After World War I he taught mostly in Germany, where from 1924 he made his most important discoveries. He wondered if the color patterns of flowers acted as signals to attract butterflies and bees. If so, bees might have a sense of color. Experiments showed that bees could be conditioned to respond not only to various colors but to odors as well. His greatest discovery was how bees communicate their findings. If the food is nearby, the scout bees do a circular dance; if further off, a tail-wagging flight. Other bees find the food supply by following these directions. "This I believe was the most far-reaching observation of my life," Frisch said. In the coming years, he deciphered further intricacies of the honeybee dance; each kind of dance relayed a message about direction, distance, or amount of food, and had a relation to the angle of the sun.

Frisch was the first major ethologist, but Tinbergen and Lorenz jointly systematized the field. The Dutchman Tinbergen was part of a rather impressive family. His physician father, Adolf, almost won a Nobel Prize in Medicine, and his brother Jan shared the first Nobel Memorial Prize in Economics in 1969. Tinbergen's interest in ethology was roused by bird-watching and reading Frisch on bees. Conventional science being irrelevant, he took a doctorate at a technical university, then went to study birds and mammals of Greenland in a fourteen-month stay there with Eskimos. Back in the Netherlands, he took up the behavior of stickleback fish and gulls.

In 1936 Tinbergen met Lorenz, and they combined ideas and forces. Like Frisch, Lorenz was from Vienna, took an M.D. degree, and shifted to zoology. At first Lorenz did the usual laboratory experiments, but he found that the artificial isolation distorted instinctual patterns. In 1934 he began his famous study of greylag geese, which showed that the first object they saw — mother goose, balloon, or box — was imprinted on them as "parent." Lorenz himself became "mother" to many such goslings; photographs of baby geese dutifully following the bearded scientist around the woods have become famous. He and Tinbergen developed a theory of "fixed action patterns" — key instinctive actions, such as parent-imprinting, that were triggered by no previous training. In a similar way, Tinbergen studied how a nestling gull's pecking against the parent's beak prompts important instinctual stimuli.

The shared award was clouded by accusations about Lorenz's political past. In 1940 and 1943 he had published two long scientific papers in German journals, one of which he coedited. Both carried remarks that seemed sympathetic to Nazi race theory. This was pointed out early on by the British biologist J. B. S. Haldane, who summed up the case: For Lorenz, human beings are "domesticated" animals, i.e., removed from their natural or instinctual setting. Domestication, however, means decadence: a domesticated human or animal loses powers of strength, sight, and response common in the wild state. Unless steps are taken to reverse this — as, say, through a politics of "racial purity" — further decadence will result. Haldane, in fact a friend of Lorenz, called this the Nazi view and denounced it.

When Lorenz won the Nobel, the same charges emerged again in scientific journals. The Nazi-hunter Simon Wiesenthal was said to have asked Lorenz to "decline the prize as a gesture of contrition."[65] On the other side, the anthropologist Margaret Mead defended Lorenz as a victim of media and mass persecution.[66] Lorenz did not renounce the prize, but claimed he had been stupidly naive about Nazi purposes. "That they meant murder when they said 'selection' was beyond the belief of anyone." It may also pass belief that anyone who had lived in Germany from 1940 to 1942 — when he taught there — could still be so naive about Nazi purposes that late. But Lorenz does seem sincere in claiming that domestication and natural "degeneracy," not racial impurity, was what he was attacking. Ethology is itself a protest against domestication, which makes unnatural, unhealthy laboratory specimens of wild beasts. Tinbergen supported this view and was no Nazi — he spent two years in a Nazi concentration camp for protesting the dismissal of Jewish professors.

Lorenz has remained the most controversial of the three laureates, partly because after the Nobel Prize he wrote best-selling books, which generated other best-sellers carrying similar views. Critics charged that he overemphasized instinctual behavior, and that he anthropomorphized his animals. Most provocative was Lorenz's view on aggression, that humans are the only species preying on their own kind. This has been widely popularized through books like Robert Ardrey's *The Territorial Imperative,* Fox and Tiger's *The Imperial Animal,* and E. O. Wilson's *Sociobiology: The New Synthesis.*

Freud — and the Two Psychiatrists Who Did Win Prizes

There have actually been two Nobel Prizes awarded for psychiatry, but Freud won neither of them. He was first nominated for the medicine Nobel by the physiologist Bárány, the 1914 medicine laureate, who did research on the inner ear. Freud was annoyed both by Bárány's winning and nominating.

> The granting of the Nobel Prize to Bárány, whom I refused to take as a pupil some years ago because he seemed too abnormal, has aroused sad thoughts about how helpless an individual is in gaining the respect of the crowd. You know it is only the money that would matter to me, and perhaps the spice of annoying some of my compatriots. But it would be ridiculous to expect a sign of recognition when one has seven-eighths of the world against one."[67]

Freud was nominated several times thereafter. The real campaigns seem to have started in the 1920s. His biographer Ernest Jones records that in 1927 the psychoanalyst Georg Groddeck agitated to secure the Nobel for Freud. Freud asked him to stop: "such an honor would not suit me." But friends and disciples kept trying. In 1930, when Freud won the prestigious Goethe Prize of Frankfurt, some hoped it would lead to Stockholm. It did not, nor did Freud seem to think the world had grown any "friendlier" to his views.[68] In 1936, when Freud turned eighty, Romain Rolland and Thomas Mann, by then both Nobelists in literature, sought to rouse interest in Stockholm. Einstein was asked to nominate Freud for a Nobel in

Medicine but refused, saying he did not think psychology suitable for that award.

When Freud fled Austria and the Nazis and settled in England in 1938, the Austrian writer Arnold Zweig began another Nobel try. Freud wrote a typically blunt reproof:

> Don't let yourself get worked up over the Nobel chimera. It is only too certain that I shall not get any Nobel Prize. Psychoanalysis has several good enemies among the authorities on whom the bestowal depends, and no one can expect of me that I hold out until they have changed their opinions or died out. Therefore, although the money would be welcome after the way the Nazis bled me in Vienna and because of the poverty of my son and son-in-law, Anna and I have agreed[,] I to renounce the prize and she the journey to Stockholm to fetch it.[69]

Freud was right, of course. His theories were too provocative for the Nobel medical committee, as well as not fitting their insistence on definitive experimental confirmation. No clinician had been honored, and the notorious Freud was hardly likely to be the first exception.

Freud himself, in the same letter, gave another reason why, after Hitler, he would never be honored by the Swedes: "It can hardly be expected that the official circles could bring themselves to make such a provocative challenge to Nazi Germany as bestowing the honor on me would be." One wonders whether the Nazis would be very exercised about an award to another Jewish exile. Freud had forgotten, or perhaps chosen to forget, that the Nobel Foundation had openly provoked the Nazis only a few years earlier, and far more seriously, by awarding the 1935 Nobel Peace Prize to the German journalist Carl von Ossietzky. Ossietzky, a militant anti-Nazi, was then in a concentration camp. Thereafter, Hitler forbade any German, or Austrian after 1938, to accept any Nobel award. Thus the 1939 Nobel medicine laureate Gerhard Domagk, who discovered the first sulfa drug, and the 1938 and 1939 chemistry laureates Kuhn and Butenandt — all Germans — were forbidden to go to Stockholm to accept their medal and their money. They got their medals after the war, but not the money.

Freud figured in a curious Nobel episode that began in 1920. The director of the psychiatric divison of the Vienna General Hospital was then Professor Julius Wagner-Jauregg. He and Freud had been schoolmates, remained friendly, used the intimate *du* with each other, and exchanged greetings on holidays. Charges of cruel treatment to soldiers with mental problems were raised against Wagner-Jauregg. In 1920 the Austrian military authorities appointed a special commission to investigate, and Freud was one of those chosen. His memorandum has been preserved. The hospitals used electric shock treatment on soldiers who claimed war trauma. According to Freud's biographer Ernest Jones,[70] the idea was to make the electric shock treatment so disagreeable that even returning to the front seemed preferable. Unfortunately, the soldiers fell ill again, and shock treatments were sometimes unbearably increased. Freud believed that Wagner-Jauregg would not personally have used electric shock treatment cruelly, whatever other doctors did. Wagner-Jauregg was ultimately exonerated. Freud had to give his testimony with Wagner-Jauregg present. He tried to be friendly and objective, but also pointed out the conflict between a doctor's duty to the patient and the military doctor's duty to get soldiers back to active duty as soon as possible. The commission condemned Freud's observation as unpatriotic.

In 1927 Wagner-Jauregg received the first Nobel Prize in Medicine for psychiatry. His prizewinning work was a new version of the old idea that temporary fevers or infections can have beneficial results. In 1917 Wagner-Jauregg had inoculated nine patients suffering from insanity caused by advanced syphilitic infection. He infected them with malaria; he claimed three were entirely cured and able to go back to work, while three had a mild and temporary improvement. Tests elsewhere showed the same thirty-percent cure rate. This therapy was developed at the same time as the shock treatments that caused Wagner-Jauregg to be investigated.

Freud congratulated Wagner-Jauregg on his Nobel award, and they maintained friendly relations. The latter's assistants, however, openly attacked psychoanalysis. And Wagner-Jauregg in his autobiography, begun the year after he won the Nobel Prize and finished in 1935 but not published till after both men were dead, accused Freud of seeking to attack him during the investigation. He claimed too that the mid-nineteenth-century French psychiatrist Charcot had really invented psychoanalysis, and Freud had lifted his ideas.[71]

Wagner-Jauregg is also reported to have said that Freud's psycho-analysis did not deserve a Nobel in medicine, but rather in literature.

Ice-Pick Psychiatry

The second Nobel medicine prize for psychiatry went in 1949 to the Portuguese neurologist António Egas Moniz, the inventor of lobotomy. He called it prefrontal leucotomy; it was his American disciple Dr. Walter Freeman who gave it the popular name "lobot-omy." Moniz carried the physical treatment of mental illness bru-tally far. In London in 1935, two American physiologists reported operations on chimpanzees that surgically removed the parts of the brain just behind the forehead, called the prefrontal lobes. Before the operation, the chimps had been able to solve puzzles that might have baffled a very young child, but they were also excitable. After-wards, as David Shutts reports in his valuable study, they became docile, but also stupid and apathetic.[72] Moniz attended this confer-ence, and decided to try the method on humans exhibiting anxiety or behavior disturbing to others.

The next year he lobotomized twenty patients. Drilling through the forehead, the surgeon cut the nerve pathways to the rest of the brain. Moniz declared that seven had been cured of their anxieties, eight improved, and five emerged neither better nor worse. The anxiety did not disappear: the patient simply became indifferent to it, and often to everything else.

The treatment almost immediately gained an enthusiastic fol-lowing, particularly in the United States. Institutions there were filled to bursting with mental patients who were treated haphaz-ardly and sometimes harshly by a staff that was always too few, too poorly trained, and certainly underpaid. In 1936 more than 430,000 psychiatric patients were in state hospitals in the U.S. Many patients lived out their lives in these places, with no treatment available that could ease their afflictions. Almost any kind of eccen-tric or bizarre behavior could be deemed lunacy by the courts or physicians. At times, "depressed" patients, whatever the cause or symptoms, were automatically considered suicidal. In some places, straitjackets were habitually used; in others, a more humane treat-ment of baths and sedatives. Almost any treatment imaginable was applied: baths, injections of fever (Wagner-Jauregg-style), overheating or chilling, extracting teeth or tonsils or sometimes glands. Restraints could be chemical — doses of chloral hydrate or opium — or padded cells and straitjackets. At Saint Elizabeth's Hospital in Washington, D.C., one of the more enlightened institutions, one-person dungeons were used for the most agitated and violent.[73] In the 1930s stronger means arrived: injections of insulin to cause shock, or direct and heavy doses of electric shock therapy.

But even compared to these and other maltreatments, lobotomy was an excessive step. Lobotomy reflected the conventional medical view that mental illness was caused by physical illness and should be treated like other physical ailments — a view opposed by Freud's belief that mental illness usually has a mental cause. Lobotomy was surgical and irreversible. Its evaluation of what a "cure" meant was uncertain and hasty, though Moniz could confidently declare someone cured of mental illness just ten days after the operation. Worse, said its critics as early as 1937, its much vaunted neurological basis "rests on pure cerebral mythology."[74]

At a meeting of the the Chicago Neurological Society in 1937, the criticism of the crude and careless surgical procedures was expert and devastating. Speaking of how, after a skull was drilled, a wire loop was inserted to pull out subcortical tissue, one surgeon said:

> On what does this procedure rest? First, this is not an operation but a mutilation. Moniz said he was unable to state the exact extent and location of the parts removed by the leucotome [the scalpel inserted into the brain]. That is evident, for there are different sizes of skulls and of brains, and there is no way of knowing what may be removed. The wire loop may strike a blood vessel.[75]

But these criticisms stayed within the profession, as doctors' ethics demanded. The press, meanwhile, praised lobotomies to the skies. The *New York Times* in 1938 ran the headline SURGERY USED ON THE SOUL-SICK; RELIEF OF OBSESSIONS IS REPORTED: *New Brain Technique Is Said to Have Aided 65% of Mentally Ill Persons*.[76] What constituted a "cure" or "aid" was left conveniently vague.

Many of the documented cases are grim reading. Joseph Kennedy, the father of JFK, had his daughter Rosemary lobotomized in her twenties. The account is all the more appalling because routine. The family is alleged to have worried that Rosemary might become pregnant or caught by a gigolo. She was claimed to be perhaps retarded or anyway willful. Her impatient and annoyed father decided to end the nuisance then and there. Dr. Walter Freeman, the foremost American practitioner of lobotomy — more than four thousand done, he proudly claimed — performed the operation. His surgery was to insert an ice pick under the upper eyelid and hammer it into the frontal lobe, then twist.[77] As the surgeon dug through her forehead until the scalpel touched her brain, Rosemary was asked to keep singing any songs she knew, or to add up numbers. As long as she did, the scalpel was pushed and scraped in further. Finally, she could no longer remember any song or how to add: her brain had been destroyed. Dr. Freeman typically used such singing-adding tests while he dug the ice pick in with boisterous good humor. But he botched the job. Far from becoming "docile," Rosemary was often violent. She spent several years confined to a convent, then was in a room with bars for nine years. Her mother never visited her. Thirty years after the lobotomy, she was found walking distractedly in Chicago streets.[78]

Whatever else it did, lobotomy pacified most patients — or mentally "castrated" them, as one physician put it — and institutions were far easier to run when patients sat dully, made no demands, and caused no bother. Unfortunately, they frequently regressed to infancy, becoming incontinent or aggressively sexual in an infantile way — often a heavier burden on their families to whom they were returned "improved" than before. In the 1950s tranquilizers achieved enough quieting effect, and helped halt lobotomizing.

Moniz was no ordinary physician. He came from a grand Portuguese family, had been ambassador from Portugal to Spain, and had the worldly finesse of a perfect diplomat. He liked to present himself as a Renaissance man — dramatist, composer, painter, historian, scientist. He was certainly covetous of the Nobel Prize. He had himself nominated for the 1928 prize in medicine, but the committee felt his work in cerebral angiography not important enough. Two medical colleagues at the University of Lisbon nominated him again in 1933. But after he invented lobotomy and it caught on, he was awarded the 1949 Nobel Prize in Medicine, shared with Walter Hess, the neurologist — but not a lobotomist. Valenstein, in his careful report, suggests that Moniz won the award because that year there happened to be unusually few nominations of merit. The *New York Times*, which seemed hypnotized by Moniz, said in an editorial of congratulations that he had taught us "to look with less awe on the brain. It is just a big organ . . . and no more sacred than the liver."[79] The esteemed *New England Journal of Medicine* went fatuously further: "A new psychiatry may be said to have been born in 1935, when Moniz took his first bold step in the field of psychosurgery."[80]

Despite mounting protests within the medical profession, the prestige of the Nobel Prize gave lobotomizing a new authority. Five thousand lobotomies are said to have been performed in the United States between 1949 and 1952. Yet within a few years, lobotomy faded quickly. Moniz died in 1955 just as his procedure became only of historical interest, like Bedlam or the straitjacket. The accounts of Moniz's death vary. One has him suffering a massive internal hemorrhage while quietly working on an article; another has him beaten to death by a deranged patient, the very last patient he intended treating before final retirement.[81] In either case, he died at age eighty-one.

8

The Peace Prize

Alfred Nobel gave over the peace prize to a committee chosen by the Norwegian parliament, the only Nobel Prize outside Swedish control. It dwells apart from the other prizes in a more important way, honoring neither an art nor a science but political activity of a special kind. As Nobel phrased it in his will, the award should go to

> the person who shall have done the most or best work for fraternity among nations, for the abolition or reduction of standing armies and for the holding and promotion of peace congresses.

This clearly meant war *between* nations, and the Nobel committees duly honored such efforts. From 1960, however, the Nobel Prizes also began to emphasize efforts for peace *within* a nation. This is a long step away from what Alfred Nobel intended, but the cause is obvious. Many nations, while at peace with their neighbors, wage war against their own citizens: Rwanda, Ethiopia, Serbia, and Cambodia are only some recent instances. Sometimes a nonviolent struggle for justice is involved, as in the U.S. campaign for civil rights. This has broadened but complicated the meaning of peace: international harmony is one thing, but peace in the form of justice within a particular nation is a quite different matter. For the Nobel Peace Prize, a sea change indeed.

A related change has been the internationalizing of the peace prize from 1950. Up to then, all prizes centered on European problems or activists, with one ambiguous exception, the 1936 prize to the Argentine Saavedra Lamas, to which we shall return. Since 1950, laureates have come from Asia, Africa, the Mideast, and Central America.

In any case, the peace prize has unfortunately coincided with the twentieth century, probably the greatest charnel house in all of human history, with hundreds of millions slaughtered. The technology that made this possible has progressed from Nobel's dynamite to the tank and airplane to the nuclear bomb and electronic weaponry. The past hundred years have seen unprecedented total and global war, the first real "world" wars. A third such war, if hydrogen bombs are used, may indeed end war altogether, along with humanity.

Toward the end of the nineteenth century, however, there was an optimistic moment in which hope arose that war might be tamed, perhaps even ended. Nobel himself shared this hope. The First World War proved it a frightful illusion. The atom and hydrogen bombs drastically changed the very measure of peace: now it is merely that the worst has not happened — humanity has not yet been exterminated. Our expectations have been lowered or cynicism raised. The eight-year Iran-Iraq War in the 1980s, for example, ruinous and futile to both sides, never threatened to turn nuclear. On that cold ultimate scale, it remained only a "minor" war. Meanwhile, however, more nations "go nuclear." At present, a dozen or more nations have that capability, with more coming, some defiant of international arms control.

Although war has thus far remained "conventional," a century of peace prizes have not made nations more fraternal. At the very end of 1999, according to the Associated Press, 65 of the world's 193 nations — one-third — were at war (international, civil, major insurgencies). This is twice as bad as the late 1980s, when only about 35 nations were in conflict. Even those at peace have increased standing armies and armaments, with some of the poorest nations squandering meager budgets arming to the teeth, and very often buying from those nations — the U.S., France, the ex-USSR — once supposed to be the vanguard in the march to peace.

Defining "peace" seems impossible. The looseness of the term is reflected in the way the peace committee has sent honors in all directions — to political figures who have achieved some practical progress, but also a Mother Teresa with her hospitals for the poor. This may seem to spread the meaning of peace too broadly, but peace is as much a spiritual matter as a political one. Certainly some curious nominations for the prize have been reported: Hitler in 1934 tops the list, unless it was a hoax. Maxim Litvinov, Stalin's hatchetman, was recommended in 1933.

The purest sort of peace advocates are the "pacifists," modeled on Jesus or Thoreau or Tolstoy. Yet the Nobel peace judges have almost entirely ignored true pacifists unless they were also political activists. This makes sense, since the peace prize is an activist award, as Nobel's will makes clear. The Dalai Lama (prize 1989) is a pacifist, and his citation said kind words about pacifism, but his prize was plainly a political protest against China's seizure of Tibet. Martin Luther King Jr., the nonviolent civil rights leader, is the Nobel's best-known example of combining activism and nonviolence. Many humanitarians have also won prizes, as "activists" who seek to help the sick or refugees, or as individual "voices of conscience": Albert Schweitzer, Mother Teresa, the International Red Cross, Father Pire and Fridtjof Nansen, Amnesty International, Elie Wiesel, Doctors without Borders. Ted Turner's biographer writes that the U.S. media king hoped to win the peace prize with his billion-dollar donation to the UN for aid to refugees and the poor.[1]

Otherwise, the Nobel Peace Prizes have largely gone to officials. Before the First World War these were usually organizers or administrators of private peace movements. With the League of Nations in 1920, governments took over the peace movement. Laureates were increasingly chosen from political leaders of nations, or officials of the League of Nations and then the UN. The U.S. secretaries of state George Marshall and Henry Kissinger, Egyptian president Anwar Sadat and Israeli premier Menachem Begin, the Soviet premier Gorbachev are some of these. Indeed, the peace prize has become coveted by politicians as the ultimate testimony of "statesmanship." Former president Jimmy Carter, who in recent years has journeyed as peacemaker to Iran, North Korea, and Haiti, among other places, has been satirized as one such hopeful. A parody by the cartoonist Garry Trudeau of a verse collection published by Carter in 1994 makes the point:

All That Glitters

Thy city, King of Kings,
Shines bright upon yon hill,
Its holy heart still sings
Of peace on earth, thy will.

When wilt thou call to me,
Commend me from thy helm,
Adorn this graceless soul
With coinage from thy realm?

O bear me to thy nation,
(Yes, swing low, chariot)
To standing reservations
At the Oslo Marriott.[2]

The Promise of Peace

Two historical factors led to a widespread hope in the nineteenth century that war might be eliminated. Alfred Nobel's peace prize is an offshoot.

On one side, never before had war been such a carnage. Armies were vastly larger. The huge French forces carrying Napoleon's wars across all Europe were made possible by the first mass draft in modern times — the French Revolution's *levée en masse.* The older, smaller armies of professionals and volunteers were on the way out. New technology also multiplied killing capacity. One million men are said to have died in the Napoleonic Wars, on the field or from untreatable wounds. The American Civil War, with industrial arsenals pouring out cannon, precision-machined rifle barrels, ironclad ships, rudimentary submarines, and devastating bombs — and new tactics — made the Napoleonic Wars of only fifty years before seem almost antique. In 1812, when Napoleon's army occupied Moscow, the Russians began burning down their own city to force him out. But Sherman burnt a path behind the lines to ruin the South economically and break the spirit of its citizens, a practice that foreshadowed twentieth-century total war.

Even "minor" wars, now all but forgotten, could be dreadful. In 1859 Austria invaded Italy and fought France and its Italian allies.

At the battle of Solferino, forty thousand were killed and wounded. A chance observer, the Swiss Henri Dunant (1828–1910), was so appalled by the slaughter that he devoted the rest of his life to the nascent peace movement: he helped found the International Red Cross, taking its emblem from the the Swiss flag. His memoirs recalled soldiers standing over dead bodies, smashing enemy skulls with their rifle butts, then disemboweling them with bayonets: "butchery."[3] Dunant shared the first Nobel Peace Prize in 1901.

On the other side, however, war seemed to be declining, at least between major European powers, since Waterloo in 1815. True, there was the Crimean War in 1854, pitting Russia against Britain and France. Then in 1864 Austria and Prussia swallowed up the Danish provinces of Schleswig-Holstein; in 1866 Prussia defeated Austria; in 1871 Prussia defeated France.

But since none of these compared with the Napoleonic Wars that convulsed all Europe from Spain to Moscow, it could seem to many that, at least among "civilized" nations, war was fading. Perhaps reason was beginning to prevail in human affairs. Some, like Tolstoy, opposed war on religious-ethical grounds. In general, however, nineteenth-century peace agitators were rationalists, tirelessly ticking off their indisputable logic and arguments. Kant had said that "the commercial spirit cannot coexist with war." Peace advocates often argued like that. Peace benefited national self-interest. Could anyone deny that war destroyed precious resources and energy or diverted them into useless armament-making, benefiting none but the armament makers? And here began the enduring modern image of the sinister warmongers loyal to no nation or creed except sales, the "merchants of death": the Krupps in Germany; Basil Zaharoff, a Turkish Greek who lived in France, beloved by the newspapers as the Mystery Man of Europe; and of course the "dynamite king" Nobel, whose prizes for peace thus naturally fascinated the public.

Reason, applied to disease, brought great cures. Why not a science of peace whose diseased form was war? Nobel himself reasoned that mankind might abandon war because weapons had become so destructive. For others, the rise of nineteenth-century democratic sentiment proved reason was in the ascendent. A free press would expose secret machinations leading to war; the spread of education would pacify wild impulses and strip war of its false glamour. Humanity had moved from primitive brutishness through tribalism and monarchy to democracy. Perhaps warlike irrationality might also evolve away, vestigial as the appendix. And nations — those ancient units whose competitiveness and exclusiveness caused most wars — might evolve into a parliament of mankind.

At times, optimism soared. Some hoped to orchestrate the separate nations into a truly international harmony. Here is Victor Hugo addressing the International Peace Congress in 1849 on "a United States of Europe":

> this sacred idea, universal peace, all nations bound together in a common bond, the Gospel for their supreme law, mediation substituted for war. . . . A day will come when you, France — you, Russia — you, Italy — you, England — you, Germany . . . will without losing your distinct qualities . . . be blended into a superior unity.[4]

There ensued scores of peace conferences, thousands of books and pamphlets, millions of words written and orated, battalions of nongovernmental international organizations, endless petitions, countless analyses of the causes of peace and war, appeals to workingmen, clerics, parliaments, and kings. From around 1870, this has continued without letup to the present day.

Peace Prizes to 1914

Before the First World War, except for a rare personage like Theodore Roosevelt, the prizes went to such unremembered figures as Charles Gobat, Frédéric Passy, Bertha von Suttner, Klas Arnoldson, and Tobias Asser. They share a general profile. War's destructiveness, madness, and wastefulness converts them to the peace cause. They work unflaggingly, inexhaustibly hopeful, ignoring all rebuffs and indifference. They achieve no stunning success and rarely win renown. For the most part, their stories are those of organizers and administrators, hard-working, practical, relentlessly single-minded people, bent on advancing their movement. After reading enough of their biographies, it is hard to keep them apart: they are like the faceless missionaries and bishops of the early Church, doing good works, sacrificing personal ambition and acclaim, and staunchly laboring in the vineyards of the Lord in happy anonymity. Like the old monks, they too sought to convert the barbarians — the war-makers — to higher views. They lived out their lives in harness, and are scarcely remembered even after winning a Nobel Prize. Indeed, several institutions have been honored with Nobel Prizes, and individuals ignored. Who can object? The peace movement is dedicated to the greater good, not private glory.

These early laureates were journalists, lawyers, merchants, writers, minor government officials who launched or labored in international peace societies: the League of Universal Brotherhood; the International Law Association; the International Arbitration League; the International Arbitration and Peace Association of Great Britain and Ireland; *Congrès international des amis de la paix; Lega di libertà, fratellanza e pace; Deutsche Friedengesellschaft.* So august and resounding are these titles that one imagines them chiseled across the porticoes of stately buildings like the U.S. Supreme Court. In fact, they were often paper organizations based on a printed letterhead, a file of correspondence, and some pamphlets and handbills, sometimes working out of their founder's home or private office. The majestic institutional titles make one forget how marginal the peace cause was to the high political chambers of the world where war and peace were really decided.

Peace agitators were apt to speak unendingly of the need for a Parliament of Man, Universal Peace, and Disarmament. But the "peace movement" up to 1914, not to mention after, was quite inwardly divided. In principle, the fight for peace ignored class lines and social differences. In practice, it didn't. Those who won peace prizes usually belonged to the same class as the government leaders they sought to influence. Some even hobnobbed with presidents or kings. After all, even Czar Nicholas II, the "greatest autocrat in Europe," in 1899 surprisingly denounced war as destroying economies and civilization and urged a conference to set up international conciliation.[5]

These conservative peace militants shunned radicals who saw peace requiring a class revolution, violent if need be. For the conservatives, peace would be a triumph of education and ethical exhortation, and they often refused to take any political stand lest it compromise their "objectivity" and neutrality — and of course irk government leaders. Peace advocates from the working classes or socialist movements obviously felt more isolated and belligerent.

At the time, however, peace activists of all stripes were likely to argue that an elite few forced war on "the people." It was assumed that once the people were educated or informed enough, war would decline: the people would refuse to fight. To quote a slogan of a few decades back, "What if they gave a war and nobody came?" Einstein once calculated that if only two percent of any nation's conscriptees refused to fight, a war would be impossible. His mathematics may have been faulty.

Pre-1914 Laureates

The first two colaureates typified the tensions of the early peace era. Dunant came from a prominent and pious Geneva family, and became a banker. His work took him to North Africa, and he wrote a book about slavery there after Harriet Beecher Stowe's writings helped convert him to abolitionism in 1853. But Algerian ranching seemed a good business venture, and he and others were prepared to invest one hundred million Swiss francs. Stupid delays by French colonial officialdom sent the impatient Dunant off in 1859 to see the French emperor himself. He found him in Italy where the French were fighting the Austrians. Dunant arrived in time for a close-up view of that horrendous battle at Solferino. Shocked, he wrote a book about it that caused a stir. Neglecting his business, he plunged into relief work for war victims and in a few years went bankrupt and was soon poverty-stricken. Still, working constantly, he gathered supporters, appealed to the famous — Dickens, Victor Hugo — and in 1863 founded the International Red Cross. The first meeting in Geneva was attended by thirty-nine people from sixteen countries. Later, no one knows why, Dunant became a recluse, so poor he had to ink his coat to hide the rips and chalk his shirt to make it whiter. A journalist found him in 1895, in time for the Nobel peace committee to honor him. He donated his prize money to the poor.[6]

Yet his winning a Nobel Prize offended a segment of the peace movement. Did not helping war victims make war more palatable, even perhaps legitimize it? His fellow laureate, the Frenchman Frédéric Passy (1822–1912), worked to prevent war, not alleviate it. Dunant was at heart a humanitarian; Passy was an organization man. He trained as an economist, worked as a French government official, and then became a full-time publicist of peace. War was economically wasteful; if nothing else, humanity's selfishness should persuade it to abandon conflict between nations. He set up the International League for Permanent Peace, just in time for it to fall apart with the Franco-Prussian War in 1870. Passy simply began another peace society. Elected to the French Chamber of Deputies, he used that position in 1889 to promote international peace arbitration among legislators in different countries. His efforts led to the Interparliamentary Union, with members from ten European nations and the U.S., and Passy as first president. This was an important toehold inside European and American legislatures, and before the First World War, his was one of the two most influential peace organizations.

The other was the International Peace Bureau at Bern, founded in 1896 to coordinate the many peace societies that seemed to be mushrooming everywhere in Europe and America. In 1903 the Nobel Peace Prize was shared by Elie Ducommun of Switzerland for the Peace Bureau and Passy's successor Charles Gobat, also of Switzerland, for the Interparliamentary Union.

But they pulled against each other, torn as the peace cause still is. One side seeks direct political influence, as Gobat's Union did, while the other fears that a political stance risks losing its moral influence. Thus Ducommun considered it unthinkable to comment publicly, much less take any position, on the Dreyfus Affair or the Russian pogroms against Jews.[7]

Then there was Bertha von Suttner (peace prize 1905). Beautiful, cultivated, aristocratic, a famous novelist, she is one of the most colorful personalities in the history of Nobel Peace Prizes. It will be recalled that she had once almost become Alfred Nobel's private secretary, but impulsively ran off to marry, clearly disappointing Nobel in more ways than one. Bertha and her husband, an impoverished Viennese aristocrat, supported themselves in Russia by teaching languages and music. They had meanwhile become devout adherents of the peace movement. With the Russo-Turkish War in 1877, Arthur von Suttner became a war correspondent, and Bertha began writing novels. In 1886 in Paris, Bertha again met Nobel, who took them about to meet important people. She was greatly disturbed by the French lust for revenge on Germany after the 1871 defeat. Her earlier novels had already emphasized world peace, liberal politics, and internationalism. In 1889 she published her most famous novel, *Die Waffen nieder* (Lay Down Your Arms). The story was of a woman's life shattered by the wars of the 1860s. The novel now seems tame, but at the time the war scenes were found shockingly realistic and powerful. Tolstoy praised the book, as did the Austrian Imperial Council, and it has been compared in impact to Harriet Beecher Stowe's *Uncle Tom's Cabin* (appropriate, as long as one registers the difference that Stowe helped foment a war, while Suttner wanted to end them all). Bertha von Suttner became the celebrity of the peace societies, a star attraction at congresses.

Not least, she is said to have persuaded Nobel to include peace in his bequest for prizes. For her, peace was a high-minded educational and moral matter to be kept firmly apart from political activism. Her ethical pacifism, her emphasis on women as nurturing and on peace as emancipating women, drew many women to the cause. But as the First World War approached, her bubble broke. Patriotic Austrians denounced her pacifism; so did the Germans although, or because, she had helped found the Anglo-German Friendship Committee in 1905. She bore the attacks with dignity. And perhaps she had a bit of luck, in dying of cancer a few weeks before the war horrors actually started.

The early peace prizes to President Theodore Roosevelt (1906) and his secretary of state Elihu Root (1912) are cases apart. Both were powerful political figures. Both were also militarists. Peace societies almost always linked disarmament with peace arbitration as two halves of the same. Roosevelt split them. On the one hand, he unabashedly flourished the "big stick" of war power. As assistant secretary of the navy, he did much to build up readiness for a war with Spain, and his secret information helped Admiral Dewey defeat the Spanish fleet in Manila, thus providing the U.S. with its first colony. As president, he enlarged the U.S. Navy to promote American influence and security. He aided Panamanian revolutionaries in their rebellion against Colombia so that the U.S. could buy rights to land for the Panama Canal. He introduced a military threat into the Monroe Doctrine: if European nations intervened in South American affairs, the U.S. would force them out by arms.

But Roosevelt also accomplished a great feat of international peace arbitration before the First World War. In 1905 he brought Russia and Japan together in a conference in Portsmouth, New Hampshire, and worked out a compromise to end the Russo-Japanese War begun in 1904. Roosevelt's motives were to maintain a balance of power. Japan's success in the war kept Russia from moving farther into Manchuria. Still, Roosevelt did not want Japan to emerge too victorious, lest it become aggressively ambitious. Hence the arbitration.

Such balance-of-power strategies, which dated back to antiquity, were anathema to many peace enthusiasts. That sort of peaceful coexistence required nations to be matched militarily, making disarmament unlikely. The peace activists thus viewed Roosevelt's peace prize with ambivalence. But his prestige and success made arbitration popular and respectable. As an arbitrator, Roosevelt acted as a private person, not officially as president of the United States — but as he later said, admitting the obvious, his being president was of course the only reason he was allowed to act at all.

Elihu Root, Roosevelt's secretary of state, had similar motives. He negotiated with Japan to keep China open to foreign nations, and to keep the status quo in the Pacific Ocean. His Nobel Prize–winning act was to repair South American distrust of Roosevelt's aggressive move into Panama. "We wish for no victories but those of peace," he told the Pan-American Peace Conference in Rio de Janeiro in 1906, to great applause. A year later, he launched what became the Central American peace arbitration court, the first of its kind in the hemisphere. In his acceptance speech for the Nobel Peace Prize, however, Root gave no satisfaction to optimistic peace activists. He declared that war was an ineradicable aspect of human nature for good and bad reasons, and could likely never be prevented. He did allow that the growing interest in international arbitration suggested a slim ray of hope.

In fact, two rays of hope had appeared. One was international arbitration. Traditionally done by diplomacy, the innovation around 1900 was to try institutionalizing it on a permanent basis. Hence the Permanent International Court of Justice at The Hague was established between 1899 and 1907, as a politically neutral tribunal to settle international disputes. For this to work, nations had to agree to a code of international law — the other hope. Unfortunately no such code existed, or ever had. Treaties and alliances had always been been done on a de facto basis. Each nation remained sovereign, which was precisely what made war possible. So, from the later nineteenth century, great effort was poured into codifying international law. The British prime minister Gladstone hailed the idea. Various institutes produced weighty legal analyses, satisfying in every respect — except that no nation was willing to surrender its right to determine its own self-interest. How then was international law and its court to enforce its decisions?

In August 1914 it became clear that Reason hadn't prevailed as hoped. None of the long list of sensible arguments against war stopped the Big Powers from a near-suicidal war of unprecedented scope and destruction.

The Great War and Peace Transformed

With the First World War, the nightmare the peace movement had hoped to exorcize or avoid arrived with a vengeance. In the next four years, nearly forty million soldiers were mobilized, and ten million of them killed.

The outbreak of war devastated the peace movement. The entire thriving international network of organizations collapsed, or fell into bitter quarrels, or turned cautiously silent. In Allied and Germanic countries, peace societies were suppressed. Or else, as with the American Peace Society, they soon switched from opposing war to patriotic boosting. Even the largest political party in the Marxist Second International, the German Social Democratic Party, quickly voted to back the German war effort.[8]

Thus skeletonized and demoralized, peace activists — and the Nobel Peace Prize with them — went through a bitter time. Once-confident hopes now seemed betrayed or self-deceiving. In countries at war, peace activists were often accused of lacking patriotism or even being treasonous. Bertrand Russell, for example, spent six months in jail for mildly criticizing the war effort. The pacifist, said the *Herald of Peace*, the influential London peace newspaper, "cannot side with his country . . . in destroying herself as well as her opponent. . . . He cannot side against her, for the same reasons."[9]

Precisely because World War I introduced so much new weaponry — tanks, airplanes, poison gas — it underlines the irony that various Nobel Prizes implicitly war with each other. The peace prizes oppose military conflict, but the physics and chemistry prizes honor discoveries that spawn the technologies expanding and intensifying war. The Russian H-bomb physicist and rights dissenter Andrei Sakharov (peace prize, 1975) declared that nuclear research must be pursued to provide us with needed energy. Contrarily, the International Physicians for the Prevention of Nuclear

War (prize 1985) warned that we are thereby dangerously becoming the servants and possible targets of our technologies.

Meanwhile, at each Nobel ceremony, science and peace are honored side by side. The 1995 peace colaureate, Joseph Rotblat, a Polish-born English physicist, had worked in Los Alamos on the atomic bomb. In 1944, when Germany was clearly losing, he resigned from the bomb project — the only physicist to do so. Later, backed by his credentials as a physicist at Los Alamos, he helped organize the Pugwash Conference on Science and World Affairs. Meeting at first in the Nova Scotia fishing village it was named after, it drew Soviet as well as Western scientists. Pugwash claims to have helped persuade the U.S. and USSR to sign the 1972 Treaty on Anti-Ballistic Missiles. Rotblat said Pugwash aimed to convince governments that "the genie can be put back into the bottle." Yet Rotblat, aged eighty-six, was honored precisely because the genie has not been put back into the bottle. The Nobel peace chairman, Francis Sejersted, admitted that "one of the reasons for Rotblat's prize is a sort of protest against testing of nuclear weapons, and nuclear arms in general."[10] Rotblat's 1995 prize — this must have been intentional — came fifty years after Hiroshima, just as France and China were conducting nuclear tests.

In 1914, 1915, 1916, and 1918, the Nobel Peace Prizes were canceled. In 1917 the International Red Cross was honored for its aid to war victims.

Yet by 1920 things looked entirely different. Before 1914 peace activists had little success in converting governments to their viewpoint. Now, with the founding of the League of Nations, governments themselves took over the peace cause. The peace lobbies working on the margins of governments no longer seemed needed. For one thing,

> the Peace Movement after the War was more truly international than it had ever been before, though the International Peace Bureau that constituted its common link declined in vigor. Secondly . . . many of its aspirations had at last been realized. There were to be no more crusades for arbitrations treaties; no more frenzied petitions for the codification of International Law. Within the framework of the League, Governments now had officially taken up the work of preserving Peace by cooperation.[11]

This was how it seemed to a perceptive observer in 1930. Only later events, such as Italy's defiance of the League in 1935, would show that crusades for arbitration treaties were still needed — and after 1945, more than ever.

The League of Nations and International Kisses

The League of Nations was established in 1919 by Woodrow Wilson and others. Nations promised to band together to punish any transgressor. If economic and other sanctions failed and violence erupted, they would make war on the war-maker. Their combined military force would outmatch the "outlaw" nation. As political scientist Frederick Schuman aptly said, this proposed to make peace by making war.[12] But the League of Nations failed abysmally here.

Where peace was involved, Wilson was Theodore Roosevelt in reverse. Roosevelt believed in military power, but was willing to arbitrate if it profited national interest. Wilson also believed in power: he sent U.S. troops into Mexico in 1916 on flimsy grounds and took America into its first European war for a variety of reasons, some dubious. But he believed in peace not simply for his nation's good but the world's. He wanted arbitration to prevent all wars. He sincerely believed his slogan "The world must be made safe for democracy."

There followed Wilson's famous Fourteen Points in 1918, which some saw as nobly idealistic, others as hopelessly naive. He envisioned a League of Nations built on ambitious but untried foundations: arbitration would be compulsory, and sanctions used if necessary; disarmament would be compulsory; a permanent international organization would be set up; a ban would be instituted on secret diplomacy that launched war without free and open discussion.

The true innovation here, at once hope and stumbling block, was the proposal to enforce peace by war sanctions if necessary. Warring nations would now have to face not only their particular chosen enemy but the combined might of the world's nations. On this decisive point, the League slowly foundered and eventually broke apart. Wilson himself, who won the peace prize in 1919 for inspiring the League, wobbled here. He wanted military sanctions if need be, yet was annoyed when Léon Bourgeois, his French colleague at the Paris Peace Conference in 1919, kept insisting that peace required a military force ready and willing to act. Bourgeois won the Nobel Peace Prize in 1920, the year after Wilson. They were the hard-headed and idealistic poles of the League, offering much room — too much — to waffle.

The painful consequences arrived very quickly. Italy had signed the League Covenant in 1920 as a founder member. In 1923 the new Fascist dictator Mussolini forcibly seized the island of Corfu from Greece. No punitive sanctions were invoked; arbitration before the Hague Court was proposed, but Italy settled outside League jurisdiction. In the 1930s the provocations became worse, the responses feebler, with the U.S. and Britain offering no support of strong action. The United States Senate in 1919 refused to ratify entry into the League of Nations or join the Hague Court, for tangled domestic reasons. Britain and the Commonwealth refused to sign the Geneva Protocol, designed to strengthen the League's authority. The protocol held that only the League as a whole could wage war, and only against an "aggressor" nation. Instead Britain opted for "regional pacts." One of these involved Germany. The reparations imposed by the vindictive Treaty of Versailles in 1919 were too steep for Germany's ruined economy. The fantastic runaway inflation in Germany up to 1923 was one outcome. Another came when Germany had to default on its reparations payments in 1923, and the French seized the Ruhr valley, Germany's industrial core.

The Versailles Treaty epitomizes how peace as well as war can be disastrously lost. While halting the most destructive war thus far in history, the treaty helped poison the future. The deep resentments it raised in Germany were soon exploited by Hitler.

Solving the German issue was important, but the Nobel peace committee rather overdid it. Prizes were awarded a small platoon of negotiators here. In 1925 the colaureates were British foreign secretary Austen Chamberlain and U.S. vice president Charles Dawes, for reducing the punitive reparations on Germany in 1924. The next year, shared prizes went to German foreign minister Gustav Stresemann and French foreign minister Aristide Briand, for the Locarno Pact, which settled German borders with France and Poland, guaranteed mutual nonaggression, and admitted Germany into the League. Again the following year, 1927, Ferdinand Buisson of France shared the peace award partly for his share in resolving French-German tensions. Finally, Nicholas Murray Butler, the president of Columbia University, took half the 1931 peace prize for his strong public championing of the Locarno Pact. This was six Nobel Peace Prizes in five years, yet the Locarno Pact probably dimmed the long-range chances for peace. It addressed itself to security problems, but remained silent about disarmament.[13]

League sentiments about disarmament tended only to be loudly vocalized. The Soviets in 1927 proposed immediate universal disarmament; that same year the League Assembly passed a resolution condemning all aggressive war; the Pan-American Union renounced war. Such lofty verbal renunciation reached its peak in the Kellogg-Briand Pact of 1928, eventually signed by sixty-five nations, all volunteering "to renounce war as an instrument of national policy." Its American sponsor was U.S. secretary of state Frank Kellogg, who won a Nobel Peace Prize in 1929 for that pact. This wondrous step forward was a setback. The pact had begun as a proposal for a nonaggression treaty between France and the United States. But this meant tying America's interests to France's, and Kellogg's pact was a gambit to avoid that. He proposed that all nations renounce war, but said nothing about how to enforce this. One U.S. senator mocked it as an "international kiss." The U.S. Senate ratified the treaty at once, only one vote dissenting.[14]

The League's Boom and Slump

In 1920 forty-one nations signed the Covenant of the new League of Nations. By 1934 the total was sixty-one. But by 1927, nations had also begun steadily withdrawing. A list of some violations suggests part of the reason:

1922–23 Collapse of naval conference (U.S., Britain, Japan), designed to set fleet sizes for the three, upon Britain refusal of parity with the U.S.

1923 French seizure of Ruhr

1926–33 U.S. Marines sent to Nicaragua to fight Sandino rebellion

1927 British troops sent into Shanghai

1931–33 Japanese occupation of Manchuria

1932 Japanese seizure of Shanghai

1935–36 Italian occupation of Ethiopia

1936 German cancellation of Locarno Pact, dismissal of League's disarmament pledge, and deployment of troops in demilitarized Rhineland

1936 Spanish Civil War, with military intervention by Germany and USSR.

The League took no punitive action in any of these cases. The Greco-Turkish hostilities involved the sack and massacre of Smyrna, but that was merely loftily denounced. France's seizure of Germany's industrial Ruhr was held justified under the Versailles Treaty. And so on.

The Japanese invasion of Manchuria was too provocative to be ignored, though the League did its best. Japan baldly claimed that no invasion had occurred; rather, the Manchurian people had themselves chosen to be Japanese subjects in a spontaneous act of national self-determination.[15] Unbelievable as this was, the League dithered. European Big Powers had their own designs on China and were loath to lose their chances, much less fight the powerful Japanese army. Depression worries also held them back: sanctioning Japan could set at risk valuable economic and financial relations with that country. Japan could have been halted, but, as one scholar summed it up,

> the European Great Powers wanted to proceed by conciliation only, the US perhaps overestimated the danger of opposing the Japanese militarists, the American association with the League was ambiguous . . . the Government in London was twice changed, and the financial blizzard broke upon the Western world; Japan was encouraged to gamble on the League's inertia.[16]

Japan set up "Manchukuo" without interference. China protested, supported by many smaller nations in the League who saw themselves as possible Manchukuos of the future and insisted that Japan be punished. The League merely condemned Japan in what was grandly but emptily called the "verdict of the world." Japan scornfully withdrew from the League.

Italy's invasion of Ethiopia in 1935 displayed as much League impotency. Though Mussolini had made clear he would invade, Britain sat tight, since "no vital British interest exists in Ethiopia," a direct affront to the League's collective purposes. Mussolini invaded in October 1935, and the Italian army scored splendid victories against Haile Selassie's army of spear carriers. The League quickly responded by declaring Italy an aggressor in violation of the League Covenant, but the only punishments were some financial sanctions, the ban of certain imports from Italy, and a leaky embargo on arms to Italy. "Italy's war," says Frederick Schuman, "could have been stopped within a week by closing the Suez Canal and banning oil exports to Italy. Neither step was taken or even seriously considered."[17] In two years, most League members recognized Italy's claim to Ethiopia.

The League did once gird itself to expel an aggressor member: Russia, for invading Finland in 1939. Japan, Italy, or Germany had never been treated so harshly. That was the League's last act before the Second World War. Its assembly met only once more, on 8 April 1946, to vote that "from this day the League of Nations shall cease to exist."

1930s Prizes

Of the Nobel Peace Prizes in the 1930s, as the next world war was visibly and ominously approaching, only two directly spoke to the threat of Nazi Germany. The first was the prize in 1935 to Carl von Ossietzky, a German journalist. Converted to peace before 1914, deepened by two years' military service in the trenches, Ossietzky in the 1920s edited a Berlin journal. He published an article claiming that the Weimar government was secretly allowing armed paramilitary groups to train, in violation of the Versailles Treaty. He spent a month in prison for libel. Once out, he published an exposé of secret German warplane training. He was arrested for treason but released. In 1931, after the Nazis won 107 seats in the Reichstag, Ossietzky laid out facts accusing them of planning war in the future. After secret hearings he was sentenced to eighteen months in prison. Prominent figures like Einstein signed protests. Ossietzky served seven months. But Hitler's assumption of power in 1933 meant the end. Ossietzky was quickly sent to a concentration camp. Meanwhile, he was nominated for the Nobel Peace Prize by Thomas Mann, Jane Addams, Bertrand Russell, Einstein, Virginia Woolf, and many others. In 1936 he was awarded the prize for 1935.

The Nazis angrily protested to the Norwegian parliament, which replied that the Nobel peace committee was independent. Ossietzky was too ill by then to travel to Stockholm or anywhere else. The German authorities mockingly said he was free to travel wherever he wished, except that they would not issue him a passport to do so. Ossietzky died under arrest in Berlin in 1938. This was the Nobel Peace Prize at its best.

The second such prize went to the 1937 laureate, Robert Cecil of Britain. He had helped found the League of Nations and been a prominent peace official and publicist. After his retirement in 1932, he asked himself why peace had not been achieved despite so much effort. He set out to warn public opinion against European appeasement and the bloodbath it was preparing. His was a voice in the wilderness.

Otherwise, the prizes remained honorific and usually retrospective. The Swedish archbishop Söderblom was honored in 1930 for organizing Christian peace conferences. The 1931 award went partly to the American reformer Jane Addams, revered for founding Hull House in 1889 in the slums of Chicago. A pacifist, she courageously opposed the U.S. entry into the First World War, an opposition for which Theodore Roosevelt, founder of the Bull Moose Party, mockingly called her a "bull mouse." In 1933 another veteran of the peace cause was honored: Norman Angell of Britain. In 1909 he wrote *The Great Illusion,* long the most famous book on peace. By "illusion," Angell meant the idea that war is profitable: on the contrary, the modern world is so economically interdependent that the victor suffers as much economic ruin as the defeated party. *The Great Illusion,* with its sturdy, simple, and simplistic argument, its array of statistics, and its appeal to economic self-interest, remained the peace "bible" for many. It sold a million copies in almost twenty languages, and begot a hundred organizations dedicated to publicizing Angell's views. In the time of Hitler and other ideological fevers, they did not seem very germane.

League of Nations efforts, though increasingly pointless, still impressed the Nobel judges. In this decade, three League officials became laureates.

The Briton Arthur Henderson (prize 1934) presided at the World Disarmament Conference in 1932, held under League auspices. Unfortunately, the conference was irrelevant before it met: Japan had embarked on its Chinese aggressions, Germany's Nazi Party was already in the government and soon to be dominant, Mussolini was arming Italy.

In 1936 the Argentine Carlos Saavedra Lamas won the prize for two semi-achievements. In 1933 he drafted an antiwar pact with a timid sanctions clause, signed by fifteen South American nations as well as the United States and Italy. Curiously, the treaty guaranteed international cooperation, yet also approved the contrary principle of neutrality. Moreover, Bolivia and Paraguay, two of the nations signing the peace treaty, had been at war with each other since 1928. Settling this war in 1935 was Lamas's other achievement. Yet by then that war had reached a weary impasse, and would have been settled one way or another. An American ambassador of the time said of Lamas that any conference entrusted to him "will be handled with a maximum of ineptitude and a minimum of hope." The prestige of his Nobel award did help elect him president of the League of Nations Assembly.

The 1938 prize to the Nansen International Office for Refugees was deserved. It had been founded by 1922 Nobel Peace Prize winner Fridtjof Nansen of Norway, the originator of the "Nansen passports" for millions of nationless people in the aftermath of the First World War. Nansen's life had an epic quality. He began as an Arctic explorer, and actually crossed Greenland on foot. It took him and his small crew one year to struggle through the subzero cold, the icy mountains and glacial formations. A world celebrity for that, he was also an oceanographer, and Norway's first ambassador to Great Britain in 1906–8. His work with refugees began in 1920. He somehow managed to repatriate almost half a million German and Austro-Hungarian ex–prisoners of war from Russia in less than a year. His famous "passports" came about when he next took on the relocation of one and a half million refugees from the Russian Revolution. The League of Nations turned down his request for funds, but Nansen's fame allowed him to make a personal worldwide appeal; the U.S. government gave him $20 million. The Nansen International Office of Refugees lasted from 1921 to 1938. Among other feats, Nansen arranged the exchange, after the bloody Greco-Turkish war ended in 1922, of a million Greeks in Turkey for half a million Turks in Greece. He died in 1930, but the Nansen Bureau continued his work.

From the Second World War to Now

From 1939 to 1943, there were no peace prizes. In 1944 the International Red Cross was honored for war relief work, although that organization knew about the Nazi death camps by late 1942 and said nothing.[18]

A number of postwar prizes went to humanitarians. The best known is still likely Albert Schweitzer (prize 1952), honored for his medical work in Lambaréné, French Equatorial Africa (now Gabon), from 1924. Over the years, he built a hospital of almost a hundred buildings with a large staff. Periodically he returned to Europe to raise funds by lectures and organ recitals — he was a great scholar of Bach. Endlessly busy, he also wrote many works expounding his philosophy of "reverence for life," which included world brotherhood and peace. Schweitzer with his crinkled smile and baggy mustache looked every inch the wise old sage, and many revered him as a saint for his African work. Others saw him as a remnant of European colonial paternalism, too authoritarian with his staff and patients, and even suggested that Lambaréné offered Schweitzer an escape from the larger and more difficult political and social problems that plagued Africa and Europe.

In more recent years the popular "saint" has been Mother Teresa (peace prize, 1979). She has been proposed for canonization, but has also been attacked for her strong opposition to abortion, even for exploiting human suffering to boost Catholic doctrine.[19] Like Schweitzer, she administered medical help to the poor. But Schweitzer had been a famous musician, theologian, and philosopher; his going to remote Africa struck the public's admiration and wonder. Mother Teresa emerged from complete obscurity to unexpected celebrity. She was born in Albania, became a nun, and decided to be a missionary in India. From her cloistered convent she could see the dreadful life outside in the Calcutta slums. She won permission to work outside the convent, studied nursing, and worked some years with the sick, poor, and abandoned. She founded a new order, the Missionaries of Charity, and eventually opened a Home for the Dying in Calcutta in 1954. She had twenty-six nuns to help her, all volunteers; they took vows to eat only the same food as the patients, and to work at least sixteen-hour shifts. Later she added an orphanage, a leper colony, a refuge for the elderly, and inoculation clinics, and she opened similar establishments in Venezuela, Rome, Tanzania, and elsewhere. Her peace prize was criticized as irrelevant to the cause of international peace, as set down in Nobel's bequest. But peace is not always won by power politics, high officials, or freedom fighters.

The United Nations

The League of Nations laid to rest, the United Nations rose from its ashes in 1945. The new showed that it had learned something crucial from the old. The UN Charter no longer spoke of all peaceful nations punishing an aggressor nation. That had unfortunately never happened, since self-interest dictated Great Power actions. The new UN accepted this fact and instead set up the Security Council, including five permanent members — the Soviet Union, the U.S., Great Britain, France, and China — any one of which could veto and thus halt the UN's ability to take collective action.

This at least brought into the open a plain fact of international life: if the UN did attempt to wage war against one of the Great Powers, the result could well be another world war.[20] On the other hand, it also seemed possible that if the Great Powers could agree, aggressor nations could be stopped.

What wasn't foreseen was the depth of the Cold War, which split the UN Assembly into two hostile camps — or that "China" by 1949 meant only Taiwan, or that Great Britain and France would quickly lose their empires and former military and political strength. The Security Council thus narrowed from five Great Powers to two superpowers, the USA and the USSR. And so it remained until the breakup of the Soviet Union in 1989.

Like the League of Nations, the United Nations immediately let its violating members go unpunished. The first provocation came fast, in 1947, when the Netherlands warred against Indonesians fighting for independence. Australia, India, and the U.S. called on the Security Council to intervene, without success — but Indonesia soon won the war on its own anyway. Then in 1976 Indonesia forcibly annexed East Timor, eventually resulting in a Nobel Peace Prize to East Timorese dissidents in 1996; the promised independence remains unsecured to this day.

In 1948 the Arab states attacked the new nation of Israel. No UN intervention or sanctions occurred. A UN official, the American

Ralph Bunche, negotiated a truce in 1949 and won the peace prize for 1950. This prize was a gesture of support for the new UN, as well as a rare instance when the prize could honor someone for actually halting a war — the only occasion before that being the prize to Theodore Roosevelt back in 1906.

With this prize, the Nobel peace committee finally shifted its focus away from Europe. From 1950, the prizes at last began to explore the globe's problems, in Asia, Africa, the Mideast, and Latin America. From 1950 to 1999, awards to these regions out-numbered those centered on Europe by about four to one, and at least twelve other prizes were broadly international in scope, as with Amnesty International.

The Cold War took hold in the UN decision to intervene in the war between North and South Korea of 1950. The Soviets accused the U.S. of starting the hostilities; the U.S. returned the accusation. The Americans persuaded the UN to act when the USSR angrily chose to be absent during the Security Council vote, a major tactical mistake, initiating the first international "police action" ever undertaken against an aggressor nation. Fifty nations were asked to send troops; only fifteen responded and the U.S. bore the massive brunt of the war. China's army entered the war to help North Korea. The war ended in a stalemate in 1953, whereupon a truce was arranged by the U.S. and USSR.

No one won a Nobel Peace Prize for anything involving the Korean War, though it was a "UN war."

Peace Prizes to UN Officials

1945 Cordell Hull (U.S.) for planning the UN

1950 Ralph Bunche (U.S.) for mediating Israeli-Arab truce

1957 Lester Pearson (Canada) for mediating truce in 1956 Suez Canal war

1961 Dag Hammarskjöld (Sweden) for peace work as secretary-general of the UN.

1974 Sean MacBride (Ireland) for work with Amnesty International and for pressing UN sanctions against South Africa over Namibia.

Peace Prizes to UN Departments

1954   Office of the UN High Commissioner for Refugees

1965   UNICEF (UN Children's Fund)

1969   International Labor Organization

1981   Office of the UN High Commissioner for Refugees

1988   UN peacekeeping forces (for observer and truce-keeping contingents in the Mideast [1948], India-Pakistan [1948], Cyprus [1964], Israel-Syria {Golan Heights} [1974], Lebanon [1978], and other conflicts)

The peace prize for Cordell Hull was strongly lobbied for by President Franklin Roosevelt, who nominated him annually. "This pleased the Secretary's ego; besides, Hull and his wife coveted the award for its cash prize of $40,000."[21] Hull was only one of several who planned the United Nations, but his prominent position made him the plausible symbolic laureate.

Bunche, Pearson, Hammarskjöld, and MacBride were the new sort of on-the-spot UN crisis managers and mediators. Their varying success encouraged a certain optimism about the new world organization. Hammarskjöld made the secretary-general's position politically more independent, and turned it into the UN's chief mediator. He improvised the first UN military force — the peacekeeping unit sent to the Suez in 1956. He was killed in a plane crash in Katanga in 1961 while trying to mediate the Belgian-Congolese war, and his peace prize was awarded posthumously, again seeming to prove that only Swedes receive Nobel Prizes when dead.

That so many UN departments have won Nobel awards is perhaps meant to stress the collective nature of peace work. UNICEF and the UN peacekeeping forces merited an award. But that the Office for Refugees won twice is an ambiguous compliment to the UN, since that bureau is designed to alleviate the horrors that the UN could or would not prevent. In 1981, High Commissioner Paul Hartling of Denmark, accepting the prize, addressed the world's refugees with no apparent irony: "Yes, this Nobel Peace Prize bears witness to the fact that your voices are being heard!"[22]

Statesmanship Prizes to Politicos

1953 U.S. secretary of state George Marshall for the Marshall Plan to rebuild Europe after the Second World War

1971 German chancellor Willy Brandt for reconciliation between West and East Germany

1973 Henry Kissinger, U.S. secretary of state, and Le Duc Tho, foreign minister of North Vietnam, for arranging a Vietnam cease-fire

1978 President Anwar al-Sadat of Egypt and Premier Menachem Begin of Israel for signing a peace treaty

1994 Israeli prime minister Yitzhak Rabin and foreign minister Shimon Peres and PLO chairman Yasir Arafat for signing a peace accord

The Marshall Plan remains an undoubted success in peacemaking. Rejecting the vindictive spirit of the Versailles Treaty, the plan set out to rebuild a war-shattered Europe, including the former enemies, for humanitarian and economic reasons — and to counter Soviet influence. Its $12-billion financing was the largest in history. Marshall was more the spokesman than the originator of the idea, but his great personal stature decisively helped ensure the plan's success.

The 1971 laureate was the German chancellor Willy Brandt, for helping to win recognition of East Germany, then a Soviet satellite, as a de facto state, setting up a mutual nonagression treaty between the divided Germanies, and establishing diplomatic relations with Poland. But the Nobel judges pointedly ignored a far more important act of reconciliation slightly earlier. For twenty years before Brandt, Konrad Adenauer was chancellor of West Germany. In the 1950s he and President Charles de Gaulle of France achieved an unprecedented reconciliation between their long-warring nations. This, rather than East-West detente, looked forward to the possible United States of Europe long hoped for by the Nobel peace committee. But the conservative de Gaulle was politically unacceptable to the liberal Norwegian peace committee (as he was to the Swedish literature prize committee: see the case of André Malraux). Yet passing over de Gaulle meant not honoring him even for saving France from civil war over Algeria — an extraordinary personal feat of peacekeeping. It also meant ignoring his partner Adenauer, of whom the Belgian prime minister Paul Spaak once said: "Without him no Coal and Steel Pool, no Common Market, and no Euratom. Without him the dream of a United Europe would not have become a reality."[23]

The 1973 prize to Henry Kissinger and Vietnam's Le Duc Tho remains one of the most controversial peace prizes. Two members of the Nobel peace committee resigned in protest; both laureates were much vilified; Le Duc Tho refused the award; Kissinger did not go to Oslo but had the American ambassador there accept the award for him. Despite the cease-fire and America's withdrawal of troops — and the Nobel award — in 1973, the war continued until 1976 when North Vietnam defeated the South and unified the country.

Other controversial peace prizes involved Israel. That small nation's crises have generated four Nobel Peace Prizes. Two of these — to Bunche, and in 1957 to another UN representative, Lester Pearson, for helping settle the Suez conflict of 1956 — were generally well received. But the prizes in 1978, to Sadat of Egypt and Begin of Israel for signing a peace treaty, and in 1994, to Israel's Rabin and Peres and the PLO's Arafat for renewing peace efforts, caused uproar and worse. One difference between the pre- and post-1950 peace prizes is reflected in the assassination of Sadat in 1981 because he had journeyed to Jerusalem for the sake of peace, and later of Rabin for the accord with the PLO. No peace laureate of the first half century ever seemed in danger of assassination for taking risky steps toward peace. The first laureate to be murdered because of peace work was Martin Luther King Jr. The Nobel peace committee had indeed ceased being a honorific agency and taken a step into dangerous political matters. Perhaps its enormous publicity also helped inflame passions and led to these murders. The aftermath of other peace prizes could be stormy: the uproar over Kissinger, the persecution of Aung San Suu Kyi and Sakharov.

These tensions infected the peace committee as well, as never in the earlier sedate period. The 1994 peace prize shared by Israel's Rabin and Peres and the PLO's Arafat caused a peace committee member to condemn Arafat as a terrorist and resign in full public view. The committee had clearly struggled for some way to avoid an uproar. It is reported they first chose Rabin, Peres, and Arafat, but then discussed giving the prize only to Peres and an assistant to Arafat, both of whom had secretly worked out the peace agreement in Norway. Further on, the committee also considered honoring only the "technicians" who had negotiated the outline of the agreement. Finally, they reverted to the original choice.[24]

Perhaps the 1974 award is the most puzzling. It was shared by Japan's premier Eisaku Sato and the UN official Sean MacBride. Sato was cited for declaring that Japan would not use or manufacture nuclear weapons, nor allow any on Japanese soil. Many well-informed Japanese and others were puzzled why Sato deserved a prize for this, since Japan had shown no intention of going nuclear. A TV reporter asked, "Is this a joke? Are they making fun of us?"[25] MacBride's award aroused similar criticism and puzzlement. South Africa had claimed Namibia, although the UN declared it held mandate in that nation. The UN sent MacBride to resolve this problem. He did not succeed. He was honored for upholding the principle of human rights, but his role as chair of Amnesty International from 1961 to 1974 was widely thought to have won him the prize, since no other compelling or substantial reason seemed to exist. Amnesty International itself won in 1977 — essentially two prizes in three years.

The Peace Prize Edges into Intervention

From 1960, the Nobel peace committee began a drastic revision of its view of peace. Up to then, peace meant the absence of war: peace occurred between nations. But why should "war" be confined to relations *between* nations? Why not as much within a nation? It might be argued — as Saint Thomas Aquinas had — that an unjust law is "a species of violence."[26] Along this line, many in our century have argued that a lack of human or civil rights, the use of secret police and imprisonment, suppression of political freedoms, censorship, and the like are "a species of war" waged by a nation against its own citizens.

The Nobel Peace Prize, with its enormous prestige and publicity, has greatly helped promote sympathy for this new type of peace activism. In general, the world has many reasons to be grateful. But the stance can be confusing and sometimes double-edged.

In 1977, as noted, Amnesty International won the prize. The world's largest independent rights organization, with a worldwide membership of over a million in a hundred or more nations, it has self-lessly fought illegal arrests, torture, and other injustices. In the Nobel acceptance speech, its representative said that "peace is not be measured by the absence of conventional war, but constructed on foundations of justice. Where there is injustice, there is the seed of conflict."

But injustice is difficult to determine. Wars end when armistice occurs. Deciding when a civil right has been fulfilled, or when a judicial system is functioning justly, is infinitely more elusive. War means that politics have broken down, leaving a no-man's-land where only brute force counts. But when peace is conceived as involving internal political change itself, the very notion of political legitimacy is at stake.

Before 1945, for example, Mussolini's violent seizure of power in Italy, and his repressive regime afterwards, did not prompt the League of Nations to act; that was only "internal" to Italy. But by invading Ethiopia, he violated international peace. Since 1960, however, a nation may be at peace with other nations, yet still be considered by the Nobel judges to be "repressive," and its right to govern "illegitimate," hence an obstacle to peace.

In these terms, "peace" can have limited goals, as with Martin Luther King Jr.'s struggle for civil rights in the United States, or it can aim at overthrowing a nation's political order itself, as with Lech Wałesa's Solidarity movement in Poland.

Peace Prizes for "Internal" Peace[27]

1960 Albert Luthuli (South Africa): nonviolent resistance to apartheid

1964 Martin Luther King Jr. (U.S.): nonviolent civil rights campaign

1975 Andrei Sakharov (USSR): nonviolent human rights campaign

1977 Mairead Corrigan and Betty Williams (Northern Ireland): Peace People movement

1980 Adolfo Pérez Esquivel (Argentina): nonviolent human rights campaign against military government

1983 Lech Wałesa (Poland): Solidarity movement

1984 Desmond Tutu (South Africa): nonviolent protests against apartheid

1989 Dalai Lama (Tibet): nonviolent effort to regain Tibet's freedom from China

1991 Aung San Suu Kyi (Mynmar, or Burma): nonviolent struggle for democracy

1992 Rigoberta Menchú (Guatemala): human rights campaign for Indians

1993 Nelson Mandela and F. W. de Klerk (South Africa): ending of apartheid

1996 José Ramos-Horta and Carlos Ximenes Belo (East Timor): campaign for civil and political rights

1998 John Hume and David Trimble (Northern Ireland): peace accords

The 1964 award to Martin Luther King Jr., one of the most famous peace prizes, illustrates the Nobel's new interventionist policy. In that year, President Johnson signed the Civil Rights Bill into law. As regards the Nobel Prize, only one side of King's familiar story needs emphasis here: in King's campaign for civil rights, international war or peace was not at stake. The campaign was specifically aimed at changing only American laws. Such an award differed entirely from the prize awarded in 1935 to the German journalist Ossietzky, who also sought reforms within his own nation by his exposés of illicit German war preparation, actions that clearly raised concrete international dangers.

In King's campaign, nonviolence was the peace prize's passport, or loophole, into a nation's internal affairs. King had adopted Gandhi's nonviolent credo and strategy. With that opening, the peace committee could escape accusations of encouraging violent revolution or civil war.

The Nobel's first step in this new direction came in 1960 with the peace prize to Albert Luthuli of South Africa, for his opposition to apartheid and his fight for civil rights. Luthuli was a Zulu, at first a teacher and then tribal chief in 1935 of the Umvoti Mission Reserve. But in 1935 the government stripped blacks of most voting rights and parliamentary seats, and restricted them to owning only a few acres of land. In 1946 apartheid was instituted: blacks needed passes to travel outside their reserves, racial intermarriage was punishable, voting rights were almost eliminated. Luthuli organized civil disobedience demonstrations, and in 1948 was elected head of the African National Congress (later headed by Nelson Mandela), which had been established in 1912 for tribal solidarity and voting rights.

Luthuli's series of nonviolent protests got him banned from major cities for two years. When that expired, he began organizing more protests and was soon arrested for treason, though the charges were dropped. But in 1960, after the police shot into a crowd of unarmed blacks gathered to protest the pass-book laws, killing some seventy and wounding nearly two hundred more in what is known as the Sharpeville Massacre, Luthuli burned his pass book. The government suppressed the ANC and arrested almost twenty thousand blacks, one of them Luthuli. Once free, he pressured Britain to deny South Africa a place in the Commonwealth. Luthuli by now had a sizable international reputation, and British public opinion was aroused. In 1961 the South African government forestalled expulsion by withdrawing from the Commonwealth. In that same year, Luthuli was awarded the delayed 1960 peace prize. He died of an accident in 1967.

In his Nobel address, Luthuli spoke of the "revolutionary stirrings" that caused his people to reclaim their land "by books, representations and demonstrations," but also if need be by "armed force provoked by the adamancy of white rule." Luthuli opposed all forms of violence, but he sought justice, not martyrdom. He thus added, "We understand those who say they have to adopt what is a last resort for them."[28]

As with King shortly after, Luthuli's actions neither aimed at nor threatened international peace: no African nation at the time had enough military force to confront South Africa and no other state in the world would have intervened. The Nobel Peace Prize had ventured onto quite new ground.

The recent extraordinary political transformation of the South African government can be called a revolution driven, though not finally accomplished, by violence — more than ten thousand people were killed since 1990. The peaceful transfer of power was presided over by the leaders of both sides, then-president F. W.

de Klerk and ANC leader Nelson Mandela, and has been orderly. Their cooperation and discouragement of violence won them a shared prize in 1993. Mandela is said to have insisted that de Klerk share the prize with him.

Other "interventionist" laureates reflect the range of global activism.

Andrei Sakharov: Sakharov, the Russian physicist and "father of the Soviet H-bomb," received the 1975 peace prize for his human rights campaign in the USSR. In the 1950s he was influential enough in Soviet science to help suspend Soviet bomb testing for almost three years. But for publicly demanding a freer Soviet society, he was stripped of his high official position and denounced as a Judas who betrayed his country for thirty pieces of silver — the Nobel prize money. He was not allowed to receive his award in person. After his Nobel Prize, Sakharov condemned the Soviet invasion of Afghanistan and was sentenced to "internal exile."

Betty Williams and Mairead Corrigan: The civil war in Northern Ireland began in 1969, with Catholic-versus-Protestant as one axis of conflict. The Catholic Corrigan and Protestant-born but Catholic-raised Williams met in what was otherwise a daily bit of violence in Belfast in 1976. British soldiers killed an IRA member trying to escape. His car, out of control, ran down Corrigan's sister, injuring her and killing her three children; the mother would commit suicide a few years later. Betty Williams witnessed the event. She had earlier been active in the IRA underground, but now began to circulate a petition for peace against the IRA. A few days later, Corrigan appeared on Belfast TV and denounced the IRA. Williams then appeared on TV as well, with a plea that all women try to halt the IRA's actions. Both thus put their lives at risk. Together, Corrigan and Williams founded the Community of Peace People. Ten thousand Catholic and Protestant women responded with a mass demonstration, and shortly after, thirty-five thousand attended. Though the civil war in Northern Ireland did not appear to threaten international peace, Williams and Corrigan shared the 1977 Nobel.

John Hume and David Trimble: The award in 1998 to Hume and Trimble was the second Nobel for Northern Ireland peace workers. The colaureates represent the opposed sides in the conflict. Negotiations, and sporadic progress, continue still.

Adolfo Pérez Esquivel: An Argentine sculptor, Pérez Esquivel was drawn into activism by the social tumult and repressions of Juan

Perón's regime. He joined a Christian peace and justice group, and then a group practicing nonviolent agitation of the Gandhian kind. In 1976, after the country suffered economic near-collapse, the army deposed Isabel Perón, Juan Perón's widow. When the Peronistas fought back, the army encouraged vigilante groups which soon terrorized the country by kidnappings — called "disappearances" — of many thousands. These were denied by the regime; years later, the government admitted to nine thousand, though the actual number may be more than double. For organizing protests, Pérez Esquivel was imprisoned in 1977 for thirteen months and tortured. Through the efforts of Amnesty International and the intercession of President Carter, he was released.

Aung San Suu Kyi: Aung leads a political party in Myanmar (formerly Burma) opposing the repressive military junta. When she won the 1991 prize, she had been under house arrest since 1989, choosing that rather than leaving the country without hope of return. On 10 June 1995, without explanation but perhaps because of her Nobel award and the resulting international publicity, the authorities released her. Her activities, however, remain severely restricted.

Rigoberta Menchú: A Quiche Indian from Guatemala, Menchú was the 1992 peace prize laureate. She won largely because of the worldwide success of her autobiography of her peace efforts, *I, Rigoberta Menchú*, published in 1983. It was translated into a dozen languages. She told movingly of being an Indian denied an education, of oppressive land seizure and witnessing people starving, of being a house servant who taught herself to read, of her brother's being doused with gasoline and burnt to death by Guatemalan soldiers, of the government's illegal arrest and torture of Indian tribespeople during the civil war there. The Guatemalan government in turn protested her peace prize, saying she advocated revolution. In December 1996 a peace treaty between the Guatemalan factions was signed, with Menchú present.

In 1999, however, a scholar of Guatemalan history published much evidence that Menchú's book was mainly lies or embellishments. In his *Rigoberta Menchú and the Story of All Poor Guatemalans*, David Stoll showed that her brother's burning never occurred, that Menchú had indeed been well educated by Belgian nuns, that she never did the backbreaking field labor she claimed — her family was too well-off — and so on. Stoll did not deny that the government was often as brutal as she claimed, but argued rather that her "autobiography" was often propaganda and fiction, not the historical truth she claimed to have lived. Her prize citation shows that she won because the peace committee accepted her published claims, especially as a victim. The committee, above the fray as usual, has declined comment. Perhaps her falsifying would not have mattered to them. As one commentator noted, 1992 was not only the year of Menchú's prize but the quincentennial of Columbus's discovery. Perhaps "Menchú struck the Nobel Committee in Norway as the perfect embodiment of the downside of the Discovery."[29]

José Ramos-Horta and Carlos Ximenes Belo: Ramos-Horta and Bishop Belo, two East Timor dissidents, shared the 1996 peace prize for seeking to end Indonesian repression and restore East Timor to independence. The matter is complicated. In 1975 Portugal left East Timor; Indonesia invaded and has repressively occupied it from 1976, despite a UN Security Council demand that it withdraw. Legally, East Timor may still be a colony of Portugal. The Indonesian regime likened the peace prizes to Hollywood Oscars, and boycotted the prize ceremonies.

Peace Prize for Peaceful Reform or Violent Revolution?

The Nobel peace jury once kept a careful distance from those who sought to overthrow an established government by force. As evident from the names just cited, that line has become increasingly hard to draw.

The earliest instance here was the award to Lech Wałesa and his Solidarity movement, which eventually brought down the Communist regime in Poland. That event happened after Wałesa won the peace prize in 1983. He was honored for what led to it: forcing the government to recognize the Danzig shipyard workers' right to strike and negotiate with the state. Unionizing was taboo in Communist nations. Fired for their part in the protests, Wałesa and others organized an illegal union which demanded free negotiating. Eventually the union was allowed to become a national organization, Solidarity, with Wałesa its chairman. In 1981 Solidarity, now a quasi political party, demanded a national referendum on whether Poland should remain Communist and stay subject to the Soviet Union. The Polish premier, General Jaruzelski, outlawed Solidarity and arrested its leaders. Wałesa spent a year in prison. When he came out, he was soon awarded the Nobel Peace Prize, and later became president of Poland.

The Nobel citation conceded that the award honored a freedom movement, and indeed all such freedom fighting:

> Lech Wałesa's contribution is more than a domestic Polish concern; the solidarity for which he is spokesman is an expression of precisely the conception of being at one with humanity . . . he stands as a shining example to all those who, under different conditions, fight for freedom and humanity.

"Fight," indeed. Solidarity's rise had scarcely been nonviolent. There had been constant riots and bloody clashes with the police. Perhaps the only thing preventing Wałesa's resort to open force was that the Polish Communist regime could call in Russian troops and tanks for the asking. Wałesa, a shrewd tactician, did nothing to make the government decide to do this. Journalists reported that he often forbade his strikers to do any drinking. Even so, violence erupted often enough.

When the Nobel citation spoke of Solidarity's struggle as more than an inner Polish concern, did the committee mean to condone civil war if it led to a democratic regime and human rights? Its award to Lech Wałesa might be seen as encouraging such a view.

One may sympathize with the Nobel peace committee here, but the assumptions behind widening the peace award from preventing war to change within a nation inevitably bump against dilemmas. It is tricky to judge "peace" by a nation's internal makeup. In the nineteenth century, Great Britain fought more than one hundred forty wars, large and small, to defend its empire. Yet through that century and half of the next, still possessed of an enormous empire, it was admired as a model of the peace-loving European nation because it was inwardly liberal.

As this suggests, the time-honored view that liberal democracy favors peace does not always obtain, nor that trade makes peace. This perspective holds that once enough commercialized republics are established, we shall have, in Kant's phrase, "perpetual peace." European democracies and the U.S. have gone to war over markets and trade advantages. Moreover, democracies can also be unpredictable: the revolving-door governments of France and Italy before and after the Second World War are examples. This leads to the irony that absolute rulers or dictators can more easily make international peace — as Sadat did with Israel.

Alfred Nobel himself seemed to have thought that peace within a nation was better served by monarchy or oligarchy than by democracy. Indeed, Nobel, though not his later peace committee, might well have approved the example of twentieth-century Portugal. Of all the larger European nations except the "official" neutrals, Sweden and Switzerland, it had the longest continuous European peace in the century. Salazar, its ruler from the late 1920s to the 1950s, kept Portugal neutral in the Spanish civil war and the Second World War. Yet Salazar would scarcely have won a peace award then or now. He ruled dictatorily and repressively.[30]

Another dilemma is that peace activity can halt war of one kind while letting it balloon out in different, even more dangerous ways. The Versailles Treaty is an example. Nobel Peace Prizes have experienced some other unpleasant surprises along this line. The 1990 peace prize was awarded to Mikhail Gorbachev, president of the USSR, whose criticism of the Stalinist crippling of the Soviet economy and approval of perestroika and glasnost set in motion the eventual breakup of the Soviet empire. At that time, the president of Lithuania was given a special peace prize by the "Norwegian people," the Lithuanians having protested Gorbachev's prize. The end of the Soviet empire indeed defused the Cold War. But in another way it has led to the invasion of Chechnya and, more, to an intensifying of nuclear war danger. From financial need, political instability, or criminal greed, Russian nuclear weapons and equipment seem to have been sold or smuggled to nations and dealers not subject to international control. The eventual consequences of this are incalculable.

Missing: Gandhi

Mohandas K. Gandhi (1869–1948) was doubtless the most famous pacifist of the twentieth century, but he was ignored by the Nobel peace committee. Why? The official Nobel history mentions him only to acknowledge complaints about honoring too few "true" pacifists. But, as noted, the reason may be that his activism came before the committee began to honor peace efforts *within* a nation. That was in 1960; Gandhi died in 1947. With his disciples Luthuli, King, and others, Gandhi has won a posthumous Nobel Peace Prize many times over.

The Holocaust

Any discussion of the Holocaust understandably arouses passionate dissent on every side. But it needs asking why the Nobel peace committee waited until 1986 — more than forty years after the Holocaust — to honor its memory and significance for peace. Perhaps the Nobel committee, like the rest of the world, needed several decades before facing the appalling facts about the death camps.

When the Holocaust was finally recognized with a prize, the Romanian-French novelist Elie Wiesel was chosen as laureate. He survived Auschwitz and other concentration camps, and his many novels about his experience have been widely read. More important with the peace prize in mind, he is also a tireless publicist of the need to remember the Holocaust, has sought to help Jews in Soviet Russia, seems an intimate of prime ministers, and presidents and popes, is a professor of Jewish studies, was chairman of the U.S. President's Commission on the Holocaust leading to the Holocaust Museum, and became widely celebrated for trying — though unsuccessfully — to dissuade President Reagan from the Bitburg fiasco in 1985, which honored some Nazi SS dead. This was likely the event that prompted his prize, making him very visible to the Nobel peace committee. Some have suggested that he campaigned for the peace prize, but many others have done the same. And if Wiesel had not striven for the award, one wonders if the peace committee would ever have named a Holocaust laureate at all.

Women and Peace

Ten women have received Nobel Peace Prizes:

1905   Bertha von Suttner (Austria)

1931   Jane Addams (U.S.)

1946   Emily Balch (U.S.)

1976   Betty Williams and Mairead Corrigan (Northern Ireland)

1979   Mother Teresa (India)

1982   Alva Myrdal (Sweden)

1991   Aung San Suu Kyi (Myanmar)

1992   Rigoberta Menchú (Guatemala)

1997   Jody Williams (U.S.)

Balch was a typical peace worker of the pre–World War II genera-tions: a tireless organizer and prominent and respected public fig-ure, but of limited influence. Addams was a major pioneering social worker who moved into the peace cause during World War I. Alva Myrdal, the wife of Sweden's famed economist Gunnar Myrdal, served on the UN Disarmament Committee (1962–73) and wrote eloquently for disarmament.

Already impressively effective are the efforts of Jody Williams, cofounder and coordinator of the International Campaign to Ban Landmines. Williams and her organization worked for six years to have 122 countries sign a treaty banning mines in 1997. The Nobel peace committee chairman, Francis Sejersted, said in Oslo that the prize to Williams and the Campaign was deliberately meant to influence the political process.[31] Its impact was bolstered by a UN claim that 110 million land mines exist in the world, though the respected Jane's military information bureau of England has called the figure inflated by as much as two-thirds. Williams's major disap-pointment is the failure of her own country to join in the ban. In interviews, she has called President Clinton a coward for refusing to sign the treaty. The adminstration counters that land mines in place between North and South Korea have prevented another war there, which would entail U.S. involvement and huge numbers of dead —

China is the other major power refusing to sign. Williams is determined to fight on.

Jody Williams is, so to speak, a frontline fighter — like that other peace laureate named Williams, Betty, and her colleague Mairead Corrigan, and like Aung San Suu Kyi. Of them all, Aung knows most acutely that her life is on the line.

Still, this is only nine awards since 1901. Why so few women laureates? The early peace movement was probably more strongly supported by women than men. But in the first fifty or so years, there were few women among the political figures, the peace administrators, the League or UN officials preferred as laureates. No prizes for Olive Schreiner, the South African peace activist and writer, or Dorothy Day of the American Catholic Workers movement.

Pacifism and feminism were often early comrades-in-arms, and deserved more recognition by the Nobel committee. One of the few great mass demonstrations against World War I occurred in 1915 when 1,200 women from fifteen countries gathered in The Hague to demand that the fighting be stopped. This has been described as something quite new in the peace movement: not only the full-fledged entry of women into the cause, but "one that was radically transnational" at a time when such a step faced the most forbidding odds.[32]

9

The Economics
Memorial Prize

The Nobel Prize in Economics is young enough to be the grandchild of the other prizes. It was established only in 1968, with the first award a year later. But it is better seen as a step-grandchild of the original prizes, since it isn't allowed the same family name as the others. The economics award's official title is segregated off as the Central Bank of Sweden Prize in Economic Sciences in Memory of Alfred Nobel. The short and usual form puts Nobel's name up front and drops the bank and thus, far more impressively, becomes the Nobel Memorial Prize in Economics. A further distancing is enforced: while laureates in all other fields have their names engraved on the surface of the Nobel medal, economists' names perch only on the outer rim. Someone — perhaps the economics Nobelist Paul Samuelson — wittily played off Nobel's handwritten will by calling this new prize "the fabricated (or 'forged') will." Among the economics prize's other distinctions has been a call for its abolition by several eminent laureates (see below).

The Central Bank of Sweden set up this award to mark its three-hundredth anniversary in 1968, and guaranteed to match the value of the existing prizes. The Swedish Academy of Sciences agreed to adjudicate the award, applying the same statutes that cover the other prizes. But the academy is reported to have hesitated before accepting the assignment. Others in the natural sciences were not altogether enthusiastic. After the first economics prize, a prominent physicist asked Murray Gell-Mann, who had won the physics Nobel that year, how the new economics laureate had been fitted into the program. When told, he replied in anguish: "You mean they sat on the platform with you?"[1]

One can understand the reaction. Why should economics have entered the Nobel temple, when it belonged with the other lesser "sciences," such as sociology, anthropology, or political science?

The West's remarkable prosperity after 1945 was doubtless a key factor. Never in history had so many been affluent. Devastating slumps, unemployment, and inflation were (almost) nowhere to be seen. Establishing a Nobel award put a seal on this extraordinary success and at the same time claimed it to be a result of advances in economic theory. Which brings us to the other reason.

In the Nobel view, only economic *theory* could deserve a prize. Here, as usual in intellectual fields, theory outranks practice. An economist like Ludwig Erhard, who engineered Germany's "economic miracle" after World War II, might have won a Nobel in peace but not in economics; he merely did "practical" economics. So does Alan Greenspan.

What carried the day with the Nobel Foundation, as the first economics citation in 1969 emphasized, was the claim that economics was becoming an "exact" science like physics or chemistry. Sociology and other social sciences were too "soft" or "subjective" for the rigor demanded of Nobel sciences. The Nobel citation put this flatly: "One essential object has been to get away from the vague, more 'literary' type of economics."

What is scientific here, and thus "Nobelizable," results from a new development in economic thought. Herbert Simon (Nobel 1978) summed it up:

> The most salient fact in the postwar history of economics was its sudden conquest by mathematics and statistics. In 1950 it was still difficult to get a paper published in the *American Economic Review* if it contained equations (diagrams were more acceptable). The Econometric Society had been founded a quarter-century earlier as a meeting ground for mathematically inclined economists. . . . I think it could be said that by 1970 mathematics had taken over economics (for better or worse); the simplest theory had to be clothed in mathematical garb before it could receive any serious attention.[2]

Mathematics has indeed become the royal road to the Nobel Prize in Economics. Simon notes that twenty-three of the first twenty-seven laureates, himself included, had been Fellows of the Econometric Society long before receiving the prize. Indeed, the first economics laureates, Ragnar Frisch and Jan Tinbergen, had helped found that body in 1930; Frisch coined the name and edited *Econometrica* for thirty years. The sophisticated equations of such formalists serve as means to measure or predict ordinary economic doings.[3] They deploy advanced probability theory (the 1992 Nobelist, Trygve Haavelmo of Norway, won his prize for work here), central limit theorems, asymptotic distribution theory, random variables known as stochastic processes, or the theory of games, to which the great mathematician John von Neumann contributed.[4] Among the ambitious formalisms honored by the prize are those of the 1980 laureate, Lawrence Klein, who constructed models in the 1950s to encompass the entire U.S. economy. His first had eighteen components, thirty-six ordering sectors, and three hundred equations; his second, his link project, used more than a thousand equations.

Whether such theorizing deserves Nobel recognition and acclaim is deeply disputed among economists themselves. Many have suggested abolishing the prize, including at least three laureates, Myrdal, Hayek, and Sen.[5] Some protest that the econometric orientation doesn't constitute an advance in knowledge, but only gives prosaic problems a scientific aura by recasting them in arcane equations. Some contend that its form makes it of little use to the real marketplace, however impressive it may be as an academic exercise. Many concede that the formulae and mathematical models may benefit stockbrokers, money managers, and the like, but question whether they meet the "benefit to humanity" requirement of the Nobel Prizes.

This can be anything but an academic matter. The 1997 prize is a prickly instance. Myron Scholes of Stanford and Robert C. Merton of Harvard became laureates for showing how to give a more precise way to value "derivatives," a risky version of "futures" or options. (Schemes that hope to diminish or hedge the risks involved are called "hedge funds.") The derivatives market in 1999 was estimated at $70 trillion, and its risks are huge. Part of the $1.64 billion loss suffered by Orange County in California in 1994 was due to hedge fund failures; in 1995, the giant Barings bank in Britain collapsed after one employee's disastrous derivatives investments. Any theory that could solve such problems would seem worth a prize. Merton and Scholes advanced an equation to help here, though a minnow compared with Klein's whale above:

$$C = SN(d) - L^{-\pi}N\left(d - \sigma\sqrt{t}\right)$$

or, loosely translated, the value equals what one hopes the stock price will be minus the cost. Developed from 1972, their theory was widely applied. Indeed, when Merton and Scholes became colaureates, they were not only professors, they were also partners in a hedge fund called Long-Term Capital Management that attracted some investors partly because of their academic and then Nobel cachet. Regrettably, their theory did not keep their company from collapsing the year after they became laureates.[6]

The economics prizes are surely the most inbred of all the Nobel Prizes. Consider the total list (1969–2000):

U.S.	30
Britain	6
Norway	2
Sweden	2
France	1
Germany	1
India	1
Netherlands	1
USSR	1

(Nationality is determined by where laureates taught when they did their prizewinning work. Thus, the 1998 laureate Amartya Sen, born in India, is listed as an Indian laureate since he did part of his work in Delhi — but he also worked in London: should he be listed as a British laureate as well?)

This list suggests that, in deep economic insight, the U.S. is light-years ahead of everyone in the world. Yet one wonders: Has Japan, so economically successful, not produced any thinker somehow worthy of Nobel notice? Or Germany only one?

Moreover, the laureates not only come exclusively from the developed democratic nations, they study exclusively that form of economy. And though liberal capitalism of the Western kind is a huge, potent arena, it is not the only sort: South Korea, Singapore, and now much of Southeast Asia are among those where capitalism can flourish without much democracy needed or even permitted.[7] If economic theory hopes to be an exact science, it is surely required to explain its subject in whatever form it occurs. The Nobelized theories have not done this, and are open to the charge of remaining parochial.[8] Chemists, after all, are not allowed to explain only the elements they prefer.

Almost all the laureates also come from a few elite universities: Chicago, Harvard, Cambridge, MIT, Stockholm and Oslo, Yale, Princeton, Stanford and Berkeley. In one six-year stretch, the University of Chicago won five times — and, by its count, claims twenty of the forty-four economics Nobelists thus far.[9]

To see how these laureates come to be, first exclude almost all the many scores of thousands of economists who work for businesses and governments, since few publish professionally. The Nobel committee will consider only candidates who have published, and these are almost always professors; theorists naturally cluster in the academy, since it sponsors work that may have no practical payoff. This is a sizable and busy group. One study of publications in one year of the 1970s found that economists, predominantly academics, published eight hundred books and more than five thousand articles.[10] As in other fields, the Nobel economics committee cannot sift the gold from the dross in this mass, and depends on the expertise of its nominators. Because such a tiny group of schools has been repeatedly honored, a self-perpetuating effect seems to have built up. Yet it isn't the schools so much as the reigning orthodoxies that bring about this narrowed result.

The Two Nobel Orthodoxies

Karl Marx is doubtless the most famous, or notorious, economic theorist. But neither he nor any adherent would ever win a Nobel Prize: after all, he tried to destroy capitalism. For the Nobel judges, as noted, free enterprise as practiced in liberal democracies of the Western type is the one true faith.

Even here, only two schools of thought have dominated the prize: neoclassicists and neo-Keynesians. The neoclassic camp emerged in the later nineteenth century. Its rebellious child and rival, neo-Keynesianism, was inspired by the 1930s work of the English theorist John Maynard Keynes. Taken together, they provide the orthodox and mainstream explanation of free enterprise in Europe and the U.S.[11] The historical evolution of these positions is tangled, but certain key elements are common to both.

Needless to insist, the free market is a teeming competitive arena of buyers and sellers, producers and consumers. In democratic capitalism, buying and selling involve endless uncertainties about raising capital, the availability of resources, the possibly erratic behavior of consumers and producers, the effect of monopoly, and shocks ranging from loss of confidence in banks or stocks to mismanagement on a local or national scale. "Practical" business is done catch-as-catch-can, a mixture of science, art, personality, and luck. Economic theory seeks the laws underlying this massive and fluid event, at once a theater, battlefield, and mechanism.

Neoclassical economics — "neo" because it revised the earlier "classical" theories of Adam Smith and others — from the nineteenth century saw free enterprise as a system of deep inner balance, despite its surface disorder. "Equilibrium" was the pivotal idea, envisioning a market where buyers and sellers are all finally satisfied and all resources employed; any change will therefore be for the worse. Here, supply governs demand: in the famous example, if water is scarce, it's valuable; if everywhere, it's worth nothing. Even if water is very scarce, the owners have to set prices that buyers accept, or else go broke. And buyers can't demand too low prices, or their suppliers will go bankrupt.

Such a market is thus a self-regulating, self-stabilizing system. Two important provisos, however, were needed. First, government must not interfere, hence "free" enterprise or laissez-faire. Through much of the nineteenth century, government generally obliged, as seen in the long fight to halt child labor and sweatshops or to allow unions to strike, not to mention unabashed political corruption by business interests. It was the age of monopolists, Rockefeller and Morgan and Alfred Nobel or his brothers the "Russian Rockefellers," bound by few laws but their own. But neoclassicists nonetheless leaned heavily, and still do, on the harmonizing principle of "perfect competition."

In the 1870s came a call to arms whose outcome was ultimately the Nobel Economics Prize. "Economics, if it is to be a science at all, must be a mathematical science," said the British theorist

W. S. Jevons, and many others echoed the sentiment.[12] This was the period when physics was formidably mathematicizing itself: why not economics?[13] After all, it too dealt with numbers and quantities — prices, costs, inventories, tax and interest rates. Data was accumulating, and only needed mathematical improvement. Moreover, a system in equilibrium conveniently lends itself to rigorous formalizing. Disequilibrium is messy.

But this yearning for mathematical rigor met a snag. When it comes to business matters, real people can be as erratic, perverse, intractable, and willfully misinformed as in everything else. A second proviso was needed. Since the self-regulating system depended on a "rational" sort of human being, neoclassicists invented the "economic individual," shaved of all human traits except commercial self-interest. They postulated people who never pay more than they think things are worth, who are such dedicated buyers that they tirelessly memorize all available prices and coolly compare them, always weighing all alternatives so as to "maximize" their "optimum" return. Neoclassical economists, without irony, call them "rational."[14]

This conceptualized figment is such a cartoon of human reality that some eminent economists protested forcefully. Karl Marx was one. Closer to the mainstream was the American Thorstein Veblen (1857–1929). He was educated in the neoclassical tradition but attacked it in his first and still most famous book, *The Theory of the Leisure Class* (1899). Veblen sought to demolish the root assumptions of neoclassicism. Far from being "rational economic agents," Veblen said, people consume in order to display their importance, power, or pride. In a deadly mock-pedantic, satirical style, he analyzed what he called "conspicuous consumption": people spend not for pleasure or utility, but to make others envious — by giving lavish parties, for example, or by having so many servants that a wife never has to lift a finger.

For Veblen, the engine of economics is not the individual but the institutions that mold individual habits of consumption in order to exploit them. Thus the immense sums spent on advertising, or the subtle pressure to conform exerted by all education. Veblen was not a professor popular with university administrators or business leaders. Nor have those who variously endorse "institutionalism" been popular with the Nobel economics committee. The Swedish economist and Nobelist Gunnar Myrdal was in important ways an institutionalist, but his Nobel citation did not mention that among the reasons for honoring him. The Canadian-American John Kenneth Galbraith and Albert O. Hirschman have affinities with institutionalism but, though likely nominated, have never been Nobelized.

A figure like Veblen offers a useful point for an overview of economics. To see economics only as another discipline is to miss some decisive reasons for its Nobel triumph. That economics, along with sociology, anthropology, political science, even history, are all now called social "sciences" — the term emerged in the nineteenth century — reflects their aspirations to become rigorous sciences like physics or biology. Karl Marx claimed that he had discovered the laws of social evolution just as Darwin did those of natural evolution. Other social scientists, in the spirit of physics, sought to split off objective "facts" from subjective "values." From the later nineteenth century, sociology and economics saw much use of statistics and other quantizations — or, failing that, at least a highly scientized terminology.

In the Nobel view, only economics succeeded. The year economics was anointed, 1968, is an interesting one. That was when the "counterculture" erupted, shaking social and cultural shibboleths in the name of more human or more enraptured truths, but triggering antagonism to science itself. Important branches of the social sciences began to shed their former scientism and strove to become more "open" and "engaged." Yet this was precisely when economics was anointed a science by the Nobel authorities. Its turn to mathematics of course helped, but was only one factor. Unlike its sister social sciences, economics deals with wealth and poverty, and these directly affect law and government. (The growing alliance between economics and law schools is a striking development.) Of the social sciences, only economics — with Nobel approval and brandishing equations — has become part of the establishment.[15]

Needless to say, neoclassicists and perhaps most neo-Keynesians insist that the hedonistic calculus is nonetheless right about the crucial point: people do want to maximize profits, and this can be measured, and mathematics can thus generalize it.

Lest the reader think the equilibrium model is not still potent in present economic theory and the Nobel Prizes, here is an example from George Stigler (Nobel 1982) of the University of Chicago. This was the case of the notorious Corn Laws in Britain, "corn" meaning cereal or grain. In the late eighteenth century, the British government decided to keep home-grown grain prices at a high level; they therefore imposed a severe duty on imports, and added a tax at home if the price fell. Landowners prospered, while consumers, especially the poor, suffered — around 1814, one bushel of wheat cost almost twice a workman's weekly wage.[16] For forty years there was agitation to repeal these laws, in vain: landowners held too many seats in Parliament. Then powerful orators like Cobden and Bright took up the cause and began to shift public opinion; Prime Minister Robert Peel began to agree. When the potato crop in Ireland failed around 1845, leading to appalling starvation in which, at its peak, ten thousand a week are said to have died, the artificially high price of grain kept the Irish from being able to buy bread. In 1846 the Corn Laws were finally repealed, and relief began to reach Ireland.

That, says Stigler, is the way the story is usually told: influential idealistic figures intervening to rectify a greedy law, and nobly succeeding at last. But Stigler, a devout neoclassical, disagrees:

> I believe, on the contrary, that if Cobden had spoken only Yiddish, and with a stammer, and Peel had been a narrow, stupid man, England would have moved toward free trade in grain as its agricultural classes declined, and its manufacturing and commercial classes grew. . . . Truly effective import prohibition would have driven grain to intolerable price levels, and it is a quite general rule that intolerable things are not tolerated. Hence, the repeal of the Corn Laws was the appropriate social response to the shift of political power.[17]

In short, the market finally regained equilibrium on its own, as theorists said it would and should and does.

Neo-Keynesians

An elegant tempter-serpent entered this demi-Paradise in 1936, when John Maynard Keynes (1883–1946) published *The General Theory of Employment, Interest and Money*. Keynes never underestimated himself. He believed his book would revolutionize how humanity thinks about economic problems. He was partly right. He became the loyal opposition to the neoclassic orthodoxy. He saw the world depressions of the 1920s and 1930s as demanding drastic revision of the equilibrium view. Keynes influentially shifted the focus to disequilibrium. For Keynes the economy as a whole, not the individual buyer or seller, became pivotal (roughly, "macroeconomics"). He also heretically claimed that demand created supply, not the other way around. But with demand and supply both stagnant, factories were idle. Keynesians recommended "pump-priming" to get things started. In short, governments must intervene.

To the reassurance that the market corrects itself "over the long run," Keynes responded: in the long run we are all dead. Keynes had been the prize pupil of the great neoclassicist Alfred Marshall, whose magisterial account of the self-regulating market appeared in 1890. Keynes described Marshall's view of equilibrium as like a "Copernican system," keeping all parts of the economic universe in place by mutual interaction. This was fine for planets, but not something mere humans could depend on. Keynes was to become the leading non-Marxist theorist to try reforming this celestial system.

After his death his followers regrouped as neo-Keynesians and were prominent, for example, in President Kennedy's administration in the early 1960s. But around 1970, as the economics Nobels began, the theory couldn't explain or solve "stagflation," in which inflation and unemployment unaccountably rose at the same time, and so the theory stalled.

Both neoclassicists and neo-Keynesians had meanwhile taken over the economics departments of leading universities, the indispensable cockpit for Nobel nominating and maneuvering.

Of the forty-four laureates thus far, almost two of three have been neoclassicists, though confusion exists because some theorists cross the lines. Why has neoclassic theory so outpaced the neo-Keynesians? The Nobel economics official Assar Lindbeck, in a 1985 article, blandly declared that the decisions of the Nobel judges had thus far been "unanimous" — indeed, "as if by some kind of invisible hand," Adam Smith's famous eighteenth-century phrase for economic Providence. That there should be such unanimity in a field as contentious as economics indeed seems to require Providence. In 1990 the American economist Robert Kuttner suggested that the invisible hand was in fact Lindbeck's own conservative one, firmly on the controls.[18] Some of the most distinguished neo-Keynesians passed away ignored, such as Joan Robinson of Britain, who died at age seventy-nine. No woman has ever won the economics award, though the Nobelist Milton Friedman claims Robinson was blackballed not from sexual bias but for her Keynesianism.[19]

Species of Laureates

Because the work honored by the Nobel judges moves inside an economic orthodoxy, debates and disagreements — with exceptions — tend to be about technicalities or method. These run from the empirical to the abstruse.

The outstanding figure among the empirics is the 1971 Nobelist Simon Kuznets. He migrated from Russia to the United States in 1922, and began learning English that summer; that fall, Columbia University accepted him. In 1923 he had his B.A. and in 1924 his M.A. It took him all the way to 1926 to receive his doctorate. Kuznets then began gathering statistics on a vast national scale. Statistics about supply and demand, income, prices, industrial development, and the like had been piling up to no great purpose, until Kuznets drew them all together. He constructed tables to show the total production of national goods, and another for total income, itemized by sources and type. He measured and correlated total national consumer expenditures and then did something similar for national income. He finally clarified the long fluctuations in how national economies waxed and waned. For the first time, using data from 1919–38, the real magnitude of total investments in the country was known, their cyclical fluctuations could be measured, as well as the relation between distribution of income and growth — a crystalline mountain of data indeed. Cautious, meticulous, and modest, Kuznets refused to make forecasts. His empirical temperament shows in his remark that mathematical abstraction "makes a lightning raid and emerges with a striking conclusion" but a close look usually shows that supportive evidence is lacking.[20]

Kuznets's stance is reflected in the Swedish laureate Gunnar Myrdal, who combined economic analysis with vast historical underpinning, as in his famous *An American Dilemma* and his three-volume *Asian Drama: An Inquiry into the Poverty of Nations* (1968). But it is also evident in Milton Friedman, often accused of being a dogmatic monetarist, who however backed up his theory with his vast *A Monetary History of the United States 1867–1960* (1963).

Another empiric laureate deserving mention is W. Arthur Lewis of Britain. Neoclassicists rarely ventured outside their self-contained systems to test their findings in global places where rules and assumptions can differ wildly. Lewis, a neoclassicist but also raised in the West Indies, did just this. He had shared the 1979 Nobel for examining what happened when two developed countries traded with each other. Then Lewis took up the more difficult issue: when one country is advanced and the other not. Third World nations have a split economy. One part is traditional, usually agricultural: people farm, run small stores, work as servants, aiming to survive on the subsistence level. The developing capitalist part, however, aims at profit surplus. This sector inevitably draws population away from the farms and traditional work. For a long while, it will also pay such people low wages, thus providing higher profits and more capital. Lewis makes clear that in developing nations, capitalism at first does not need a free market — more likely, a state-controlled economy. Eventually, the cheap labor supply runs out. Growth slows. Strikingly, what emerges is a neoclassical market: supply and demand begin to fall into a balance. Now Lewis provides his other model, involving trade between rich and poor countries. Both produce what Lewis calls "food." But only the industrialized country produces "steel" (his symbol for high-tech products), while the poor country's main product is symbolized as "coffee" (a single product on which the whole economy depends, like sugar in Cuba). Unlike many in the West, Lewis does not believe that investing in Third World industrial plants is the answer; it may well cause harm. The better way is to raise the agricultural productivity of the poorer nation, so it can feed itself, improve its balance of payments, and thereby gain capital to invest in its own industrial sector. But this will require a heavy investment in education, something Nobel economic theory has thought little about; Lewis's colaureate, Theodore Schultz, is one of the few. It also requires thinking about economic planning, as Lewis has done, under such extreme conditions as dictatorships.

Among the formalists is Paul Samuelson, the 1970 laureate and the first American, the foremost prodigy and greatest generalist in later twentieth-century economic theory. Here he is remembering himself around age twenty, and why he became an economist:

> Because the analysis was so interesting and easy — indeed so easy that at first I thought there must be more to it than I was recognizing, else why were my older classmates making such heavy weather over supply and demand?[21]

His first famous book was *Foundations of Economic Analysis*, his dissertation written when he was twenty-two. It is at once a manifesto and a brilliant demonstration of the need for advanced mathematical treatment of economics, which otherwise would be only "mental gymnastics of a peculiarly depraved type."[22]

The Nobel citation rightly said that he had single-handedly rewritten much of economics: both Keynesian and equilibrium theory, international trade, linear programming, maximization. A mathematical virtuoso, he can seemingly translate any economic problem into a strong web of equations. He has impressively tackled a remarkable number of thorny problems by way of innovative mathematical methods, some of which he describes as

> turnpike theorems and osculating envelopes; nonsubstitutability relations in Minkowski-Ricardo-Leontief-Metzler matrices of Mosak-Hicks type; balanced budget multipliers under conditions of balanced uncertainty in locally impacted topological spaces and molar equivalences.[23]

His textbook *Economics* (1948) was an international best-seller through many editions and perhaps a dozen languages, made him a multimillionaire, and gave the coming generations of economics students a common vocabulary and outlook. Endlessly prolific, Samuelson also wrote a popular column in *Newsweek*, was an adviser to President Kennedy, and grew so prominent that a German Marxist, Marc Linder, published a four-volume work simply called *The Anti-Samuelson*, while the young right-wing William Buckley attacked him from the other side in *God and Man at Yale* as fostering a value-free scientistic attitude.[24] Far from being doctrinaire, however, Samuelson's open-mindedness sometimes leads to his embracing contrary views. This pure formalist, for instance, also espouses an "economics of the heart." If anyone is the theorist of the "mixed" economy, or perhaps the mixed-up economy, it is Samuelson, so much so that his constant balancing of neoclassical–neo-Keynesian alternatives can seem to leave him hovering.[25]

His predictions could be famously wrong. He forecast a worldwide depression after World War II, just as prosperity blossomed as never before. In 1967, reversing himself, he declared that though social security was indeed "actuarially unsound," this should worry no one "since the national product is growing at compound interest and can be expected to do so as far ahead as the eye cannot see."[26] Alas, that was just before the economy hit such roadblocks as stagflation and skyrocketing oil prices.

Samuelson is an example of the paradox that a theorist who does one big thing may be remembered longer than someone who has done many major things but none popularly remembered. It is hard to identify him with any particular striking achievement. It might be argued that he has not opened any important field, as did Friedman with monetarism or Frisch with national planning. His central contribution is probably in methodology — in sharpening and vastly extending the mathematical analysis of economic theory.

Kenneth Arrow of the U.S. (Nobel 1972) and the French-American Gerard Debreu (Nobel 1983) are two formalists whose prizewinning work outdid even Samuelson in ambition. They generalized a theory to cover all variables in any self-balancing market. The butcher, baker, candlestick-maker, and every other sort of consumer and producer are dissolved into equations, in hopes of transparently exhibiting the inner structure of the market's equilibrium. Such an all-encompassing formalism is necessarily abstract: everyone and all economic activity must become a generalized variable. To gain as simple and consistent a model as possible, Arrow and Debreu eliminated all but a few unavoidable "primitive" assumptions (i.e., assumed as true rather than proved). These included "commodity," which can be measured; the idea that buyers and producers acted "rationally" in their commercial behavior; and "price" or the money-value.

The daunting mathematics was rigorously axiomatic, and used sophisticated and novel methods. The model as such is very impressive.[27] It can formally integrate static equilibrium, consumer behavior, the theory of capital and economic actions under uncertainty conditions.[28] But the theory's abstract method and narrow assumptions have raised doubts about its usefulness and relation to reality. The American economist Roy Radner analyzed Arrow's theory in 1968 and concluded that it breaks down decisively "in the face of the limits of agents to compute optimal strategies."[29] Or more plainly said, it doesn't work quite as well when real people replace the xs and ys.

No economic model is as unconventional or formally sophisticated as the theory of games. This was honored in 1994, when John Nash and John Harsanyi of the U.S. and Reinhard Selten of Germany were made laureates. The theory was pioneered by John von Neumann (1903–1957) and the Austro-American economist Oskar Morgenstern (1902–1977) with their *Theory of Games and Economic Behavior*, published in 1944. But that work then found few theorists equipped to follow its difficult mathematical innovations and unfamiliar approach.

The theory of games is not about games, but uses that device to explore strategy of all kinds, economic, political, and military. It has been called the formalizing of "second-guessing." Morgenstern in 1935 compared it to Sherlock Holmes trying to outguess his great rival, the master criminal Dr. Moriarty. If Holmes seems about to do X, he may then expect Moriarty to second-guess him, perhaps by assuming that Holmes is faking and will really do Y. Holmes, realizing this, may do X or Y or even Z. And so on endlessly, until both disappear into the Reichenbach Falls.

The implications for military planning or international negotations are evident, as well as for management decisions, sales campaigns, leveraged-buyout sieges, or ordinary buying and selling. Governments took it up: the RAND think tank did game theory for the U.S. military, and corporations involved in complex deals occasionally hired an in-house games theorist.

But the theory languished somewhat. The mathematics needed more clarifying and improving, which was accomplished by the Princeton mathematician John Nash. In the early 1950s, just a few years after the Morgenstern–von Neumann book, he managed in a single page to link the theory of games with neoclassical equilibrium.[30] Nash assumed, as game theorists tend to, that both rivals — as with equally matched chess players — know what the other can do and might do. In economic life, however, people have far less perfect knowledge. In the late 1960s, Harsanyi of Berkeley fenced in this difficulty: he let rivals swim about in uncertainty, as long as probability laws generally apply. Another difficulty is that in real life, competition can end in several different ways. In chess, you win, lose, or draw. In business, many other things are possible. This was Selten's contribution: in the 1960s, he managed to find a mathematical way to make only certain decisions reasonable.

This Nobel Prize received unusual publicity because of the personal tragedy of John Nash. He clearly has mathematical genius: his doctoral dissertation at Princeton written at age twenty-two was the work the Nobel judges honored in 1994. By the late 1950s, before he was thirty, Nash suffered a mental illness and was unable to work for the next thirty-five years. But in recent years he has recovered; Princeton gave him a part-time research post, and a film about his life has been planned.[31]

Other laureates worked on more limited, specific problems.

The first economics Nobel in 1969 went to Ragnar Frisch of Norway and Jan Tinbergen of the Netherlands. Frisch developed the first national planning system, for Norway. He "talked about planning as if it were . . . almost a religion." Appropriately, beekeeping was his hobby.[32] Tinbergen in turn drew up a planning model for the Netherlands, using twenty-seven equations and fifty variables; in 1939, he used a more complex scheme to analyze the U.S. economy from 1919 to 1929.

Wassily Leontief (Nobel 1973) introduced input-output concepts. Russian-born, he emigrated to Berlin in 1922 and then, by way of China, came to the U.S. and soon to Harvard. Before Leontief, for example, the effect of the defense industry on employment often ignored its effect on the economy as a whole, or even on related industries such as oil production. No integrating method was available. Leontief invented one, by treating the output of one industry as the input of another. Thus coal, the output of coal mining, is an input of the electric power industry. In his formalisms, the economy's factors broke down into components; his first version used forty-four sectors, with data then tabulated and fitted into equations. The outcome describes, quite precisely, how much is needed for each sector to produce just one more item of output — assuming, as such models do, static conditions, unvarying rate of production, perfectly free competition, and the rest. Leontief's scheme was soon adopted by the U.S. Commerce Department, the UN, the World Bank, and at least fifty other countries including the Soviet Union.

Econometrics as the Key to History, Life, and Everything

Those mentioned thus far have confined themselves to the market. Others have since won the prize for trying to apply econometric theory to the far reaches of other subjects.

The 1993 colaureates, Robert Fogel and Douglass North, were honored for founding a "new brand of scientific history" called cliometrics. For them, mathematical models are the proper and reliable guide to history. As Fogel explains,

> The approach sometimes leads cliometricians to represent historical behavior by mathematical equations and then to seek evidence, usually quantitative, capable of verifying the applicability of these equations or of contradicting them.[33]

Fogel argues that all historians use models — a highly debatable view. But this allows Fogel to argue that the only question is whether such models will be "implicit, vague, incomplete and internally inconsistent — or explicit and formally rigorous." The new cliometricians propose to use equations to "represent" historical events; then they seek quantitative evidence to verify or disprove their equations.

One might think this goes at history backwards. Shouldn't one ascertain the facts and then, cautiously, begin to generalize? Fogel in fact claims he is following the great nineteenth-century German historian Ranke, who urged going at history "as it really happened." Fogel's method, however, in the Nobel's formalist spirit, leads him radically away from old "literary" Ranke. Traditional historians, says Fogel, focused on individuals; cliometricians focus on "collections of individuals, categories of institutions, and on repetitive occurrences." Naturally, the "collective" fits more easily into equations. In fact, cliometrics is not the first effort to emphasize the "collective" side of history. In the late nineteenth and middle twentieth centuries, Galton and Namier of Britain respectively studied psychology and political history stressing "large populations" of data, with much use of statistics. The innovation of Fogel and North is to start from neoclassical economic assumptions. They do not deny that the "stochastic" (i.e., randomness) plays an enormous role in human life — though apparently not so enormous that cliometrics must take account of that unsettling fact.

Fogel and North pale in audacity alongside the work that won the 1992 prize for Gary Becker of Chicago. For this laureate, neoclassical economics can clarify a flabbergasting list of topics and problems: the human family, racial discrimination, crime, the basis of gender conflict, child-parent relations, marriage, and altruism and egoism. That however is only a start. The same explanation is extended to families of "birds, mammals and amphibians."[34]

This grandiose enterprise once more begins, not surprisingly, deep in the heart of equilibrium theory. More than other behavioral approaches, Becker notes, economics emphasizes "maximizing" behavior. But this has been used too timidly, he says: "The combined assumptions of maximizing behavior, market equilibrium, and stable preferences, used relentlessly and unflinchingly, form the heart of the economic approach as I see it."[35] Relentlessly and unflinchingly, then, he generalizes the notion of market maximizing as far as possible.

For example, construe a household or family as a factory: it inputs food purchases and outputs them into meals and so on. An educated family — or, rather, "factory" of this sort — will devote more time to "production": they will try to get the kids to do homework, and they will calculate how much "quality time" in the "factory" will be released, say, by hiring a maid.

Becker proceeds to nonhuman families. All species must "decide" whether to mate in monogamous or polygamous systems.[36] Like Disney in stern uniform, the animals are presented as if "calculating" whether to have many offspring and devote little care to each, or to have fewer and give them more time — in short, the economic ape or amphibian must decide if selfishness or altruism is more optimal. Market competition relentlessly presides over all creatures, great and small. "Members of a species compete against one another for food, mates, and other limited resources," and the strong, clever, and attractive win out, the weak perish. Becker's world is a bleak marketplace, where animals like humans are all utilitarians and keep maximizing advantages constantly; survival and market-biological gratifications are the only rewards in sight.

In his *Economic Behavior of Human Nature*, Becker praises the nineteenth-century utilitarian Jeremy Bentham for his "pleasure-pain calculus," which is "applicable to all human behavior." But he chides Bentham for wanting to reform humanity, rather than remain a value-free behavioral scientist. Any such protests, much less passionate ones, are not for Becker. He quite coolly announces that his approach

> does not draw conceptual distinctions between major and minor decisions, such as those involving life and death in contrast to the choice of a brand of coffee; or between decisions said to involve strong emotions and those with little emotional involvement, such as

choosing a mate or the number of children in contrast to buying paint.[37]

This is nihilism, but of a tepid sort. Becker elsewhere attacks racism, but one wonders why: on his premises, it is hard to see why he thinks racial discrimination is more important than buying paint.

Becker's analyses often provide unintended and inimitable pedantic comedy. He tells us that not only humans but "fireflies, locusts, grouse, antelopes, and mountain sheep" also form efficient "mating markets." Moreover, especially with fish, "males usually can fertilize the eggs of females cheaply." It takes a rare single-mindedness to think of price coefficients while contemplating fish fertilizing.[38] Back in the human world, discussing the division of labor in households and families, he says that virtually all societies have developed long-term protection for married women. "One can even say that 'marriage' is defined by a long-term commitment between a man and a woman." This sounds so ironic, though such a word fits nothing in Becker, that it could have been written by Thorstein Veblen, that great deadpan satirist of economic folly.[39]

Science or Scientizing

Gary Becker once sought to answer this question: Why do dominant and deferential people tend to marry each other? This happened, he explained, "because the dominant person's time can be used when the household encounters situations calling for dominance, and the deferential person's time can be used when deference is needed."[40] As Paul Samuelson once suggested, arcane mathematical models and jargon can intimidate the nonspecialist. Scientized language, or jargon, are also useful here.

Leonid Kantorovich of the USSR and Tjalling Koopmans of the Netherlands shared the Nobel award in 1975, for independently solving this sort of problem. The method is called linear programming. When cargo is shipped, a slow ship or inefficient crew or bad weather can eat away full profit. Kantorovich and Koopmans, proper mathematical economists, sought a model that would cover all possible cases here of "maximizing" under a constraint. They found a way to set up equations whose solutions equal the price of an "input"; cargo is an "input"; the ship delivers a certain amount of "output." Their model has been useful in matching resources to equipment, as in shipping and trucking, or running assembly lines. Yet this seems like an everyday problem that cargo shippers have been solving for centuries, albeit "practically," not formally. For this, a Nobel Prize?

In 1978 Herbert Simon won the prize. His prizewinning work developed the popular "decision-making" approach to administrative problems. People, he argued in *Administrative Behavior* (1947), have only imperfect knowledge of alternatives. Group decision-making demonstrates this: decisions result from give-and-take, stumbling progress, and compromise. Simon went further. Organization thinking is the individual's only way out of the limited view that any one person possesses: "the rational individual is, and must be, an organized and institutionalized individual."

Simon called this "satisficing." The human mind can solve only a few of the immense and varied problems facing it. Satisficing doesn't pretend to fully satisfy, i.e., "maximize" knowledge; it seeks only knowledge that is "good enough." Good enough for what? Simon never gives a clear answer. Good enough for management decisions, certainly, since those involve compromise based on specific practical problems. Simon wishes to "reconstruct the theory of the rational." But satisficing hardly seems to do more than legitimize opinions people happen to reach.

Simon's views have been praised for correcting the usual hyper-rationalized ideas found in economic theory.[41] This is a recurrent point of praise in this field (see Lucas and "rational expectations" below). But where, except in such a hyperrationalized context, could anyone win a Nobel Prize for stating the obvious?

In 1995 Robert Lucas of the University of Chicago won the prize for his theory of "rational expectations." This was originally an idea of Paul Muth (b. 1930), who did not mean the older neoclassic dogma that buyers and sellers act on their best information. He asked a prior question: What can people know economically? The obvious answer, in general, is the given marketplace world they inhabit. People come to expect certain things to happen there, and they act accordingly. Now, can a self-regulating system, constantly returning to equilibrium, actually meet people's expectations and seem "rational" to them? Unlikely, said Muth. Buyers keep changing their minds after various experiences, and sellers have to keep adapting to the new expectations. No invariable model can do this.

Lucas developed this perception. For example, no invariable model can ever predict the distressing booms and busts of business. Even if the fluctuation of money supply were shown to be the cause, à la Friedman, people quickly adapt. They notice local bank interest rates and the like. Lucas and Muth thus newly emphasized how buyers and sellers and the rest stay afloat by watching what is happening around them. This naturally cast grave doubt on the idea of economic agents who simply believe the information sent out by markets and governments. It has been said that with Lucas and Muth, "uncertainty" entered the heart of the theories most favored by the Nobel Prizes. Whether that is so or not, uncertainty seems to have entered the Stockholm decision on this award. Muth did not share the prize.[42]

Economics and Politics

Economics began as a branch of political thought ("political economy"), and still decisively affects political policy and vice versa. This is how theorists are inevitably but realistically described and self-described: the Communist Marx, the liberal Keynes, the conservative Stigler or Hayek, the libertarian Milton Friedman. Beyond the how of technical methods, the why sits waiting to be answered: What sort of political and therefore moral order ought economic theory to try to achieve or improve?

The 1986 American laureate James Buchanan emphatically insists that an economist aspiring to exact and thus neutral scientific status should express no political or moral preferences. The discovery of "what is" must not be contaminated by "what ought to be." In this way Buchanan, among many others, seeks to turn public policy into a value-free subject.[43]

Paul Samuelson is more sensitive to both sides of the issue. Mathematics can endorse no moral "ought," but Samuelson argues that economics must also be "normative," otherwise why bother? And, "you can't have normative economics without norms, without ethics, without prejudices."[44]

Despite many efforts to show that economic theories can be divorced from political or moral consequences, no value-free economics is anywhere in sight. Gunnar Myrdal made this point sharply:

Modern establishment economists have retained the welfare theory [not charity for the poor but "consumer satisfaction"] from the earliest neoclassical authors, but have done their best to conceal and forget its foundation upon a particular and now obsolete moral philosophy [i.e., utilitarianism]. They have thus succeeded in presenting what appears to be an amoral economic theory, and they are proud of stressing this as "professionalism."[45]

These are fighting words, but Myrdal was attacking assumptions that were and still are dominant. The Nobel citations gloss over this problem, focusing instead on technical accomplishment.

What Myrdal was driving at can be seen in the two most contentious episodes in the short history of the economics Nobels. Both involved the American laureate Milton Friedman (Nobel 1976). He is the famous advocate of monetarism, and his doctrine can be simply stated, though at some risk: changing the supply of money is the one crucial act that influences what happens in an economy. The central bank controls the money supply, and by increasing or decreasing the amount of money available to banks, which raise or lower interest rates accordingly, it can nourish the economy's health by supplying money only at the same rate as the economy's growth.

Friedman is combative. When traditional economists called his view unheard-of and fanciful, Friedman wrote a vast historical survey of the topic to prove his point. A master of publicity and controversy, he became courted by government and business leaders, and has probably had more public influence than any single economist of the last half century. As a columnist for *Newsweek* for almost twenty years from 1966, and the subject of a ten-part TV series, his name became "known probably to more people than that of any economist who had ever lived with the exception of Karl Marx."[46]

It surely helped that, compared with others' hypersophisticated theorems, monetarism seemed understandable: money supply influenced prices but not production. His theory also appeared at an opportune moment. Stagflation had arrived: unemployment and inflation were both rising at once. Government efforts to hold back either had little effect. It seemed that both neoclassicism and neo-Keynesianism must give way to this newer, bolder approach. Friedman postulated a "natural rate of unemployment" during which inflation would hold steady.

Friedman's combative political views have made him a flashpoint. He strongly affirms individual freedom and wants government to keep hands off the free enterprise system. Yet, as often remarked, he seems inconsistent here. If, as he urges, a central bank should control the supply of money, isn't that an instrument of external and coercive intervention in the free economy — the very stopper in the bunghole of the whole huge vat, which alone can decide whether things go at a trickle or a flood? For such reasons, Friedman has been classed among the "bastard progeny" of Keynes.[47]

Samuelson once wonderfully described Friedman's role in economics as like the eel that sea captains used to put into a barrel of fish to keep them lively and fresh on long voyages.[48] Certainly Friedman, on one side, often uses his economics to support provocative and extreme political positions, as in his opposition to Social Security, farm legislation, pure food and drug laws, the licensing of doctors, minimum wages, and so on. On the other side, Friedman can, with blithe inconsistency, declare that an economist's political views — like a physicist's — are merely personal. Others are troubled by his championing of and by repressive regimes — Taiwan, South Korea, Chile, Argentina: civil freedoms were suppressed in those countries, though capitalism might flourish.[49] In 1973 a military junta overthrew the Marxist Allende government in Chile. Friedman's economic advising and support of the repressive junta set off many protests. His 1975 Nobel Prize was denounced by four American Nobelists.[50] In Stockholm two thousand "leftists," so described by the *New York Times*, marched in protest outside the Nobel ceremony hall. Inside, as Friedman accepted his prize, a man shouted objections and was ejected.[51]

In early 1977, a few months after Friedman's award, Gunnar Myrdal publicly called for an end to the Nobel economics awards.

This had been boiling up since 1974, when Myrdal and the Austrian-British Friedrich Hayek shared the Nobel award. Of all the laureates, they stand out for taking up broad social and political problems. Myrdal's most famous book is *An American Dilemma: The Negro Problem and American Democracy* (1944), which urged government action against segregation as a desperately needed measure. Also in 1944, Hayek published his most widely read book, *The Road to Serfdom*, which strongly opposed state central planning and control of the market as a threat to individual liberty.

When the joint award to Myrdal and Hayek was announced, it did not go over well with Myrdal, or perhaps with Hayek either, as Myrdal's daughter Sissela Bok noted:

> Sharing the prize in this way was probably as much of a cold shower for von Hayek as for Gunnar. The two were polar opposites from a political point of view. Neither they nor anyone else could avoid thinking that the prize was the result of an ideological balancing act. Many among their colleagues even surmised that the choice reflected a condescending joke on the part of the Swedish economics establishment. Although they could hardly avoid giving their brilliant but cosmopolitan and flamboyantly un-Swedish compatriot a prize, they had it in their power to do so in a way that prevented him from relishing the honor or feeling truly recognized in his home country. . . . From then on, Gunnar [argued] that it might be best to abolish prizes in which [Nobel committee] politics played such an intrusive role.[52]

Friedman's Nobel award in 1975 made Myrdal go public. He wrote an open letter to a Swedish newspaper calling for an end to the Nobel economics prize. This was no ordinary complaint. Myrdal was Sweden's most prestigious intellectual. He might have softened the attack by attacking Friedman or Nobel committee bias. Instead he directly attacked economic theory's claim to deserve a Nobel Prize because of its supposed scientific rigor and use. Myrdal portrayed it as an inexact field which must address political and social needs and aims, or else be irresponsible. He had long insisted that to detach economics from policy-making responsibilities is pernicious. Ironically, Myrdal had been a prime force in setting up the Nobel economics awards in the first place, probably hoping that economic thought would be activist in posture.

One theorist who strongly agreed with Myrdal here was none other than his political opposite and co-Nobelist, the "conservative" Hayek. In his toast to the king and queen, Hayek announced he would have "decidedly advised against" instituting the economics prize, if he had been asked. Both Hayek and Myrdal came to believe that their efforts to broaden economic theory had discredited them in the eyes of their colleagues, as not being "technical" economists. Hayek said this was why he migrated from Britain to the U.S. in the 1950s.

The Nobel Prize obviously survived. But since Myrdal's protest, it has not ventured to honor laureates as prominent, outspoken, and provocative as Myrdal, Hayek, or Friedman. The prizes usually go to highly technical work, most typically pertaining to market and investment problems. The Nobel judges seem to have been surprised by protests that the award to Fogel's cliometric work constituted support for racism.

Perhaps Myrdal and Hayek did make an impact. In 1998 the prize went to the Indian-British Amartya Sen. He studies not the market but welfare economics. The problems here, as Sen makes clear, are many and overwhelming: how societies, especially in the Third World, should apportion their scarce resources in helping the poor; how to prevent famines caused by floods and droughts; how to measure the inequality of incomes in a realistic way. Sen provocatively argues that scarcity of food does not cause many famines. Rather, people lose "entitlement" to food supplies. Surprisingly, considering the long line of laureates proclaiming the necessity of a "value-free" science, the Nobel economics committee praised Sen in its citation for having "restored an ethical dimension to the dicussion of vital economic problems." Sen told a reporter that he had always been "sceptical" of the prize, but hesitated to say so before being honored because people would think it "sour grapes." His prize has been attacked from opposite sides, as merely another mainstream exercise and too formalist, and also as only left-wing establishment economics.

But the 1999 prize seemed a return to business as usual for the economics committee: it went to Robert Mundell, an early enthusiast of supply-side economics, for clarifying how a government's shift from a flexible to a fixed monetary policy will cause fluctuations in exchange rates. This has implications for the Euromarket currency. A native Canadian, he is now also another U.S. laureate, from Columbia University.

Summing Up

Does economic theory, neoclassic or neo-Keynesian, deserve Nobel Prizes even in the Central Bank's simulacrum of them? The evidence, as suggested, is not encouraging. On the more empirical side,

Kuznets's work stands as a solid accomplishment. The national planning and accounting schemes of Tinbergen or the British Richard Stone (prize 1984), or linear programmming (Kantorovich, Koopmans) or input-output methods (Leontief) are useful.

Too many Nobelized achievements, however, seem perilously close to scientizing the commonsensical: portfolio choices (Tobin), or corporate debt-equity financing (Modigliani-Miller), or the "human resources/Third World interpretations" (Schultz, Ohlin, Meade). George Stigler was a brilliant teacher and an eminence in American academic economics, but the deregulation analyses that won him the 1982 prize, based partly on an analysis of Interstate Commerce Commission codes, seem rather thin for so exalted an award.

On the high formalist side, the same problem exists. For all their mathematical prowess, the question is whether the elegant and impressive models of Samuelson, Hicks, Arrow, Simon, or Nash provide a "firm cornerstone both for further theoretical work and empirical testing" — this is quoted from the Nobel laudation for Ohlin and Meade, but similar praise is bestowed on almost every economics laureate. Thus far, any fundamental advance into a new science of economics has not materialized.

Samuelson and his like were the kind of bold, powerful theoreticians seemingly needed by any exact science of economics. But, as the history of science shows, elegantly mathematicized theories are not necessarily good science, or even science at all. Economic theory gives off a sense of high expectations unfulfilled. The economic historian Jurg Niehans, after surveying the field, writes that despite extraordinary technical advance,

> it is sobering to observe, however, that after forty years of effort, hardly any economic arguments had been settled by econometric methods. Perhaps it will later be realized that these methods were not well suited for the analysis of the everchanging complexities of human history.[53]

Samuelson himself confesses to such pessimism. He had once expected

> the new econometrics would enable us to narrow down the uncertainties of our economic theories . . . this expectation has not worked

out. . . . it seems objectively to be the case that there does not accu-mulate a convergent body of econometric findings, convergent on a testable truth.[54]

Myrdal spoke of the proud Nobel formalisms as merely "the concept market, which has no resemblance to the real market." Keynes, himself a great master of probability theory, long ago warned that the "bare bones" of economics expressible in mathematics are easy, compared to interpreting the incompletely known facts about economic experience.[55]

Econometricians can naturally be impatient with such a portrait. Lawrence Klein (1980 Nobelist) was unrepentant: "Nonmathematical contributions to economics [are] fat, sloppy and vague."[56] But Milton Friedman says that "there is of course no sharp line between the empirical scientist and the theorist — we are dealing with a continuum."[57]

As for the charge that such theorizing really benefits mankind very little — nor often even the marketplace — some econometricians note, fairly enough, that all fundamental thought begins like this. Its meaning and benefit can take decades to demonstrate — look at quantum physics. Unless basic principles are clarified, progress will never happen.

Meanwhile, worry persists that Nobel theory mainly inhabits the universities — too much so, say many critics, since thereby it becomes inbred and cut off from marketplace realities and tests. Some have worried, and it seems rightly, that while the Nobel Prizes keep coming each year, there may not be or already have not been enough worthy achievements to sustain it. The talent pool may be running thin, considering some of the recent awards. Perhaps it should be given only every few years or so.

Arjo Klamer summarizes the situation:

> To the outsider, theoretical discourse in economics may appear to be an esoteric, if not absurd affair. The assumptions economists use sound unreal, and their technical language deters further reading. Nonacademic economists and new students in economics tend to speak in non-technical terms about economic questions. . . . Economists look for a systematic theory to expound more clearly the conditions under which an event takes place. . . . it facilitates arguments in academic discourse.[58]

The business media illustrate Klamer's point. There, the figures who loom most important are not economics laureates but "analysts" — experts who study the performances of some industry or company — or Federal Reserve chairs, or important money managers or CEOs. The marketplace remains oddly indifferent, often even dismissive of its theoreticians, particularly those ambitious formalists that the Nobel economics judges often laud for "pioneering discoveries" or "pathfinding breakthroughs."

Perhaps expectedly so. Nobelized theories have not been exactly famous for reliable predictions. The *Economist* asked: why not a Nobel Prize for business itself? As the *Economist* argued, actual prosperity serves the public good more than theories about it.[59] But since such a prize would be impossible to implement, the Central Bank of Sweden's intrusion into the Nobel Prize might soon come to an end. Which may have been the point of the suggestion of that journal aptly named the *Economist*.

Conclusion

The Nobel Prizes are now a century old, and their future lies open. Any assessment can only be an interim report.

Not surprisingly, the response to the Nobel Prizes is mixed. On one extreme, some wish all the prizes away as a plague of celebrity that corrupts the ambitions of writers and scientists, and the peace prize as a trophy coveted by self-parading politicians and activists. Meanwhile, the public cheers those glorified by the media circus as "great," little comprehending or caring why. On the other extreme, the prizes are admired as reliably honoring truly major achievements and progress. As nothing else can, the Nobel certifies what is important in science, writing, and peace work. It stands as a model of integrity, above the fray — like the king who bestows its medals. It thus provides a desperately needed symbol of authority and coherence in an age when all standards are under attack. Between the nay- and yea-sayers, the moderates, as usual, agree and disagree with both sides. The reader will already have guessed that this report is by one of the moderates.

Moderate, because after studying the Nobel Prizes award by award and field by field, the effect is both disquieting and encouraging. Everyone's education enforces specialization and pens one in: scientists have little time for literature, literary people have little patience with mathematics and molecules, and so on. But the prizes spread over our self-imposed enclosures and offer a view from higher ground. And to see things from the heights is always a liberating experience. The Nobel list is surely a constant reminder that at least some of the riches of human reason and spirit are not exhausted. On the contrary, the sheer prodigiousness of discovery and creativity can soon become overwhelming. Try — as just one step in becoming more familiar with the long line of prizes in one small group of achievements — to gain some intimacy with such Nobelized marvels as Schrödinger's equation, or Perse's poem *Anabase*, which seems as eerily archaic as the era it evokes, or to conjure what it cost the Northern Irish laureates Betty Williams and Mairead Corrigan — Protestant and Catholic — to be enclosed in fear and scorn for breaking with both sides to protest the killings. After not too much of this, it soon may seem better to tend our own gardens and let the Nobel judges cope with all that. The Swedish and Norwegian committees around 1900 could hardly have imagined what they were getting into when they agreed to administer the awards.

Many demurrals are registered in the foregoing chapters. Still, one must conclude that the Nobel Prizes in their venerable hundredth year are healthier than ever. The laureate lists in physics, chemistry, and medicine certainly deserve applause. Precisely because high expectations have so consistently been satisfied here, any lapse causes much disappointment. How could they have ignored Lise Meitner's role in discovering nuclear fission, or Ralph Alpher, who cofounded the theory of the Big Bang, or Albert Schatz, who codiscovered streptomycin? Or dismissed Freud while honoring psychiatry with awards to lobotomy and malaria inoculations for mental illness? Yet, across a long century, the scientific list is a glittering one, and crucially helped save the Nobel Prize's reputation from 1901 to 1950 and later, when the literature and peace prizes were in the doldrums.

For reasons discussed, good literary prizes are much more difficult to choose than science prizes. One need only think how long it took for Whitman, Melville, and Emily Dickinson to win wide acceptance, among experts as well as ordinary readers. The history of taste proves the point again and again, if anyone still needs convincing. George Steiner has made this point forcefully in his attacks on the Nobel committee system, and he doesn't even dwell on the well-known fractiousness within the Swedish Academy.

Yet something there must be working right, since literary awards in the last thirty years are better than ever. Prizes are still too often overlong delayed, or go to safe choices. But only the prizes to William Golding and Dario Fo have been greeted with deeply felt catcalls. The literature prize has begun to live up to itself more impressively than before. "Difficult" greatness still makes the judges wary, as with the poet Paul Celan. Still, literary history has its peaks and flats, and we may be in one of the flats. The surpassing greatness found in Joyce or Proust may simply be absent now. That also means that the judges are less apt to make grandly embarrassing mistakes. The nagging possibility remains that remarkable literature may exist in Asia or Africa or one of the vast linguistic reaches scarcely explored by the Nobel jury. Here all of us depend too much on the Nobel jury to find these treasures. Few scholars or critics even begin to undertake such a daunting task, but that rarely stops anyone from complaining that the Nobel judges are too Europe-centered.

The peace prize spent its first half century honoring far too many functionaries, interrupted only now and then by a compelling prize. But in 1960, when the peace prize took a bold new step to honor peace efforts within a nation, with its award to Albert Luthuli of South Africa for opposing apartheid, and later to the Polish Solidarity movement or the U.S. civil rights campaign, it revitalized itself. Since the peace prize is essentially political, and often crisis-driven, the Oslo committee is always in someone's line of fire. In the terrible arena of the twentieth century, one wishes they had done better. But decency adds the wish that we had all done better.

The late-arrived economics prize is a case apart. It has its many defenders, though mostly in the academy, and especially in those few universities which have taken almost all the prizes. But even some of its laureates have voiced doubt about the point of such a prize. There is also a sceptical feeling that economics, its equations notwithstanding, is no more a "hard" science than sociology and other non-Nobelized "soft" social sciences. A majority of the prizes have rewarded advice to the investment market, which seems inappropriate to the caliber and benefit-to-humanity criterion that Nobel Prizes demand elsewhere. And, while the literature and science prizes face an embarrassment of riches, with too many deserving candidates to honor, the economics prize — after only thirty years — seems already running short of worthy candidates. In what other Nobel field could one win prizes for urging an econometric interpretation of history, or for speculations about human, animal, and fish "economic" behavior, or for a theory whose "experimental" test — actual stock market performance — ended in a quick bankruptcy?

The celebrity and authority of the prizes have assuredly brought some neglected or specialist work to wide public attention. It gave the Icelandic novelist Halldór Laxness a well-deserved international reputation; it made the new quantum mechanics of 1925–26 far more visible than it would otherwise be. The lists of laureates in all fields, and of those omitted, provide a historical gloss on how these fields have developed and how attitudes about their worth and meaning have changed. One can see scientific enthusiasms, or literary trends, prosper and recede and others emerge. Even the Nobel's often puzzling delays are useful in this respect. But how the Nobel Prizes illuminate modern scientific, literary, and peace history is still confined to a handful of scholars. One of the most eminent of these, Elisabeth Crawford, points out that most of twentieth-century science's dramas involving politics also involved Nobel Prize winners. This is as true of the literary prize and its omissions, not only during the Cold War but throughout the century.[1]

Deeper and unsettling questions hover about the Nobel Prize. To start, why should any prizes be given for serious intellectual and artistic work? Shouldn't artists and scientists find the work its own reward? But, as once and wisely said, if men were angels, government would not be needed — and, one must add, neither would prizes. Humanly fallible scientists indeed do their work for its own sake, but also seek priority and recognition. As for writers, only one comes to mind who never sought publication for brilliant work — the French essayist Joseph Joubert (1754–1824). The rest want to be published, and many write best or only when spurred by the hope of recognition. Prizes have anyway existed since antiquity, and the likes of Sophocles and Jean-Jacques Rousseau did not hesitate to seek and accept them. No sensible person can think that a prize makes any work intrinsically better, much less the "best" of its kind. As noted several times, the celebrity bestowed by any Nobel Prize is usually fleeting. For proof, identify Zewail or Veltman or Saramago or Bobel; answer: all were laureates in 1998 or 1999. This is not unfair. The achievements that win a Nobel Prize are after all only made possible by long traditions of mind and spirit — the high disciplines of science, literature, political justice — maintained and developed from antiquity by their devotees as if life itself depended on it. Honoring these disciplines that sustain great human achievements is the true justification and glory of the Nobel Prizes.

Nothing could be more misleading than reducing such matters to an academic speciality. The cult of Einstein is helpful here. His theories are puzzles to most, and attention thus shifts to his personality.

Yet why should this man's personality particularly interest anyone? Celebrity worship unquestionably plays its part. But beyond all vulgarizing, the answer leads back to his astonishing views about the heavens, and the time and space we inhabit. "Einstein" ultimately argues that a widespread sense of wonder at the universe — and at the marvels of human reason — is still alive. Considering the many diagnoses proclaiming the opposite, this is heartening. Now substitute "Nobel Prize" for "Einstein": at least something of the same is at work. The prizes make us a bit more open to or reverent of greatness, and that is important.

In very limited ways, the future of the Nobel Prizes seems predictable. Scientific discoveries of Nobel caliber can be expected to continue as far as one can see: too little is yet understood about too much. Peace prizes will hardly lack laureates, since war and injustice are permanent as death, though the character of the awards may change as circumstances do. The literary prize may undergo more radical change. Thus far, it is rooted in the tradition of the book. But in the dawning electronic age, the book or text may find itself rivaled in a number of ways: one familiar example is the "hypertext," whose free-floating bits or bytes can be assembled as whim dictates to the laptop. What the literary prize will look like in fifty years is anyone's guess. Perhaps the 1997 award to the performing artist Dario Fo is a portent.

One of the most vexing questions involves literature and the sciences. These have been the backbone of the prizes, but relations between them may bring grave dilemmas. This is not the school-teacherly dispute called the Two Cultures, which urges literary folk to learn the second law of thermodynamics and scientists to read more Shakespeare or Flaubert. That takes "literature" too narrowly. The Nobel Prize itself uses literature to stand for all serious writing, including philosophy and history — witness the prizes to Bergson and Churchill — and in principle also theology or political thought. But modern thought, taken this broadly, may have sustained a wound which gives every sign of getting worse. The physicist J. Robert Oppenheimer in 1959 warned not only of technological dangers, as one might expect from the man who had directed the building of the atom bomb. He also emphasized "an increasing estrangement between the world of science and that of common language." The "world of science has impoverished, intimidated and emasculated" the common world, "depriving it of its legitimacy and condemning it to a kind of permanently arbitrary condition," he wrote. "A great chasm has appeared between the intellectual world of the scientist and that of the men who, at the level of common language, are busy with fundamental human problems."[2]

Far from scientific arrogance, Oppenheimer deeply lamented this outcome, but could not see how to solve it. By "common language" and "fundamental human problems," he invoked our whole vital heritage of literature, philosophy, religion, history, morality, and political justice. He gave as an example the fact that although twentieth-century physics has been an epic of great intellectual adventure, sadly no epic poem will ever be written celebrating human grandeur here. The equations of physics defy translation into ordinary words. Quantum physics and relativity refer to experiences that common language grasps or conveys only poorly.

For similar reasons and at about the same time, the literary critic Lionel Trilling drew an equally distressing conclusion. Literature and philosophy once confidently occupied the center: even Newton's universe and calculus were not beyond the grasp of the cultivated person. But now science commands knowledge that brings untold power but also a rich order of reality previously unimagined. This has pushed the traditional writer and reader to the margins in important ways. One proof, Trilling said, is "the extreme attenuation of the authority of literary culture" in our time. And precisely the common language that writers and philosophers share with all humanity but deploy with such subtle skill — that great instrument itself — has cut off access to the mathematical and hyperspecialized realm of science (he was thinking of the ascendency of physics after World War II). Nor is there any way, Trilling said, to give a comprehension of science to those who have not studied it professionally, or who lack the special gifts needed. "This exclusion of most of us from the mode of thought which is habitually said to be the characteristic achievement of the modern age is bound to be experienced as a wound to our intellectual self-esteem."[3] Trilling was too circumspect to add the obvious possibility that such deep wounds often lead to ruinous hostilities.

The same problem has prompted some hopeful prophecies. William Faulkner, accepting his 1949 prize, also warned that the new fear of human extinction brought by the atom bomb has made writers forget that the problems of the spirit are deeper than any politics, however seemingly apocalyptic. Because humanity has a soul, he proclaimed, as only Faulkner could, it will not only endure but prevail.

The Nobel ceremony is the most celebrated and visible place where science and literature stand side by side, honored as equals. The citations carefully avoid noticing any of the unpleasant possibilities just mentioned. The Nobel assignment after all is to award honorifics in a celebratory mood. Perhaps Oppenheimer and Trilling were too pessimistic, and Faulkner too optimistic. Even so, their warnings suggest that the future may hold some unwelcome surprises for the harmony, not to mention the coherence, of the Nobel Prizes. The ceremony and medals and pomp, the great names of the past, the tuxedos and gowns, the gracious royal family, and the resulting media applause — all of it makes us forget that the Nobel Prizes ultimately celebrate deep and potent forces in the human soul. If that soul begins speaking two different languages past each other, the Nobel may become a flashpoint or else an irrelevant parody of itself. Or it may find a way, as it has done before, to live up to itself. After all, the Nobel Prize has by now existed longer than almost anyone alive. It has become part of the common memory shared by humanity across the globe. We are used to it. But in truth, with whatever reservations and reluctance, we also depend on it.

CHRONOLOGY OF PRIZES

LITERATURE

1901 **Sully Prudhomme** (pseud. of René F. A. Prudhomme) (1839–1907), France. Poetry.

1902 **C. M. Theodor Mommsen** (1817–1903), Germany. History.

1903 **Bjørnstjerne Bjørnson** (1832–1910), Norway. Poetry.

1904 **Frédéric Mistral** (1830–1914), France. Poetry in Provençal language.

José Echegaray y Eizaguirre (1832–1916), Spain. Drama.

1905 **Henryk Sienkiewicz** (1846–1916), Poland. Fiction.

1906 **Giosuè Carducci** (1835–1907), Italy. Poetry.

1907 **Rudyard Kipling** (1865–1936), Britain. Poetry, fiction.

1908 **Rudolf Eucken** (1846–1926), Germany. Philosophy.

1909 **Selma Lagerlöf** (1858–1940), Sweden. Fiction.

1910 **Paul Heyse** (1830–1914), Germany. Poetry, drama, fiction.

1911 **Maurice Maeterlinck** (1862–1949), Belgium. Poetry, drama.

1912 **Gerhart Hauptmann** (1862–1946), Germany. Drama.

1913 **Rabindranath Tagore** (1861–1941), India. Poetry.

1914 No award.

1915 **Romain Rolland** (1866–1944), France. Fiction.

1916 **Carl Verner von Heidenstam** (1859–1940), Sweden. Poetry, fiction.

1917 **Karl Gjellerup** (1857–1919), Denmark. Poetry.

Henrik Pontoppidan (1857–1943), Denmark. Fiction.

1918 No award.

1919 **Carl Spitteler** (1845–1924), Switzerland. Poetry.

1920   **Knut Hamsun** (pseud. of Knud Hamsund) (1859–1952), Norway. Fiction.

1921   **Anatole France** (pseud. of Jacques Thibault) (1844–1924), France. Fiction.

1922   **Jacinto Benavente y Martínez** (1866–1954), Spain. Drama.

1923   **William Butler Yeats** (1865–1939), Ireland. Poetry.

1924   **Władysław Reymont** (pseud. of Władysław Rejment) (1867–1925), Poland. Fiction.

1925   **George Bernard Shaw** (1856–1950), Ireland-Britain. Drama.

1926   **Grazia Deledda** (1871–1936), Italy. Fiction.

1927   **Henri Bergson** (1859–1941), France. Philosophy.

1928   **Sigrid Undset** (1882–1949), Norway. Fiction.

1929   **Thomas Mann** (1875–1955), Germany. Fiction.

1930   **Sinclair Lewis** (1885–1951), U.S. Fiction.

1931   **Erik Karlfeldt** (1864–1931), Sweden. Poetry.

1932   **John Galsworthy** (1867–1933), Britain. Fiction, drama.

1933   **Ivan Bunin** (1870–1953), Russia. Fiction.

1934   **Luigi Pirandello** (1867–1936), Italy. Drama, fiction.

1935   No award.

1936   **Eugene O'Neill** (1888–1953), U.S. Drama.

1937   **Roger Martin du Gard** (1881–1958), France. Fiction.

1938   **Pearl Buck** (1892–1973), U.S. Fiction.

1939   **Frans Sillanpää** (1888–1964), Finland. Fiction.

1940–43   No award.

1944   **Johannes V. Jensen** (1873–1950), Denmark. Fiction.

1945   **Gabriela Mistral** (pseud. of Lucila Godoy Alcayaga) (1889–1957), Chile. Poetry.

1946   **Hermann Hesse** (1877–1962), Germany-Switzerland. Fiction.

1947   **André Gide** (1869–1951), France. Fiction.

1948   **Thomas Stearns Eliot** (1888–1965), U.S.-Britain. Poetry.

1949   William Faulkner (1897–1962), U.S. Fiction.

1950   Bertrand Russell (1872–1970), Britain. Philosophy.

1951   Pär Lagerkvist (1891–1974), Sweden. Fiction, drama.

1952   François Mauriac (1885–1970), France. Fiction.

1953   Winston Churchill (1874–1965), Britain. History.

1954   Ernest Hemingway (1899–1961), U.S. Fiction.

1955   Halldór Laxness (pseud. of Halldór Gudjónsson) (1902–1998), Iceland. Fiction.

1956   Juan Ramón Jiménez (1881–1958), Spain. Poetry.

1957   Albert Camus (1913–1960), France. Fiction, criticism.

1958   Boris Pasternak (1890–1960), USSR. Poetry, fiction.

1959   Salvatore Quasimodo (1901–1968), Italy. Poetry.

1960   Saint-John Perse (pseud. of Alexis Saint-Léger Léger) (1887–1975), France. Poetry.

1961   Ivo Andrič (1892–1975), Yugoslavia. Fiction.

1962   John Steinbeck (1902–1968), U.S. Fiction.

1963   George Seferis (pseud. of Giorgios Seferiades) (1900–1971), Greece. Poetry.

1964   Jean-Paul Sartre (1905–1980). France. Fiction, drama, philosophy.

1965   Mikhail Sholokhov (1905–1984), USSR. Fiction.

1966   Shmuel Y. Agnon (pseud. of Shmuel Czaczkes) (1888–1970), Israel. Fiction.

Nelly Sachs (1891–1970), Germany-Sweden. Poetry.

1967   Miguel Angel Asturias (1899–1974), Guatemala. Fiction.

1968   Yasunari Kawabata (1899–1972), Japan. Fiction.

1969   Samuel Beckett (1906–1989), Ireland-France. Fiction, drama.

1970   Aleksandr Solzhenitsyn (1918–), USSR. Fiction.

1971   Pablo Neruda (pseud. of Ricardo Reyes y Basoalto) (1904–1973), Chile. Poetry.

1972   **Heinrich Böll** (1917–1985), Germany. Fiction.

1973   **Patrick White** (1912–1990), Australia. Fiction.

1974   **Eyvind Johnson** (1900–1976), Sweden. Fiction.

Harry Martinson (1904–1978), Sweden. Fiction, poetry.

1975   **Eugenio Montale** (1896–1981), Italy. Poetry.

1976   **Saul Bellow** (1915–), Canada-U.S. Fiction.

1977   **Vicente Aleixandre** (1898–1984), Spain. Poetry.

1978   **Isaac Bashevis Singer** (1904–1991), Poland-U.S. Fiction.

1979   **Odysseus Elytis** (pseud. of Odysseus Alepoudelis) (1911–1996), Greece. Poetry

1980   **Czesław Miłosz** (1911–), Poland-U.S. Poetry.

1981   **Elias Canetti** (1905–1994), Bulgaria-Austria-Britain. Fiction, essays.

1982   **Gabriel García Márquez** (1928–), Colombia. Fiction.

1983   **William Golding** (1911–1993), Britain. Fiction.

1984   **Jaroslav Seifert** (1901–1986), Czechoslovakia. Poetry.

1985   **Claude Simon** (1913–), France. Fiction.

1986   **Wole Soyinka** (1934–), Nigeria. Fiction, drama.

1987   **Joseph Brodsky** (1940–1996), USSR-U.S. Poetry.

1988   **Naguib Mahfouz** (1911–), Egypt. Fiction.

1989   **Camilo José Cela** (1916–), Spain. Fiction.

1990   **Octavio Paz** (1914–1998), Mexico. Poetry, criticism.

1991   **Nadine Gordimer** (1923–), South Africa. Fiction.

1992   **Derek Walcott** (1930–), Jamaica. Poetry, drama.

1993   **Toni Morrison** (pseud. of Chloe Wofford) (1931–), U.S. Fiction.

1994   **Kenzaburo Oe** (1935–), Japan. Fiction.

1995   **Seamus Heaney** (1939–), Northern Ireland. Poetry.

1996   **Wisława Szymborska** (1923–), Poland. Poetry.

1997   **Dario Fo** (1926–), Italy. Drama.

1998   **José Saramago** (1922–), Portugal. Fiction.

1999   **Günter Grass** (1927–), Germany. Fiction.

2000   **Gao Xingjian** (1942–), China-France. Fiction.

PHYSICS

1901   **Wilhelm Röntgen** (1845–1923), Germany. Discovery of X-rays [1895].

1902   **Hendrik Lorentz** (1853–1928), Netherlands. Explanation of Zeeman effect [1896].

        Pieter Zeeman (1865–1943), Netherlands. Discovery of Zeeman effect of spectral line splitting [1896].

1903   **Henri Becquerel** (1852–1908), France. Discovery of radioactivity [1896].

        Marie Skłodowska Curie (1867–1934), Poland-France, and **Pierre Curie** (1859–1906), France. Research on radioactivity [1898].

1904   **John W. Strutt, Lord Rayleigh** (1842–1919), Britain. Discovery of argon [1894].

1905   **Philipp Lenard** (1862–1947), Germany. Cathode ray research [c. 1902].

1906   **Joseph John Thomson** (1856–1940), Britain. Discovery of electron [1897].

1907   **Albert A. Michelson** (1852–1931), U.S. Precision measurements [c. 1890].

1908   **Gabriel Lippmann** (1845–1921), France. Color photography improvement [1890].

1909   **Guglielmo Marconi** (1874–1937), Italy. Wireless radio [1895–1901].

        Karl F. Braun (1850–1918), Germany. Radio transmitter improvements [1897].

1910   **Johannes van der Waals** (1837–1923), Netherlands. Equation of gas and liquid states [1873].

1911   **Wilhelm Wien** (1864–1928), Germany. Laws of heat radiation [1896].

1912   **Nils Dalén** (1869–1937), Sweden. Lighthouse illumination [1907].

1913   **Heike Kamerlingh Onnes** (1853–1926), Netherlands. Super-conductivity in low-temperature experiments [1907–8].

1914   **Max von Laue** (1879–1960), Germany. X-ray diffraction [1912].

1915   **William Henry Bragg** (1862–1942) and **William Lawrence Bragg** (1890–1971), Britain. X-ray analysis of crystals [1912].

1916   No award.

1917   **Charles Barkla** (1877–1944), Britain. "Secondary radiation" of X-rays [1905].

1918   **Max Planck** (1858–1947), Germany. Quantum law [1900].

1919   **Johannes Stark** (1874–1957), Germany. Spectral line splitting by electricity [1913].

1920   **Charles Guillaume** (1861–1938), France. Alloys [c. 1895]

1921   **Albert Einstein** (1879–1955), Germany-Switzerland-U.S. "Theoretical Physics, and especially . . . the photoelectric effect" [1905].

1922   **Niels Bohr** (1885–1962), Denmark. Quantum theory of atom [1913].

1923   **Robert A. Millikan** (1868–1953), U.S. Measurement of electron charge [1909–11] and photoelectric effect [1912–16].

1924   **Karl Manne Siegbahn** (1886–1978), Sweden. X-ray spectroscopy [1922].

1925   **James Franck** (1882–1964), Germany-U.S., and **Gustav Hertz** (1887–1975), Germany. Laws governing electron-atom collisions [1915].

1926   **Jean Perrin** (1870–1942), France. Suspension equilibrium [1908].

1927   **Arthur H. Compton** (1892–1962), U.S. Experimental proof of light as particle [1923].

        Charles T. R. Wilson (1869–1959), Britain. Cloud chamber detector [1911].

1928   **Owen Richardson** (1879–1959), Britain. Thermionic phenomena [1910].

1929 **Louis de Broglie** (1892–1987), France. Wave nature of electron [1923].

1930 **Chandrasekhara V. Raman** (1888–1970), India. Explanation of scattering of light [1928].

1931 No award.

1932 **Werner Heisenberg** (1901–1976), Germany. Quantum mechanics, uncertainty principle [1925–27].

1933 **Erwin Schrödinger** (1887–1961), Austria. Wave mechanics [1926].

Paul A. M. Dirac (1902–1984), Britain. Quantum theory [1925–28].

1934 No award.

1935 **James Chadwick** (1891–1974), Britain. Discovery of neutron [1932].

1936 **Victor Hess** (1883–1964), Austria. Discovery of cosmic rays [1911].

Carl Anderson (1905–1991), U.S. Discovery of positron [1932].

1937 **Clinton Davisson** (1881–1958), U.S., and **George P. Thomson** (1892–1975), Britain. Independently, proof of wave property of electrons [1927].

1938 **Enrico Fermi** (1901–1954), Italy. "Slow" neutron nuclear reactions [1934].

1939 **Ernest O. Lawrence** (1901–1958), U.S. Cyclotron [1932].

1940–42 No award.

1943 **Otto Stern** (1888–1969), Germany-U.S. Discovery of proton's magnetic moment [1920].

1944 **Isidor I. Rabi** (1898–1988), U.S. Magnetic moment recording by resonance method [1937].

1945 **Wolfgang Pauli** (1900–1958), Germany-Switzerland. Exclusion principle [1925].

1946 **Percy Bridgman** (1882–1961), U.S. High-pressure physics [1909–30s].

1947 **Edward Appleton** (1892–1965), Britain. Discovery of ionosphere [1924].

1948 **Patrick M. S. Blackett** (1897–1974), Britain. Cloud chamber improvement and cosmic ray research [1933].

1949 **Hideki Yukawa** (1907–1981), Japan. Prediction of meson [1935].

1950 **Cecil Powell** (1903–1969), Britain. Discovery of pi-meson [1947].

1951 **John Cockcroft** (1897–1967), Britain, and **Ernest T. S. Walton** (1903–1995), Ireland. First accelerator [1932].

1952 **Felix Bloch** (1905–1983), Switzerland-U.S., and **Edward M. Purcell** (1912–1997), U.S. Independently, new methods of nuclear magnetic resonance or NMR [c. 1945].

1953 **Frits Zernike** (1888–1966), Netherlands. Phase-contrast microscope [c. 1932].

1954 **Max Born** (1882–1970), Germany. Statistical interpretation of quantum theory [1926].

Walther Bothe (1891–1957), Germany. "Coincidence" method [1924].

1955 **Willis E. Lamb** (1913–), U.S. New measurement of hydrogen spectrum ("Lamb shift") [1947].

Polykarp Kusch (1911–1993), U.S. New measurement of electron magnetic moment [1947].

1956 **John Bardeen** (1908–1991), **Walter H. Brattain** (1902–1987), and **William B. Shockley** (1910–1989), U.S. Transistor [1948–49].

1957 **Chen Ning Yang** (1922–) and **Tsung-Dao Lee** (1926–), China-U.S. Theory that parity not conserved in weak interactions [1956].

1958 **Pavel Cherenkov** (1904–1990), **Igor Tamm** (1895–1971), and **Ilya Frank** (1908–1990), all USSR. "Cherenkov effect" [1935–37].

1959 **Emilio Segrè** (1905–1989), Italy-U.S., and **Owen Chamberlain** (1920–), U.S. Discovery of antiproton [1955].

1960 **Donald Glaser** (1926–), U.S. Bubble chamber [1952].

1961 **Robert Hofstadter** (1915–1990), U.S. Nucleon structure [1955].

Rudolf Mössbauer (1929–), Germany. Resonance absorption [1958].

1962 **Lev Landau** (1908–1968), USSR. Theory of superfluidity [c. 1941].

1963 **Eugene Wigner** (1902–1995), Hungary-U.S. Nuclear theory [1927–32].

Maria Goeppert Mayer (1906–1972), Germany-U.S., and **Johannes Hans Daniel Jensen** (1907–1973), Germany. Independently, nuclear shell model [1948].

1964 **Nikolai G. Basov** (1922–) and **Aleksandr M. Prokhorov** (1916–), USSR; **Charles H. Townes** (1915–), U.S. Work leading to maser and laser [1952–54].

1965 **Richard P. Feynman** (1918–1988), U.S. [1949]; **Julian S. Schwinger** (1918–1994), U.S. [1948]; **Shinichiro Tomonaga** (1906–1979), Japan [1945]. Independent contributions to renormalizing of quantum electrodynamics or QED.

1966 **Alfred Kastler** (1902–1984), France. Optical study of resonance in atoms [by 1950].

1967 **Hans Bethe** (1906–), Germany-U.S. Explanation of nuclear reactions in stars [1938].

1968 **Luis Alvarez** (1911–1988), U.S. Improved bubble chamber [1962].

1969 **Murray Gell-Mann** (1929–), U.S. "Eightfold" particle classifying [1962–64].

1970 **Hannes O. Alfvén** (1908–1995), Sweden. Plasma physics [c. 1948].

Louis Néel (1904–), France. Solid-state magnetism [1932–48].

1971 **Dennis Gabor** (1900–1979), Hungary-Britain. Holograph [1948].

1972 **John Bardeen** (1908–1991), **John Robert Schrieffer** (1931–), and **Leon N. Cooper** (1930–), all U.S. Superconductivity theory [1957].

1973   **Leo Esaki** (1925–), Japan, and **Ivar Giaever** (1929–), Norway-U.S. Independent work on quantum tunneling phenomenon [1958–60].

Brian Josephson (1940–), Britain. Superconducting tunneling [1962].

1974   **Antony Hewish** (1924–), Britain. Discovery of pulsars [1967].

Martin Ryle (1918–1984), Britain. Improvements in radio astronomy [1954].

1975   **James Rainwater** (1917–1986), U.S. [1950]; **Aage Bohr** (1922–), Denmark [1953], and **Ben Mottelson** (1926–), U.S.-Denmark [1953]. Inclusive model of nuclear shell.

1976   **Burton Richter** (1931–) and **Samuel Ting** (1936–), U.S. Independent discovery of J/psi meson (charm quark) [1974].

1977   **John Van Vleck** (1899–1980), U.S. Paramagnetic theory [1932].

Philip Anderson (1923–), U.S., and **Nevill Mott** (1905–1996), Britain. Amorphous superconductors [1960s].

1978   **Pyotr Kapitsa** (1894–1984), USSR. Discovery of superconductivity [1937–38].

Arno Penzias (1933–), and **Robert W. Wilson** (1936–), U.S. Discovery of cosmic background radiation [1965].

1979   **Sheldon Glashow** (1932–), U.S. [1960], **Steven Weinberg** (1933–), U.S. [1967], and **Abdus Salam** (1926–1996), Pakistan-Britain [1967]. Independent development of electroweak theory.

1980   **James Cronin** (1931–) and **Val L. Fitch** (1923–), U.S. Theory of CP parity violation [1964].

1981   **Nicolaas Bloembergen** (1920–), Netherlands-U.S., and **Arthur Schawlow** (1921–1999), U.S. Laser spectroscopy [1950s].

Kai M. Siegbahn (1918–), Sweden. Electron spectroscopy [1950s].

1982   **Kenneth Wilson** (1936–), U.S. Phase transition theory [1970].

1983   **Subrahmanyan Chandrasekhar** (1910–1995), India-U.S. White dwarf structure [1934].

William A. Fowler (1911–1995), U.S. Nuclear reactions in element formation in space [c. 1960].

1984   **Carlo Rubbia** (1934–), Italy-U.S., and **Simon van der Meer** (1925–), Netherlands. W and Z particles of electroweak force [1983].

1985   **Klaus von Klitzing** (1943–), Germany. Quantum Hall effect [1980].

1986   **Gerd Binnig** (1947–), Germany, and **Heinrich Rohrer** (1933–), Switzerland. Scanning tunnel microscope [1981].

Ernst Ruska (1906–1988), Germany. Electron microscopy [1933].

1987   **Karl Alexander Müller** (1927–), Switzerland, and **Johannes Georg Bednorz** (1950–), Germany. High-temperature super-conductivity [1986].

1988   **Leon Lederman** (1922–), **Melvin Schwartz** (1932–), and **Jack Steinberger** (1921–), U.S. Experimental finding of second neutrino [1962].

1989   **Norman Ramsey** (1915–), U.S. Cesium atomic clock [1950s].

Wolfgang Paul (1913–1993), Germany [1950s], and **Hans Georg Dehmelt** (1922–), Germany-U.S. [1973]. Ion trapping.

1990   **Henry W. Kendall** (1926–1999), U.S., **Richard E. Taylor** (1929–), Canada, and **Jerome Friedman** (1930–), U.S. Confirmation of quarks [1967–73].

1991   **Pierre-Gilles de Gennes** (1932–), France. Liquid crystals [1974].

1992   **Georges Charpak** (1924–), Poland-France. Wire chamber detector [1970s].

1993   **Russell Hulse** (1950–) and **Joseph H. Taylor** (1941–), U.S. Discovery and measurement of first binary pulsar [1974].

1994   **Clifford G. Shull** (1915–), U.S., and **Bertram N. Brockhouse** (1918–), Canada. Independently, neutron scattering techniques [c. 1960].

1995   **Martin Perl** (1927–), U.S. Tau lepton [1974].

Frederick Reines (1918–1998), U.S. First neutrino [1956].

1996   **David M. Lee** (1931–), **Robert C. Richardson** (1945–), and **Douglas Osheroff** (1945–), U.S. He-3 superfluid [1972].

1997   **William Phillips** (1948–) and **Steven Chu** (1948–), U.S.; **Claude Cohen-Tannoudji** (1933–), France. Atom trapping [1980s].

1998   **Daniel Tsui** (1939–), U.S., and **Horst L. Störmer** (1949–), Germany-U.S.; **Robert Laughlin** (1950–), U.S. Independently, fractional quantum Hall effect [1982].

1999   **Martinus J. G. Veltman** (1937–) and **Gerardus 't Hooft** (1945–), Netherlands. Renormalization of electroweak theory [1960–70s].

2000   **Zhores Alferov** (1930–), Russia, **Jack S. Kilby** (1923–), U.S., and **Herbert Kroemer** (1928–), Germany-U.S. Basic information and communications technology, using rapid transistors and integrated circuits.

CHEMISTRY

1901   **Jacobus van't Hoff** (1852–1911), Netherlands. Chemical dynamics [1884].

1902   **Emil Fischer** (1852–1919), Germany. Sugar, purine synthesis [1882–98].

1903   **Svante Arrhenius** (1859–1927), Sweden. Electrolytic dissociation [1884–87].

1904   **William Ramsay** (1852–1916), Britain. Discovery of inert elements [1894–1904].

1905   **Adolf von Baeyer** (1835–1917), Germany. Research on organic dyes [1870s].

1906   **Henri Moissan** (1852–1907), France. Isolation of fluorine [c. 1886].

1907   **Eduard Buchner** (1860–1917), Germany. Cell-free fermentation [1897].

1908   **Ernest Rutherford** (1871–1937), New Zealand-Britain. Transmutation of elements [1902].

1909   **Wilhelm Ostwald** (1853–1932), Germany. Chemical equilibria and reaction rates [1880s].

1910   **Otto Wallach** (1847–1931), Germany. Alicylic compounds [1880s].

1911   **Marie Skłodowska Curie** (1867–1934), Poland-France. Discovery of radium and polonium [1898].

1912   **Victor Grignard** (1871–1935), France. Grignard reagent [1901].

       Paul Sabatier (1854–1941), France. Catalytic hydrocarbon syntheses [1897].

1913   **Alfred Werner** (1866–1919), Switzerland. New valence theory for inorganic chemistry [1893].

1914   **Theodore Richards** (1868–1928), U.S. Measurement of atomic weights [1890s–1912].

1915   **Richard Willstätter** (1872–1942), Germany. Explanation of chlorophyll [1905–14].

1916–17   No award.

1918   **Fritz Haber** (1868–1934), Germany. Ammonia process [1901–8].

1919   No award.

1920   **Walther Nernst** (1864–1941), Germany. Thermodynamics and heat theorem [1889–1906].

1921   **Frederick Soddy** (1877–1956), Britain. Discovery of radioactive isotopes [1913].

1922   **Francis Aston** (1877–1945), Britain. Discovery of nonradioactive isotopes; mass spectroscope [1919].

1923   **Fritz Pregl** (1869–1930), Austria. Microanalysis [1913].

1924   No award.

1925   **Richard Zsigmondy** (1865–1929), Austria. Ultramicroscope. [1903].

1926   **Theodor Svedberg** (1884–1971), Sweden. Ultracentrifuge [1923–24].

1927   **Heinrich Wieland** (1877–1957), Germany. Bile acid structure [1912].

1928 **Adolf Windaus** (1876–1959), Germany. Structure of sterols and link to vitamins [1919].

1929 **Arthur Harden** (1865–1940), Britain. Fermentative enzyme research [1904–5].

Hans von Euler-Chelpin (1873–1964), Sweden. Yeast enzyme [1924–28].

1930 **Hans Fischer** (1881–1945), Germany. Hemin synthesis [1929].

1931 **Carl Bosch** (1874–1930), Germany. Improvement of Haber process [1910].

Friedrich Bergius (1884–1949), Germany. High pressure chemistry [1913].

1932 **Irving Langmuir** (1881–1957), U.S. Surface chemistry [c. 1916].

1933 No award.

1934 **Harold C. Urey** (1893–1981), U.S. "Heavy hydrogen" [1931].

1935 **Frédéric Joliot-Curie** (1900–1958) and **Irène Joliot-Curie** (1897–1956), France. Artificial radioactivity [1934].

1936 **Peter Debye** (1884–1966), Netherlands. Atomic dipole moments [c. 1912–16].

1937 **Walter Haworth** (1883–1950), Britain. Vitamin C [1932].

Paul Karrer (1889–1971), Switzerland. Vitamin A [1930–35].

1938 **Richard Kuhn** (1900–1967), Germany. Carotenes and vitamin B_2 [1931–36].

1939 **Adolf Butenandt** (1903–1994), Germany. Sex hormones [1931–35].

Leopold Ružička (1887–1976), Croatia-Switzerland. Complex terpenes and relation to bile and sex hormones [1920s].

1940–42 No award.

1943 **George de Hevesy** (1885–1966), Hungary-Denmark. Isotope tracers [1934].

1944 **Otto Hahn** (1879–1968), Germany. Theory of fission of heavy nuclei [1939].

1945   **Artturi Virtanen** (1895–1973), Finland. Agricultural chemistry [1920–30s].

1946   **James B. Sumner** (1887–1955), U.S. Crystallizing of enzyme, shown to be a protein [1926].

        John H. Northrop (1891–1987), U.S. Confirmation of Sumner [1930s].

        Wendell M. Stanley (1904–1971), U.S. Crystallizing of first virus [1935].

1947   **Robert Robinson** (1886–1975), Britain. Alkaloid research [1917–20s].

1948   **Arne Tiselius** (1902–1971), Sweden. Electrophoresis [1936].

1949   **William Giauque** (1895–1982), U.S. Adiabatic process [1924–32].

1950   **Otto Diels** (1876–1954) and **Kurt Alder** (1902–1958), Germany. Diene synthesis [1928].

1951   **Edwin McMillan** (1907–1991) and **Glenn Seaborg** (1912–1999), U.S. First artificial elements, beyond uranium [1940–44].

1952   **Archer J. P. Martin** (1910–) and **Richard L. M. Synge** (1914–1994), Britain. Partition chromatography [1944].

1953   **Hermann Staudinger** (1881–1965), Germany. Theory of macromolecules [1920s].

1954   **Linus Pauling** (1901–1994), U.S. Quantum chemical bonding theory [1928–32].

1955   **Vincent du Vigneaud** (1901–1978), U.S. Polypeptide hormone synthesis [1953].

1956   **Nikolai Semenov** (1896–1986), USSR, and **Cyril Hinshelwood** (1897–1967), Britain. Collaborated on chemical chain reactions [1928–40].

1957   **Alexander Todd** (1907–1997), Britain. Nucleotides [1940–50s].

1958   **Frederick Sanger** (1918–), Britain. First analysis of a protein [1943–55].

1959   **Jaroslav Heyrovsky** (1890–1967), Czechoslovakia. Polarography [1922].

1960   **Willard Libby** (1908–1980), U.S. Carbon-14 dating [1947].

1961   **Melvin Calvin** (1911–1997), U.S. Carbon dioxide assimilation in plants [1953].

1962   **Max Perutz** (1914–), Austria-Britain. Analysis of hemoglobin [1938–59].

   John Kendrew (1917–1997), Britain. Analysis of myoglobin [1946–59].

1963   **Karl Ziegler** (1898–1973), Germany [1952], and **Giulio Natta** (1903–1979), Italy [1954]. Artificial polymers.

1964   **Dorothy Crowfoot Hodgkin** (1910–1994), Britain. X-ray analysis of vitamin B_{12} and penicillin [1940–50s].

1965   **Robert B. Woodward** (1917–1979), U.S. Organic syntheses [1940s–1950s].

1966   **Robert S. Mulliken** (1896–1986), U.S. Molecular orbital bonding theory [1930s].

1967   **Manfred Eigen** (1927–), Germany; **Ronald Norrish** (1897–1978) and **George Porter** (1920–), Britain. Studies of very fast chemical reactions [1950s].

1968   **Lars Onsager** (1903–1976), Norway-U.S. Thermodynamics of irreversible processes [1930s].

1969   **Odd Hassel** (1897–1981), Norway. "Chair" configurations [1930s].

   Derek Barton (1918–1998), Britain. Conformational analysis [1950–98].

1970   **Luis Leloir** (1906–1987), Argentina. Carbohydrate biosynthesis [1957].

1971   **Gerhard Herzberg** (1904–1999), Germany-Canada. Clarification of free radicals [1950s].

1972   **William H. Stein** (1911–1980) and **Stanford Moore** (1913–1982), U.S. Sequence structure of RNA enzyme [1939–60].

   Christian Anfinsen (1916–1995), U.S. Ribonuclease configuration [1950s].

1973   **Geoffrey Wilkinson** (1921–1996), Britain [1952], and **Ernst Otto Fischer** (1918–), Germany [1951]. Independent explanation of organometallic compounds.

1974   **Paul Flory** (1910–1985), U.S. Macromolecules [1948].

1975   **John Cornforth** (1917–), Australia-Britain. Stereochemistry of enzyme-catalyzed reactions [1950s].

       Vladimir Prelog (1906–1998), Yugoslavia-Switzerland. Molecule stereochemistry [c. 1947].

1976   **William Lipscomb** (1919–), U.S. Theory of three-center chemical bonding [1950s].

1977   **Ilya Prigogine** (1917–), Belgium. Nonequilibrium thermodynamics [1950–60s].

1978   **Peter Mitchell** (1920–1992), Britain. Chemiosmotic theory [1961].

1979   **Herbert C. Brown** (1912–), U.S. Hydroboration [1955].

       Georg Wittig (1897–1987), Germany. Rearrangement reaction [1950s].

1980   **Paul Berg** (1926–), U.S. Recombinant DNA [1956].

       Frederick Sanger (1918–), Britain. Base sequence of chromosome [1977].

       Walter Gilbert (1932–), U.S. Base sequence in DNA [1970].

1981   **Kenichi Fukui** (1918–1998), Japan. "Frontier" orbital theory [1960s].

       Roald Hoffmann (1937–), Poland-U.S. Molecular orbital theory for organic reactions [1965–69].

1982   **Aaron Klug** (1926–), South Africa-Britain. Crystallographic electron microscopy [1968].

1983   **Henry Taube** (1915–), Canada-U.S. Electron transfer in metal complexes [1954].

1984   **Robert Bruce Merrifield** (1921–), U.S. Automatized synthesis of amino acids [1962–65].

1985   **Herbert A. Hauptman** (1917–) and **Jerome Karle** (1918–), U.S. Mathematical methods of analyzing molecules [1950].

1986   **Dudley Herschbach** (1932–), U.S., and **Yuan Tseh Lee** (1936–), Taiwan-U.S. Molecular collision methods [1967].

       John C. Polanyi (1929–), Hungary-Canada. Chemiluminescence method [1967].

1987 Charles J. Pedersen (1904–1989) and Donald J. Cram (1919–), U.S.; Jean-Marie Lehn (1939–), France. Independent development of "host-guest" chemistry [1960–70s].

1988 Hartmut Michel (1948–), Robert Huber (1937–), and Johann Deisenhofer (1943–), Germany. Three-dimensional structure of proteins in photosynthesis [1982–85].

1989 Sidney Altman (1939–), Canada-U.S., and Thomas Cech (1947–), U.S. Independent discovery of catalytic properties of RNA [1978–81].

1990 Elias James Corey (1928–), U.S. Synthesis of complex molecules for medical use [1960s].

1991 Richard R. Ernst (1933–), Switzerland. NMR spectroscopy [1970].

1992 Rudolf A. Marcus (1923–), Canada-U.S. Mathematics of electron transfer [1956–65].

1993 Kary B. Mullis (1944–), U.S. Polymerase chain reaction [1983].

Michael Smith (1932–), Britain-Canada. Genetic engineering [1978].

1994 George A. Olah (1927–), Hungary-U.S. Hydrocarbon research [1960s].

1995 Paul Crutzen (1933–), Netherlands-Sweden. Demonstration of damage to ozone from nitrogen oxides [1970s].

Mario Molina (1943–), Mexico-U.S., and Frank Sherwood Rowland (1927–), U.S. Chlorofluorocarbon threat to ozone [1974].

1996 Robert F. Curl Jr. (1933–), U.S., Harold Kroto (1939–), Britain, and Richard E. Smalley (1943–), U.S. Carbon-60 molecule ("buckyball") [1985].

1997 Paul D. Boyer (1918–), U.S. [1950s], Jens C. Skou (1918–), Denmark [1957], and John E. Walker (1941–), Britain [1980–90s]. New models of ATP enzyme.

1998 Walter Kohn (1923–), U.S. [1964], and John A. Pople (1925–), Britain [1970]. Computer means to predict reactions.

1999   **Ahmed H. Zewail** (1946–), Egypt-U.S. Femtosecond spectroscopy, bonding theory [1980s].

2000   **Alan J. Heeger** (1936–), U.S., **Alan G. MacDiarmid** (1927–), U.S., and **Hideti Shirakaw** (1936–), Japan. Development of conductive polymers.

PHYSIOLOGY OR MEDICINE

1901   **Emil von Behring** (1854–1917), Germany. Immunization against tetanus, diphtheria [1890–91].

1902   **Ronald Ross** (1857–1932), Britain. Work on malaria vector [1897–98].

1903   **Niels Finsen** (1860–1904), Denmark. Phototherapy [1893–94].

1904   **Ivan Pavlov** (1849–1936), Russia. Digestive physiology [1890s].

1905   **Robert Koch** (1843–1910), Germany. Discovery of and test for tuberculosis pathogen [1880–90s].

1906   **Camillo Golgi** (1843–1926), Italy. Discovery of nerve synapses [1873].

   Santiago Ramón y Cajal (1852–1934), Spain. Structure of nervous system [1887].

1907   **Charles-Louis-Alphonse Laveran** (1845–1922), France. Malaria cause [1882].

1908   **Elie Metchnikoff** (1845–1916), Russia-France. Phagocytes [1882].

   Paul Ehrlich (1854–1915), Germany. Chemotherapy [1890s].

1909   **Emil Theodor Kocher** (1841–1917), Switzerland. Thyroid gland discoveries [1880s].

1910   **Albrecht Kossel** (1853–1927), Germany. Cell chemistry of proteins and nucleic acids [c. 1880].

1911   **Allvar Gullstrand** (1862–1930), Sweden. Eye dioptrics [c. 1896].

1912   **Alexis Carrel** (1873–1944), France. Vascular suturing [1906–10].

1913   **Charles Richet** (1850–1935), France. Anaphylaxis [1901–3]

1914   **Robert Bárány** (1876–1936), Austria. Inner ear physiology [c. 1910].

1915–18   No award.

1919   **Jules Bordet** (1870–1961), Belgium. Immunity findings [1896–1906].

1920   **August Krogh** (1874–1949), Denmark. Capillary mechanism [1915–20].

1921   No award.

1922   **Archibald V. Hill** (1886–1977), Britain. Muscular heat [c. 1920].

   Otto Meyerhof (1884–1951), Germany. Muscle metabolism [c. 1920].

1923   **Frederick Banting** (1891–1941), Canada, and **John J. R. Macleod** (1876–1935), Britain. Discovery of insulin [1922].

1924   **Willem Einthoven** (1860–1927), Netherlands. Electrocardiogram [1901].

1925   No award.

1926   **Johannes Fibiger** (1867–1928), Denmark. Theory of cancer cure [1913].

1927   **Julius Wagner-Jauregg** (1857–1940), Austria. Inoculative treatment of paresis [1917].

1928   **Charles Nicolle** (1866–1936), France. Typhus cause [1902].

1929   **Christiaan Eijkman** (1858–1930), Netherlands. Beriberi cause [1897].

   Frederick G. Hopkins (1861–1947), Britain. Vitamin factors [1906–12].

1930   **Karl Landsteiner** (1868–1943), Austria. Blood types [1901].

1931   **Otto Warburg** (1883–1970), Germany. Respiratory enzyme [1920s].

1932   **Charles S. Sherrington** (1857–1952), Britain. Integrative action of nervous system [1900s].

       Edgar D. Adrian (1889–1977), Britain. Nerve impulse research [1920s].

1933   **Thomas H. Morgan** (1866–1945), U.S. Chromosome role in heredity [1911–1930s].

1934   **George H. Whipple** (1878–1976), **George R. Minot** (1885–1950), and **William P. Murphy** (1892–1987), U.S. Liver therapy for anemia [1920s].

1935   **Hans Spemann** (1869–1941), Germany. Organizer effect in embryonic development [c. 1922].

1936   **Otto Loewi** (1873–1961), Germany-U.S. [1921], and **Henry Dale** (1875–1968), Britain [1929–36]. Independent explorations of chemical transmission of nerve impulses.

1937   **Albert von Szent-Györgyi** (1893–1986), Hungary-U.S. Vitamin C [1930s].

1938   **Corneille Heymans** (1892–1968), Belgium. Sinus and aortic mechanisms in respiration [1924–27].

1939   **Gerhard Domagk** (1895–1964), Germany. First sulfa drug [1932–35].

1940–42   No award.

1943   **C. P. Henrik Dam** (1895–1976), Denmark. Vitamin K [1935].

       Edward A. Doisy (1893–1986), U.S. Synthesized vitamin K [1940].

1944   **Joseph Erlanger** (1874–1965) and **Herbert Gasser** (1888–1963), U.S. Differentiation of nerve fiber properties [1921–32].

1945   **Alexander Fleming** (1881–1955), Britain. Penicillin [1928].

       Ernst Chain (1906–1979), Germany-Britain, and **Howard W. Florey** (1898–1968), Britain. Purified penicillin as antibiotic [1938–41].

1946   **Hermann J. Muller** (1890–1967), U.S. X-ray mutations [1926].

1947   **Gerty Cori** (1896–1957) and **Carl Ferdinand Cori** (1896–1984), Czechoslovakia-U.S. Catalytic conversion of glycogen [1930s].

Bernardo Houssay (1887–1971), Argentina. Hormone role in sugar metabolism [1920s].

1948   **Paul H. Müller** (1899–1965), Switzerland. DDT [c. 1939].

1949   **Walter R. Hess** (1881–1973), Switzerland. Interbrain findings [1925–48].

António Egas Moniz (1874–1955), Portugal. Lobotomy [1935].

1950   **Edward C. Kendall** (1886–1972) and **Philip S. Hench** (1896–1965), U.S. Cortisone isolated [Kendall, 1930s] and applied to arthritis [Hench, 1940s].

Tadeus Reichstein (1897–1996), Poland-Switzerland. Independent research on cortisone [1930s].

1951   **Max Theiler** (1899–1972), South Africa-U.S. Yellow fever cause [1937].

1952   **Selman Waksman** (1888–1972), Russia-U.S. Streptomycin [1943].

1953   **Hans A. Krebs** (1900–1981), Germany-Britain. Citric acid cycle [1937].

Fritz Lipmann (1899–1986), Germany-U.S. Coenzyme-A [1947].

1954   **John Enders** (1897–1985), **Thomas H. Weller** (1915–), and **Frederick C. Robbins** (1916–), U.S. Studies of polio virus growth [1947–48].

1955   **Axel Theorell** (1903–1982), Sweden. Oxidation enzymes [1930s].

1956   **Werner Forssmann** (1904–1979), Germany. Heart catheterization [1929].

André Cournand (1895–1988), France-U.S., and **Dickinson W. Richards** (1895–1973), U.S. Improvement of catheter [1929–40s].

1957   **Daniel Bovet** (1907–1992), Switzerland-Italy. Antihistamines [1937].

1958   **George W. Beadle** (1903–1989) and **Edward L. Tatum** (1909–1975), U.S. One-gene-one-enzyme law [1940s].

Joshua Lederberg (1925–), U.S. Proof that chromosomal matter passes between cells [1952].

1959   **Severo Ochoa** (1905–1993), Spain-U.S. Enzymes in catalysis of nucleic acid molecules [1955].

Arthur Kornberg (1918–), U.S. Enzymes in synthesis of DNA [1953].

1960   **Frank Macfarlane Burnet** (1899–1985), Australia. Immunological tolerance [1940s].

Peter B. Medawar (1915–1987), Britain. Application of Burnet's theory to transplants [1953].

1961   **Georg von Békésy** (1899–1972), Hungary-U.S. Cochlea mechanism [1950s].

1962   **Francis Crick** (1916–), Britain, and **James D. Watson** (1928–), U.S. Double-helix structure of DNA [1953].

Maurice Wilkins (1916–), Britain. X-ray crystallography in double-helix discovery [1950s].

1963   **Alan Hodgkin** (1914–1998) and **Andrew Fielding Huxley** (1917–), Britain. Electrical network in nervous system [1940s].

John C. Eccles (1903–1997), Australia. Measurement of electrical transmission in synapses [1951].

1964   **Konrad E. Bloch** (1912–), Germany-U.S., and **Feodor F. Lynen** (1911–1979), Germany. Cholesterol mechanism [1930s].

1965   **André Lwoff** (1902–1994), France. Bacteriophage [1930s].

François Jacob (1920–) and **Jacques L. Monod** (1910–1976), France. "Messenger" RNA [1950s].

1966   **Francis Peyton Rous** (1879–1970), U.S. Virus as a cause of cancer [1911].

Charles B. Huggins (1901–1997), Canada-U.S. Hormone therapy of prostate cancer [1941].

1967   **Ragnar Granit** (1900–1991), Finland-Sweden. Electrical properties of vision [1930s].

George Wald (1906–1997), U.S. Proof of Granit's theory [1950s].

Haldan Hartline (1903–1983), U.S. Retinal neurons [1950s].

1968 **Marshall Nirenberg** (1927–), U.S. Base triplet of gene sequence [1961].

Robert W. Holley (1922–1993), U.S. Nucleotide sequence of tRNA [1958–65].

Har Gobind Khorana (1922–), India-U.S. Synthesis of all 64 triplets of genetic code [1960].

1969 **Max Delbrück** (1906–1981), Germany-U.S., and **Salvador Luria** (1912–1991), Italy-U.S. Proof that viruses recombine genetic material [1943].

Alfred D. Hershey (1908–1997), U.S. Proof that DNA carries genetic information [1952].

1970 **Bernhard Katz** (1911–), Germany-Britain. [1954], **Ulf S. von Euler** (1905–1983), Sweden [1946], and **Julius Axelrod** (1912–), U.S. [1950s]. Electrical mechanisms of nervous system.

1971 **Earl W. Sutherland Jr.** (1915–1974), U.S. Hormonal action [1950s].

1972 **Rodney Porter** (1917–1985), Britain, and **Gerald Edelman** (1929–), U.S. Independently, biochemistry of immunology [1959–62].

1973 **Karl von Frisch** (1886–1982), Austria, **Konrad Lorenz** (1903–1989), Austria-Germany, and **Nikolaas Tinbergen** (1907–1988), Netherlands-Britain. Ethology [1920s–1930s].

1974 **Albert Claude** (1898–1983), Belgium. RNA in viruses as cause of cancer [1930s].

Christian de Duve (1917–), Belgium. Transmission of amino acids in cells [1950].

George Palade (1912–), Romania-U.S. Ribosome, site of protein synthesis [1956].

1975 **Howard Temin** (1934–1994), U.S., and **Renato Dulbecco** (1914–), Italy-U.S.; **David Baltimore** (1938–), U.S. Independently, proof that RNA can copy itself back into DNA [1970].

1976   **Baruch S. Blumberg** (1925–), U.S. Spread of infectious diseases, especially hepatitis [1960s].

        D. Carleton Gajdusek (1923–), U.S. Possible new group of virus diseases [1968].

1977   **Roger Guillemin** (1924–), France-U.S., and **Andrew V. Schally** (1926–), Poland-U.S. Independent work on production of peptide hormones in brain [1966–71].

        Rosalyn Yalow (1921–), U.S. Radioimmunoassay method [1950s].

1978   **Werner Arber** (1929–), Switzerland [1962]; **Daniel Nathans** (1928–1999) and **Hamilton Smith** (1931–), U.S. [1968]. Cutting of DNA by enzymes.

1979   **Allan M. Cormack** (1924–1998), South Africa-U.S. [1963]; **Godfrey Hounsfield** (1919–), Britain [1973]. Independent development of computer-assisted tomography (CAT scan).

1980   **George D. Snell** (1903–1996), U.S. [1930s]; **Jean Dausset** (1916–), France [1952]; **Baruj Benacerraf** (1920–), Venezuela-U.S. [1960s]. Influence of genetics of cell surface on immunology.

1981   **Roger W. Sperry** (1913–1994), U.S. Left-right brain hemispheres [1950s].

        David H. Hubel (1926–), Canada-U.S., and **Torsten N. Wiesel** (1924–), Sweden-U.S. Brain's visual cortex [1960s].

1982   **Sune K. Bergström** (1916–) and **Bengt Samuelsson** (1934–), Sweden. Prostaglandin research [1950s–60s].

        John R. Vane (1927–), Britain. Effect of prostaglandins on blood vessels [1950s].

1983   **Barbara McClintock** (1902–1992), U.S. Mobile genetic elements [1940s].

1984   **Niels K. Jerne** (1911–1994), Britain-Denmark. Advances in immunology [1955–73]. **Georges Köhler** (1946–1995), Germany, and **César Milstein** (1927–), Argentina-Britain. Theory of monoclonal antibodies [1975].

1985   **Michael S. Brown** (1941–) and **Joseph Goldstein** (1940–), U.S. Cholesterol mechanisms [1972–73].

1986   **Stanley Cohen** (1922–), U.S., and **Rita Levi-Montalcini** (1909–), Italy-U.S. Nerve growth factors [1950s].

1987   **Susumu Tonegawa** (1939–), Japan-U.S. Genetics of antibody diversity [1970s].

1988   **James W. Black** (1924–), Britain. Beta-blockers [1950s].

Gertrude Elion (1918–1999) and **George H. Hitchings** (1905–1998), U.S. Design of new pharmaceuticals [1950s].

1989   **John Michael Bishop** (1936–) and **Harold E. Varmus** (1939–), U.S. Cell origin of retroviral oncogenes [1976].

1990   **Joseph E. Murray** (1919–) and **Edward Donnall Thomas** (1920–), U.S. Independent progress in kidney and bone marrow transplants [1950s].

1991   **Erwin Neher** (1944–) and **Bert Sakmann** (1942–), Germany. Passage of electricity through ion membrane [mid-1970s].

1992   **Edmond H. Fischer** (1920–), France-U.S., and **Edwin G. Krebs** (1918–), U.S. Enzyme activity and cancer [1950–60s].

1993   **Richard J. Roberts** (1943–), Britain-U.S., and **Phillip A. Sharp** (1944–), U.S. Independent discovery of "nonsense" segments in gene messages [1977].

1994   **Martin Rodbell** (1925–1998) and **Alfred G. Gilman** (1941–), U.S. Independent discovery of G-proteins [1960s].

1995   **Edward Lewis** (1918–), U.S., **Christiane Nüsslein-Volhard** (1942–), Germany, and **Eric Wieschaus** (1947–), U.S. Mechanism of genetic birth defects [1970s–80s].

1996   **Peter C. Doherty** (1940–), Australia, and **Rolf Zinkernagel** (1944–), Switzerland. Immune system recognition of virus-infected cells [1970s].

1997   **Stanley Prusiner** (1942–), U.S. Theory of prions [1970s–80s].

1998   **Robert Furchgott** (1916–), **Louis J. Ignarro** (1941–), and **Ferid Murad** (1936–), U.S. Independent discoveries in cell signal transmission [1977–80].

1999   **Günther Blobel** (1936–), Germany-U.S. Signal mechanisms of protein movement in cells. [1980s]

2000   **Arvid Carlsson** (1923–), Sweden, **Paul Greengard** (1925–), and **Eric Kandel** (1929–), U.S. Signal transduction in the nervous system.

PEACE

1901   **Henri Dunant** (1828–1910), Switzerland. Red Cross [1863].

     Frédéric Passy (1822–1912), France. First French peace society [1867].

1902   **Elie Ducommun** (1833–1906), Switzerland. International Peace Bureau.

     Charles Gobat (1843–1914), Switzerland. Interparliamentary Union [1892].

1903   **William R. Cremer** (1828–1908), Britain. Workingmen's Peace Association [1870].

1904   **Institute of International Law** (founded 1873), Geneva.

1905   **Bertha Kinsky von Suttner** (1843–1914), Austria. Pacifist leadership and writings.

1906   **Theodore Roosevelt** (1858–1919), U.S. Russo-Japanese treaty [1905].

1907   **Ernesto Moneta** (1833–1918), Italy. International Peace Congress [1906].

     Louis Renault (1843–1918), France. Contributions to Hague Conferences.

1908   **Klas Arnoldson** (1844–1916), Sweden. Swedish neutrality, Norwegian independence.

     Fredrik Bajer (1837–1922), Denmark. Danish Peace Society.

1909   **Auguste Beernaert** (1829–1912), Belgium. Peace efforts.

     Paul d'Estournelles de Constant (1852–1924), France. Association for International Conciliation [1905].

1910   **Permanent International Peace Bureau** (founded 1891), Bern.

1911   **Tobias Asser** (1838–1913), Netherlands. Hague Conferences [1893–1904].

     Alfred Fried (1864–1921), Austria. Peace societies and journals.

1912   **Elihu Root** (1845–1937), U.S. Peace negotiations as secretary of state.

1913   Henri LaFontaine (1854–1943), Belgium. Peace activism.

1914–16   No award.

1917   **International Committee of the Red Cross.** War relief work.

1918   No award.

1919   **Woodrow Wilson** (1856–1924), U.S. Cofounding of League of Nations.

1920   **Léon Bourgeois** (1851–1925), France. Work to establish League of Nations.

1921   **Karl Hjalmar Branting** (1860–1925), Sweden. Peace work.

Christian Lange (1869–1938), Norway. Service to Interparliamentary Union.

1922   **Fridtjof Nansen** (1861–1930), Norway. Repatriation of war refugees, Nansen passports [1922].

1923–24   No award.

1925   **J. Austen Chamberlain** (1863–1937), Britain. Locarno Pact [1925].

Charles G. Dawes (1865–1951), U.S. Dawes Plan [1924].

1926   **Aristide Briand** (1862–1932), France. Locarno Pact [1925].

Gustav Stresemann (1878–1929), Germany. Locarno Pact [1925].

1927   **Ferdinand Buisson** (1841–1932), France. League of the Rights of Man [1898].

Ludwig Quidde (1858–1941), Germany. Munich Peace Society, German Peace Cartel.

1928   No award.

1929   **Frank B. Kellogg** (1856–1937), U.S. Kellogg-Briand Pact outlawing war [1928].

1930   **Nathan Söderblom** (1866–1931), Sweden. World Union of Churches [1914].

1931   **Jane Addams** (1860–1935), U.S. Women's International League for Peace and Freedom [1919].

Nicholas Murray Butler (1862–1947), U.S. Carnegie Endowment for International Peace.

1932 No award.

1933 **Norman Angell** (1873–1967), Britain. Book *The Great Illusion* [1909], peace activism.

1934 **Arthur Henderson** (1863–1935), Britain. World Disarmament Conference [1932–34].

1935 **Carl von Ossietzky** (1889–1938), Germany. Journalism protesting German militaristic acts.

1936 **Carlos Saavedra Lamas** (1878–1959), Argentina. South American Antiwar Pact [1933], Bolivia-Paraguay peace [1935].

1937 **E. A. Robert Cecil** (1864–1958), Britain. Peace Ballot [1934], International Peace Campaign [1936].

1938 **Nansen International Office for Refugees** (1921–1939), Geneva.

1939–43 No award.

1944 **International Committee of the Red Cross.** War relief work.

1945 **Cordell Hull** (1871–1955), U.S. Help in founding United Nations.

1946 **Emily Balch** (1867–1961), U.S. Women's peace movements.

John Mott (1865–1955), U.S. Service as head of YMCA [1888–1931] and International Missionary Council [1921–42].

1947 **Friends Service Council** (founded 1927), London, and **American Friends Service Committee** (founded 1917), Philadelphia. War and peacetime relief by Quaker groups.

1948 No award.

1949 **John Boyd Orr** (1880–1971), Britain. World food plan through UN.

1950 **Ralph Bunche** (1904–1971), U.S. UN mediation in 1948 Israeli-Arab war.

1951 **Léon Jouhaux** (1879–1954), France. Founding and leadership of International Labor Organization [1919–51].

1952   **Albert Schweitzer** (1875–1965), France. Humanitarian.

1953   **George C. Marshall** (1880–1959), U.S. Marshall Plan to reconstruct Europe after Second World War.

1954   **Office of UN High Commissioner for Refugees** (founded 1951), Geneva.

1955–56   No award.

1957   **Lester Pearson** (1897–1972), Canada. UN mediation in Suez War [1956].

1958   **Georges Pire** (1910–1969), Belgium. Housing for refugees [1950s].

1959   **Philip Noel-Baker** (1889–1982), Britain. Disarmament activism.

1960   **Albert Luthuli** (1898–1967), South Africa. Leadership of African National Congress in fight against apartheid [1952–1960s].

1961   **Dag Hammarskjöld** (1905–1961), Sweden. UN mediation of Suez crisis [1956] and Congo [1960–61].

1962   **Linus Pauling** (1901–1994), U.S. Campaign for nuclear test ban treaty [1963].

1963   **International Committee of the Red Cross** and **League of Red Cross Societies.**

1964   **Martin Luther King Jr.** (1929–1968), U.S. Civil rights leadership [1955–64].

1965   **UNICEF.**

1966–67   No award.

1968   **René-Samuel Cassin** (1887–1976), France. UN Declaration of Human Rights [1948].

1969   **International Labor Organization** (founded 1919), Geneva.

1970   **Norman Borlaug** (1914–), U.S. Disease-resistant wheat for Green Revolution.

1971   **Willy Brandt** (1913–1992), Germany. De facto recognition of East Germany and mutual renunciation of war [1970].

1972   No award.

1973   **Henry Kissinger** (1923–), Germany-U.S., and **Le Duc Tho** (1911–1990), Vietnam. Cease-fire agreement [1973].

1974   **Sean MacBride** (1904–1988), Ireland. Human rights work. [1961–74].

          Eisaku Sato (1901–1975), Japan. During premiership, stress on international cooperation.

1975   **Andrei Sakharov** (1921–1989), USSR. Human rights activism.

1976   **Betty Williams** (1943–) and **Mairead Corrigan** (1944–), Northern Ireland. Peace People movement [1976].

1977   **Amnesty International** (founded 1961).

1978   **Anwar al-Sadat** (1918–1981), Egypt, and **Menachem Begin** (1913–1992), Israel. Camp David peace treaty [1978].

1979   **Mother Teresa** (1910–1997), Albania-India. Missionaries of Charity, in Calcutta [1950], then worldwide.

1980   **Adolfo Pérez Esquivel** (1931–), Argentina. Protests of abductions by Argentine regime [1970s].

1981   **Office of the UN High Commissioner for Refugees.**

1982   **Alva Myrdal** (1902–1986), Sweden. Disarmament activism.

          Alfonso García Robles (1911–1991), Mexico. Latin-American Treaty for Prohibition of Nuclear Weapons [1967].

1983   **Lech Wałesa** (1943–), Poland. Solidarity movement.

1984   **Desmond Tutu** (1931–), South Africa. Protests against apartheid.

1985   **International Physicians for the Prevention of Nuclear War** (founded 1980).

1986   **Elie Wiesel** (1928–), Romania-France-U.S. Work for oppressed peoples, especially Holocaust victims.

1987   **Oscar Arias Sánchez** (1941–), Costa Rica. Central America peace efforts.

1988   **UN Peacekeeping Forces.**

1989   **Dalai Lama** (1935–), Tibet. Nonviolent campaign to end China's occupation of Tibet.

1990 **Mikhail Gorbachev** (1931–), USSR. During presidency, efforts for peace.

1991 **Aung San Suu Kyi** (1945–), Myanmar (Burma). Opposition to Myanmar regime.

1992 **Rigoberta Menchú** (1959–), Guatemala. Human rights in her country.

1993 **Frederik Willem de Klerk** (1936–) and **Nelson Mandela** (1918–), South Africa. End to apartheid and transfer of political power.

1994 **Yasir Arafat** (1929–), Palestine, and **Shimon Peres** (1923–) and **Yitzhak Rabin** (1922–1995), Israel. Oslo peace accord.

1995 **Pugwash Conferences on Science and World Affairs** (founded 1957) and **Joseph Rotblat** (1908–), Poland-Britain, director of Pugwash.

1996 **Carlos Ximenes Belo** (1948–) and **José Ramos-Horta** (1949–), East Timor. Efforts for peaceful achievement of self-determination in East Timor.

1997 **International Campaign to Ban Landmines** and **Jody Williams** (1950–), U.S., cofounder and coordinator.

1998 **David Trimble** (1944–) and **John Hume** (1937–), Northern Ireland. Peace accords in Northern Ireland.

1999 **Doctors without Borders** (founded 1971).

2000 **Kim Dae Jung** (1924–), South Korea. Efforts toward peace between North and South Korea.

ECONOMICS

1969 **Ragnar Frisch** (1895–1973), Norway. National economic models.

Jan Tinbergen (1903–1994), Netherlands. Models for economic analysis.

1970 **Paul Samuelson** (1915–), U.S. Mathematical contributions to economic analysis.

1971 **Simon Kuznets** (1901–1985), U.S. Gross national product models.

1972   **John R. Hicks** (1904–1989), Britain. Equilibrium theory.

Kenneth Arrow (1921–), U.S. General equilibrium theory.

1973   **Wassily Leontief** (1906–1999), USSR-U.S. Input-output analysis.

1974   **Gunnar Myrdal** (1898–1987), Sweden. Social aspects of economics.

Friedrich von Hayek (1899–1992), Austria-Britain. Theory of capital and social aspects.

1975   **Leonid Kantorovich** (1912–1986), USSR. Linear programming.

Tjalling Koopmans (1910–1985), Netherlands-U.S. Optimum allocation theory.

1976   **Milton Friedman** (1912–), U.S. Monetary theory.

1977   **Bertil Ohlin** (1899–1979), Sweden. International trade.

James E. Meade (1907–1995), Britain. International capital.

1978   **Herbert Simon** (1916–), U.S. Decision-making.

1979   **Theodore Schultz** (1902–1998), U.S. Economic theory for developing countries.

W. Arthur Lewis (1915–1991), West Indies-Britain. Economic theory for developing countries.

1980   **Lawrence R. Klein** (1920–), U.S. National economic models.

1981   **James Tobin** (1918–), U.S. Portfolio selection theory.

1982   **George Stigler** (1911–1991), U.S. Economic regulations.

1983   **Gerard Debreu** (1921–), France-U.S. General equilibrium theory.

1984   **Richard Stone** (1913–1991), Britain. National income accounts.

1985   **Franco Modigliani** (1918–), Italy-U.S. Analysis of saving and markets.

1986   **James M. Buchanan Jr.** (1919–), U.S. "Consent" theory.

1987   **Robert M. Solow** (1924–), U.S. Theory of economic growth.

1988   **Maurice Allais** (1911–), France. Market theory, utilization of resources.

1989   **Trygve Haavelmo** (1911–1999), Norway. Econometric probability theory.

1990   **Harry Markowitz** (1927–), U.S. Portfolio theory.

         William F. Sharpe (1934–), U.S. Capital asset pricing model.

         Merton Miller (1923–2000), U.S. Miller-Modigliani theory.

1991   **Ronald Coase** (1910–), Britain. Economic firms, social cost.

1992   **Gary Becker** (1930–), U.S. Economic theory and human behavior.

1993   **Robert W. Fogel** (1926–) and **Douglass C. North** (1920–), U.S. Cliometrics (econometric model of history).

1994   **John Nash** (1928–), U.S., **John C. Harsanyi** (1920–), Australia-U.S., and **Reinhard Selten** (1930–), Germany. Economic theory of games.

1995   **Robert E. Lucas Jr.** (1937–), U.S. Rational expectation theory.

1996   **James Mirrlees** (1936–), Britain, and **William Vickrey** (1914–1996), U.S. Economic theory of incentives.

1997   **Robert C. Merton** (1944–), U.S., and **Myron Scholes** (1941–), Canada-U.S. Formula for valuation of options.

1998   **Amartya Sen** (1933–), India-Britain. Social welfare in Third World.

1999   **Robert A. Mundell** (1932–), Canada-U.S. Common market currency theory.

2000   **James J. Heckman** (1944–) and **David L. McFadden** (1937–), U.S. Theory and methods of analyzing selective samples and discrete choice.

APPENDIX A:

VALUE OF PRIZES

1901	c. $40,000 each
1923	$30,000
1931	$46,000
1951	$31,000
1970	$77,000
1972	$100,000
1975	$143,000
1976	$180,000
1985	$225,000
1990	almost $1 million
1992	$1.2 million
1993	$880,000
1994	$600,000
1996	$600,000
1998	$940,000
1999	$960,000

Laureates who did not appear in Stockholm to claim their prizes the year awarded forfeited their prize money, though not the medals and diplomas, which they could claim later. This happened in Nazi times to German laureates forbidden by Hitler to attend the Nobel ceremonies, and to certain Soviet laureates for a like reason. Sartre, having refused his prize for literature, forfeited the money as well.

Accounts of how the Nobel manages its finances are rare. In his 1974 article "Movers and Shakers," Martin Sherwood stated that the "two major bankers in Sweden" were on the Nobel Foundation's board — the only outsiders. Also that until about 1945 the Nobel funds were invested in government bonds, but after that in stocks. The board favors "big international enterprises," and thus does not reflect the "idealism" shown in the prizes.

The Nobel Gold Medal was worth about $2,000 in 1945. During World War II, several laureates had their medals melted down and hidden at Niels Bohr's Institute of Theoretical Physics in Copenhagen, to prevent their being seized by the Nazis. After the war they were recast.

APPENDIX B:

PRIZES BY NATION

National identity here, when it can be ascertained, is based solely on where prizewinning work was mainly done. Country of birth, education, or residence at time of award are excluded.

In literature, an arbitrary time division takes World War II as one cutoff point, with another a few decades later, to help see more clearly how countries fared in certain periods.

In the sciences, a dividing line of 1933 is taken because of the massive emigration from Europe to Britain, the U.S., and elsewhere to escape Nazism and the war. If prize work was done in Germany, the recipient is listed as German, and likewise for Austria. Thus Germany's prizes after 1933 include three in physics from the 1920s (Stern, Born, Bothe); West Germany's first prize came in 1961, to Mössbauer.

PHYSICS

	1901–33	1934–2000
U.S.	3	65
Germany	9	18
Britain	8	13
France	6	5
USSR		6
Netherlands	4	2
Austria	2	2
Sweden	2	2
Switzerland	2	2
Canada		3
Denmark	1	2
Italy	1	2
Japan		3
India	1	
Pakistan		1
Russia		1

Note: In the whole 100 years, experiments won 91 physics prizes and theories 42. In some cases — von Laue, Felix Bloch — experiment and theory were both involved. Rubbia is counted as Italian. Tsui, born in China, did his prizewinning work in Canada. Charpak did his cited work at CERN, which is not a nation, and he is counted as French.

CHEMISTRY

	1901–33	1934–2000
U.S.	2	47
Germany	13	13
Britain	5	18
France	4	3
Switzerland	1	4
Sweden	2	2
Canada		3
Austria	2	
Netherlands	1	1
Argentina		1
Belgium		1
Czechoslovakia		1
Denmark		1
Finland		1
Italy		1
Japan		2
Mexico		1
Norway		1
South Africa		1
USSR		1

Note: Peter Debye, laureate in 1936, did his prizewinning work in the Netherlands, Switzerland, and Germany; he is included in the Swiss total above.

MEDICINE

	1901–33	1934–2000
U.S.	1	91
Britain	5	15
Germany	7	11
Switzerland	1	10
France	4	5
Sweden	1	7
Denmark	3	3
Austria	2	2
Australia		3
Netherlands	2	1
Belgium	1	1
Canada	2	
Italy	1	1
Russia	2	
Argentina		1
Hungary	1	
Portugal		1
Spain	1	

LITERATURE

	1901–39	1940–74	1975–2000
France	6	5	1
U.S.	3	3	3
Britain	3	3	1
Germany	5	1	1
Italy	3	1	2
Sweden	3	3	

	1901–39	1940–74	1975–2000
Spain	2	1	2
Russia/USSR	1	3	
Denmark	2	1	
Norway	3		
Poland	2		1
Chile		2	
Greece		1	1
Ireland	1		1
Japan		1	1
Switzerland	1	1	

Note: Countries with one winner each were: (1901–39) Belgium, Finland, India; (1940–74) Australia, Guatemala, Iceland, Israel, Yugoslavia; (1975–99) China, Colombia, Czechoslovakia, Egypt, Mexico, Nigeria, South Africa.

Writers especially difficult to place nationally are: Elias Canetti, with work done mainly in Vienna and Britain; Samuel Beckett, who worked in France in both English and French; Derek Walcott, of the West Indies but much of whose prize work was done in the U.S.; Nelly Sachs, of German birth but whose poetry in German was written in Sweden from 1940; Czesław Miłosz, who writes in Polish, helps translate his poetry into English, and has resided in the U.S. since 1960 (he is usually cross-listed as Polish-U.S.); and Joseph Brodsky, whose poetry was written in the USSR and the U.S. These are not counted above. Ivan Bunin, who left for France in 1920, is still listed as Russian. Hermann Hesse is considered Swiss.

PEACE

	1901–20	1921–46	1947–2000
U.S.	3	7	6
Britain	1	5	2
France	3	2	3
Sweden	1	2	2
Northern Ireland			4

	1901–20	1921–46	1947–2000
South Africa			4
Belgium	2		1
Germany		2	1
Israel			3
Switzerland	3		
Austria	2		
East Timor			2
Norway		2	
USSR			2
Argentina		1	
Canada			1
Costa Rica			1
Denmark	1		
Egypt			1
Guatemala			1
India			1 (Mother Teresa)
Ireland			1
Italy	1		
Japan			1
Myanmar			1
Netherlands	1		
North Vietnam			1
Poland			1
South Korea			1
Tibet			1

Note: Peace Prizes have been awarded to sixteen organizations, such as the Red Cross or the UN or Doctors without Borders, which are not nations. Yasir Arafat of the Palestinian Liberation Organization shared the 1994 prize, but the PLO is not yet a nation. Albert Schweitzer resided in Africa when he became a laureate, but he is usually counted as German (he is not included in the totals above). Elie Wiesel is included in France's totals.

APPENDIX C:

WOMEN LAUREATES

In the list below, "shared" means the individual was cited as a collaborator in a team. "Separately cited" means that a separate contribution was singled out for honor. Unless otherwise noted, laureates won the entire prize for that year (e.g., Curie, 1911).

PHYSICS

Marie Curie, Poland-France (shared, 1903)
Maria Goeppert Mayer, Germany-U.S. (separately cited, 1963)

CHEMISTRY

Marie Curie, Poland-France (1911)
Irène Joliot-Curie, France (shared, 1935)
Dorothy Crowfoot Hodgkin, Britain (1964)

MEDICINE

Gerty Cori, Czechoslovakia-U.S. (shared, 1947)
Rosalyn Yalow, U.S. (separately cited, 1977)
Barbara McClintock, U.S. (1983)
Rita Levi-Montalcini, Italy-U.S. (shared, 1986)
Gertrude Elion, U.S. (shared, 1988)
Christiane Nüsslein-Volhard, Germany (shared, 1995)

PEACE

Bertha von Suttner, Austria (1905)
Jane Addams, U.S. (separately cited, 1931)
Emily Balch, U.S. (separately cited, 1946)
Betty Williams and Mairead Corrigan, Northern Ireland (1976)

Mother Teresa, Albania-India (1979)
Alva Myrdal, Sweden (separately cited, 1982)
Aung San Suu Kyi, Myanmar (1991)
Rigoberta Menchú, Guatemala (1992)
Jody Williams, U.S. (separately cited, 1997)

ECONOMICS

None.

LITERATURE

Selma Lagerlöf, Sweden (1909)
Grazia Deledda, Italy (1926)
Sigrid Undset, Norway (1928)
Pearl Buck, U.S. (1938)
Gabriela Mistral, Chile (1945)
Nelly Sachs, Germany-Sweden (separately cited, 1966)
Nadine Gordimer, South Africa (1991)
Toni Morrison, U.S. (1993)
Wisława Szymborska, Poland (1996)

APPENDIX D:

FAMILY LAUREATES

Curies. The first married couple to be jointly honored were Marie and Pierre Curie (physics, 1903). In 1911 the widowed Marie won again, alone, in chemistry. The year after Marie's death, the Curies' elder daughter, Irène, shared the 1935 chemistry prize with her husband, Frédéric Joliot-Curie, who also joined his name to his wife's. The younger Curie daughter, Eve, got a trip to the Nobel awards too: the 1965 peace prize was accepted on behalf of UNICEF by its director, Henry R. Labouisse, Eve's husband.

Braggs. With the 1915 physics award, William Henry Bragg and William Lawrence Bragg became the only father-son team to share a Nobel Prize.

Thomsons. Joseph John Thomson (physics, 1906) had the unique pleasure of living to see his son, George Paget Thomson, join the ranks of Nobel laureates (physics, 1937).

Coris. A second husband-wife research team jointly cited were Carl Friedrich and Gerty Cori (medicine, 1947).

von Eulers. Hans von Euler-Chelpin, 1929 chemistry cowinner, was the father of Ulf Svante von Euler, colaureate in medicine, 1970.

Tinbergens. With prizes just four years apart, Jan's in economics in 1969 for being a founder of econometrics, Niko's in physiology in 1973 for being a founder of ethology, the Tinbergens pulled off the only brother act in Nobel history.

Bohrs. The great Niels Bohr (physics, 1922) also fathered a Nobelist, Aage Bohr (physics, 1975).

Siegbahns. Karl Manne Siegbahn (physics, 1924) and Kai Manne Siegbahn (physics, 1981) were likewise father and son.

Myrdals. The Nobel Peace Prize to Alva (1982) following the economics award to Gunnar (1974) made the Myrdals the only married couple to win for work in separate fields.

Chandrasekhars. When Subrahmanyan C. shared the 1983 physics prize, nepotism was not a factor, as his uncle Chandrasekhara V. Raman (physics, 1930) was no longer alive.

(non-)Hodgkins. Alan Hodgkin (medicine, 1963) was not married to Dorothy Crowfoot Hodgkin (chemistry, 1964). Dorothy's husband was Alan's first cousin Thomas, a historian like most of that family. Alan's wife was Marion, daughter of Peyton Rous (medicine, 1966).

APPENDIX E:
JEWISH LAUREATES

Some listed below, such as Bergson, are always seen as Jews, though sometimes of only half-Jewish parentage. According to traditional Jewish law,
the mother must be Jewish for the child to be considered Jewish; Bergson's
mother was not Jewish, nor was Wolfgang Pauli's, among other cases.

LITERATURE

Paul Heyse, Germany
Henri Bergson, France
Boris Pasternak, USSR
S. Y. Agnon, Israel
Nelly Sachs, Sweden
Saul Bellow, Canada-U.S.
Isaac Bashevis Singer, Poland-U.S.
Elias Canetti, Bulgaria-Austria-Britain
Joseph Brodsky, USSR-U.S.
Nadine Gordimer, South Africa

PHYSICS

Albert A. Michelson, U.S.
Gabriel Lippmann, France
Albert Einstein, Germany-Switzerland-U.S.
Niels Bohr, Denmark (mother was Jewish)
James Franck, Germany-U.S.
Gustav Hertz, Germany (father was Jewish)
Otto Stern, Germany-U.S.
Isidor I. Rabi, Austria-U.S.
Wolfgang Pauli, Austria-U.S. (father was Jewish)
Felix Bloch, Switzerland-U.S.
Max Born, Germany-Britain
Ilya Frank, USSR
Igor Tamm, USSR
Emilio Segrè, Italy-U.S.
Donald Glaser, U.S.

Robert Hofstadter, U.S.
Lev Landau, USSR
Eugene Wigner, Hungary-U.S.
Richard Feynman, U.S.
Julian Schwinger, U.S.
Hans Bethe, Germany-U.S. (mother was Jewish)
Murray Gell-Mann, U.S.
Dennis Gabor, Hungary-Britain
Brian Josephson, Britain
Ben Mottelson, U.S.-Denmark
Burton Richter, U.S.
Arno Penzias, Germany-U.S.
Sheldon Glashow, U.S.
Steven Weinberg, U.S.
Leon Lederman, U.S.
Jack Steinberger, Germany-U.S.
Melvin Schwartz, U.S.
Jerome Friedman, U.S.
Georges Charpak, Poland-France
Martin Perl, U.S.
Frederick Reines, U.S.
Claude Cohen-Tannoudji, France

CHEMISTRY

Adolf von Baeyer, Germany (mother was Jewish)
Henri Moissan, France
Otto Wallach, Germany
Richard Willstätter, Germany
Fritz Haber, Germany
George de Hevesy, Hungary-Sweden
Melvin Calvin, U.S.
Max Perutz, Austria-Britain
Gerhard Herzberg, Germany-Canada
William H. Stein, U.S.
Ilya Prigogine, USSR-Belgium
Herbert C. Brown, U.S.
Paul Berg, U.S.
Roald Hoffmann, Poland-U.S.
Aaron Klug, Lithuania-South Africa
Herbert A. Hauptman, U.S.

Jerome Karle, U.S.
Sidney Altman, Canada-U.S.
Rudolf A. Marcus, Canada-U.S.
Walter Kohn, U.S.
Walter Gilbert, U.S.

MEDICINE

Elie Metchnikoff, Russia-France (mother was Jewish)
Paul Ehrlich, Germany
Robert Bárány, Austria
Otto Meyerhof, Germany
Willem Einthoven, Netherlands
Karl Landsteiner, Austria-U.S. (mother was Jewish)
Otto Warburg, Germany
Otto Loewi, Germany-U.S.
Joseph Erlanger, U.S.
Ernst Chain, Germany-Britain
Tadeus Reichstein, Poland-Switzerland
Selman Waksman, Russia-U.S.
Hans A. Krebs, Germany-Britain
Fritz Lipmann, Germany-U.S.
Joshua Lederberg, U.S.
Arthur Kornberg, U.S.
François Jacob, France
André Lwoff, France
George Wald, U.S.
Marshall Nirenberg, U.S.
Salvador Luria, Italy-U.S.
Bernhard Katz, Germany-Britain
Julius Axelrod, U.S.
Gerald Edelman, U.S.
David Baltimore, U.S.
Howard Temin, U.S.
Baruch S. Blumberg, U.S.
Rosalyn Yalow, U.S.
Daniel Nathans, U.S.
Baruj Benacerraf, Venezuela-U.S.
César Milstein, Argentina-Britain
Joseph Goldstein, U.S.
Stanley Cohen, U.S.

Rita Levi-Montalcini, Italy-U.S.
Gertrude Elion, U.S.
Martin Rodbell, U.S.
Stanley Prusiner, U.S.
Alfred Gilman, U.S.
Hermann J. Muller, U.S.

PEACE

Alfred Fried, Austria
Henry Kissinger, Germany-U.S.
Menachem Begin, Israel
Elie Wiesel, Romania-France-U.S.
Shimon Peres, Israel
Yitzhak Rabin, Israel
Joseph Rotblat, Poland-Britain

ECONOMICS

Ragnar Frisch, Norway
Paul Samuelson, U.S.
Simon Kuznets, U.S.
Kenneth Arrow, U.S.
Leonid Kantorovich, USSR
Milton Friedman, U.S.
Herbert Simon, U.S.
Franco Modigliani, Italy-U.S.
Robert M. Solow, U.S.
Harry Markowitz, U.S.
Gary Becker, U.S.
Robert W. Fogel, U.S.
Myron Scholes, U.S.

NOTES

INTRODUCTION

1. Quinn, *Curie*, chapter 7. This biography is highly recommended. The fountainhead biography is by Marie's younger daughter Eve: *Madame Curie*, published in 1937 in French, an international bestseller for years.

2. Pflaum, *Grand Obsession*, 75.

3. Crawford, *Beginnings*, 195. Professor Crawford's pioneering historical studies on the Nobel scientific institutions and prizes — she was one of the very first to have access to hitherto sealed archives — remain indispensable for any investigation, and the present study is indebted to all her work on the subject.

4. Crawford, *Beginnings*, 194.

5. For the prejudice against women scientists around 1900, see Quinn, *Curie*, 243. See also 153, where Quinn reports that when Marie won the 1898 Gegner Prize, Pierre alone was notified and told to inform his wife. Also 187–88: on her American tour, Marie Curie was awarded ten honorary degrees — she was after all a two-time Nobelist — but the Harvard physics department voted against honoring her.

6. Quinn, *Curie*, 191–97 gives many quotes from newspapers of the time.

7. Forman, Heilbron, and Weart, "Physics circa 1900," 3, cited in Pais, *Inward Bound*, 5.

8. Nye, *From Chemical Philosophy*, 25–26.

9. Kevles, *The Physicists*, 9.

10. Crawford, *Beginnings*, 17–18.

11. Crawford, *Beginnings*, 193.

12. Harvard has annual spoofs of the Nobels called "Ig-Nobels," where awards are given for parodies of scientific discoveries. They often feature genuine laureates.

13. See Crawford, *Nationalism and Internationalism*, ch. 3, pp. 48–79.

14. Quoted from a letter of 1908, in Crawford, *Beginnings*, 162.

15. Crawford, *Beginnings*, 195–96.

16. The Nobel Foundation has privately communicated explanations to certain protesting parties, usually about the Nobel's unwitting lack of adequate information at the time of the award. But no award has ever been qualified or reversed as a result.

17. Nigel Williams, "Newspaper Backs Down," *Science*, 22 September 1995.

18. Sweden's freedom-of-information law applies to all public institutions. One of these is the Karolinska Institute, which administers the Nobels in medicine. The Swedish Academy, for the literature Nobels, is a private institution, as is the Royal Academy of Sciences, for physics, chemistry, and economics. The Norwegian peace committee is of course outside Swedish law. A compromise was worked out in 1974 whereby the Karolinska could keep its Nobel deliberations secret but, along with the other Nobel-awarding groups, agreed to unseal archives more than fifty years old at their discretion. See Crawford, "Secrecy."

19. Crawford, "Secrecy," 416.

20. For fuller description, see Morrison, "So You Want to Win."

21. Heilbron, "Creativity and Big Science." Heilbron notes that the contemporary sense of the word "genius" (e.g., Einstein) came into vogue just about the time the Nobels began.

22. Quoted in *Time*, 3 July 1972, 53.

23. *New York Times*, 19 January 1988. The 1986 Peace Nobelist Elie Wiesel helped organize this conference and describes it in his *And the Sea Is Never Full: Memoirs 1969*. Translated from the French by Marion Wiesel. New York: A. A. Knopf, 1999. 277–87.

24. Taylor, *Science of Life*, 229.

1. THE FOUNDING FATHER

1. Ödelberg, *Nobel*, 36. This is the Nobel's official history of the prizes. It has gone through three editions — see Bibliography for details — and the second edition was franker about lapses and gaffes than the other two. Unless noted, we refer to the third edition, which is more up-to-date.

2. Tolf, *The Russian Rockefellers*, 10.

3. Reader, *Imperial Chemical*, 1:19.

4. Reader, *Imperial Chemical*, 1:12.

5. Schuck and Sohlman, *Nobel*, 192. This is a biography of Nobel by the executors he appointed.

6. Schuck and Sohlman, *Nobel*, 13.

7. Reader, *Imperial Chemical*, 1:32.

8. Ödelberg, *Nobel*, 36.

9. Ödelberg, *Nobel*, 33.

10. Halasz, *Nobel*, 232.

11. Reader, *Imperial Chemical*, 1:68 and 1:75, for causing his own firm to compete. See also 1:80, where Nobel acted to help his manufacturers stop "waging war against each other" and preparing to commit "collective suicide."

12. Halasz, *Nobel*, 178.

13. Halasz, *Nobel*, 187–88.

14. Reader, *Imperial Chemical*, 1:87.

15. Halasz, *Nobel*, 178.

16. Crawford, *Beginnings*, 28.

17. Sohlman and Schuck, *Nobel*, 20.

18. Halasz, *Nobel*, 179.

19. Halasz, *Nobel*, 180.

20. Ödelberg, *Nobel*, 12.

21. Halasz, *Nobel*, 193.

2. THE NOBEL PRIZE INVENTS ITSELF

1. Crawford, *Beginnings*, 64.

2. Estimates of how much such sums were worth inevitably vary. The actual buying power at the time and inflation since then must be factored in, always hard to do. The buying power of $9 million in 1900

would equal about $61 million in 1975 dollars, according to Zuckerman, *Scientific Elite*, 1. Crawford, *Beginnings*, 64, estimates that in 1900 buying power one million kronor was worth about $270,000.

3. Details in this paragraph are from Crawford, *Beginnings*, 64, 66, 206.

4. Crawford, *Beginnings*, 4.

5. For details in the next four paragraphs, see Crawford, *Beginnings*, 69–70, 61.

6. Crawford, *Beginnings*, 69; for institutes mentioned in next paragraph, 70.

7. Crawford, *Beginnings*, 31, 43.

8. Crawford, *Beginnings*, 57.

9. Ödelberg, *Nobel*, 486–87.

10. McLachlan, "Defining Physics."

11. Crawford, "Secrecy," 414. Crawford also invented the "chauvinism index" to analyze how often physics and chemistry nominators proposed fellow citizens. Up to 1937, again, France and Great Britain had most nominated their own (60 on a scale of 100), with the U.S. and Germany rating 44 and 37 on the scale, and Sweden unexpectedly low at 5.

12. Ödelberg, *Nobel*, 51–52.

3.   THE NOBEL PRIZE IN LITERATURE

1. Wallace, *Writing of a Novel*, 161. The novel referred to in the title is *The Prize*.

2. In these same decades (1910–40) the Pulitzer Prizes in the U.S. chose the same sort of middlebrow writers: Booth Tarkington, Edna Ferber, Louis Bromfield, Julia Peterkin, Oliver LaFarge, Pearl Buck, Margaret Mitchell, J. P. Marquand, and Marjorie Kinnan Rawlings (of *The Yearling* fame). Like the Nobels, the Pulitzers occasionally landed a good one: Cather, Sinclair Lewis (who refused the prize), Thornton Wilder. But in this same period they blackballed Fitzgerald, Hemingway, Dos Passos, and Faulkner.

3. Frenz, "What Prize Glory?" 44.

4. Brown, "Twenty Years and Two Laureates," 208.

5. Kjell Espmark, *The Nobel Prize in Literature* (1986) is the indispensable study of the voting and nominating records of the Nobel literary committees from 1901 to 1986. This chapter is crucially indebted to his work. His book resulted from unrestricted access to the otherwise sealed Nobel archives. He has been chair of the Nobel literary committee since 1988. In every sense an insider, he views the Nobel awards in terms of the various committees' historical biases, needs, and constraints. He writes neither to defend nor to attack the Nobel choices and fairly gives evidence on both sides, but places them in the historical context of the Nobel committees. This is a healthy corrective to any naive notion of how the prize originates. But besides seeing how the prizes reflect the personalities of the committees, they must finally be judged on their own terms, and that is a different story. On that side, the Nobel Prizes do present themselves to the public in terms of "timeless" excellence. The history of the American presidency cannot be understood in terms of election campaigns. See Herbert Howarth's trenchant comment in the text for the limitations of an approach like Espmark's, and also the Finale section.

6. Ödelberg, *Nobel*, 91.

7. Espmark, *Nobel Prize in Literature*, 153.

8. Ödelberg, *Nobel*, 136.

9. Espmark, *Nobel Prize in Literature*, 79.

10. For "the Boyg," see Levin, *Memories of the Moderns*, 115–16.

11. Specter, "The Nobel Syndrome," 48. The next quote in the text about Sture Allen is also from Specter, 48.

12. Perhaps this animosity is why Sture Allen remains permanent secretary, while Kjell Espmark has chaired the committee since 1988. Up to 1986, the permanent secretary also chaired the committee.

13. Oppenheimer, *The Open Mind*, 119.

14. Espmark, *Nobel Prize in Literature*, 146.

15. Howarth, "Petition to the Swedish Academy," 6.

16. Espmark, *Nobel Prize in Literature*, 64.

17. One of the most successful awards of prizes without a committee occurred in 1914, when the philosopher Ludwig Wittgenstein, whose family was wealthy, decided to give 100,000 Austrian crowns

(then worth about approximately £4,000 or $20,000, almost the size of a Nobel Prize) to needy Austrian artists. Wittgenstein asked an Austrian editor, Ludwig von Ficker, to decide. Ficker split the money among three artists: Rilke, Georg Trakl, and Carl Dallago.

18. Espmark, *Nobel Prize in Literature*, 4–5.

19. Ödelberg, *Nobel*, 77.

20. Ibid., 9.

21. Ruth, "Second New Nation," 53.

22. These quotes, respectively, are from Espmark, *Nobel Prize in Literature*, 10–11, 17, 18, 25.

23. Ibid., 16–17.

24. The classical scholar G. W. Bowersock, in a review of a translation of Mommsen's *History of Rome*, claims the work still had relevance when honored in 1902, and that perhaps the Nobel jury believed it could push the eighty-five-year-old author into finishing his missing volume 4. They were wrong. See Bowersock, "Rendering unto Caesar."

25. See Espmark, *Nobel Prize in Literature*, 164–65.

26. Coleman, "Why Asturias?" 1–3.

27. Sommer, "The Air You Breathe."

28. Heaney, *Redress of Poetry*, 2.

29. *Nobel Lectures in Literature 1901–67*, 196.

30. Wallace, *Writing of a Novel*, 17. Wallace claims he was told that Buck scarcely bowled over the academy. Ten of the eighteen members voted against her, but Sven Hedin and Selma Lagerlöf changed their minds. Hedin was Wallace's informant.

31. Ödelberg, *Nobel*, 115.

32. Vowles, "Twelve Northern Authors."

33. Howarth, "Petition to the Swedish Academy," 5.

34. The influential Swedish critic Sven Delblanc, writing in 1982, claimed that saga fiction appealed so much to the Nobel judges and Swedish readers because Swedish writers were more comfortable dealing with their country's past than its present. But this past is painted darkly, so that readers — while escaping the present — can

also say that things aren't so bad now. Quoted in Gustafsson, "Silences of the North," 97.

35. Espmark, *Nobel Prize in Literature*, 38.

36. Contat and Rybalka, *Writings of Jean-Paul Sartre*, 455. For Sartre's pro-Communism and Nobel "objectivity," see Espmark, *Nobel Prize in Literature*, 109–12.

37. Contat and Rybalka, *Writings of Jean-Paul Sartre*, 453.

38. Sholokhov wrote *The Quiet Don* (more than a thousand pages) between the ages of twenty-two and twenty-five. The first volume appeared in 1928, and there were immediate charges that Sholokhov had plagiarized a Cossack writer; evidence for and against has been advanced, but the case remains unsettled. His writing during the rest of his life never came near matching the *Don* work. See Scammell, "The Don Flows Again."

39. Espmark, "Nobel Prize in Literature" on Nobel website, 8.

40. Bizzarro, *Pablo Neruda*, 135

41. Specter, "The Nobel Syndrome," 52.

42. Espmark, *Nobel Prize in Literature*, 108. Also Espmark, "Nobel Prize in Literature," Nobel website, 4, states that Hammarskjöld negotiated "on the Academy's commission" for Pound's release from St. Elizabeth's Hospital, where he was confined after World War II. Espmark cites this as an instance of the academy's "generosity." But if the Swedish Academy thought Pound not mentally ill — and thus fit to be released from the mental asylum — shouldn't they have concluded he had committed treason against his country and belonged in jail?

43. Espmark, *Nobel Prize in Literature*, 109.

44. Ibid.

45. On Céline, see Steiner, "Cry Havoc," 35–46.

46. Espmark, *Nobel Prize in Literature*, 115.

47. Ziolkowski, "German Literature and the Prize," 1.

48. See Bahti and Fries, *Jewish Writers*, for a general discussion; for Sachs's mental suffering, 35; for Domin, 3 and 49 (Sachs's "poetry belongs to the best produced in the German language during this century"); for the German isolation of Sachs as a Holocaust poet, 8, 49–50, and passim.

49. Miłosz, *Witness of Poetry*, 7. For a survey of the nations and writers involved, see Czerwinski, "For Whom the Nobel Tolls."

50. Dutta and Robinson, *Tagore*, report that in the 1920s and 1930s he was one of the most popular lecturers in the world.

51. Ödelberg, *Nobel*, 94.

52. Dates and comments on Claudel are given in Espmark, *Nobel Prize in Literature*, 54, 59, and 161.

53. The film critic Stanley Kauffmann suggested Nobel awards for screenplays, with Ingmar Bergman or Akira Kurosawa as eligibles.

54. Ödelberg, *Nobel*, 97.

55. Espmark, *Nobel Prize in Literature*, 67.

56. Ödelberg, *Nobel*, 123.

57. Österling in Ödelberg, *Nobel*, 1st ed., 132: the prizes "obviously cannot serve as a representative picture of the literary standards in each country."

58. Espmark, *Nobel Prize in Literature*, 42, 152; for "not a single legitimate proposal," 190.

59. Ellmann, *James Joyce*, 546. For Joyce's non-nominations, see Espmark, *Nobel Prize in Literature*, 152.

60. Edel, *Henry James: The Master*, 476.

61. Espmark, *Nobel Prize in Literature*, 26.

62. Ibid., 106.

63. Ibid., 74, on Valéry as "difficult"; 59 and 80 on earlier Nobel evaluations of Valéry.

64. In a letter to the *New York Times* (18 October 1981), the German literature scholar Roman Karst protested that the *Times* had described Canetti as "the first Bulgarian" to win the Nobel in Literature. Karst pointed out that Canetti left Bulgaria at age six, lived in Austria from 1921 to 1938 and wrote his major works there, and, alluding to his debt to that city's writers Nestroy and Karl Kraus, said, "I am a Viennese writer."

65. Ragusa, "Carducci, Deledda, Pirandello, Quasimodo."

66. More intriguing gossip from Irving Wallace: a Nobel committee member told him that Mistral was chosen over Croce, Hesse, Sand-

burg, Jules Romains, and others because a Nobel judge and poet, Hjalmar Gullberg, fell in love with her verse and translated it all into Swedish — and single-handedly swayed the entire vote. See *Writing of a Novel*, 19.

67. Yoshio Iwamoto, "The Nobel Prize in Literature, 1967–87: A Japanese View," 218.

68. Espmark, *Nobel Prize in Literature*, 141.

69. Preminger, *Princeton Encyclopedia of Poetry*, 389–90. For Ngugi, see Sturrock, *Oxford Guide to Contemporary Writing*, 13.

70. See Espmark for the Bengali scholar. Espmark thus claims that the academy's "linguistic competence has, as a rule, been high," in "Nobel Prize in Literature," Nobel website, 7.

71. Espmark, *Nobel Prize in Literature*, 142.

4.   THE NOBEL PRIZE AND THE SCIENCES

1. Pais, *Inward Bound*, 5. In the 1880s, only seventeen colleges in the U.S. employed more than twenty science professors in any field; the physicist Henry Rowland, who taught at Johns Hopkins from 1876 until 1901, called them "a cloud of mosquitoes, instead of eagles": quoted in Kevles, *The Physicists*, 43. J. L. Heilbron gives a table of physics faculty in the world in 1900 in Weiner, *Twentieth Century Physics*, 49: he counts 700 members, from full professors to Privat-dozent. In 1966 the staff of CERN was almost 2,490, of whom 413 were "scientists." Jeremy Bernstein relates that in the 1950s, theoretical physicists on both the Harvard and MIT faculties were so few they could all sit around one small table at lunch. See his *Theory for Everything*, 251.

2. In 1894 the first volume of *Physical Review*, the major American journal in physics, consisted of 480 pages and twenty articles. By 1980 it ran to two volumes of almost 30,000 pages, with 3,400 articles. Since 1970 each volume of *Physical Review* appears in four subvolumes. In 1985 the American Institute of Physics (AIP) published more than forty journals, almost half of which were translations of research done in the USSR. All figures cited from Pais, *Inward Bound*, 5–6. (This is still the best history of particle physics from 1895 to 1983, for its technical expertise, biographical insights, and superb coverage.)

3. Glasser, *Roentgen*, cited in Pais, *Einstein Lived Here*, 138.

4. Farmelo, "Discovery of X-rays," 86. For the medical treatment mentioned, see Crease and Mann, *Second Creation*, 10.

5. Heilbron "Fin-de-Siècle Physics," 61, and 51 for inventions mentioned in text.

6. Ibid., 68, quoting Jacobus van't Hoff (first laureate in chemistry) in 1902.

7. See Merton, *Sociology of Science*, for a famous but different comparison, where the moral character of the pure scientist is stressed: selfless, devoted to truth against any preconception, and indifferent to worldly gain but seeking instead to promote communal benefit by making all knowledge freely public. Edison et al. failed the last requirement.

8. Quoted in Gaston, *Originality and Competition*, 71.

9. See also Feynman, *Surely You're Joking*. But this is light-hearted fun alongside the recent tract-as-autobiography by Kary Mullis (shared chemistry prize, 1993), *Dancing Naked in the Mind Field*. "Because of the Nobel Prize," he writes, "I am a free agent. I don't owe anything to anybody." He goes on to urge the study of astrology and rejects HIV as the cause of AIDS, among other ideas.

10. G. Johnson, "What a Physicist Finds Obscene."

11. Pais, *Subtle Is the Lord*, 316. The assassination in 1922 by right-wing elements of Walter Rathenau, the German foreign minister and a Jew, convinced Einstein that "a long absence from Germany" would be helpful to his personal safety. Hence the world tour during which he won the Nobel Prize.

12. Quoted from the *New York Times* in Christianson, *Hubble*, 204–5.

13. Pais, *Bohr's Times*, 14.

14. Elisabeth Crawford writes: "In general, the drama of science in the making has been played out long before the works reached the Prize juries." See "Secrecy," 418.

15. Galison, *How Experiments End*, 127.

16. Ziman, *Prometheus Bound*. Ziman contrasts science's earlier "growth" phase with the emerging "steady-state" condition on these grounds: the new corporate Big Science is local (as against older science's universality); it is authoritarian (as against individualistic); it commissions research of "target" importance (rather than remaining disinterested); it is proprietary or government-funded (rather than

free, with original work open to the community of science for any purpose or use).

17. For a full account, see Rhodes, *Deadly Feasts*, Afterword, especially 250–56 for the effect of the Nobel award on funding in this matter.

18. Merton, *Sociology of Science*, 367. For statement immediately following, see Medawar, *Art of the Soluble*, 106.

19. Medawar, *Art of the Soluble*, 97.

20. Crease and Mann, *Second Creation*, 290.

21. Quoted in Crowther, *British Scientists*, 68. Niels Bohr, one of the most modest and humble of scientists, also worried that someone might beat him out when working on his epochal quantum model of the atom in 1912–13.

22. Taylor, *Science of Life*, 220.

23. Merton, *Sociology of Science*, 306.

24. The last three quotations of Darwin are from Merton, *Sociology of Science*, 306–7.

25. Alvarez, *Adventures of a Physicist*, 118.

26. Schweber, *QED*, 456, and 657 (note 175).

27. This was the V-A theory (of weak interactions) which Feynman and Gell-Mann independently developed and then wrote up in a joint paper in 1958. See Feynman, *Surely You're Joking*, 251. For background, see Gleick, *Genius*, 336–38.

28. Crease and Mann, *Second Creation*, 213–14.

29. Julian Schwinger, who shared the 1965 prize (with Feynman and Tomonaga) for the QED theory, was surprised that he won the Nobel for that. "It's splashy and all that, but it was an obvious development in the air. Frankly, I much prefer [my] work centering on the action principle, spin statistics, TPC. These are fundamental results." Quoted in Schweber, *QED*, 355. Hans Bethe thought his most important work wasn't on the energy sources of stars (cited by the Nobel) but his 1930 theory on the passage of fast corpuscular radiation through matter: see Galison, *How Experiments End*, 101. Zuckerman, *Scientific Elite*, 210–11, reports that half the American laureates she interviewed (a total of 41) did not think the Nobel honored their best work.

30. Hager, *Force of Nature*, 450.

31. Pais, *Inward Bound*, 283. See Wali, *Chandra*, 248, for more on Bose.

32. Stephan and Levin, *Striking the Mother Lode*, 69.

33. It is worth noting that two of the IBM Nobelists, Georg Bednorz and K. A. Müller, established their priority by publishing in obscure journals unlikely to be read by rivals, thus giving them time to improve their findings. See Schechter, *Path of No Resistance*, 82–83.

34. M. Wilson, "How Nobel Winners Get That Way," 73.

35. Pais, *Bohr's Times*, 386.

5. THE NOBEL PRIZE IN PHYSICS

1. Crawford and Friedman, "Context of Swedish Science," 324–27. Also Friedman, "Americans as Candidates," 277.

2. Elisabeth Crawford, "*Scientific Elite* Revisited," in Goldberg and Stuewer, *Michelson Era*, 260.

3. Friedman, "Americans as Candidates," 282, 279–80.

4. Friedman, "Physics Prizes in Perspective," 796.

5. For a vivid account of how the physics committee contrived to enforce their wishes, see Friedman, *Appropriating the Weather.*

6. Christianson, *Hubble*, 249, reports that in the 1930s Fred Hoyle, the British astrophysicist, told Hubble "it was well known in England that the Nobel Prize committee had discussed the legal possibility of amending the statutes, which contained no provision for astronomy, so that science's highest award could go to Edwin." But astronomy was still eligible according to the Statutes. About the same time, Christianson relates (317), Robert Millikan told Marconi the same thing. Hubble much wanted to win, and even hired a press agent. Christianson mistakenly reports (362) that Fermi and Chandrasekhar were members of the Nobel committee; they could only have been nominators, but they may, as Christianson reports, have nominated Hubble. Hubble died in September 1953 — still officially, but unknowingly, eligible for the prize.

7. MacLachlan, "Defining Physics," 171. MacLachlan also mentions the Nobel bias against geophysics in the case of the Norwegian geophysicist Fredrik Carl Størmer, with seven nominations between 1915 and 1934.

8. The landmark study of experimental physics is Galison, *Image and Logic*. This is at once the most wide-ranging and vivid history of what Galison calls "the machines of physics" in laboratory work through this century, and a defense of experiment against the vaunts of theory. More than a corrective, the book opens an entirely new sense of the discipline. See also Galison, *How Experiments End*, 137–45, 244.

9. Snow, *The Physicists*, 39.

10. Schweber, *QED*, 67, citing P. M. S. Blackett. As early as 1907, Rutherford thought a "divorce" already existed between experimenters and mathematical physicists. See Wilson, *Rutherford*, 230.

11. Kragh, *Dirac*, 257–58.

12. T. H. Huxley in the nineteenth century is said to have recommended strangling scientists at sixty, as too fixed in their thinking.

13. Jungnickel and McCormmach, *Now Mighty*, xv, 113, and 341–45 for the new mathematics reshaping physics.

14. Jungnickel and McCormmach, *Now Mighty*, 371.

15. Friedman, "Americans as Candidates," 276. Kragh, *Quantum Generations*, 432–33, notes that in Sweden between 1890 and 1920, of 77 Ph.D.s from Swedish universities, 67 were mainly experimental and only 10 theoretical. Jungnickel and McCormmach, *Now Mighty*, 320–21, note that around 1880 experimenters were often divided into two kinds: some found new data from which theory could arise, and some were "measuring physicists" who improved the accuracy of calculations and units of already existing theories.

16. When he won the 1902 prize, Lorentz was widely seen as the greatest theorist of the time and could have been honored for several important contributions. But the Nobel jury chose to honor a theory Lorentz formulated in response to an experiment by Pieter Zeeman. They became colaureates, although by 1902 Lorentz's theory was known to be "incomplete," not to say wrong, according to Pais, *Bohr's Times*, 198. Pais wondered why Lorentz won the Nobel for that particular theory. The Nobel committee's attitude seems the only answer.

17. Lederman, *God Particle*, 13.

18. Galison, *How Experiments End*, ix.

19. Riordan, *Hunting of the Quark*, 12.

20. The last two sentences rely on Bunch, *Handbook*, 625.

21. Ne'eman and Kirsh, *Particle Hunters*, 102.

22. Said by the French physicist Langevin, as reported in Pflaum, *Grand Obsession*, 106.

23. Pais, *Inward Bound*, 437–38.

24. Snow, *The Physicists*, 35–36.

25. Chadwick, "Rutherford."

26. Pais, *Inward Bound*, 84–86, argues that Thomson was the discoverer only when he completed measurement of the e/m value of the cathode rays in 1899. Kragh, *Quantum Generations*, 51, argues instead that Thomson's measurements were not as accurate as those of the Germans Wiechert and Kaufmann. But Wiechert didn't see that the electron was corpuscular; Kaufmann saw that, but missed seeing it was within the atom.

27. Andrade, "Rutherford."

28. Perrin's "proof" was inevitably indirect. As the scientific historian Stephen Brush notes, Erwin Mueller in 1955 was the first person ever to "see" an atom, using a field-ion microscope — no Nobel Prize. See Brush, *Statistical Physics*, 97.

29. For the remarks on Freud and Princeton, see Pais, *Einstein Lived Here*, 200.

30. Pais, *Subtle Is the Lord*, 477.

31. See Gleick, *Genius*, 312.

32. Pais, *Subtle Is the Lord*, 372.

33. The question of how Einstein and Planck won their Nobel Prizes has been much discussed. The present section relies on what seem the two most authoritative and illuminating accounts — for Einstein: Pais, *Subtle Is the Lord*, chapter 30, and *Einstein Lived Here*, 70ff.; for Planck: Nagel, "Discussions," 353–76.

34. Pais, *Inward Bound*, 134.

35. Pais, *Subtle Is the Lord*, 30; also for quote immediately following.

36. The photoelectric effect occurs when a quantum of light (called a photon from 1926) hits an electron on a metal surface, causing it to be displaced from its atom. Electric eyes and remote control devices now use the photoelectric effect. Brightness of the light is irrelevant;

the effect depends on the photon's wavelength: shorter frequencies, on the high-intensity side of the spectrum, provide more energy to the photon. Since the photon's energy is fixed according to frequency levels, it is a quantum effect. For a survey of the photoelectric effect in modern physics, see Pais, *Subtle Is the Lord*, 379–82.

37. G. Holton, "On the Hesitant Rise of Quantum Physics Research," in Goldberg and Stuewer, eds., 203, notes 81 and 82.

38. Planck's letter is quoted in Pais, *Subtle Is the Lord*, 382. For Planck's vacillations about light-quanta, see Brush, *Statistical Physics*, 156–57.

39. Quoted in Pais, *Subtle Is the Lord*, 399.

40. Nagel, "Discussions," provides extracts from nomination letters and Nobel deliberations.

41. Crawford, *Beginnings*, 236, 172–73.

42. Nagel, "Discussions," 371.

43. MacLachlan, "Defining Physics," 166–74; 170 quotes Crawford.

44. Crawford and Friedman, "Context of Swedish Science," 323.

45. Pais, *Einstein Lived Here*, 74.

46. Crawford and Friedman, "Context of Swedish Science," 323–24.

47. Pais, *Subtle Is the Lord*, chapter 32, gives a full discussion of Einstein's nominations for the physics prize. A few highlights: In 1918 he nominated Planck, who in 1919 won the prize for 1918. He nominated Compton for the third time in 1927, the year he won. In 1931 Einstein nominated Schrödinger and Heisenberg; Heisenberg won the 1932 prize, while Schrödinger shared the 1933 prize with Dirac, whom Einstein never nominated. He did nominate Born, who won only in 1954. His two 1940 nominees, Otto Stern and I. I. Rabi, both won, Stern in 1943 and Rabi in 1944. Einstein's 1945 choice, Pauli for his 1925 "exclusion principle," won that same year; likewise Walther Bothe in 1954, when he shared the prize with Born.

48. Pais, *Einstein Lived Here*, 35.

49. Heisenberg, *Physics and Beyond*, 73.

50. Pais, *Bohr's Times*, 299. For a list of Bohr's nominations for the physics prize between 1920 and 1939, see 216.

51. Pais, *Bohr's Times*, 275.

52. Pais, *Bohr's Times*, 201, for Pauli; for Heisenberg's meeting with Bohr, 262–63.

53. Cassidy, *Uncertainty*, 151–52.

54. Schweber, *QED*, 21.

55. Weiner, *Twentieth Century Physics*, 120.

56. Lederman, *God Particle*, 168: the equation was cited 100,000 times by 1960.

57. Kuhn, interview with Dirac, April 1962, in *Source*.

58. Kragh, *Dirac*.

59. Pais, *Bohr's Times*, 178–79.

60. Brown and Hoddeson, *Birth of Particle Physics*, 46.

61. Born, *My Life*, 226.

62. Pais, *Inward Bound*, 286–92, for a superb though technical account of the Dirac equation.

63. Kragh, *Dirac*, 117.

64. When X-rays were deflected by carbon, some of the deflections showed an increased wavelength. Compton decided that the X-rays, like particles, collided with electrons and lost energy doing so, lowering their frequency. The wave-particle duality thus came to puzzling sight, never to disappear. Since X-rays are a form of light, Compton's experiment helped confirm Einstein's 1905 light-quanta theory.

65. Kragh, *Dirac*, 115.

66. Andrade, E. N. da C., "Rutherford," 111.

67. These numbers involve protons and neutrons in a nucleus: in each, the total of protons or neutrons adds up to 2, 8, 20, 28, 82, and 126 (with some exceptions).

68. Kragh, *Quantum Generations*, 282.

69. Kragh, *Quantum Generations*, 198–201.

70. Schweber, *QED*, 212.

71. Lamb, "Fine Structure." For such major articles in physics, see Ezhela et al., *Particle Physics*. This is an invaluable record of virtually every significant article from 1895 to 1996, with summaries and abstracts.

72. At Columbia, Lamb was part of Rabi's team. In 1937 Rabi was able to make atoms shift their spin orientations, "flipping" their internal atomic magnets by applying radio frequencies. The medical procedure called MRI exploits Rabi's "flipping" method to photograph tissues. Rabi's theory applied best to molecules and gases. In 1946 Felix Bloch of Stanford and Edward Purcell of Harvard (independently) improved Rabi's method and extended it to solids and liquids.

73. To give a sense of how minute the divergences were: Dirac's 1928 equation gave the magnetic moment as 2. The 1948 experiments by Lamb measured 2.00236. Schwinger's theoretical calculation, based on the new data, came out to 2.00232. See Kragh, *Quantum Generations*, 333. Kusch also revised the old assumption (since the discovery of spin) that the electron's "orbital" magnetic strength equaled its "spin" magnetic strength. Kusch showed that spin's strength is always greater by one-tenth of a percent. This was another tiny figure, but of huge proportions on the minuscule quantum level.

74. Absorbed by an atom, an electron jumps to a higher energy level; emitted, it moves down. The "jumps" also release energy in the form of photons (quanta of light). But because they exist for a fraction of a trillionth of a second, they are "virtual" — too quick and small to be observed. Still, in their bare instant of existence, they hover as a "cloud" over the particles, and make the field swarm with energy. This is no freak event, but the normal situation. Mesons and antimesons, antielectrons, and protons are endowed with this curiously spectral life. But if an electron keeps creating and swallowing virtual photons, its energy becomes infinite. Yet electrons have only finite energy. The physicists could not eliminate the infinities in the calculations. The mathematics said one thing, physical reality another. This helped balk QED for two decades.

75. Bernstein, *Tenth Dimension*, 30–32.

76. Dyson, *From Eros to Gaia*, 306.

77. Schweber, *QED*, 71.

78. Brown and Hoddeson, *Birth of Particle Physics*, 52–53. Dirac's remarks on renormalization were made in 1980, four years before he died.

79. Schweber, *QED*, 218.

80. Schweber, *QED*, 575.

81. Pais, *Inward Bound*, 430.

82. For Anderson's reminiscences, see Brown and Hoddeson, *Birth of Particle Physics*. Bernstein, *Tenth Dimension*, 20, discusses the events before and after Powell's discovery of the correct meson.

83. Crease and Mann, *Second Creation*, 165, from interview; Pais, *Inward Bound*, 453, 468 (note 45); and Ne'eman and Kirsh, *Particle Hunters*, 80–81.

84. In later terms, what happens in Yukawa's strong force is something like this: As the pion moves between the proton and neutron, it changes one into the other. Weaving and unweaving thus, the strong force restrains the positively charged protons from pulling apart.

85. Fermi's model was Maxwell's electromagnetic theory, where no mediating ("exchange") particle was involved. Force was simply exchanged when electrically charged particles directly collided with each other. See Bernstein, *Tenth Dimension*, 97; also Galison, *How Experiments End*, 151.

86. Fermi, "Theorie der B-Strahlen," 576. Author's translation.

87. Pais, *Inward Bound*, 533, gives references to texts providing this data.

88. Bernstein, *Tenth Dimension*, 7. Also Pais, *Inward Bound*, 570.

89. Crease and Mann, *Second Creation*, 203.

90. Mulvey, *Nature of Matter*, 110; for end of paragraph, 111.

91. Crease and Mann, *Second Creation*, 248.

92. Quoted from Sidney Coleman in Galison, *How Experiments End*, 157.

93. Franklin, *Neglect of Experiment*, 11.

94. Crease and Mann, *Second Creation*, 210.

95. The ignored included Lee and Yang's chief collaborator, Chen-Shiung Wu (1912–) of Columbia, who did the "official" experiment. Madame Wu, as she was usually called, won no share of the prize perhaps because, in the Nobels as elsewhere, too many cooks can spoil the broth. Leon Lederman of Columbia, his graduate student Marcel Weinrich, and Richard Garwin of IBM independently found experimental proof of parity violation as quickly as Wu and her team, and told her so. ("She was of course less than delighted by our clean, unequivocal result," Lederman remembers.) Valentine Telegdi at Chicago was another claimant. Indeed, the reports of Lederman-Garwin, Wu, and Telegdi appeared in the same volume (105) of *Physical Review*, but Wu and Garwin were published in the issue of 15

February 1957, and Telegdi in 1 March 1957 — though the "received date" noted only two days' difference. *Physical Review* explained that for "technical reasons" Telegdi's paper had to be delayed. Telegdi resigned in protest from the American Physical Society, which publishes *Physical Review*. See Franklin, *Neglect of Experiment*, 27 ff., for untangling these experiments.

96. Parity involves three symmetries: "charge-conjugation" (roughly, that every particle can be replaced by its antiparticle without changing the laws of nature), mirror-image (left and right are interchangeable), and time-reversal (reactions can run forward or backward with the same effect). Wang and Lee proved that in weak interactions mirror-image parity was not conserved. Cronin and Fitch found that charge and mirror-image parity were not conserved when taken together either. Thus only the three combined properties are conserved. This has vast consequences for symmetry principles, which underlie much recent work.

97. Pais, *Inward Bound*, 405.

98. The unit of accelerator energy is the electron-volt (the energy an electron receives from one volt). The alpha rays that Rutherford discovered around 1900 possessed a "natural" power of about five million electron-volts. The first accelerator, by Cockcroft and Walton in 1932, sped protons at three to four hundred thousand eV in the first "artificial" splitting of an atom. By 1970 an accelerator could reach almost two trillion eV. The canceled SSC project was planned to deliver forty trillion eV.

99. Lederman, *Nobel Lectures in Physics, 1981–1990*, 511–12.

100. Ibid., 514. For Blackett, see Pais, *Inward Bound*, 363.

101. Galison, *How Experiments End*, 140.

102. Dodd, *Ideas of Particle Physics*, 57; for the next two paragraphs, 59–60.

103. Povh et al. *Particles and Nuclei*, 112.

104. Technically, it used internal symmetry, which builds on mathematical group theory. Special Unitary groups (abbreviated to SU) involve transformation by unitary matrices in two or three dimensions, hence SU(2) and SU(3). SU(2) has three charged currents and involves the strong forces. SU(3) turned out to be the right group, because SU(2) is its subgroup, and because SU(3) also contains five currents of its own, thus totaling eight with SU(2) added in. The eight numbers refer to quantum numbers for spin and hypercharge.

105. Ne'eman and Kirsh, *Particle Hunters*, 204.

106. Unlike electrons, quarks always have fractional electrical charges: plus or minus 2/3 or 1/3. "Up" quarks always have +2/3; down have –1/3.

107. Such as Harry Lipkin of Tel Aviv University: "The Nobel Prize for QCD as a description of strong interactions might have been awarded to Sakharov, Zel'dovich and Nambu. They had it all figured out in 1966.... All subsequent developments leading to QCD were just mathematics and public relations, with no new physics. But the particle physics establishment refused to recognize the beginnings of new physics and had to wait until new fancy names like color chromodynamics, confinement and so on, were invented — together with a massive public-relations campaign. Then they claimed they had discovered it all." In Hoddeson et al., *Rise of the Standard Model*, 552.

108. Bernstein, *Tenth Dimension*, 92–93.

109. These theorists are: 1) Kazuhiko Nishijima of Japan, who in 1953 (only a few months after Gell-Mann) independently developed the strangeness theory; 2) Yuval Ne'eman, who independently discovered the Eightfold Way and also predicted the omega-minus particle; 3) George Zweig, who independently discovered the quark theory (Gell-Mann published in 1964, while Zweig only circulated two unpublished preprints that year. Richard Feynman is said to have nominated Gell-Mann and Zweig for the 1977 Nobel Prize; perhaps he felt that the fully developed quark theory deserved a second award for Gell-Mann, and a first for Zweig. No prize resulted.); 4) Moo Young Han and Yochiro Nambu, who in 1965 spelled out a theory of strong interactions, later called quantum chromodynamics (QCD) in quark terminology; the Han-Nambu theory attracted little attention until 1973, and by then other theories had caught up.

110. Eckert and Schubert, *Crystals*, 73.

111. For a lucid historical account, see Riordan and Hoddeson, *Crystal Fire*.

112. Brush, *Statistical Physics*, 214.

113. See Livanova, *Landau*, and Ryutova-Kemoklidze, *Quantum Generation*. See also Gorelik, "Top-Secret Life," 73–77, for what KGB archives reveal about Landau's troubles.

114. Livanova, *Landau*, for Landau's work here. Also Brush, *Statistical Physics*, 181–97.

115. Gleick, *Genius*, 300.

116. Wilson, building on Onsager's contributions, was honored for work on phase transitions, where the scale of the phenomena being probed changes. This requires a formidable mathematical procedure using renormalizing-group theory. His work moves into low-temperature physics. Wilson has claimed that the mathematical difficulties in his work are as great as any in physics, and it would be hard to argue.

117. For background, see Kirtley and Tsuei, "Probing High-Temperature Superconductivity."

118. Wali, *Chandra*, 295; for Chandrasekhar's remembrance that physics, not astrophysics, was the "center" when he was young, 98.

119. Alvarez, *Adventures of a Physicist*, 214.

120. Riordan, *Hunting of the Quark*, 278. Riordan's book is a full history of these two simultaneous, important experiments, and of the experiments and theory that prepared the way. It is invaluable as an insider's account of what such experiments are really like. Riordan himself is an experimental physicist who worked at Stanford's SLAC high-energy apparatus.

121. Ibid., 277. Richter's team made their discovery on 9–10 November 1974. Ting reported his on 11 November. Both teams' findings were confirmed on 15 November. See also the account of the Richter experiment by Gerson Goldhaber, "From the Psi to Charmed Mesons," in Hoddeson et al., *Rise of the Standard Model*, 57–78, and chronology on 61.

122. Taubes, *Nobel Dreams*. Taubes's account is technically lucid, fully up to the larger-than-life Rubbia and his behavior. His book quickly disposes of the notion that scientific experiments are dull compared with money-making, emergency rooms, or crime.

123. Taubes, *Nobel Dreams*, 89, 100.

124. Taubes, *Nobel Dreams*, 55 (epigraph).

125. Alvarez, *Adventures of a Physicist*, 73–74, for details in next paragraph.

126. For a vivid account of Fermi's path here, see Rhodes, *Making of the Atomic Bomb*, 208–32, 258–62.

127. Pais, *Inward Bound*, 363.

128. Hanson, *Concept of the Positron*, 140; all of ch. 9.

129. Pflaum, *Grand Obsession*, 304.

130. Alvarez, *Adventures of a Physicist*, 61.

131. Victor Weisskopf, *The Joy of Insight* (New York: Basic Books, 1991), 168–69.

132. Crease and Mann, *Second Creation*, 109.

133. Lederman, *God Particle*, 315–16.

134. Jeremy Bernstein claimed that Penzias and Wilson's "was a discovery without a context," in *A Theory for Everything*. Helge Kragh says that the physics community seemed to have considered Gamow's more a "model" than a "theory." The case for Alpher is discussed by D'Agnese, "Last Big Bang Man." Alpher's own full account is in preparation.

135. Schweber, *QED*, 577.

136. Brown and Hoddeson, *Birth of Particle Physics*, 74.

137. For Stueckelberg's biography and scientific work, see Schweber, *QED*, 576–79. For quotation from Feynman, see Mehra, *Beat of a Different Drum*, 577.

138. Shapley, "Nobelists: Piccioni Lawsuit," 1405–6.

139. Heilbron, "Creativity and Big Science," 42–47.

140. In 1979 Segrè and Chamberlain's Nobel Prize work was again attacked. J. C. Cooper published a paper accusing Segrè and Chamberlain of fraud, and Cooper circulated unpublished papers, one of them titled "Fraudulent Experiment Won 1959 Nobel Prize." Cooper charged that Segrè and Chamberlain hid the fact that their data actually showed that faster-than-light particles (tachyons) existed — and accused the physics community of conniving in this cover-up. Cooper's charges, as analyzed by the physicist Allan Franklin in *Neglect of Experiment*, 239–43, appear to be baseless.

141. There are many accounts of this. See Brown and Hoddeson, *Birth of Particle Physics*, 40.

142. Pais, *Inward Bound*, 280.

143. Kronig, "Turning Point"; also G. E. Uhlenbeck, "Personal Reminiscences," *Physics Today* 29 (June 1976). The American theorist John Slater (1900–1976) seems to have independently discovered spin at the same time. Or, rather, according to the physicist Philip Morse, he would have done so if he had "terminated his 1925 paper" with a simple statement about "a spin doublet[,] which could have been made in a sentence." Instead he spoke vaguely about duality of states. Slater never won a Nobel Prize. Morse is quoted by the

Nobelist John Van Vleck in *National Academy of Sciences*, vol. 53, (Washington, D.C.: National Academy Press, 1982), 300.

144. The matter involves assigning quantum numbers to the atom, which describe its electrons. Pauli systematized earlier efforts that assigned quantum numbers for energy levels, angular momentum, and magnetic energy, and he threw in a fourth number vaguely called a "two-valued" number in an attempt to account for lines on the spectroscope that were split into "doublets." The reason they were split was explained in 1925 by Uhlenbeck and Goudsmit's newly discovered "spin." See Crease and Mann, *Second Creation*, 42.

145. Pais, *Inward Bound*, 631. In 1929 Heisenberg in a letter mentions Pauli's neutrino hypothesis. The usual date is 1931, when Pauli mentioned the neutrino hypothesis in a half-joking letter to colleagues.

146. Pais, *Inward Bound*, 314.

147. Alvarez, *Adventures of a Physicist*, 78. For a recent defense of Oppenheimer's contributions to physics, see Rigden, "Oppenheimer."

148. Crease and Mann, *Second Creation*, 107, on Serber; Schweber, *QED*, 245–47, on Oppenheimer and the Dancoff incident.

149. M. Wilson, "How Nobel Winners Get That Way," 69.

150. Moore, *Schrödinger*, 286.

151. Ziman, *Force of Knowledge*, 122.

152. Bernstein, *Theory for Everything*, 142.

6. THE NOBEL PRIZE IN CHEMISTRY

1. Mulvey, *Nature of Matter*, 169.

2. For Kelvin and Boltzmann, see Nye, *From Chemical Philosophy*, 276. But Kragh, *Quantum Generations*, 446, notes that "it soon turned out that not even simple molecules could be reduced to quantum physics without empirical input from the chemists."

3. Ball, *Designing*, 4.

4. Knight, *Ideas*, 11–12.

5. Brock, *Norton History*, 507.

6. Mendelssohn, *The World of Walther Nernst*, 38.

7. Crawford, *Beginnings*, 99.

8. The Debye-Hückel theory replaced Arrhenius's explanation of acids, bases, and salts in very dilute solution, but couldn't explain strong electrolytes. Debye-Hückel gave a statistical treatment of electrolytes (liquids that conduct electricity because ions are present, as when silver coats metal). When the atoms are fully in solution, ions are formed — an ion being an atom that has lost or gained one or more electrons than its normal complement. These ions are encircled by ions of the opposite charge. Electrostatic reactions occur. The theory predicts how electrolytes will behave. Lars Onsager in the 1940s immensely refined such theories mathematically, and gave them further application. See also Leicester, *Source Book*, 182.

9. Hiebert, "Developments in Physical Chemistry," 105, for Ostwald, the early history of physical chemistry, and the early prizes; also Crawford and Friedman, "Context of Swedish Science," 312–18.

10. Ödelberg, *Nobel*, 287.

11. Crawford, *Beginnings*, 119.

12. Hiebert, "Developments in Physical Chemistry," 97–115.

13. Ibid., 98–99.

14. Crawford, *Beginnings*, 124–26; Crawford and Friedman, "Context of Swedish Science," 317.

15. Quoted in Joseph S. Fruton, "The Interplay of Chemistry and Biology at the Turn of the Century" in *Science, Technology*, eds. Bernhard, Crawford, and Sorbom, 82.

16. This section on biochemistry's history is indebted to the overview provided by Kohler, "History of Biochemistry."

17. In 1982 Michel crystallized proteins in the photosynthesis reaction center. In 1985 Deisenhofer and Huber analyzed the structure of these proteins — involving the location of 10,000 atoms — and showed that the center's complex chemistry made it possible for light to be stored as energy. When a photon is absorbed, a cholorophyll molecule releases an electron. The result is a positive charge. Photosynthesis thus occurs.

18. Crawford, *Beginnings*, 94; Crawford and Friedman, "Context of Swedish Science," 319.

19. For the conflict between Arrhenius and Nernst, see Crawford, *Beginnings*, 126–28. Crawford notes that neither Arrhenius, van't Hoff, nor Ostwald ever nominated Nernst. For Arrhenius's insinuations about Nernst's money-making immorality, see Mendelssohn, *The World of Walther Nernst*, 44–49.

20. Medawar and Medawar, *Life Sciences*, 84.

21. Leicester, *Source Book*, 33.

22. Servos, *Physical Chemistry*, 135.

23. Servos, *Physical Chemistry*, 132. See also Irving Langmuir, *Collected Works*, ed. G. Suits (New York: Pergamon Press, 1960–62), 12:111.

24. Brock, *Norton History*, 477.

25. See Nye, *From Chemical Philosophy*, 228, for the context of these developments.

26. Pauling, "Fifty Years of Progress," 290–91.

27. Molecular orbitals give a way of representing electron distribution in a molecule and its energy levels. When different orbitals are filled, different properties result.

28. In the 72d annual issue of the *CRC Handbook of Chemistry and Physics* (1991), the kind of information any chemist may now need is exhaustively listed in a thick volume of 2,300 pages. It is full of solid empirical laboratory methods but also mathematical-quantum formulas. Here one can find the structures of 15,000 organic compounds and also the physical constants of thousands of inorganic compounds, plus their order of refraction, the electronic bonding energies, lengths, and angles of the elements, their magnetic susceptibilities and magnetic rotatory power, a table of how much energy is needed to break a particular chemical bonding, and interatomic distances. There are tables for the fundamental vibrational frequencies of small molecules and for lattice energies in crystals. A long section exposits the biochemistry of the three main components of living matter — carbohydrates, fats, and proteins. A detailed list is given of the properties of solids, polymers, isotopes, and particles like mesons.

29. Ball, *Designing*, 91.

30. Brock, *Norton History*, 549.

31. Hahn, *My Life*, 86.

32. Servos, *Physical Chemistry*, 310.

33. Nevill Mott, in footnote to Nye, *From Chemical Philosophy*, 261.

34. Knight, *Ideas*, 177.

35. Pauling, "Theory of Resonance," 7.

36. Roald Hoffmann, *The Same and Not the Same*. Since Pauling and Mulliken have just been mentioned, it deserves note that Hoffmann won his Nobel award for work done with Robert Woodward, who died before that Nobel was awarded, otherwise he would have won another one. This involved the way atoms bond through electron orbitals. Woodward suspected that the orbitals had to be "in phase" for the molecules to twist and bend appropriately. Heat alone couldn't do this; it would only excite the electrons. But photons could enable electrons to rise to levels of higher energy per Pauli's exclusion principle. Between 1965 and 1969, Woodward and Hoffmann worked this out quantitatively in their principles of orbital symmetry.

37. Brock, *Norton History*, 621.

38. Asimov, *New Guide to Science*, 564.

39. Schwartz, *Chemistry in Context*, 452.

40. *Nobel Lectures in Chemistry 1901–70*, 4:651.

41. Wasson, *Nobel Prize Winners*, 693.

42. Ball, *Designing*, 162; also 160 on the work of Cram, Pedersen, and Lehn.

43. For a comprehensive biography, see Stoltzenberg, *Fritz Haber*. For background, see Johnson, *The Kaiser's Chemists*. For a discerning essay on Haber, see Fritz Stern, *Dreams and Delusions: The Drama of German History* (New York: Knopf, 1987), ch. 2.

44. Hahn, *My Life*, 131.

45. Haber, *The Poisonous Cloud*, 18. (The author was Fritz Haber's son.) See also Shea, *Otto Hahn and the Rise of Nuclear Physics*.

46. *Leo Baeck Institute* has much personal information on Haber.

47. Haber, *Poisonous Cloud*, 292.

48. Ibid., 392, note 87.

49. Crawford, *Nationalism and Internationalism*, 78.

50. *Operation Epsilon.*

51. *Operation Epsilon*, 70.

52. Hahn, *My Life*, 177.

53. Meitner's deserving a full share in Hahn's discovery and Nobel Prize is convincingly argued in the biography by Sime, *Lise Meitner.*

54. Crawford, *Beginnings*, 163.

7. THE NOBEL PRIZE IN PHYSIOLOGY OR MEDICINE

1. Claude Bernard, *Introduction to the Study of Experimental Medicine* (1865). For background, see Borje Uvnas, "The Rise of Physiology during the Nineteenth Century," in Bernhard, Crawford, and Sorbom, *Science, Technology*, 135–45.

2. See the illuminating essay by Claire Salomon-Bayet, "Bacteriology and the Nobel Prize Selections."

3. Ibid.

4. In 1999 an editorial in the respected British journal *Lancet* argued that the Nobel emphasis on laboratory research has gone too far, and that clinical and epidemiological ["real world" or "field"] research needs to be recognized by the Nobel jury. See "Narrowness of Nobel Awards."

5. From Rothschuh, *History of Physiology*. A rebuttal is advanced in McLennan, *Advances in Physiological Research*, 96, along lines such as: "What else is pharmacology but physiology with molecular tools?" For a historical view supporting Rothschuh's conclusion, see Borje Uvnas, "The Rise of Physiology during the Nineteenth Century," in Bernhard, Crawford, and Sorbom, *Science, Technology*, 135–45.

6. R. A. Gregory, "The Gastrointestinal Hormones," in Hodgkin et al., *Pursuit of Nature*, 108–9.

7. It has been argued that both Pavlov and Starling and Bayliss were right. In 1912 one of Pavlov's Russian pupils (Anrep) demonstrated in the laboratory of Starling and Bayliss that stimulating the vagal nerve could cause secretion of pancreatic juices. See Gray, *Ivan Pavlov.*

8. Ödelberg, *Nobel*, 223.

9. Ödelberg, *Nobel*, 247.

10. See Witkop, "Paul Ehrlich," with many useful references.

11. Salomon-Bayet, "Bacteriology," 384, 388 (note 22).

12. Ibid., 386.

13. Köhler, *From Medical Chemistry*, 323.

14. Taylor, *Science of Life*, 280.

15. For a survey, see Fruton, *Molecules and Life*.

16. H. J. Muller, "Variation Due to Change in Individual Gene."

17. Quoted in Olby, *Path to the Double Helix*, 235.

18. Cairns, Stent, and Watson, *Phage*, 3–4.

19. Luria, *A Slot Machine*, 74.

20. Allen, *Life Science*, 208.

21. Judson, *Eighth Day*, 40; Crick, *What Mad Pursuit*, 37.

22. Crick, *What Mad Pursuit*, 55.

23. Crick, *What Mad Pursuit*, 58.

24. Judson, *Eighth Day*, 123.

25. Crick, *What Mad Pursuit*, 6.

26. Crick, *What Mad Pursuit*, 68.

27. Watson, *Double Helix*, 107.

28. Crick, *What Mad Pursuit*, 75.

29. Fischer and Lipson, *Thinking about Science*, 263.

30. Crick, *What Mad Pursuit*, 87; for Franklin as "unfairly treated," 82.

31. Judson, *Eighth Day*, 67.

32. Judson, *Eighth Day*, 195.

33. Dyson, *From Eros to Gaia*, 151–52. The road to the Nobels was perhaps more chancy. James Watson partly contradicts Dyson about Bragg's building up molecular biology. In a letter to Max Delbrück, Watson describes the situation just after the DNA discovery. "Until we produced the model Bragg did not know what either DNA or genes were and his reaction to our original *Nature* note was 'it's all Greek to me.' After we convinced him that DNA might be interest-

ing, he then got out of control and I spend much of my time deemphasizing it since I have not infrequent spells of seriously worrying about whether it is correct." Quoted in Judson, *Eighth Day*, 232–33.

34. Watson, *Double Helix*.

35. *New Scientist*, 3 October 1974.

36. Quoted in Schweber, *QED*, 468.

37. Borek, *Atoms within Us*, 186.

38. Lehninger, *Biochemistry*, 156.

39. Bartusiak, *A Positron Named Priscilla*, 101.

40. Borek, *Atoms within Us*, 215.

41. Medawar and Medawar, *Life Science*, 29, 31.

42. Ibid., 103.

43. The story of Gajdusek's and Prusiner's work is told by Richard Rhodes in *Deadly Feasts*. The neurologist Oliver Sacks in a review of this book in the *New Yorker*, 14 April 1997, called TSE "potentially the deadliest diseases on earth," because they can develop without any warning to the infected body.

44. Rhodes, *Deadly Feasts*, Afterword; for Prusiner's pursuit of the prize, 160–68; for Gajdusek's background and research, ch. 2.

45. Taylor, *Science of Life*, 242.

46. Crick, *What Mad Pursuit*, 146.

47. Angier, *Natural Obsessions*, 66.

48. Medawar and Medawar, *Life Science*, 117.

49. Bliss, *Insulin*, 111 and 121 for tests on patients; 107–8 and 263 for rivalry between Banting and Macleod.

50. Bliss, *Insulin*, 18–19.

51. Bliss, *Insulin*, 168.

52. Bliss, *Insulin*, 212.

53. Ödelberg, *Nobel*, 224.

54. Fleming, "Nobel's Hits and Errors."

55. Zuckerman, *Scientific Elite*, 55.

56. Wainwright, "Streptomycin." Professor Wainwright's pioneering analysis of the case is indispensable for this discussion. For background, see also Swann, *Academic Scientists and the Pharmaceutical Industry.*

57. Wainwright, "Streptomycin," 102.

58. Wainwright, "Streptomycin," 111.

59. Wainwright, "Streptomycin," 119.

60. These began in the *New York Times* on 11 March 1950 with a report that Schatz had sued, claiming to have participated in the discovery. On 13 March, Schatz is reported as winning, getting 3% of royalties and a $125,000 settlement. On 29 April 1950, Waksman is reported as having received $350,000 in royalties.

61. Sharif, "Pioneer of TB Drug Recognized."

62. Taylor, *Science of Life*, 392.

63. Nisbett, *Lorenz*, 8–9.

64. Nisbet, *Lorenz*, 221, examines the relation between ethology and medicine.

65. *New York Times*, 15 December 1973.

66. Evans, *Lorenz*, xv.

67. Jones, *Freud*, 3:202. See also Eissler, *Expert Witness*.

68. Jones, *Freud*, 3:202.

69. Jones, *Freud*, 3:234.

70. Jones, *Freud*, 3:21–22.

71. Jones, *Freud*, 3:24.

72. Shutts, *Lobotomy*, 37–38.

73. Shutts, *Lobotomy*, xvi.

74. Valenstein, *Great and Desperate Cures*, 99.

75. Ibid., 146.

76. Ibid., 156.

77. See Vertosick, "Lobotomy's Back." Vertosick, a neurosurgeon, describes a new form of "psychiatric surgery" done between 1991 and 1995 which uses a computer to guide an electrode into the frontal lobe. The results seem at best tentative.

78. A detailed account, not for the squeamish, is Leamer, *Kennedy Women*, 319–23.

79. Valenstein, *Great and Desperate Cures*, 226.

80. Shutts, *Lobotomy*, 195.

81. Shutts, *Lobotomy*, 228; Valenstein, *Great and Desperate Cures*, 239.

8. THE PEACE PRIZE

1. Bibb, *It Ain't as Easy as It Looks.* The *New Republic*, 26 January 1997, 19, claims that the entire $1 billion may finally cost nothing as a tax write-off.

2. *New York Times*, 2 October 1994.

3. Dunant, *A Memory of Solferino.* For the most complete history of the Red Cross, see Moorehead, *Dunant's Dream.*

4. Chatfield and Ilukhina, *Peace/Mir*, 100.

5. Beales, *History of Peace*, 231–32.

6. Moorehead, *Dunant's Dream.*

7. Simon, "International Peace Bureau," 69.

8. Chatfield and Ilukhina, *Peace/Mir*, 117.

9. Beales, *History of Peace*, 279.

10. *Time*, 23 October 1995.

11. Beales, *History of Peace*, 317.

12. Schuman, *Commonwealth.* This approach, as Schuman points out, is a variation on the old balance of power.

13. Beales, *History of Peace*, 315.

14. Ibid., 317.

15. Woolf, *Intelligent Man's Way*, 100.

16. Ibid., 301.

17. Schuman, *Commonwealth*, 364, 366–67 for this and next paragraph.

18. See Moorehead, *Dunant's Dream*, for detailed evidence.

19. Hitchens, *Missionary Position*, passim.

20. Schuman, *Commonwealth*, 371–72.

21. Gellman, *Secret Affairs*, 93.

22. Wasson, *Nobel Prize Winners*, 777.

23. Laqueur, *Europe Since Hitler*, 149.

24. *New York Times*, 11 October 1994.

25. Wasson, *Nobel Prize Winners*, 927–28.

26. Saint Thomas Aquinas, *Summa Theologica*, 1a–2ae, Q xcii, art 3, ad 2.

27. To these, one should add figures widely reported in the media as serious candidates for the peace prize, each noted for efforts to promote democracy within a nation or area: Leyla Zana, a Kurd imprisoned by the Turks for agitating for freedom and rights for Turkish Kurds; Samuel Ruiz, a Catholic bishop in Mexico; Wei Jingsheng, a Chinese activist for civil and human rights; Sergei Kovalyov, a human rights activist in Russia.

28. Thee, *PEACE!*, 515–21.

29. Stoll, *Menchú and the Story*. See Charles Lane, "Deceiving Is Believing," *New Republic*, 8 March 1999, 36, for review of Stoll's book.

30. Hugh Kay, an admiring biographer of Salazar, presents him as a lover of peace: see *Salazar and Modern Portugal*, 65, for Salazar's admiration of Aquinas's view of war.

31. *New York Times*, 11 October 1997, A1.

32. Chatfield and Ilukhina, *Peace/Mir*, 152.

9. THE ECONOMICS MEMORIAL PRIZE

1. Simon, *Models of My Life*, 319.

2. Simon, *Models of My Life*, 325–26.

3. For discussion, see Baumol, "Economic Models and Mathematics," 88–101.

4. See for example Davidson, *Stochastic Limit Theory*.

5. As examples, see R. Samuelson, "Booby Prize"; "A Nobel Prize for Business"; Bergmann, "Abolish the Nobel Prize for Economics."

6. On the other hand, some Nobel laureates are said to invest their money in Dimensional Fund Advisors, which "insists that each of its funds follow a strategy based on rigorous academic research." See Tully, "How the Really Smart Money Invests."

7. The 1975 prize went to Leonid Kantorovich, the only Soviet economist ever honored. But he was no Marxist. The Nobel citation took the opportunity of his award to preach that scientific economics "is independent of the society under consideration." It then immediately contradicted itself by praising Kantorovich for helping move the Soviet economy toward "decentralization" — which is to say, free enterprise.

8. In the 1960s Lawrence Klein set up an ambitious model to cover twelve national areas, a global interrelationship integrating Third World and also socialist and Communist economies. Called Project Link, this model consisted of 1,178 simultaneous nonlinear equations. The very ambitiousness of such efforts has raised questions about their usefulness. Getting empirical verification from these models has also been a problem.

9. Many eminent economists shared the same background and might well have won the prize if they had lived long enough. Within a decade of the first economics prize in 1969, however, most had died unhonored. A short list with death dates includes: (from Britain) Michael Kalecki in 1970, Roy Harrod in 1976, Joan Robinson in 1983; (from the U.S.) Joseph Schumpeter in 1950, Jacob Viner in 1970, Frank Knight in 1972, Ludwig von Mises in 1973, Jacob Marschak in 1977, Oskar Morgenstern in 1977.

10. Stigler, *The Economist as Preacher*, 223.

11. In academic taxonomy, there are also "post-Keynesians" such as Michael Kalecki, Nicholas Kaldor, and Stanley Weintraub, but the Nobel has ignored these.

12. The Frenchman Léon Walras (1834–1910) and the French-Italian Vilfredo Pareto (1848–1923) are important examples.

13. The mid-nineteenth-century development in physics of the law of the conservation of energy also influenced the neoclassical economists who took up equilibrium theories.

14. The English theorist Thomas Balogh, an acerbic guide to economic follies, summed up what this ideal type implied:

A consumer's behavior must not be impulsive; he must be assumed to have considered all the possible choices open to him and to have fully understood their implications. The consumer must not only be rational, but his tastes must be constant; any change in tastes would make [the equilibrium] impossible. Hence, this "ideal" consumer does not explore new possibilities; nor can he be influenced by persuasive advertising. In particular, he must not be influenced in his own choice by the consumption, conspicuous or otherwise, of others.

See Balogh, *Irrelevance of Contemporary Economics.* To which may be added, from Ormerod, *Death of Economics,* "The appropriation of the word 'rational' to describe the basic postulates of orthodox economic theory was a propaganda coup of the highest order. The world's most expensive public-relations firm could not have done better. It carries the implication that any criticism of it, or any alternatives put forward, are by definition irrational."

15. Compressed in these two paragraphs is a long historical development that has been explored in countless studies, philosophical, historical, sociological, and otherwise. One might only mention the German sociologist Max Weber, who most influentially tried to separate facts from values, a position endorsed by many Nobel laureates in economics. The works of the Harvard sociologist Talcott Parsons are an instance of the scientizing of sociological language minus mathematics. The literature on how the counterculture influenced social sciences to turn activist is vast. For a glimpse into the recent antagonism to science, see essays by Gerald Holton and Theodore Roszak, among others, in "Science and Its Public: The Changing Relationship," *Daedalus* 103, no. 3 (1974). For a highly approving view of the alliance between law and economics — and of Becker's variety — see books by Richard Posner, a federal judge.

16. Heilbroner, *Worldly Philosophers,* 63.

17. Stigler, *The Economist as Preacher,* 64.

18. Kuttner, "Invisible Hand."

19. Breit and Spencer, *Lives of the Laureates,* 77.

20. Spiegel and Samuels, *Contemporary Economists in Perspective,* 2: 524.

21. Szenberg, *Eminent Economists,* 236.

22. Silk, *The Economists,* 3.

23. Ibid.

24. Linder, *The Anti-Samuelson*. Buckley's book was published in Chicago by Regnery in 1951.

25. For "economics of the heart," see Niehans, *History*, 422. Kuttner, *Economic Illusion*, 27, castigates Samuelson's synthesis as "nothing but the old classical economics with the ingestion of as little Keynesianism as possible, an antitoxin to inoculate against further infection."

26. Quoted in Sobel, *Worldly Economists*, 101–2.

27. John Geanakoplos, "Arrow-Debreu Theory of General Equilibrium," in Eatwell, Millgate, and Newman, *New Palgrave*, 1:116–23.

28. Lindbeck, "Prize in Economic Science," 42.

29. Roy Radner, "Competitive Equilibrium under Uncertainty," *Econometrica* 36 (1968), has been called "perhaps the single most devastating technical critique of the concept of general equilibrium": see Ormerod, *Death of Economics*, 90, 218.

30. Niehans, *History*, 399.

31. Nasar, *A Beautiful Mind*, gives a full biography.

32. Niehans, *History*, 373.

33. Fogel and Elton, *Which Road to the Past?* 26.

34. Becker, *Treatise on the Family*, 307.

35. Becker, *Economic Approach to Human Behavior*, 5.

36. Becker, *Treatise on the Family*, 307.

37. A reviewer in the *Economist*, 30 April 1977, tapped Becker on the wrist very politely for claiming that criminals break the law or don't, depending on their calculation of getting caught and punished. The reviewer wondered whether such a view might even encourage criminality: don't most people obey the law because they believe being law-abiding is a good in itself, and not because of costs and benefits on the margin?

38. Becker, *Treatise on the Family*, 309, 312.

39. After Becker won the Nobel, Arjo Klamer decided that his work represented something new in economic theory — not exact science but a move into "storytelling": "We can think of the Nobel more as a literary prize than a scientific prize" (*Business Week*, 11 October 1993).

One recalls that the first Nobel citation in 1969 proclaimed the time long past due for economists to give up the "literary" approach.

40. Becker, *Treatise on the Family*, 117.

41. For an acute criticism of Simon's theories, see Storing, "Science of Administration."

42. Paul Muth should have shared Lucas's Nobel. Niehans, *History*, 505–6, says: "Muth's contribution is one of the relatively few instances in which there is no indication that the history of economics would have taken the same course in its absence." It was a novel and ingenious idea, not "in the air."

43. See Buchanan and Tullack, *Calculus of Consent*. His Nobel was for developing "constitutional economics," or public choice theory. In his view, the essence of economics is not buying and selling but property rights. The social contract spells out these rights and guarantees them to each individual. But the individual and the government thereafter may diverge greatly. Here Buchanan himself diverges crucially from the neoclassical economics he otherwise espouses. "Passionately individualistic," as he calls himself, he opposes most of his fellow Nobelists, whom he sees as mostly "elitist" and "collectivist." Buchanan's effect on policy has been influential, especially as regards balanced budgets, tax cuts, and the general problem of whether and how government should dominate individual choice. This despite his value-free credo.

44. Silk, *The Economists*, 35, 38.

45. Myrdal, *Political Element*, vii.

46. Niehans, *History*, 499–500.

47. It should be noted that Friedman importantly differs from Keynes by claiming that the Keynesian "tradeoff" between unemployment and inflation was false. There is no such tradeoff. Rather, according to Friedman, a "natural rate of unemployment" exists whenever inflation doesn't rise or fall. This is one of the appeals of Friedman's views to conservative political leaders facing unemployment problems: see Eatwell, Millgate, and Newman, *New Palgrave*, 2: 425.

48. Sobel, *Worldly Economists*, 144.

49. M. Friedman, *Capitalism and Freedom*, 169.

50. They were Linus Pauling (chemistry, 1956, and peace, 1962); George Wald (medicine, 1967), Salvador Luria (medicine, 1969), and

David Baltimore (medicine, 1975). No economics laureate or theorist, except Gunnar Myrdal later, as seen, seems to have made a public protest.

51. See *New York Times Index* for 1976 under "Nobel Prize."

52. Bok, *Alva Myrdal*, 305–6. Mrs. Bok's mother, Alva Myrdal, shared a Nobel in peace in 1982.

53. Niehans, *History*, 315.

54. See Silk, *The Economists*, 42; Sobel, *Worldly Economists*, 103; Szenberg, *Eminent Economists*, 243.

55. Quoted in Bell and Kristol, *Crisis in Economic Theory*, 290 (note). Leontief, who used far more mathematics in his work than Keynes ever did, also warned that fascination with equations can lead to imagined rather than observed reality (cited in Balogh, *Irrelevance of Contemporary Economics*, 8).

56. Szenberg, *Eminent Economists*, 238.

57. Silk, *The Economists*, 50.

58. Klamer, *Conversations with Economists*, 240.

59. *Economist*, 15 October 1994, 16.

CONCLUSION

1. Crawford, "Secrecy," 419.

2. Oppenheimer, "Science and Our Common Language," 146.

3. Trilling, "Mind in the Modern World," 108.

SELECTED BIBLIOGRAPHY

Allen, Garland. *Life Science in the Twentieth Century.* New York: Wiley, 1975.

Alvarez, Luis. *Adventures of a Physicist.* New York: Basic Books, 1987.

Andrade, E. N. DaC. "Rutherford." In *Rutherford at Manchester,* edited by J. B. Birks. New York: W. A. Benjamin, 1963.

Angier, Natalie. *Natural Obsessions: The Search for the Oncogene.* New York: Houghton Mifflin, 1988.

Asimov, Isaac. *New Guide to Science.* New York: Basic Books, 1984.

Bahti, T., and M. S. Fries, eds. *Jewish Writers, German Literature: The Uneasy Examples of Nelly Sachs and Walter Benjamin.* Ann Arbor: University of Michigan Press, 1995.

Ball, Philip. *Designing the Molecular World: Chemistry at the Frontier.* Princeton: Princeton University Press, 1994.

Balogh, Thomas. *The Irrelevance of Conventional Economics.* New York: Liveright, 1982.

Bartusiak, Marcia, ed. *A Positron Named Priscilla: Scientific Discovery on the Frontier.* Washington, D.C.: National Academy Press, 1994.

Baumol, William J. "Economic Models and Mathematics." In *The Structure of Economic Science,* edited by Sherman Roy Krupp. New York: Prentice-Hall, 1966.

Beales, Arthur C. F. *The History of Peace: A Short Account of the Organised Movements for International Peace.* London: G. Bell, 1931.

Becker, Gary. *The Economic Approach to Human Behavior.* Chicago: University of Chicago Press, 1976.

———. *Treatise on the Family.* Cambridge: Harvard University Press, 1981.

Bell, Daniel, and Irving Kristol, eds. *The Crisis in Economic Theory.* New York: Basic Books, 1981.

Bensaude-Vincent, Bernadette, and Isabelle Stengers. *A History of Chemistry.* Translated by Deborah van Damm. Cambridge: Harvard University Press, 1996.

Bergmann, Barbara. "Abolish the Nobel Prize for Economics." *Challenge*, March–April 1999, 52–57.

Bernhard, C. G., E. Crawford, and P. Sorbom, eds. *Science, Technology and Society in the Time of Alfred Nobel: Nobel Symposium 52*. New York: Pergamon, 1982.

Bernstein, Jeremy. *The Tenth Dimension*. New York: McGraw-Hill, 1989.

———. *A Theory for Everything*. New York: Copernicus, 1996.

Bibb, Porter. *It Ain't as Easy as It Looks: Ted Turner's Amazing Story*. New York: Crown, 1993.

Bizzarro, Salvatore. *Pablo Neruda*. Metuchen, N.J.: Scarecrow Press, 1979.

Bliss, Michael. *The Discovery of Insulin*. Chicago: University of Chicago Press, 1982.

Bok, Sissela. *Alva Myrdal: A Daughter's Memoir*. New York: Addison-Wesley, 1991.

Borek, E. *Atoms within Us*. New York: Columbia University Press, 1980.

Born, Max. *My Life: Recollections of a Nobel Laureate*. New York: Scribner, 1978.

Bowersock, G. W. "Rendering unto Caesar." *New Republic*, 16 December 1996, 42–45.

Breit, William, and Roger Spencer, eds. *Lives of the Laureates: Seven Nobel Economists*. Cambridge: MIT Press, 1986.

Brian, Denis. *Genius Talk: Conversations with Nobel Scientists and Other Luminaries*. New York: Plenum Press, 1995.

Brock, William H. *The Norton History of Chemistry*. New York: W. W. Norton, 1992.

Brown, John L. "Twenty Years and Two Laureates: Francophone Nobel Prizes 1967–87." *World Literature Today*, spring 1988, 207–11.

Brown, Laurie M., ed. *Renormalization: From Lorentz to Landau (and Beyond)*. New York: Springer, 1993.

Brown, Laurie, and Lillian Hoddeson. *The Birth of Particle Physics*. Cambridge: Cambridge University Press, 1983.

Brush, Stephen G. *Statistical Physics and the Atomic Theory of Matter, from Boyle and Newton to Landau and Onsager*. Princeton: Princeton University Press, 1983.

Buchanan, James. *Constitutional Economics*. Cambridge: Blackwell, 1991.

Buchanan, James, with Gordon Tullock. *The Calculus of Consent: Logical Foundations of Constitutional Democracy*. Ann Arbor: University of Michigan Press, 1962.

Bunch, Bryan. *Handbook of Current Science and Technology*. Detroit: Gale, 1996.

Cairns, John, Gunther Stent, and J. D. Watson, eds. *Phage and the Origins of Molecular Biology*. New York: Cold Spring Harbor Laboratory Press, 1992.

Carlson, E. A. *Genes, Radiation and Society: The Life of H. J. Muller.* Ithaca: Cornell University Press, 1981.

Cassidy, David. *Uncertainty: The Life and Science of Werner Heisenberg*. New York: Freeman, 1991.

Chadwick, James. "Rutherford." *Nature* 140 (1937): 749.

Chargaff, Erwin. *Heraclitean Fire: Sketches from a Life before Nature..* New York: Rockefeller University Press, 1978.

Chatfield, Charles, and Ruzanna Ilukhin. *Peace/Mir: An Anthology of Historic Alternatives to War.* Syracuse: Syracuse University Press, 1994.

Chatfield, Charles, and Peter van den Dungen, eds. *Peace Movements and Political Cultures*. Knoxville: University of Tennessee Press, 1968.

Christianson, Gail. *Edwin Hubble: Mariner of the Nebulae*. New York: Farrar, Straus & Giroux, 1995.

Coleman, Alexander. "Why Asturias?" *New York Times Book Review*, 19 November 1967, VIII, 1–3.

Contat, Michel, and Michael Rybalka, comps. *The Writings of Jean-Paul Sartre*. Evanston, Ill.: Northwestern University Press, 1974.

Crawford, Elisabeth. "Arrhenius, the Atomic Hypothesis, and the 1908 Nobel Prizes in Physics and Chemistry." *Isis* 75 (1984): 503–22.

———. *The Beginnings of the Nobel Foundation: The Science Prizes 1901–15*. New York: Cambridge University Press, 1984.

———. "The Secrecy of the Nobel Prize Selections in the Sciences and Its Effect on Documentation and Research." *Proceedings of the American Philosophical Society* 134, no. 4 (1990): 408–19.

———. *Nationalism and Internationalism in Science: Studies of the Nobel Population*. New York: Cambridge University Press, 1992.

Crawford, Elisabeth, and Robert Marc Friedman. "The Prizes in Physics and Chemistry in the Context of Swedish Science." In *Science, Technology and Society in the Time of Alfred Nobel,* edited by C. G. Bernhard, E. Crawford, and P. Sorbom. New York: Pergamon, 1982.

Crawford, Elisabeth, J. L. Heilbron, and Rebecca Ulrich. *The Nobel Population 1901–37: A Census of the Nominators and Nominees for the Prizes in Physics and Chemistry.* Berkeley and Los Angeles: University of California Press, 1987.

CRC Handbook of Chemistry and Physics. Cleveland: CRC Press, 1991.

Crease, Robert P., and Charles C. Mann. *The Second Creation: Makers of the Revolution in Twentieth Century Physics.* New York: Collier, 1986.

Crick, Francis. *What Mad Pursuit: A Personal View of Scientific Discovery.* New York: Basic Books, 1988.

Crowther, J. G. *British Scientists of the 20th Century.* London: Routledge & Kegan Paul, 1952.

Curie, Eve. *Madame Curie.* Translated by Vincent Sheean. New York: Garden City Publishing, 1940. Reprint.

Czerwinski, E. J. "For Whom the Nobel Tolls: The Nationless." *World Literature Today,* spring 1988, 211–14.

D'Agnese, Joseph. "The Last Big Bang Man." *Discover* 20, no. 7 (1999): 60–67.

Dansel, Michel. *Les Nobel français de littérature.* Paris: A. Bonne, 1967.

Davidson, J. *Stochastic Limit Theory: An Introduction for Econometricians.* New York: Oxford University Press, 1994.

Dodd, James E. *The Ideas of Particle Physics: An Introduction for Scientists.* New York: Cambridge University Press, 1984.

Dunant, Henri. *Mémoires.* Paris: Institut Henri-Dunant, 1971.

———. *A Memory of Solferino.* Washington, D.C.: American Red Cross, 1939.

Dutta, K., and A. Robinson. *Rabindranath Tagore: The Myriad-Minded Man.* New York: St. Martin's, 1995.

Dyson, Freeman. *From Eros to Gaia.* New York: Pantheon, 1992.

Eatwell, J., M. Millgate, and P. Newman, eds. *The New Palgrave: A Dictionary of Economics.* 4 vols. London: Macmillan, 1987.

Eckert, Michael, and Helmut Schubert. *Crystals, Electrons, and Transistors: From Scholar's Study to Industrial Research.* Translated by Thomas Hughes. New York: AIP, 1990.

Edel, Leon. *Henry James: The Master 1901–1916.* Philadelphia: Lippincott, 1972.

Eissler, Kurt. *Freud as an Expert Witness: The Discussion of War Neuroses between Freud and Wagner-Jauregg.* Translated by Christiane Trollope. New York: International Universities Press, 1986.

Ellmann, Richard. *James Joyce.* New York: Oxford University Press, 1959.

Elzinga, Aant. "Einstein in the Land of Nobel: An Episode in the Interplay of Science, Politics and Popular Culture." In *Physics, Philosophy and the Scientific Community,* edited by Kostas Gavroglu, John Stachel, and Marx Wartofsky. New York: Elsevier, 1995.

Epstein, Gene. "Economic Beat: Is It Really Reasonable to Assume That the Newest Nobelist Deserved the Prize?" *Barron's,* 19 October 1998, 44:1.

Espmark, Kjell. *The Nobel Prize in Literature: A Study of the Criteria behind the Choices.* New York: G. K. Hall, 1986.

———. "The Nobel Prize in Literature." www.nobel.se

Evans, Richard I. *Konrad Lorenz: The Man and His Ideas.* New York: Harcourt Brace, 1975.

Eve, A. S. *Rutherford.* New York: Macmillan, 1939.

Ezhela, V. V., et al, eds. *Particle Physics: One Hundred Years of Discoveries. An Annotated Chronological Bibliography.* Woodbury, N.Y.: AIP, 1996.

Farmelo, Graham. "The Discovery of X-rays." *Scientific American,* November 1995, 86–91.

Fermi, Enrico. "Versuch einer Theorie der B-Strahlen (Toward a theory of beta rays)." In *Collected Papers,* 1:575–90. Chicago: University of Chicago Press, 1962.

Fermi, Laura. *Illustrious Immigrants: The Intellectual Migration from Europe 1930–41.* Chicago: University of Chicago Press, 1968.

Feynman, Richard, as told to Ralph Leighton. *Surely You're Joking, Mr. Feynman! Adventures of a Curious Character.* Edited by E. Hutchings. New York: W. W. Norton, 1985.

Fischer, Ernst P., and Carol Lipson. *Thinking about Science: Max Delbrück and the Origins of Molecular Biology.* New York: W. W. Norton, 1988.

Fleming, Donald. "Nobel's Hits and Errors." *Atlantic Monthly*, 218:53–57.

Fogel, Robert, and G. R. Elton. *Which Road to the Past? Two Views of History.* New Haven: Yale University Press, 1983.

Forman, Paul, J. L. Heilbron, and Spencer Weart. "Physics circa 1900: Personnel, Funding and Productivity of the Academic Establishments." *Historical Studies in Physical Sciences* 5 (1975): 1–185.

Franklin, Allan. *The Neglect of Experiment.* Cambridge: Cambridge University Press, 1986.

French, Warren G. *American Winners of the Nobel Literary Prize.* Norman: University of Oklahoma Press, 1968.

Frenz, Horst. "What Prize Glory?" *Yearbook of Comparative and General Literature*, no. 23 (1973): 42–46.

Friedman, Milton. *Capitalism and Freedom.* Chicago: University of Chicago Press, 1962.

Friedman, Robert Marc. "Americans as Candidates for the Nobel Prize: The Swedish Perspective." In *The Michelson Era in American Science: 1870–1930*, edited by Stanley Goldberg and Roger H. Stuewer. New York: AIP, 1988.

———. *Appropriating the Weather.* Ithaca, N.Y.: Cornell University Press, 1989.

———. "Nobel Physics Prizes in Perspective." *Nature* 292 (August 1981): 793–98.

Fruton, Joseph S. *Molecules and Life: Essays in the History of Biochemistry.* New York: Wiley, 1973.

Galbraith, J. K. *Economics in Perspective: A Critical History.* New York: Houghton Mifflin, 1987.

Galison, Peter. *How Experiments End.* Chicago: University of Chicago Press, 1987.

———. *Image and Logic: A Material Culture of Microphysics.* Chicago: University of Chicago Press, 1997.

Gaston, Jerry. *Originality and Competition in Science: A Study of the British High-Energy Physics Community.* Chicago: University of Chicago Press, 1973.

Gellman, Irwin F. *Secret Affairs: Franklin Roosevelt, Cordell Hull and Sumner Welles*. Baltimore: Johns Hopkins University Press, 1995.

Gillispie, Charles C., ed. *Dictionary of Scientific Biography*. 18 vols. New York: Scribner, 1970–81.

Glasser, Dr. O. *W. C. Roentgen*. Translated by C. C. Thomas. 2d edition. Springfield, Ill.: C. C. Thomas, 1972.

Gleick, James. *Genius. The Life and Science of Richard Feynman*. New York: Pantheon, 1992.

Goldberg, Stanley, and Roger H. Stuewer, eds. *The Michelson Era in American Science: 1870–1930*. New York: AIP, 1988.

González Rodas, Pablo. *Premios Nobel latinoamericanos de literatura*. Zaragoza: Libros Portico, 1999.

Gorelick, Gennady. "The Top-Secret Life of Lev Landau." *Scientific American*, August 1997, 73–77.

Gray, Jeffrey. *Ivan Pavlov*. New York: Viking, 1979.

Gregory, R. A. "The Gastrointestinal Hormones." In *The Pursuit of Nature*, edited by Alan L. Hodgkin et al. New York: Cambridge University Press, 1977.

Gustafsson, Madeleine. "The Silences of the North." *Daedalus*, spring 1984, 94–105.

Haber, Fritz. "Letters to Chaim Weizmann." In *Leo Baeck Institute of Jews from Germany Yearbook*, vol. 8, 103–11. New York: East and West Library, 1963.

Haber, L. F. *The Poisonous Cloud: Chemical Warfare in the First World War.* Oxford: Oxford University Press, 1986.

Hager, Thomas. *Force of Nature: The Life of Linus Pauling*. New York: Simon and Schuster, 1995.

Hahn, Otto. *My Life: The Autobiography of a Scientist*. New York: Herder and Herder, 1970.

Halasz, Nicholas. *Nobel: A Biography*. New York: Orion, 1959.

Hanson, Norwood R. *The Concept of the Positron*. New York: Cambridge University Press, 1963.

Heaney, Seamus. *The Redress of Poetry*. New York: Farrar, Straus & Giroux, 1995.

Heilbron, J. L. "Creativity and Big Science" *Physics Today,* November 1992, 42–47.

———. *The Dilemmas of an Upright Man: Max Planck as Spokesman for German Science.* Berkeley and Los Angeles: University of California Press, 1986.

———. "Fin-de-siècle Physics." In *Science, Technology and Society in the Time of Alfred Nobel: Nobel Symposium 52,* edited by C. G. Bernhard, E. Crawford, and P. Sorbom, 51–73. New York: Pergamon, 1982.

Heilbroner, Robert. *The Worldly Philosophers: The Lives, Times and Ideas of the Great Economic Thinkers.* New York: Simon and Schuster, 1953.

Heisenberg, Werner. *Physics and Beyond: Encounters and Conversations.* New York: Harper, 1971.

Hermann, Armin, et al., eds. *German Nobel Prizewinners: German Contributions to the Fields of Sciences, Letters and International Understanding.* Munich: Moos, 1968.

Hiebert, E. N. "Developments in Physical Chemistry at the Turn of the 19th Century." In *Science, Technology and Society in the Time of Alfred Nobel: Nobel Symposium 52,* edited by C. G. Bernhard, E. Crawford, and P. Sorbom, 97–115. New York: Pergamon, 1982.

Hitchens, Christopher. *The Missionary Position: Mother Teresa in Theory and Practice.* New York: Verso, 1995.

Hoddeson, Lillian, et al., eds. *The Rise of the Standard Model: Particle Physics in the 1960s and 1970s.* New York: Cambridge University Press, 1997.

Hodgkin, Alan L., et al., eds. *The Pursuit of Nature: Informal Essays in the History of Physiology.* New York: Cambridge University Press, 1977.

Hoffmann, Roald. *The Same and Not the Same.* New York: Columbia University Press, 1995.

Holton, Gerald, ed. *The Scientific Imagination: Case Studies.* Cambridge: Harvard University Press, 1978.

———. *Thematic Origins of Scientific Thought: Kepler to Einstein.* Cambridge: Harvard University Press, 1973.

———. *The 20th Century Sciences in Perspective.* New York: W. W. Norton, 1972.

———. "On the Hesitant Rise of Quantum Physics Research in the United States." In *The Michelson Era in American Science: 1870–1930,* edited by Stanley Goldberg and Roger H. Stuewer. New York: AIP, 1988.

Howarth, Herbert. "A Petition to the Swedish Academy." *Books Abroad.* Norman: University of Oklahoma Press, 1967.

Iwamoto, Yoshio. "The Nobel Prize in Literature, 1967–1987: A Japanese View." *World Literature Today.* Norman: University of Oklahoma Press, 1988, 217–19.

Jacob, François. *The Statue Within: Autobiography.* New York: Basic Books, 1988.

Johnson, George. "What a Physicist Finds Obscene." *New York Times,* 6 February 1997, E4.

Johnson, Jeffrey. *The Kaiser's Chemists: Science and Modernization in Imperial Germany.* Chapel Hill: University of North Carolina Press, 1990.

Jones, Ernest. *The Last Phase: 1919–1939.* Vol. 3 of *The Life and Work of Sigmund Freud.* New York: Basic Books, 1957.

Judson, Horace Freeland. *The Eighth Day of Creation.* New York: Simon and Schuster, 1979.

Jungnickel, Christa, and Russell McCormmach. *The Now Mighty Theoretical Physics: 1870–1925.* Vol. 2 of *The Intellectual Mastery of Nature.* Chicago: University of Chicago Press, 1986.

Kay, Hugh. *Salazar and Modern Portugal.* New York: Hawthorn, 1970.

Kevles, Daniel. *The Physicists. The History of a Scientific Community in Modern America.* Cambridge: Harvard University Press, 1971.

———. "Robert A. Millikan." *Scientific American,* January 1979, 142.

Kidd, Walter, ed. *British Winners of the Nobel Literary Prize.* Norman: University of Oklahoma Press, 1968.

Kipnis, A. Ya., B. E. Yaevlov, and J. S. Rowlinson. *Van der Waals and Molecular Science.* Oxford: Oxford University Press, 1996.

Kirtley, John R., and Chang C. Tsuei. "Probing High-Temperature Superconductivity." *Scientific American,* August 1996, 68–73.

Klamer, Arjo. *Conversations with Economists: New Classical Economists and Opponents Speak Out on the Current Controversy in Macroeconomics.* Totowa, N.J.: Rowman & Alanheld, 1984.

Klaw, Spencer. *The New Brahmins: Scientific Life in America.* New York: Morrow, 1968.

Kleinkauf, Jorst, Hein von Dungen, and Lothar Jaenicke, eds. *The Roots of Modern Biochemistry: Fritz Lipmann's Squiggle and Its Consequences.* New York: de Gruyter, 1988.

Knight, David M. *Ideas in Chemistry: A History of the Science.* New Brunswick, N.J.: Rutgers University Press, 1992.

Köhler, Robert. *From Medical Chemistry to Biochemistry: The Making of a Biomedical Discipline.* New York: Cambridge University Press, 1982.

———. "The History of Biochemistry: A Survey." *Journal of the History of Biology* 8, no. 2 (1975): 275–318.

Kragh, Helge. *Dirac: A Scientific Biography.* Cambridge: Cambridge University Press, 1990.

———. *Quantum Generations: A History of Physics in the Twentieth Century.* Princeton: Princeton University Press, 1999.

Kronig, Ralph. "The Turning Point." In *Theoretical Physics in the 20th Century,* edited by M. Fierz and Victor Weisskopf. New York: Interscience, 1960.

Krupp, Sherman Roy, ed. *The Structure of Economic Science: Essays in Methodology.* New York: Prentice-Hall, 1966.

Kuhn, Thomas, et al. *Source for the History of Quantum Physics: An Inventory and Report.* Philadelphia: American Historical Society, 1967.

Kuttner, Robert. *The Economic Illusion: False Choices between Prosperity and Social Justice.* Philadelphia: University of Pennsylvania Press, 1987.

———. "The Invisible Hand Guiding the Nobel Prize in Economics." *Business Week,* 12 November 1990, 20.

Kwan-Terry, John. "Chinese Literature and the Nobel Prize." *World Literature Today* 63 (1989): 385–89.

Lamb, Willis. "Fine Structure of the Hydrogen Atom by a Microwave Method." *The Physical Review* 72 (1947): 241.

Laqueur, Walter. *Europe Since Hitler.* London: Penguin, 1982.

Leamer, Laurence. *The Kennedy Women.* New York: Villard Books, 1994.

Lederman, Leon, with Dick Teresi. *The God Particle.* New York: Dell, 1993.

Lehninger, Albert. *Biochemistry: The Molecular Basis of Cell Structure.* 2d ed. New York: Worth Publishing, 1975.

Leicester, Henry M., ed. *Source Book in Chemistry 1900–1950.* Cambridge: Harvard University Press, 1968.

Leo Baeck Institute of Jews from Germany Yearbook. Vol. 8. New York: East and West Library, 1963.

Levin, Harry. *Memories of the Moderns.* New York: New Directions, 1980.

Liao, Kang. *Pearl S. Buck: A Cultural Bridge across the Pacific.* Westport, Conn.: Greenwood Press, 1997.

Lindbeck, Asser. "The Prize in Economic Science in Memory of Alfred Nobel." *Journal of Economic Literature* 23 (March 1985), 37–55.

Linder, Marc. *The Anti-Samuelson: Macroeconomics, Basic Problems of the Capitalist Economy.* Abridged from 4-volume German original. New York: Urizen, 1997.

Lindfors, Bernth. "South Africa and the Nobel Prize." *World Literature Today,* spring 1988, 222–24.

Livanova, Anna. *Landau: A Great Physicist and Teacher.* New York: Pergamon, 1980.

Lonnroth, Lars. "The Intellectual Civil Servant: The Role of the Writer and the Scholar in Nordic Culture." *Daedalus,* spring, 1984, 107–36.

Luria, Salvador. *A Slot Machine, a Broken Testtube: An Autobiography.* New York: Harper, 1984.

Magill, Frank N. *The Nobel Prize Winners: Literature.* 3 vols. Englewood Cliffs, N.J.: Salem Press, 1987.

Mattson, James, and Merrill Simon. *The Pioneers of NMR and Magnetic Resonance in Medicine: The Story of MRI.* Ramat Gan, Israel: Bar-Ilan University Press, 1996.

McGrayne, Sharon Bertsch. *Nobel Prize Women in Science: Their Lives, Struggles, and Momentous Discoveries.* Secaucus, N.J.: Carol Publishing Group, 1993.

MacLachlan, James. "Defining Physics: The Nobel Prize Selection Process 1901–37." *American Journal of Physics* 5, no. 2 (1991): 166–73.

McLennan, H., ed. *Advances in Physiological Research.* New York: Plenum Press, 1987.

Medawar, Peter. *The Art of the Soluble.* New York: Penguin, 1967.

Medawar, Peter, and J. S. Medawar. *The Life Science: Current Ideas of Biology.* New York: Harper and Row, 1977.

Mehra, Jagdish. *Beat of a Different Drum.* New York: Oxford University Press, 1994.

———, ed., *Werner Heisenberg: A Physicist's Conception of Nature.* Dordrecht: Reidel, 1973.

Mendelssohn, Kurt. *The Quest for Absolute Zero: The Meaning of Low Temperature Physics.* 2d ed. London: Taylor and Francis, 1977.

———. *The World of Walther Nernst: The Rise and Fall of German Science 1864–1941.* Pittsburgh: University of Pittsburgh Press, 1973.

Merrifield, Bruce. *Life during a Golden Age of Peptide Chemistry: The Concept and Development of Solid-Phase Peptide Synthesis.* Washington, D.C.: American Chemical Society, 1993.

Merton, Robert K. *The Sociology of Science.* Chicago: University of Chicago Press, 1973.

Mills, Robert. "Tutorial on Infinities in QED." In *Renormalization*, edited by Laurie Brown. New York: Springer, 1993.

Miłosz, Czesław. *The Witness of Poetry.* Cambridge: Harvard University Press, 1983.

Moe, Ragnvald. *Le Prix Nobel de la paix et l'institut Nobel norvégien, rapport historique et descriptif accompagné d'une histoire du mouvement pacifiste de 1896 à 1930.* Oslo: H. Achehoug, 1932.

Moore, Walter. *Schrödinger: Life and Thought.* Cambridge: Cambridge University Press, 1989.

Moorehead, Caroline. *Dunant's Dream.* New York: Carroll & Graf, 1998.

Morrison, Blake. "So You Want to Win a Nobel Prize." *New York Times Magazine,* 1 October 1995, VI, 62–65.

Mulliken, Robert S. *Life of a Scientist.* New York: Springer, 1989.

Muller, Hermann J. "Variation due to Change in the Individual Gene." *The American Naturalist* 56 (Jan.–Feb. 1922): 48–54.

Mullis, Kary. *Dancing Naked in the Mind Field.* New York: Pantheon, 1998.

Mulvey, J. H. *The Nature of Matter.* New York: Oxford University Press, 1981.

Myrdal, Gunnar. *The Political Element in the Development of Economic Theory.* Translated by P. Streeten. Cambridge: Harvard University Press, 1954.

Nagel, Bengt. "The Discussions Concerning the Nobel Prize for Max Planck." In *Science, Technology, and Society in the Time of Alfred Nobel: Nobel Symposium 52*, edited by C. G. Bernhard, E. Crawford, and P. Sorbom, 355–76. New York: Pergamon, 1982.

"Narrowness of Nobel Awards for Physiology or Medicine." *Lancet* 354, no. 9188 (1999): 1399.

Nasar, Sylvia. *A Beautiful Mind: A Biography of John Forbes Nash Jr., Winner of the Nobel Prize in Economics 1994.* New York: Simon and Schuster, 1998.

Ne'eman, Yuval, and Yorem Kirsh. *The Particle Hunters*. 2d ed. New York: Cambridge University Press, 1996.

Niehans, Jurg. *A History of Economic Theory: Classic Contributions 1720–1980*. Baltimore: Johns Hopkins University Press, 1990.

Nisbett, Alan. *Konrad Lorenz*. London: Dent, 1976.

Nobel Lectures in Chemistry 1901–70. 4 vols. New York: Elsevier, 1964–70.

Nobel Lectures in Chemistry 1971–80. Edited by Tore Frangsmyr. River Edge, N.J.: World Scientific, 1992.

Nobel Lectures in Chemistry 1981–90. Edited by Bo G. Malmstrom. River Edge, N.J.: World Scientific, 1992.

Nobel Lectures in Chemistry 1991–95. Edited by Bo G. Malmstrom. River Edge, N.J.: World Scientific, 1997.

Nobel Lectures in Economic Sciences 1969–80. Edited by Asser Lindbeck. River Edge, N.J.: World Scientific, 1999.

Nobel Lectures in Economic Sciences 1981–90. Edited by Karl-Goran Maler. River Edge, N.J.: World Scientific, 1999.

Nobel Lectures in Economic Sciences 1991–95. Edited by Torsten Persson. River Edge, N.J.: World Scientific, 1999.

Nobel Lectures in Literature 1901–67. Edited by Horst Frenz. New York: Elsevier, 1969.

Nobel Lectures in Literature 1968–80. Edited by Sture Allen. River Edge, N.J.: World Scientific, 1994.

Nobel Lectures in Literature 1981–90. Edited by Sture Allen. River Edge, N.J.: World Scientific, 1994.

Nobel Lectures in Literature 1991–95. Edited by Sture Allen. River Edge, N.J.: World Scientific, 1999.

Nobel Lectures in Peace 1901–70. 4 vols. Amsterdam: Elsevier, 1964–70.

Nobel Lectures in Peace 1971–80. Edited by Irwin Abrams. River Edge, N.J.: World Scientific, 1997.

Nobel Lectures in Peace 1981–90. Edited by Irwin Abrams. River Edge, N.J.: World Scientific, 1997.

Nobel Lectures in Peace 1991–95. Edited by Irwin Abrams. River Edge, N.J.: World Scientific, 1999.

Nobel Lectures in Physics 1901–21. New York: Elsevier, 1967.

Nobel Lectures in Physics 1922–41. New York: Elsevier, 1965.

Nobel Lectures in Physics 1942–61. New York: Elsevier, 1965.

Nobel Lectures in Physics 1962–70. New York: Elsevier, 1972.

Nobel Lectures in Physics 1971–80. Edited by Stig Lundqvist. River Edge, N.J.: World Scientific, 1992.

Nobel Lectures in Physics 1981–90. Edited by Gosta Ekspong. River Edge, N.J.: World Scientific, 1993.

Nobel Lectures in Physics 1991–95. Edited by Gosta Ekspong. River Edge, N.J.: World Scientific, 1997.

Nobel Lectures in Physiology and Medicine 1901–70. 4 vols. Amsterdam: Elsevier, 1974.

Nobel Lectures in Physiology and Medicine 1971–80. Edited by J. Lindsten. River Edge, N.J.: World Scientific, 1984.

Nobel Lectures in Physiology and Medicine 1981–90. Edited by J. Lindsten. River Edge, N.J.: World Scientific, 1994.

Nobel Lectures in Physiology and Medicine 1991–95. Edited by Nils Ringertz. River Edge, N.J.: World Scientific, 1999.

"A Nobel Prize for Business." *Economist,* 15 October 1994.

"Nobel Prize Symposium II: Choices and Decisions 1967–87." *World Literature Today,* spring 1988, 197–241.

"Nobel Symposium" *Books Abroad* 41 (winter 1967): 5–45.

Nye, Mary Jo. *From Chemical Philosophy to Theoretical Chemistry.* Berkeley and Los Angeles: University of California Press, 1986.

———. "Gustave Le Bon's Black Light: A Study in Physics and Philosophy in France at the Turn of the Century." *Historical Studies in Physical Sciences* 4 (1974): 163–95.

————. "N-rays: An Episode in the History and Psychology of Science." *Historical Studies in the Physical Sciences* 11 (1980).

Ödelberg, W., ed. *Nobel: The Man and His Prizes.* 1st ed. Norman: University of Oklahoma Press, 1950; 2d ed. Amsterdam: Elsevier, 1962: 3d ed. New York: American Elsevier, 1972.

Olby, Robert. *The Path to the Double Helix.* Seattle: University of Washington Press, 1974.

Operation Epsilon: The Farm Hall Transcripts. Berkeley and Los Angeles: University of California Press, 1993.

Opfell, Olga S. *The Lady Laureates: Women Who Have Won the Nobel Prize.* Metuchen, N.J.: Scarecrow Press, 1978.

Oppenheimer, J. Robert. *The Open Mind.* New York: Simon and Schuster, 1955.

————. "Science and Our Common Language." Transcript of conversation with Raymond Aron in *L'Express* (Paris), 15 October 1959. Translated by Patrick Evans. In *Robert Oppenheimer,* by Michel Rouze. Greenwich, Conn.: Fawcett, 1965.

————. *Science and the Common Understanding.* New York: Simon and Schuster, 1954.

Ormerod, Paul. *The Death of Economics.* New York: St. Martin's, 1994.

Pais, Abraham. *Einstein Lived Here.* New York: Oxford University Press, 1994.

————. *Inward Bound.* Oxford: Oxford University Press, 1986.

————. *Niels Bohr's Times: In Physics, Philosophy and Polity.* New York: Oxford University Press, 1991.

————. *Subtle Is the Lord: The Science and the Life of Albert Einstein.* New York: Oxford University Press, 1982.

Partington, J. R. *A History of Chemistry.* 4 vols. New York: St. Martin's, 1961–64.

Paul, Henry W. *The Sorcerer's Apprentice: The French Scientist's Image of Germany 1840–1919.* Gainesville: University of Florida Press, 1972.

Pauling, Linus. "Fifty Years of Progress in Structural Chemistry and Molecular Biology." In *The 20th Century Sciences in Perspective,* edited by Gerald Holton. New York: W. W. Norton, 1972.

————. "The Nature of the Theory of Resonance" In *Perspectives in Organic Chemistry*, edited by Alexander Todd. New York: Interscience, 1956.

Peyre, Henri. "What's Wrong with the Nobel Prize?" *Books Abroad*, 1951.

Pflaum, Rosalyn. *Grand Obsession: Marie Curie and Her World*. New York: Doubleday, 1989.

Posner, Richard. *The Economics of Justice*. Cambridge: Harvard University Press, 1981.

Povh, Bogdan, et al., eds. *Particles and Nuclei: An Introduction to the Physical Concepts*. 2d ed. New York: Springer, 1999.

Preminger, Alex, ed. *Princeton Encyclopedia of Poetry and Poetics*. Princeton: Princeton University Press, 1993.

Price, Derek. *Little Science, Big Science*. New York: Columbia University Press, 1963.

Prusiner, Stanley B. "The Prion Diseases." *Scientific American*, January 1995, 48–57.

Quinn, Susan. *Madame Curie: A Life*. New York: Simon and Schuster, 1995.

Radner, Roy. "Competitive Equilibrium under Uncertainty." *Econometrica* 36 (1968): 31–58.

Ragusa, Olga. "Carducci, Deledda, Pirandello, Quasimodo." *Books Abroad* 41 (1967): 28–30.

Reader, William J. *Imperial Chemical Industries, 1871–1926*. 2 vols. Oxford: Oxford University Press, 1970–75.

Reuss, Alejandro. "Nobel Prize Winner Tweaks Free Marketeers." *Dollars and Sense*, no. 221 (1999): 9–10.

Rigden, John S. "J. Robert Oppenheimer: Before the War." *Scientific American*, July 1995, 75–78.

Riordan, Michael. *The Hunting of the Quark: A True Story of Modern Physics*. New York: Simon and Schuster, 1987.

Riordan, Michael, and Lillian Hoddeson. *Crystal Fire: The Birth of the Information Age*. New York: W. W. Norton, 1997.

Rhodes, Richard. *Deadly Feasts: Tracking the Secrets of a Terrifying New Plague*. New York: Simon and Schuster, 1997.

————. *The Making of the Atomic Bomb*. New York: Simon and Schuster, 1986.

Rossiter, Margaret W. *Women Scientists in America: Before Affirmative Action 1940–72.* Baltimore: Johns Hopkins University Press, 1995.

Rothschuh, Karl E. *History of Physiology.* Translated by B. G. B. Risse. New York: Robert Krieger, 1973.

Rozental, S., ed. *Niels Bohr.* New York: Wiley, 1967.

Ruth, Arne. "The Second New Nation: The Mythology of Modern Sweden." *Daedalus,* spring 1984, 53–96.

Ryutova-Kemoklidze, Margarita. *The Quantum Generation: Highlights and Tragedies of the Golden Age of Physics.* Translated by J. Hine. New York: Springer, 1995.

Salomon-Bayet, Claire. "Bacteriology and the Nobel Prize." In *Science, Technology and Society in the Time of Alfred Nobel: Nobel Symposium 52,* edited by C. G. Bernhard, E. Crawford, and P. Sorbom, 377–400. New York: Pergamon, 1982.

Samuelson, Robert. "Booby Prize." *New Republic,* 3 December 1990, 18.

Scammell, Michael. "The Don Flows Again." *New York Times Book Review,* 25 January 1998.

Schechter, Bruce. *The Path of No Resistance: The Story of the Revolution in Superconductivity.* New York: Simon and Schuster, 1989.

Schimanski, F. "The Nobel Experience: The Decision Makers." *New Scientist* 64, no. 917 (3 Oct. 1974): 10–13.

Schlessinger, Bernard, and June Schlessinger, eds. *The Who's Who of Nobel Prize Winners 1901–1995.* New York: Oryx Press, 1996.

Schuck, Henrik, and Ragnar Sohlman. *Nobel: Dynamite and Peace.* New York: Cosmopolitan, 1929.

Schuman, Frederick L. *The Commonwealth of Man: An Inquiry into Power Politics and World Government.* New York: Knopf, 1952.

Schwartz, A. Truman. *Chemistry in Context.* New York: W. C. Brown, 1994.

Schweber, Silvan. *QED and the Men Who Made It: Dyson, Feynman, Schwinger and Tomonaga.* Princeton: Princeton University Press, 1994.

Segrè, Emilio. *Enrico Fermi: Physicist.* Chicago: University of Chicago Press, 1970.

———. *From X-rays to Quarks: Modern Physicists and Their Discoveries.* Berkeley and Los Angeles: University of California Press, 1980.

Servos, John. *Physical Chemistry from Ostwald to Pauling: The Making of a Science in America*. Princeton: Princeton University Press, 1990.

Shapley, D. "Nobelists: Piccioni Lawsuit Raises Question about the 1959 Prize." *Science* 176 (30 June 1972): 1405–6.

Sharif, Dara. "Pioneer of TB Drug Recognized. Rutgers Honors Researcher — 50 Years Later." *Record* (Northern New Jersey), 29 April 1994, a10.

Shea, W. R., ed. *Otto Hahn and the Rise of Nuclear Physics*. Dordrecht and Boston: Reidel, 1983.

Sherwood, Martin. "Life at the Top." *New Scientist* 64, no. 917 (3 Oct. 1974): 13–17.

Shutts, David. *Lobotomy: Resort to the Knife*. New York: Van Nostrand, 1982.

Silk, Leonard. *The Economists*. New York: Basic Books, 1976.

Sime, Ruth Lewin. *Lise Meitner: A Life in Physics*. Berkeley and Los Angeles: University of California Press, 1996.

Simon, Herbert A. *Models of My Life*. New York: Basic Books, 1991.

Simon, Werner. "The International Peace Bureau, 1892–1917: Clerk, Mediator or Guide?" In *Peace Movements and Political Cultures*, edited by Charles Chatfield and Peter van den Dungen. Knoxville: University of Tennessee Press, 1968.

Snow, C. P. *The Physicists*. Boston: Little, Brown, 1981.

Sobel, Robert. *The Worldly Economists*. New York: Free Press, 1980.

Solomey, Nickolas. *The Elusive Neutrino*. New York: Scientific American Library, 1997.

Sommer, Piotr. "The Air You Breathe." *Times Literary Supplement* (London), 18 October 1996.

Soyinka, Wole. *Art, Dialogue and Outrage*. Princeton: Princeton University Press, 1993.

Specter, Michael. "The Nobel Syndrome." *New Yorker*, 5 October 1998, 46–55.

Spiegel, Henry, and Warren Samuels, eds. *Contemporary Economists in Perspective*. 2 vols. Greenwich, Conn.: JAI Press, 1984.

Steiner, George. "Cry Havoc." In *Extraterritorial*. New York: Atheneum, 1971.

————. "The Scandal of the Nobel Prize." *New York Times Book Review*, 30 September 1984, VII, 1:1.

Stent, Gunther. *The Coming of the Golden Age*. New York: Atheneum, 1971.

Stephan, Paula E., and Sharon G. Levin. *Striking the Mother Lode in Science: The Importance of Age, Place and Time*. Oxford: Oxford University Press, 1992.

Stern, Rudolf. "Fritz Haber, Personal Recollections." In *Leo Baeck Institute of Jews from Germany Yearbook*, vol. 8, 70–102. New York: East and West Library, 1963.

Stigler, George. *The Economist as Preacher, and Other Essays*. Chicago: University of Chicago Press, 1982.

Stoll, David. *Rigoberta Menchú and the Story of All Poor Guatemalans*. New York: HarperCollins, 1999.

Stoltzenberg, Dietrich. *Fritz Haber: Chemiker, Nobelpreisträger, Deutscher, Jude*. Weinheim: VCH, 1994.

Storing, Herbert. "The Science of Administration: Herbert A. Simon." In *Essays on the Scientific Study of Politics*, edited by Herbert Storing. New York: Holt, Rinehart and Winston, 1962.

Sturrock, J., ed. *The Oxford Guide to Contemporary Writing*. Oxford: Oxford University Press, 1996.

Swann, John Patrick. *Academic Scientists and the Pharmaceutical Industry: Cooperative Research in Twentieth-Century America*. Baltimore: Johns Hopkins University Press, 1988.

Swenson, Lloyd. *The Ethereal Aether: A History of the Michelson-Morley Ether-Drift Experiments 1880–1930*. Austin: University of Texas Press, 1972.

Szenberg, Michael, ed. *Eminent Economists*. New York: Cambridge University Press, 1992.

Tagore, Rabindranath. *Gitanjali*. Introduction by W. B. Yeats. New York: Macmillan, 1913.

Taubes, Gary. *Nobel Dreams: Power, Deceit and the Ultimate Experiment*. New York: Random House, 1986.

Taylor, Gordon Rattray. *The Science of Life*. New York: McGraw-Hill, 1963.

Thee, Marek, ed. *PEACE! By the Nobel Peace Laureates*. Paris: UNESCO Publishing, 1995.

Tinbergen, Jan. *Econometrics*. Translated by H. R. van Olst. London: George Allen & Unwin, 1951.

Tolf, R. *The Russian Rockefellers: The Saga of the Nobel Family and the Russian Oil Industry.* Stanford: Hoover Institution, 1976.

Trilling, Lionel. "Mind in the Modern World." In *The Last Decade, Essays and Reviews 1965–75,* edited by Diana Trilling. New York: Harcourt Brace Jovanovich, 1981.

Tully, Shawn. "How the Really Smart Money Invests." *Fortune,* 6 July 1998, 148–52.

Uhlenbeck, G. E. "Personal Reminiscences." *Physics Today,* 29 June 1976, 43–47.

Valenstein, Elliott. *Great and Desperate Cures: The Decline of Psychosurgery and Other Medical Treatments for Mental Illness.* New York: Harcourt Brace, 1986.

Vertosick, Frank T. "Lobotomy's Back." *Discover,* October 1999, 66–72.

Vowles, Richard B. "Twelve Northern Authors." *Books Abroad* 41 (1967): 17–23.

Wade, Nicholas. *The Nobel Duel: Two Scientists' 21-Year Race to Win the World's Most Coveted Research Prize.* Garden City, N.Y.: Anchor Press, 1981.

Wainwright, Milton. "Streptomycin: Discovery and Resultant Controversy." *History and Philosophy of the Life Sciences* 13 (1991): 97–124.

Wali, K. C. *Chandra: A Biography of S. Chandrasekhar.* Chicago: University of Chicago Press, 1991.

Wallace, Irving. "Those Explosive Nobel Prizes." *Collier's,* 5 November 1949, 22–25, and 12 November 1949, 21–23.

———. *The Writing of a Novel.* New York: Simon and Schuster, 1968.

Wasson, Tyler, ed. *Nobel Prize Winners.* New York: H. W. Wilson, 1987.

Watson, James. *The Double Helix.* New York: Atheneum, 1968.

Weinberg, Steven. "The Search for Unity: Notes for a History of Quantum Field Theory." *Daedalus,* fall 1977, 17–35.

Weiner, Charles, ed. *History of Twentieth Century Physics.* New York: Academic Press, 1977.

"What's Wrong with the Nobel Prize?" (A Symposium)." *Books Abroad* 25 (spring 1951).

Williams, Nigel. "Newspaper Backs Down over Allegation of Impropriety." *Science* 269, no. 5231 (1995): 1663–64.

Wilson, David. *Rutherford: Simple Genius*. Cambridge: Cambridge University Press, 1983.

Wilson, Mitchell. "How Nobel Winners Get That Way." *Atlantic Monthly*, no. 224 (1970): 69–74.

Witkop, Bernhard. "Paul Ehrlich: His Ideas and His legacy." In *Science, Technology and Society in the Time of Alfred Nobel*, edited by C. G. Bernhard, E. Crawford, and P. Sorbom, 146–66. New York: Pergamon, 1982.

Woolf, Leonard, ed. *The Intelligent Man's Way to Prevent War*. Reprint, New York: Garland, 1973.

World Encyclopedia of Peace. Edited by E. Laszlo et al.; Linus Pauling, hon. ed. New York: Pergamon, 1989.

Yuan, Luke, ed. *Nature of Matter: Purposes of High-Energy Physics*. Upton, N.Y.: Brookhaven National Laboratory, 1965.

Zahka, William. *The Nobel Economics Lectures: A Cross-Section of Current Thinking*. Brookfield: Avebury, 1992.

Ziman, John. *The Force of Knowledge. The Scientific Dimension of Society*. Cambridge: Cambridge University Press, 1976.

———. *Knowing Everything about Nothing*. Cambridge: Cambridge University Press, 1987.

———. *Prometheus Bound: Science in a Dynamic Steady State*. Cambridge: Cambridge University Press, 1994.

Ziolkowski, Theodore. "German Literature and the Prize." *Books Abroad* 41 (1967): 13–17.

Zuckerman, Harriet. *Scientific Elite: Nobel Laureates in the US*. New York: Free Press, 1977.

INDEX

Names of Nobel laureates are displayed in SMALL CAPS.